S0-BDG-708

Hungary
a country study

Federal Research Division
Library of Congress
Edited by
Stephen R. Burant
Research Completed
September 1989

On the cover: Esztergom, 1916

Second Edition, 1990; First Printing, 1990.

Library of Congress Cataloging-in-Publication Data

Hungary: A Country Study.

Area Handbook Series, DA Pam 550-165
"Research completed September 1989."
Bibliography: pp. 275-301.
Includes index.
Supt. of Docs. no. : D 101.22:550-165/991
1. Hungary I. Burant, Stephen R., 1954-   . II. Keefe, Eugene
K. Area Handbook for Hungary. III. Library of Congress. Federal
Research Division. IV. Series. V. Series: Area Handbook Series:
DA Pam 550-165.

DB906.H86   1990   943.9—dc20   90-6426   CIP

Headquarters, Department of the Army
DA Pam 550-165

For sale by the Superintendent of Documents, U.S. Government Printing Office
Washington, D.C. 20402

Foreword

This volume is one in a continuing series of books now being prepared by the Federal Research Division of the Library of Congress under the Country Studies—Area Handbook Program. The last page of this book lists the other published studies.

Most books in the series deal with a particular foreign country, describing and analyzing its political, economic, social, and national security systems and institutions, and examining the interrelationships of those systems and the ways they are shaped by cultural factors. Each study is written by a multidisciplinary team of social scientists. The authors seek to provide a basic understanding of the observed society, striving for a dynamic rather than a static portrayal. Particular attention is devoted to the people who make up the society, their origins, dominant beliefs and values, their common interests and the issues on which they are divided, the nature and extent of their involvement with national institutions, and their attitudes toward each other and toward their social system and political order.

The books represent the analysis of the authors and should not be construed as an expression of an official United States government position, policy, or decision. The authors have sought to adhere to accepted standards of scholarly objectivity. Corrections, additions, and suggestions for changes from readers will be welcomed for use in future editions.

Louis R. Mortimer
Acting Chief
Federal Research Division
Library of Congress
Washington, D.C. 20540

Acknowledgments

The authors wish to express their appreciation to a number of people who assisted in the preparation of this study. Paul Marer of Indiana University furnished his considerable expertise on the Hungarian economy. Thanks go to Sharon Schwartz, who edited the chapters, and to Cissie Coy, who performed the final prepublication review. The index was prepared by Shirley Kessell. Malinda B. Neale of the Library of Congress Composing Unit prepared the camera-ready copy under the supervision of Peggy Pixley.

A number of members of the Federal Research Division of the Library of Congress made significant contributions to the preparation of this book. Special thanks are owed to Richard F. Nyrop, who supplied help and suggestions on chapters 1 through 4, and to Sandra W. Meditz, who reviewed Chapter 5. The authors are also grateful to Raymond E. Zickel, who assisted in research and writing. Martha E. Hopkins ably oversaw editing, and Marilyn Majeska managed production of the book. Elizabeth A. Yates, Barbara Edgerton, and Izella Watson assisted in numerous phases of manuscript preparation. Helen Fedor gathered and helped select the photographs, and Walter R. Iwaskiw assembled the materials for the maps. Invaluable graphics support was given by David P. Cabitto, assisted by Sandra K. Ferrell (who did the cover and chapter illustrations) and Kimberly A. Lord. Stanley M. Sciora furnished information on the ranks and insignia of the Hungarian armed forces.

Finally, the authors wish to note the generosity of those individuals who provided photographs for this book. All photographs are original work not previously published.

Contents

Chapter 2. The Society and Its Environment . 63
Becky Gates

Chapter 3. The Economy 109
Charles Sudetic

Chapter 4. Government and Politics 167
Stephen R. Burant

List of Figures

Preface

Since the mid-1970s, few countries in the world have experienced such rapid and extensive change as Hungary. The political system has moved from an authoritarian regime dominated by the Hungarian Socialist Workers' Party (HSWP) to a multiparty republic. The HSWP itself split, in October 1989, and most of its leaders organized a new party, the Hungarian Socialist Party. In the late 1980s, relations with Western countries improved dramatically, and the Hungarians also received significant support for their reform efforts from the Soviet Union. By contrast, until late 1989 tensions between Hungary and Romania were rising over the latter's treatment of its Hungarian minority, but, after the December 1989 revolution in Romania, the chances for the resolution of that problem improved. Although sporadic efforts had been undertaken since the late 1960s to introduce elements of a market economy into a socialist command economy, Hungarian leaders in 1989 declared their intention to create a full-fledged capitalist economy. The government has also reduced the defense budget, and it has taken steps to make the police apparatus accountable to the people and to their elected representatives. Yet, the discontent that emerged from pressures stemming from the economy's precipitous decline continued. This discontent, coupled with the regime's need to widen its support to sustain the transition from a state socialist to capitalist economy, led the Hungarian regime to undertake political reform efforts.

These changes have necessitated a new edition of *Hungary: A Country Study*, which supersedes the edition published in 1973. Virtually everything discussed in the previous edition has been overtaken by events. Like the earlier edition, this study attempts to present the dominant historical, social, economic, political, and national security aspects of Hungary. Sources of information included books and scholarly journals, official reports of governments and international organizations, foreign and domestic newspapers, and numerous periodicals. A brief annotated bibliographic note on sources recommended for further reading appears at the end of each chapter, and more detailed chapter bibliographies appear at the end of the book. Measurements are given in the metric system; a conversion table is provided to assist those readers who are unfamiliar with metric measurements (see table 1, Appendix). A glossary is also provided.

The Hungarian people are descendants of the Magyars, an Asiatic tribe whose origins lie in what is today central Russia. The word *Hungary* appears to derive from a Slavicized form of the Turkic words *on ogur,* meaning "ten arrows," which may have referred to the number of Magyar tribes. Unlike most Europeans, Hungarians do not speak an Indo-European language. Hungarian is a member of the Finno-Ugric language family, which also includes such languages as Estonian and Finnish.

The illustration on the cover and those that introduce each chapter merit a word of explanation. These drawings were adapted from Andre Kertesz's poignant photographs of his native land, which were published in *Hungarian Memories: Nineteen Twelve to Nineteen Twenty-Five*.

Table A. Chronology of Important Events

Date	Events
EARLY HISTORY ca. A.D. 100–600	Magyar tribes, a pagan Finno-Ugric people, begin migration from Urals south onto Russian steppes and continue west, to area between Don and lower Dnepr rivers, where they fall under the sway of the Bulgar-Turkish people.
ca. A.D. 600–900	Magyars fall under the control of the Khazars but are later freed from Khazar rule in the ninth century. Magyars join Byzantine armies to fight the Bulgars in 895. Magyars migrate farther west into the Danube-Tisza Basin, 895 or 896. Árpád is chosen as chieftain; his male descendants become hereditary heirs of this kingdom, which became known as Hungary.
MEDIEVAL PERIOD Árpád Dynasty ca. 900–1301	Magyars besiege Europe and the Byzantine Empire but are defeated by Moravian and German armies in 955. Chieftain Géza (972–97) is baptized into Roman Catholic Church. Géza's son, Stephen I (997–1038), is recognized by Pope Sylvester II as king of Hungary, ensuring independence from Byzantium and the Holy Roman Empire. Latin alphabet is devised for Hungarian language. Magyars occupy Transylvania. László I (1077–95) occupies Slavonia in 1090, and Kálmán I (1095–1116) takes the title of king of Croatia in 1103. Under Béla III (1173–96), Hungary becomes one of the leading powers in southeastern Europe. Nobles force Andrew II (1205–35) to sign Golden Bull (1222) limiting crown's power. Mongols rout Hungarian army at Mohi in 1241. Mongols withdraw in 1242. Árpád line expires in 1301.
RENAISSANCE AND REFORMATION 1301–1699	Charles Robert (1308–42) wins prolonged succession struggle. Dynastic marriages link Hungary to Naples and Poland. Louis I (1343–82) reconfirms Golden Bull. First university is founded in 1367. Hungary's fortunes begin to decline under Sigismund (1387–1437). Social turmoil erupts because of higher taxes and pressures from the magnates on the lesser nobles. Wars against Ottoman Turks are waged in reigns of Albrecht V (1437–39) and Ulászló I (1439–44). János Hunyadi rules Hungary as regent for infant king, László V. Hunyadi defeats the Turks in Transylvania in 1442 and in Serbia in 1443, is defeated at Varna in 1444, and defeats the Turks again in 1456 near Belgrade. Nobles crown Hunyadi's son Mátyás Corvinus (1458–90) king. Mátyás enacts numerous

Table A.—Continued

reforms. After the death of Mátyás, an oligarchy of magnates takes control, and the country remains in a state of anarchy until 1526, when the Turks defeat Hungary at Mohács. Hungary is partitioned between the Turks and the Habsburgs in 1541. Habsburgs invade Transylvania in 1591. Habsburgs rout a Turkish army in 1664 at St. Gotthard in Hungary. Hungarians rebel against Habsburg rule in 1681. Turks attack Habsburgs but are routed near Vienna in 1683. Western campaign drives Turks from Hungary, and Turks lose almost all Hungarian possessions in Peace of Karlowitz (1699), which ends partition.

HUNGARY UNDER THE HABSBURGS
1700–1867

Vienna assumes control of Hungary's foreign affairs, defense, and tariffs, and it treats Transylvania as separate from Hungary. Peasant rebellion in 1703 provokes an eight-year uprising led by Ferenc Rákóczi against Habsburg rule. Treaty of Szatmár (1711) ends rebellion. Under Pragmatic Sanction (1723), Habsburg monarch agrees to rule Hungary as a king subject to restraints of Hungary's constitution and laws. Under Charles VI (1711–40) and Maria Theresa (1740–80), the economy declines. Joseph II (1780–90), an enlightened despot, attempts various changes, but the nobles resist and thus inspire a renaissance of Hungarian culture. Leopold I (1790–92) softens Habsburg policy. Under Francis I (1792–1835), Hungary stagnates. Toward the end of Francis's rule, liberal reformers István Széchenyi and Lajos Kossuth emerge; they increasingly press their demands under Ferdinand V (1835–48). In March 1848, a revolution against the absolute monarchy breaks out in Vienna and quickly spreads to Budapest. The Hungarians declare independence in April 1849, but with the help of Russian troops the Habsburgs reimpose control. Franz Joseph (1848–1916) revokes the Hungarian constitution and assumes absolute power. Austria is defeated by Sardinia and France in 1859 and by Prussia in 1866, resulting in the Compromise of 1867, which creates the Dual Monarchy of Austria-Hungary, also known as the Austro-Hungarian Empire.

DUAL MONARCHY
1867–1918

Under the Dual Monarchy, the Habsburg emperor reigns as king of Hungary. A Hungarian government administers domestic affairs, while Vienna manages foreign policy, defense, and finance. Croatia gains autonomy

Table A.—Continued

Date	Events
	from Hungary over its domestic affairs in 1868. Kálmán Tisza serves as prime minister 1875–90. Economic modernization begins, accompanied by rise of a middle class. István Tisza serves as prime minister 1903–05 and 1912–17. The June 28, 1914, assassination of Archduke Franz Ferdinand precipitates World War I (1914–18). Bourgeois-democratic revolution in Budapest, October 31, 1918. Mihály Károlyi, a liberal, assumes power. Hungary loses territory to Yugoslavia, Romania, Austria, and Czechoslovakia. A coalition of Social Democrats and communists takes power. Hungarian Soviet Republic is proclaimed under Béla Kun, March 21, 1919. Romanian forces occupy Budapest. Anticommunist government seizes control and imposes "white terror."
TRIANON HUNGARY 1920–45	Admiral Miklós Horthy is named regent of Hungary, March 21, 1920. Under Treaty of Trianon (June 4, 1920), Hungary loses more than two-thirds of its prewar territory, 60 percent of its prewar population, and most of its natural-resource base. Count István Bethlen serves as prime minister, 1921–31. Hungary joins League of Nations in 1922. Bethlen promotes industrial development, but economic progress is halted by Great Depression, 1929. Gyula Gömbös, a right-wing dictator, is in power, 1932–36. Gömbös forges close ties with Germany and Italy. Right-wing governments are in power under Kálmán Darányi (1936–38) and Béla Imrédy (1938–39). Pál Teleki serves as prime minister, 1939–41. Hungary joins Hitler's invasion of the Soviet Union in June 1941 and declares war against the Western Allies in December 1941. László Bárdossy prime minister, 1941–42, followed by Miklós Kállay, 1942–43. Nazi Germany occupies Hungary in April 1943. Pro-Nazi Döme Sztójay serves as prime minister, April 1943–August 1944, followed by Géza Lakatos, August–October 1944. Leader of fascist Arrow Cross Party, Ferenc Szálasi, serves as prime minister, October 1944–April 1945. Soviet troops drive all German troops out of Hungary by April 4, 1945.
POSTWAR HUNGARY 1945–	Allied Control Commission, with Soviet, American, and British representatives, holds sovereignty in Hungary, with Soviet chairman in absolute control. Second, expanded Provisional National Assembly chosen in which

Table A.—Continued

Country Profile

Formal Name: Republic of Hungary (the name was Hungarian People's Republic from August 1949 until October 1989).

Short Form: Hungary.

Term for Citizens: Hungarian(s).

Capital: Budapest.

Geography

Size: Approximately 92,103 square kilometers.

Topography: Lies in the central Danube Basin. Rolling foothills in the west; hilly region north of Budapest; remainder of the country to the east and south has a variety of terrains. Highest point: Mount Kékes, 1,008 meters.

Climate: Continental and mild.

Society

Population: Approximately 10.6 million in 1989; average annual growth rate, negative 0.2 percent.

Ethnic Groups: Magyars more than 95 percent of population. Minorities include Gypsies, Germans, Jews, Slovaks, Serbs, Slovenes, Croats, Romanians, and Greeks.

Language: Modern Hungarian spoken by all. Various dialects used at home. Minorities bilingual.

Religion: Religious freedom guaranteed by Constitution. About 67.5 percent Roman Catholic, 20 percent Reformed (Calvinist), 5 percent Lutheran, and 5 percent unaffiliated. Small numbers of other Protestant sects, Uniates, Orthodox, and Jews.

Education: Free, compulsory education from ages six to sixteen. About half of students get vocational and technical training. About 10 percent of population aged eighteen to twenty-two enrolled in regular daytime courses in higher education.

Welfare: Social insurance program includes free health care, unemployment compensation, and retirement benefits. Health care good, with decline in infant mortality and incidence of communicable diseases. High proportion of elderly; pensions low relative to wages.

Economy

Gross National Product: Estimated at US$84 billion in 1986; US$7,910 per capita, with 1.3 percent growth rate.

Energy and Mining: Country energy deficient; relies on imported crude oil and natural gas from Soviet Union and domestic lignite. Coal reserves plentiful, but energy a major problem for the 1990s. Dependent on imports for iron and nonferrous metals.

Industry: Manufacturing and chemicals predominate, with light industry and food processing also important. Emphasis on heavy industry in postwar period.

Agriculture: Largely collectivized, but with decentralized, loose restrictions on self-financing, much emphasis on private-plot production, and no obligatory targets. Very efficient by East Euroean standards; net exporter of grain, meat, and meat products.

Foreign Trade: Most important trading partner Soviet Union, but about half of foreign trade with Western countries. Principal imports: fuels, raw materials and semifinished products, agricultural and forestry products, light industrial goods. Principal exports: agricultural products, pharmaceuticals, bauxite, machine tools, and lighting equipment. Balance of trade negative in 1986: exports US$9.2 billion; imports US$9.6 billion.

Exchange Rate: Exchange rate in July 1989 about sixty-two forints per US$1.

Fiscal Year: Calendar year.

Fiscal Policy: Central planning with market reforms in the late 1980s to decentralize economic decision making and broaden scope for private ownership.

Transportation and Communications

Railroads: 7,769 kilometers total in 1986, of which 7,513 kilometers standard gauge, 221 narrow gauge, and 35 kilometers broad gauge; 1,128 kilometers double-tracked and 1,918 kilometers electrified.

Roads: 140,163 kilometers total in 1986, of which 29,796 kilometers concrete, asphalt, and stone block.

Inland Waterways: 1,622 kilometers in 1986.

Pipelines: 1,204 kilometers in 1986 for crude oil; 600 kilometers in 1986 for refined products; and 3,800 kilometers in 1986 for natural gas.

Ports: Budapest's Csepel the principal port; also Dunaújváros.

Airports: Eighty total in 1986, with ten having permanent surface runways. Budapest's Ferihegy the principal airport and only international airport.

Telecommunications: 770,200 telephones in 1986, or about 145 per 1,000 persons. Severe shortage of telephone lines.

Government and Politics

Politics: Monopolized by Hungarian Socialist Workers' Party (HSWP), the communist party. Other parties reappeared in liberalized conditions of late 1980s, including Independent Smallholders' Party and Social Democratic Party. Opposition Roundtable engaged in talks with HSWP to reform political system.

Government: Constitution of 1949 substantially amended in 1972. National Assembly met infrequently but was gaining importance in 1989. Presidential Council and Council of Ministers principal government bodies. Important posts occupied by high-ranking HSWP members.

Foreign Relations: Diplomatic relations with most countries. Allied with Soviet Union in international affairs. Relations with United States throughout postwar period; since late 1970s, these relations have warmed considerably and in late 1980s have blossomed.

International Agreements: Participation in Council for Mutual Economic Assistance (Comecon), Warsaw Pact, and United Nations. Signatory to Helsinki Accords and Mutual and Balanced Force Reduction Agreement.

National Security

Armed Forces: Hungarian People's Army in 1989 included ground forces (77,000 with 58 percent conscripts); air force (22,000 with 36 percent conscripts); Danube Flotilla (700); and Border Guards (11,000 with 70 percent conscripts). All forces organized under Ministry of Defense. Soviet Southern Group of Forces stationed in Hungary numbered 65,000 troops.

Ground Forces: Three corps, with combined total of five tank brigades and ten motorized rifle brigades; independent artillery and surface-to-surface missile brigades; one airborne battalion; one antitank regiment; one antiaircraft regiment; and surface-to-air missile regiments. Danube Flotilla had eighty-two vessels in 1988.

Air Force: One air division and one air defense division. Air division had three fighter or fighter-bomber regiments, one helicopter regiment, and one reconnaissance squadron. Air defense division had three surface-to-air regiments in late 1980s.

Equipment: Primarily Soviet.

Paramilitary: Included Security Police apparatus (15,000) and Workers' Guard (60,000) in 1988. Both forces received some military training.

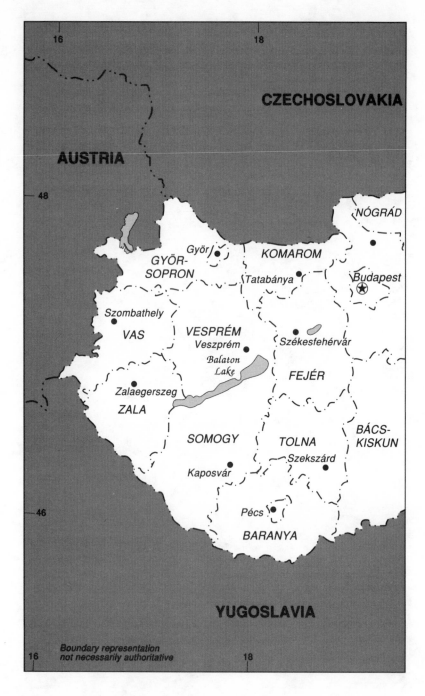

Figure 1. Administrative Divisions of Hungary, 1989

20

22

SOVIET
UNION

BORSOD-ABAUJ-
ZEMPLÉN

Salgótarján●

●Miskolc

SZABOLCS-
SZATMÁR

48

Eger ●

HEVES

●Nyíregyháza

Debrecen ●

PEST

SZOLNOK

HAJDÚ-
BIHAR

●Szolnok

Kecskemét ●

BÉKÉS

ROMANIA

●Békéscsaba

CSONGRÁD

●Szeged

—··—	International boundary
—·—	Megyes (counties)
⊛	National capital
●	Megye (county) capital

*Six cities have megye (county) status
and also serve as administrative
centers for surrounding megyes.*

0   25   50   **Kilometers**

0   25   50   **Miles**

20

22

Introduction

THE HUNGARIAN PEOPLE'S REPUBLIC came into existence in 1949 when, with Soviet support, the Hungarian Workers' Party (HWP) eliminated the last of its rivals and proclaimed the country a "people's democracy." The proclamation of the Hungarian People's Republic was part of Soviet dictator Joseph Stalin's plan to enforce total Soviet domination over the countries in Eastern Europe that Soviet armies had occupied in their war against Nazi Germany.

Like other countries in Eastern Europe, Hungary was completely Sovietized. The Constitution of 1949 established the leading role of the HWP in all aspects of Hungarian life. In turn, the HWP took its orders from Stalin. Hungary was also forced to adopt the Soviet model in its economy and society. Hungary embarked on an ambitious drive to industrialize its economy, and the new regime collectivized agriculture. The property of the prewar ruling classes was expropriated, and the regime undertook a reign of terror against its perceived political enemies, who eventually included a number of prominent communists. The Hungarian military was subordinated to the Soviet military, and the regime established a large secret police force, which answered to Moscow, not Budapest.

On October 23, 1989, the Hungarian People's Republic came to an end. Acting President Mátyás Szűrős proclaimed the new republic: "As provisional president of our Republic, I greet . . . the citizens of our country, our friends abroad. I ceremonially announce that, with the declaration of the Constitution amended by the National Assembly, as from today, October 23, 1989, our country's state form and name is the Republic of Hungary." New amendments to the Constitution asserted "the values of both bourgeois democracy and democratic socialism," eliminated the clause of the Constitution that established the leading role of the communist party in government and society, and proclaimed a regime based on the rule of law. These new amendments followed the Fourteenth Party Congress of the Hungarian Socialist Workers' Party (HSWP—the Hungarian Workers' Party had been renamed the Hungarian Socialist Workers' Party on November 1, 1956), in which the party split between reformers and conservatives. Out of this congress, which had convened October 6, a new party emerged—the Hungarian Socialist Party (HSP)—which was modeled on the socialist parties of Western Europe and was designed to operate within a multiparty system. Thus, in 1989 Hungary experienced a political transformation. With Poland, it was in the forefront of communist countries attempting to reform their polity, economy, and social relations.

A number of internal economic and social factors led to the crisis that brought about this transformation. A Soviet leadership itself attempting to carry through far-reaching reforms allowed Hungary to implement radical reforms. The example of wide-ranging political and economic reforms in Poland also spurred Hungary's leaders to action.

The economic crisis had been brewing since the mid-1970s. Beginning in 1973, world oil prices rose precipitously, having a devastating effect on Hungary, which was almost completely dependent on foreign energy suppliers, mainly the Soviet Union. Hungary's leaders responded to higher energy prices with a plan to accelerate economic growth and launched a number of major economic projects, but they could not carry them out efficiently. These efforts were designed to produce goods that could be exported in return for energy. Moreover, spending on consumption and investment also rose. To cover the costs of energy, consumption, and investment, Hungary borrowed from abroad, but, because its exports were unable to cover the costs of its hard-currency borrowings, the country ran up a large foreign currency deficit. Conservatives in the leadership used these problems to win support for the reversal of economic reforms that had been instituted in the late 1960s.

Similar problems arose in the late 1970s and early 1980s. Again, world energy prices rose, and Western banks limited the flow of credits as a result of the crackdown on the Solidarity labor movement in Poland and the insolvency in Romania. Increases in interest rates caused problems for Hungary's balance of payments.

Hungary joined the International Monetary Fund (IMF—see Glossary) and the World Bank (see Glossary) in 1982. These institutions compelled Hungary to introduce a new stabilization program, which called for reductions in spending on investment and consumption. Although by 1985 spending on investment was 21.8 percent less than it had been in 1981, prices rose. The Sixth Five-Year Plan (1981–85) called for economic growth of 14 percent to 17 percent over the previous plan period, but in fact growth rose only 7 percent. Industrial production increased a mere 12 percent, although the plan called for growth of 19 percent to 22 percent. Exports were to rise 37 to 39 percent but in fact rose only 27 percent.

Performance fell far short of the plan in the late 1980s as well. In 1986 national income, industrial production, and agricultural production did not meet the levels called for in the plan. In 1987 the economy fared somewhat better, but in 1988 inflation far exceeded the rate for the previous year. Hungary's foreign currency debt rose from US$8.6 billion in 1985 to US$18 billion by December 1987.

In 1989 the country's economic problems continued. By the end of 1989, Hungary had a state budget deficit of approximately 62.2 billion forints (for value of the forint—see Glossary), more than three times the planned budget deficit of 19.5 billion forints. The foreign debt stood at US$20 billion. Hungary had to cut its deficit or forego the last installment of a loan it had obtained from the IMF in May 1988. Inflation continued as well. Wages rose 12 to 13 percent rather than the planned 6 to 7 percent. Prices rose 15 to 16 percent rather than the planned 12 to 15 percent. From January through September 1989, industrial production was only 98.4 percent of what it had been during the same period in 1988. Output of the manufacturing sector fell 5.1 percent. Exports rose by about 22 percent in 1989, but the need to increase exports to the West forced enterprises to forego profitability in the interests of earning hard currency. As a result, bills owed to Hungarian firms went unpaid. In 1989 domestic debt stood at 950 billion forints.

Society felt the effects of the country's economic problems. To make ends meet, most Hungarians had to work very hard; in many cases, they worked more than one job. Western analysts estimated that between 25 and 40 percent of the population lived below the poverty level (about 5,200 forints per month). Average monthly wages were a mere 6,000 forints. Official statistics classed between 1.5 million and 3 million people (out of a population of 10.6 million) as "socially poor." This group included a large share of retired persons, about half of families with two children, and 70 to 90 percent of families with three or more children. Single heads of households and people working on less productive collective farms or living on isolated homesteads were also likely to be living below the poverty line.

Economic problems took their toll on the family. In the 1980s, every third marriage ended in divorce, and single parents headed about 12 percent of all families. In addition to the heavy work load needed to achieve a decent standard of living, another source of strain on the family was the shortage of housing, especially for young families. Having reduced its direct role in the provision of housing, the government encouraged private individuals to construct their own homes. By the late 1980s, most new housing units were privately constructed, but the country had a long way to go to meet the housing needs of its citizens.

In 1989 the government took steps to solve these problems. In contrast to the Soviet reaction to the 1956 uprising in Hungary and the 1968 Prague Spring in Czechoslovakia, when it invaded these countries to ensure continued communist party domination, the Soviet Union in 1989 announced support for Hungary's political and economic reform efforts. Such reforms included the introduction of a capitalist market economy and the emergence of a multiparty system, anathema to the old communist system.

In addition, Hungary could count on Poland to join it in a pro-reform bloc within the Warsaw Pact alliance (see Glossary). In June 1989, the first free elections in the history of postwar Eastern Europe took place in Poland. These elections eventually brought to power a Solidarity-led government that intended to institute many of the same political and economic reforms in Poland that Hungary's leaders, as well as Hungary's opposition groups, envisaged for their country. In late 1989, the reform bloc within the Warsaw Pact was strengthened as the German Democratic Republic (East Germany), Bulgaria, and Czechoslovakia began their own reform efforts.

Although the most important steps toward creating a democracy were taken in late 1989, the effort actually began with a number of measures in the first half of the year. On January 11, 1989, the National Assembly passed laws on associations and assembly, the first in a series of steps aimed at introducing a multiparty system in Hungary. On March 15, 1989, for the first time in postwar history, the government allowed commemoration of the anniversary of the 1848 revolt against the Habsburg Empire. About 100,000 people attended the demonstration in Budapest, and smaller demonstrations took place throughout the country. The demonstrators called for government recognition of civil and political rights and political pluralism. Shortly thereafter, Imre Mécs, a member of the dissident Committee for Historical Justice, said that a return to the old ways of ruling the country would be very difficult "after hundreds of thousands of people throughout the country have shouted out demands for their rights." On March 22, 1989, the National Assembly passed a law that granted the right to strike (although within strictly defined limits).

The reburial of Imre Nagy and his associates on June 16 marked the most important symbolic break with Hungary's past in the first half of 1989. Most Hungarians had never accepted the regime's verdict that the events of 1956 represented a counterrevolution against Marxism-Leninism. The massive attendance at the reburial and the millions who watched the events on television showed that Hungarians rejected the regime that had been placed in power by Soviet troops in 1956.

The media were becoming more open as a consequence of the reforms. In late 1988, a number of independent publications had been established, including *Kapu* (Gate), which had a circulation of more than 35,000 by January 1989; *Reform,* part of a joint venture with media magnate Axel Springer's conglomerate in the Federal Republic of Germany (West Germany), which by early 1989 had a circulation of 256,000; and *Hitel* (Credit), which covered social and political issues and literature.

It was the HSWP that set the stage for more profound changes. Party leaders Imre Pozsgay and Rezső Nyers sought to manage the country's severe economic, social, and political problems by sharing power with organizations representing other sectors of the population. Indeed, the party's reformist wing—which was headed by Pozsgay and Nyers—had accepted the ideas and program of the opposition.

The strength of the reformers became apparent at a February 10, 1989, plenum of the Central Committee of the HSWP. At that plenum, the party set as its goal the achievement of popular sovereignty and a constitutional state. At a February 20 plenum, the party Central Committee approved a draft of a new constitution that contained no clause on the leading role of the party. At its March 1989 plenum, the party Central Committee came out in support of a multiparty system, free elections, and independent trade unions; recognized certain individual freedoms; and called for the creation of a state governed by a democratic socialist constitution and characterized by an independent judiciary, representative democracy, and depoliticized military. The party's new Action Program "offered cooperation and agreement on national issues of vital importance to all citizens and organizations that think in a progressive manner and accept responsibility for the country." In line with its changed outlook, the Central Committee gave up its *nomenklatura* (see Glossary) authority. According to one party spokesman, this right had become "obsolete." Indeed, on May 10, 1989, the National Assembly approved a government reshuffle involving five ministers and one state secretary with ministerial rank. Chairman of the Council of Ministers Miklós Németh himself, rather than the Central Committee of the HSWP, selected the new officials.

The Central Committee also outlined a reform program for the economy. At its February 10 plenum, the Central Committee determined to end the country's "economic, political, and moral crisis" by creating a market economy based on mixed ownership. On

May 4, 1989, the Central Committee released its "Proposal for a Three-Year Transformation and Stabilization Program," which called for opening up Hungary to world markets and trade and maintaining the country's solvency and creditworthiness. The proposal advocated a change from state ownership to stock companies and limited partnerships and "the sale of state-owned [enterprises] to foreigners and private individuals." State subsidies to enterprises would be drastically reduced. The proposal stressed the importance of small- and medium-sized companies. For agriculture, the proposal advocated private ownership, easy lease terms, and the purchase of land by private individuals.

The new legislation on political parties and the liberalized atmosphere in the country led to the formation of many new political parties. Indeed, with the decisions made by the HSWP in the late winter of 1988 and spring of 1989, it was clear that the HSWP was taking many aspects of its own reform program from the programs of other parties and organizations promoting fundamental political and economic changes. Many of these parties were not altogether new, however; they were revivals of historical parties that had been disbanded in the late 1940s. Other parties were indeed new, formed largely by dissident intellectuals and students.

The first historical party to reemerge after years of inactivity was the Independent Smallholders' Party, which was refounded in November 1988. In August 1989, the Smallholders had an estimated 6,000 members grouped into 230 chapters. The party called for privatization of the economy and free enterprise; returning land to the peasants from whom it had been seized during Hungary's campaign to collectivize agriculture in the late 1940s; free elections in a pluralistic multiparty political system; and a new constitution that would include a clause establishing Hungary's neutrality.

Another historical party that reestablished itself was the Hungarian Independence Party, which was refounded on April 24, 1989. The members of the original Hungarian Independence Party had broken with the Smallholders' Party in 1947 because they believed that the Smallholders were too willing to cooperate with the Hungarian Communist Party. In 1989 the main political goal of the Hungarian Independence Party was "the purest democracy." It advocated government recognition of individual political and civil rights; the removal of communist party control over the army, police, and judiciary; the expansion of legislative power at the expense of the executive; a free market system; strong support for private sector entrepreneurship; tax relief to encourage entrepreneurs; the reprivatization of agriculture; and "perpetual neutrality" for Hungary.

The Democratic People's Party was active in Hungarian politics in the late 1940s but was banned in 1949. In 1989 this party reappeared as the Christian Democratic People's Party, which grew out of the Aron Márton Association (named after a Catholic bishop in Transylvania). The draft program of the Christian Democratic People's Party defined it as "a political organization with a Christian worldview that is, however, independent of the Churches." It called for multiparty democracy, parliamentary government, full guarantees for human and civil rights, and autonomy for local communities. For the economy, this party advocated free enterprise combined with a welfare system to help those disadvantaged by a free market system. In foreign policy, the Christian Democratic People's Party called for accelerating Hungary's integration into Europe and the country's return to the fold of Christian civilization.

Finally, among the historical parties, the Social Democratic Party was refounded on January 9, 1989. Originally founded in 1890, the Social Democratic Party was forced to merge with the Hungarian Communist Party in June 1948 to create the Hungarian Workers' Party. Leaders of the reemergent Social Democratic Party claimed 30,000 members, but the actual figure was closer to 3,000. The party was weakened by a split between those who had belonged to the party before 1948 and younger members who sought leadership positions. The Social Democratic Party advocated a West European-style social democracy for Hungary.

Of the new political parties, the largest at the end of 1989 was the Hungarian Democratic Forum, which was founded on September 27, 1987. In November 1989, the forum had approximately 20,200 members organized into 327 local organizations in 306 localities across Hungary. This party was largely the creation of the provincial intelligentsia and was closely identified with Hungarian populism (an interwar political movement that distrusted Western capitalism and favored an economy based on small agricultural producers and independent peasant entrepreneurs; it also included antirationalist and anti-semitic strains). It advocated free and democratic elections, a multiparty system, an increase in funding for education and culture, improvement of social security, and a greater role for the church in providing social services. The Hungarian Democratic Forum came out for a "third road" for the economy: an economy neither capitalist nor socialist. It proposed dismantling the state sector in a "socially controlled and economically rational way" and encouraging the emergence of an entrepreneurial stratum. However, the entrepreneurs were to be groups, not individuals.

The Alliance of Free Democrats was founded on December 13, 1988. In July 1989, the alliance had about 3,000 members, who were organized into twenty chapters in Budapest and fifteen in the counties. This party was largely the creation of the Budapest intelligentsia. Two ideological strains made up the alliance: democratic socialists, who favored state intervention in the economy and a mixture of both state and private property; and classical liberals, who supported an unrestrained free market and the denationalization of the economy. The party's program called for a new constitution to end the communist party's monopoly of power, to secure the sovereignty of the people, and to limit the power of the state by separating the powers of the executive, legislature, and judiciary. In the economic realm, the alliance's program called for the "denationalization of the economy," the expansion of private ownership, cuts in military expenditure, and state assistance to the poorest members of the population to minimize poverty. In foreign policy, the alliance advocated neutrality for Hungary and the withdrawal of Soviet troops.

The Federation of Young Democrats, founded in 1988, was made up of 4,000 to 5,000 members between the ages of sixteen and thirty-five. Members were mainly college and university students. The party advocated a multiparty system, political and military independence, the evolution of the Warsaw Pact into a political alliance, and the privatization of economic assets.

In the spring of 1989, several opposition parties joined together to form the Opposition Roundtable to establish new rules for the conduct of politics as Hungary entered the era of reform. The roundtable was made up of the Alliance of Free Democrats, the Hungarian Democratic Forum, the Social Democratic Party, the Independent Smallholders' Party, the Hungarian People's Party, the Federation of Young Democrats, and the Endre Bajcsy-Zsilinszky Society (an organization dedicated to environmental protection and the defense of Hungarian minority rights in Romania). (The Democratic League of Free Trade Unions had observer status at the roundtable.) The Opposition Roundtable had two basic objectives: to enter into talks with the HSWP to determine the principles and rules that would govern the transition to a pluralist democracy, and to discuss the means necessary to overcome Hungary's social and economic crisis.

In June 1989, the Opposition Roundtable entered into formal talks with the HSWP and the so-called "third side," which was made up of the Patriotic People's Front, the National Council of Trade Unions, and other organizations allied with the HSWP. In the negotiations, one committee dealt with political matters, including constitutional changes, establishment of a presidency, setting of a date for elections to the National Assembly, revisions of the penal code, creation of a new law on information, and securing of guarantees against a violent rollback of the reform process. A second committee dealt with economic problems, including the reform of property rights, the introduction and strengthening of market mechanisms in the economy, and, most generally, "strategic questions of dealing with the economic crisis" and the means of treating the social consequences of the crisis.

The Opposition Roundtable and the party had different objectives in the negotiations. The former negotiated on the premise that the roots of the economic crisis lay in the political system; it therefore sought to emphasize constitutional changes and overall political reform. By contrast, the HSWP emphasized measures to alter the economy. Thus, the party sought to make the opposition groups in the roundtable share responsibility for the dislocations, unemployment, and inflation that would accompany the effort to pull Hungary out of its economic crisis. The party hoped to share political responsibility and yet give up as little power as possible. The HSWP hoped to exact agreement to its economic reform program by threatening to effect political reforms without the participation of the Opposition Roundtable. About 75 percent of the delegates to the National Assembly were HSWP members, and the party leadership believed it could ram through reforms using its vast majority in the legislature.

The parties that made up the Opposition Roundtable represented only a very small fraction of the population. Further, the HSWP, although numbering several hundred thousand members, had little claim to legitimacy within society. The members of the "third side" also had little support among society as a whole. Thus, in the summer of 1989 a number of critics complained that the population as a whole had no say in the negotiations that were determining Hungary's political and economic future.

In several elections to fill seats in the National Assembly that had been vacated, the population did have the chance to make its voice heard. The HSWP lost every election.

On July 22, 1989, Gábor Rozsik was the first opposition candidate elected to the National Assembly. He ran for election in the town of Gödöllő, near Budapest, and won 69.5 percent of the vote. Rozsik was a candidate of the Hungarian Democratic Forum but also had the support of the Alliance of Free Democrats and the Federation of Young Democrats.

In other elections held on July 22, either less than the required 50 percent of the eligible voters of the election district participated or else none of the candidates managed to receive a majority of the votes cast. In Szeged the Hungarian Democratic Forum's candidate won 59.4 percent of the vote, but the turnout was less than the required 50 percent. In the repeat election on August 5, the Hungarian Democratic Forum's candidate won with about 62 percent of the vote, while the HSWP's candidate received 22 percent of the vote. In Kecskemét no candidate received the majority of votes, but in the August 5 runoff election, the Hungarian Democratic Forum's candidate won with about 70 percent of the vote. In the July 22 election in Kiskunf-élegyháza, 61 percent of the people voted, but no candidate received a majority. The HSWP's candidate, however, won 44.7 percent of the votes, the highest vote total. In the repeat election, only 46 percent of eligible voters participated, and the result was therefore invalid.

Finally, in a September 16 election for a National Assembly seat in Zala County, the HSWP candidate received less than one-third of the votes cast. The Hungarian Democratic Forum, the Alliance of Free Democrats, and the Federation of Young Democrats all supported the winner, who received more than 59 percent of the vote.

These elections demonstrated serious weaknesses on the part of the HSWP. In all locales, despite almost a total monopoly of the media and overwhelming advantages over the opposition in funds available to run campaigns, HSWP candidates showed poorly. These elections served as yet another reminder that the HSWP had either to transform itself fundamentally or to resign itself to a marginal role in Hungary's new political system.

Other evidence for the lack of support for the HSWP came from poll data. A survey conducted by János Simon and László Bruszt of the Sociological and Social Science Institute of the Hungarian Academy of Sciences found that only 36.5 percent of those surveyed would vote for the HSWP. Most of that support came in the villages and small towns. The support of the remainder of those surveyed was divided among the Social Democratic Party (13 percent); the Hungarian Democratic Forum (11. 4 percent); the Alliance of Free Democrats (5.6 percent); the Smallholders' Party (5.4 percent); the Hungarian People's Party (4.3 percent); and the Christian Democratic People's Party (4.3 percent).

The lack of public support for the HSWP did not deter it from attempting to carry through its objectives in negotiations with the Opposition Roundtable. In September an agreement was signed that seemed at least in the short run to have met the HSWP's objectives. In addition, this agreement caused a split in the roundtable itself, thereby seeming to bring additional benefits to the party.

The agreement between the HSWP and the Hungarian Democratic Forum, the Independent Smallholders' Party, the Hungarian People's Party, and the Endre Bajscy-Zsilinszky Society was to establish "the political and legal conditions for a peaceful transition to a multiparty system." It contained six draft laws dealing with the following issues: the establishment of a constitutional court to ensure the constitutionality of legislation; the acceptance by the HSWP of the values of bourgeois democracy and democratic socialism; a draft electoral law; amendments to the penal code and criminal code to ensure that they "conform to the accepted norms of human and civil rights"; an increase in the amount of state aid for election campaigns from 35 million forints to 100 million forints; and the surrender by the HSWP of some 2 billion forints of its assets to finance other political parties.

The agreement also called for the creation of a presidency that would embody the unity of the nation, exercise authority through the Council of Ministers, and act as commander in chief of the armed forces in peacetime. Any party or group with 50,000 supporting signatures could nominate candidates for president and vice president. The winning candidate would have to receive at least half the votes with a minimum turnout of half to two-thirds of the electorate. If no candidate received the necessary number of votes, a second round of voting would be held. According to the agreement, the presidential election was to take place before new elections to the National Assembly.

The Alliance of Free Democrats and the Federation of Young Democrats did not sign the agreement. First, they argued that it failed to require the withdrawal of the HSWP from the workplace, a presence that lay at the basis of the party's substantial control over the economy. Second, these two parties maintained that the agreement did not call upon the HSWP to render a full accounting of its finances and property. Third, the Alliance of Free Democrats and the Federation of Young Democrats also believed that the agreement was inadequate because it did not call for the dissolution of the Workers' Guard, the HSWP's private army.

Fourth and perhaps most important, the Alliance of Free Democrats and the Federation of Young Democrats held that the agreement was seriously flawed in setting the elections for president before the elections to the National Assembly. The HSWP wanted the elections for president to be held relatively quickly because its candidate—Imre Pozsgay—was the most popular political figure in the country at the time. For its part, the Hungarian Democratic Forum minimized the importance of Pozsgay's candidacy because of the difficulty of even a well-known politician's winning an absolute majority, the damage already caused to Pozsgay's candidacy by his role in the HSWP leadership, and the fact that Pozsgay could not count on the support of the conservative and centrist factions of the HSWP. The Alliance of Free Democrats argued, by contrast, that election of a president before the elections to the National Assembly would distort the parliamentary elections, that only the new National Assembly should have the power to define the role of the elections to the National Assembly, and that the new president could unduly influence the outcome of the elections to the National Assembly. Finally, the Alliance of Free Democrats and the Federation of Young Democrats underscored the dangers of electing a communist president in a fledgling democracy.

The Alliance of Free Democrats and the Federation of Young Democrats decided to call for the resolution of these four issues by a popular referendum. According to a law passed on June 15, 1989, 100,000 signatures would be sufficient to call for a binding popular referendum on matters subject to political dispute. The two parties managed to collect almost 200,000 signatures, and a referendum was scheduled for November 26. The Alliance of Free Democrats and the Federation of Young Democrats both urged Hungarians to render a vote of "yes" on the following issues: disbanding the Workers' Guard, abolishing party cells in the workplace, demanding that the HSWP give a full account of its assets, and requiring that the newly elected National Assembly elect the president.

On September 18, 1989, negotiations on the economy began between the Opposition Roundtable and the HSWP. Talks were quickly suspended in the third committee, which was charged with discussing changes in ownership and determining how many enterprises should remain under state control. Talks proceeded in the other five committees, which dealt with the state budget deficit, major state investments, social welfare, land reform, and ownership reform.

HSWP losses in the four valid National Assembly elections, the agreement with elements of the Opposition Roundtable, and the widespread dissatisfaction with the agreement reached between the roundtable and the party set the stage for the Fourteenth Party Congress of the HSWP, which began on October 6, 1989. These events demonstrated that Hungary had entered a new political era in which the methods and structure of a Marxist-Leninist party were no longer relevant. The decisions reached at the Fourteenth Party Congress marked an attempt by the party leadership to adapt to this new era.

The party had undergone some significant changes prior to the congress. The most important among these changes was the emergence of factions within the party. Marxist-Leninist parties had long condemned factions within their ranks; decision making was carried out via democratic centralism, which required a unified party position in support of the leadership on all issues of theory and practice.

In late 1988 and 1989, factions did indeed arise within the party, whose leadership was split between reformers (who encouraged the rise of factions) and conservatives (who condemned the incipient factions). Factions in support of reforms within the party—known as the "reform circles"—had been growing rapidly since November 1988, when the first groups were organized by József Géczi of the Department of Political Theory at Attila József University in Szeged. The first national conference of reform circles took place in Szeged on May 21-22, 1989, and was attended by more than 400 representatives of 110 reform groups. The manifesto produced by the conference maintained that problems in Hungary were part of a "crisis of Asiatic despotism." The document called for the building of a new organization based on the values of the Hungarian progressive movement, the socialist movement, progressive bourgeois traditions, and Hungarian populism. The manifesto demanded the reform of the HSWP. The reform circles also held a second conference in Budapest on September 2-3 to prepare for the party congress.

By contrast, the Ferenc Münnich Society (named after the minister of the armed forces and internal affairs who came to power with János Kádár in 1956) was a faction formed by party conservatives in November 1988. Retired army officers, retired state security officers, members of the Workers' Guard, and conservative party members predominated among its 10,000 to 20,000 members. According to Róbert Ribánszki, who was one of the society's leaders, "the primary goal of the [Ferenc Münnich Society] is to stop the further deterioration of socialist achievements . . . and to lend support to the development and strengthening of socialism." The Ferenc Münnich Society sought the retention of the HSWP's leading role in social, economic, and governmental institutions. It strongly criticized the reform circles and the party's reform leaders, chiefly Pozsgay and Nyers.

Delegates to the Fourteenth Party Congress of the HSWP came from the different party factions. In fact, the rules for election of delegates expressly called for the representation of these factions at the congress. Every party member could "propose delegates and be eligible for election." The guidelines stressed that members were to acquaint themselves with the views of candidates prior to the election of delegates, so they could vote for the representatives of the faction of their choice. At the congress itself, Pozsgay stated that "our party will respect the freedom of platforms and trends, and respect the protection of minority rights more strongly" than the former party. The guidelines for delegate selection and Pozsgay's sentiments starkly contrasted with election procedures for previous congresses.

To be sure, party leaders did not always follow the guidelines in carrying out the delegate selection. Nevertheless, a number of platforms were strongly represented at the congress. At the beginning of the proceedings, the Reform Alliance had 464 delegates; the People's Democratic Platform (a centrist grouping), 68 delegates; the For the Equality of Chances of the Provinces Platform, 35 delegates; the For the HSWP Platform, 35 delegates; the Young People's Platform, 28 delegates; and the Agricultural and Food Processing Platform, 28 delegates. In addition, in another departure from previous congresses, delegates from districts south of Lake Balaton and the southwest met to decide on a common approach to the interests of their regions (see fig. 1).

The Reform Alliance was the best organized of the factions, and it had the most elaborate program. By the end of the second day of the congress, the Reform Alliance had 511 members, about 40 percent of the total. This faction played an important role in the outcome of the congress. It called for an open break with the past, as well as for a repudiation of the HSWP's crimes and mistakes, and it sought to staff leadership positions with new personnel who would promote new kinds of policies. The Reform Alliance also advocated the democratization of party decision making.

Indeed, in large measure the congress produced the new policies called for by the Reform Alliance. To begin with, the party changed its name to the Hungarian Socialist Party (HSP). The party's statutes still defined it as a "Marxist political organization," but it fully accepted "the values of human development, humanism, freedom, and democracy." The term *Leninist* did not appear in any of the documents emanating from the congress.

The HSP's manifesto dedicated the organization to building a "democratic, law-governed state marked by direct democracy" and the creation of a "market-based economy." The party also called for a social welfare policy to moderate extreme differences in living standards but at the same time advocated a system of wages and salaries to reward productivity. The party's program sought an "undisturbed and balanced relationship" with the Soviet Union but at the same time obligated the party to work for mutually advantageous political and economic relations with every country and with every "integrating and cooperative organization." Finally, the HSP came out firmly in support of minority rights within Hungary and castigated the violation of the rights of Hungarians elsewhere.

The HSP's rejection of Leninist organizational principles was clearly apparent in its new organizational structure. The bylaws allowed freedom of choice in joining or leaving the party; freedom of conscience, expression, and action; and tolerance of different views, opinions, and trends within the party. It also located in the will of the membership the source of every decision and action by the party. According to the bylaws, any minority view that had the support of at least 10 percent of the membership was to be stated along with the position of the majority. Terms of office for party officials were to be decided by the electing forum; nominations were to take place by open ballot, and elections were to be held by secret ballot.

The party congress was to be the HSP's highest representative and decision-making organ. The National Steering Committee replaced the Central Committee to act as "the party membership's representative and control organ between the congresses." The National Presidium, consisting of twenty-five people, was to lead the party between congresses. Except for the chairman of the HSP, members of the National Presidium could not be members of the Steering Committee. The party leader, called the chairman, was to be elected by a secret ballot of the party congress. Rezső Nyers was elected chairman of the HSP with 87 percent of the vote. The chairman and the leader of the party's bloc in the National Assembly served as ex officio members of the National Presidium; all others were elected from a slate of candidates prepared by the delegates to the congress, by a nominating committee, or by the chairman. The National Conciliation Committee was set up to protect party members' rights and to ensure that the actions of national and local party organs conformed to the HSP's bylaws. The Central Financial Committee was established to manage the party's finances and property.

At the bottom of the HSP's organizational pyramid were the basic organizations, which required a minimum of three members. Local organizations were to be set up in election districts throughout the country. Regional party organs were to be established at the county level and in Budapest. According to the bylaws, these party organs were independent of the national organization. They were to decide on their own which candidates to nominate for election to local representative bodies within their jurisdictions, and they could nominate candidates from their jurisdictions for election to the National Assembly.

At the Fourteenth Party Congress, the leadership gave each HSWP member until October 31, 1989, to decide whether or not to accept membership in the new party. The HSWP's membership had declined throughout 1989. In mid-1988 the HSWP had approximately 817,000 members; by September 1989, its membership stood at 725,000. However, relatively few members of the old party decided to join the new organization. As a result, the leadership decided to extend the deadline for old HSWP members to December 31. As of mid-December, the HSP claimed about 51,000 members.

Reactions of Hungary's opposition groups to the changes in the HSWP were decidedly mixed. The Hungarian Democratic Forum stated that "reform of the ruling party is a long-awaited and important event" but believed that the party had failed to make a clear break with the past. The Alliance of Free Democrats feared that "the setting up of the HSP does not mean genuine change. The first resolutions of the new party and the composition of its presidium do not indicate, for the time being, a break away from its past as a state party." The Social Democratic Party stated that it "did not consider the new socialist party, which carries certain social democratic features, a real political rival" and that free elections would show whether the public considered the changes to be credible.

Conservative party members decided to maintain the existence of the HSWP. Former General Secretary Károly Grósz was to become a member, as was János Berecz, the former HSWP ideology secretary. The conservatives held their own Fourteenth Party Congress of the HSWP in mid-December 1989. The HSWP leadership dedicated itself to creating a "unified Marxist party of workers, peasants, and intellectuals" to retain the achievements of the past four decades, to overcome the country's "stifling crisis," and to find paths leading to the realization of socialist ideals.

Shortly after the HSP congress, the National Assembly took action on three measures that were the subject of the November 26 referendum called for by the Alliance of Free Democrats and the Federation of Young Democrats. In a session on October 17–18, the National Assembly voted to ban all party organizations from the workplace. At the same session, the legislature passed a law on political parties, which called for redistribution of some of the HSP's assets to other political parties and the selling off of other party assets to help finance the government's health and education systems. Finally, on October 20 the National Assembly disbanded the Workers' Guard, without naming a successor organization.

In October the National Assembly also passed a number of other measures that would have a significant impact on Hungary's political future. The country's name was changed to the Republic of Hungary. A new amendment to the Constitution vested legislative power solely in the National Assembly, which henceforth would have the power to draft and enact laws, confirm the government, and pass a budget. A second new amendment abolished the Presidential Council and in its place established the presidency. The president of the republic, who was given a term of office of four years, was granted extensive powers: to serve as commander in chief of the armed forces; to declare war or a state of emergency if the National Assembly were prevented from doing so; to represent Hungary in foreign relations; to sign international agreements; and to nominate the president of the Supreme Court (who then required confirmation by the National Assembly).

A third amendment created the Constitutional Court to review the constitutionality of laws. It was to have power to annul laws deemed unconstitutional. Individuals and institutions could turn to the court with grievances against the state. The Constitutional Court consisted of fifteen judges, who were to be nominated by a committee of the National Assembly made up of representatives of various parties and then confirmed by the whole National Assembly.

Yet another amendment stated that "the Hungarian Republic recognizes the inalienable and inviolable rights of man" and that the state's foremost duty is to protect those rights. The Constitution explicitly endorsed the freedoms of speech, press, and assembly.

Finally, an amendment on the economic system defined it as "a market economy that also makes use of the advantages of economic planning, and in which public and private property are equal and receive equal protection." More detailed legislation that would transform the economy from a command system to a market-based system was to be dealt with later.

Other laws concerned the election system. A party assets law stipulated that party assets must be paid for exclusively through membership fees, state support, and after-tax profits of companies and limited companies founded by the parties. All parties represented in the National Assembly were to be entitled to state budget support: 25 percent of the funds were to be shared equally, while 75 percent of the funds were to be divided according to the number of seats held by each party. The amount of funds would be determined by the availability of money in the budget.

According to the new electoral law, the National Assembly to be elected in 1990 will have 386 members chosen in a two-part secret ballot. One ballot will elect 176 deputies from individual electoral districts each having about 350,000 people. Parties and individuals nominate candidates for these seats. If no candidate wins a majority in a given district, a second round of balloting is held. Those parties that are able to enter candidates in at least 25 percent of the electoral districts in a given county (and in Budapest, which has the status of a county) can nominate a party list for that county (or for Budapest). In the second ballot, voters will choose a party as such, that is, they will cast a ballot for one of the county-level lists, from which another 152 deputies will be elected. Parties that are able to put forward seven or more of these lists or that win 66 percent of the vote for the county-level list in any given county can enter a slate for the national list of deputies. Fifty-eight deputies will be named from the national list; seats will be distributed in proportion to the total number of votes secured by losing parties on the county-level ballot. However, those parties that fail to win at least 4 percent of the votes cast for the county-level lists will not qualify for party representation in the National Assembly, although their individual members could win seats in the district-level elections.

Approximately one month after the National Assembly enacted these momentous changes, the national referendum called for by the Alliance of Free Democrats and the Federation of Young Democrats was held. The questions on the removal of the HSP from the workplace, the nature of the HSP's assets, and the disbanding of the Workers' Guard were moot at this point because the National Assembly had already passed laws resolving these issues. However, 50.1 percent of those who voted supported the proposition that the presidential election should take place *after* the elections to the National Assembly. Subsequently, district elections to the National Assembly were set for March 25, 1990.

Hungary's political transformation during 1989 was reflected in military and foreign policy developments. In May Hungary removed the barbed wire fence that marked the border with Austria. In September Hungary proposed establishment of a border security zone with Austria and Yugoslavia, as well as a number of steps to reduce its military presence along the borders with these two countries. Specifically, the proposal called for a fifty-kilometer-wide "confidence building zone" on either side of the boundaries with Austria and Yugoslavia. The number of tanks in these areas would be halved, and Austria and Yugoslavia would be given details of Hungary's deployments. Military exercises would be curtailed, and the Austrians and Yugoslavs would be invited to observe any exercises that were held.

The budget deficit led to defense budget cuts. In 1990 the military budget was to be reduced by 30 percent compared with 1989. In addition, the Ministry of Home Affairs—responsible for the police and the Border Guards—was to have a 1990 budget of 900 million forints less than it asked for. Armed forces were to be reduced from about 100,000 troops to less than 80,000 troops by 1991. Also beginning in 1991, military service was to be cut from eighteen months to one year. HSP organizations were withdrawing from the armed forces and attempting to set up organizations in residential areas.

These budget cuts and reductions in force levels were accompanied by the reorganization of the Ministry of Defense. First, the Main Political Administration (see Glossary), which supervised political and ideological work in the military, was disbanded. New education officers were to work side by side with commanders and to train soldiers in civics and educate them about social policy problems. Second, some of the functions of the Ministry of Defense were transferred to the new "Command of the Hungarian People's Army," which was to assume responsibility for actual military assignments. A smaller Ministry of Defense continued to function, but it had responsibility for military policy and other administrative and theoretical matters only. The minister of defense was accountable to the prime minister, and the commander of the Hungarian People's Army was responsible to the president, who was commander in chief of the armed forces.

On February 2, 1990, following talks between the Soviet Union and Hungary, Moscow agreed to withdraw all of its troops from Hungary. The communiqué that resulted from the talks stated that the two sides "agreed that the withdrawal of Soviet troops will be carried out on the basis of an intergovernmental agreement to be concluded within the shortest possible time." On March 10, 1990, Budapest and Moscow signed an agreement for the withdrawal of all Soviet forces from Hungary by June 30, 1991. The withdrawal began on March 11, 1990, and two-thirds of Soviet troops and equipment were to be removed by the end of 1990.

In foreign policy, Hungary continued to adhere to its semi-independent stance within the Warsaw Pact. In the early 1980s, Hungary had attempted to halt the deterioration of relations between East and West by seeking constructive relations with the leading states of the North Atlantic Treaty Organization (NATO). Hungary also attempted to develop relations with some states considered pariahs by other members of the Warsaw Pact, notably the

Republic of Korea (South Korea) and Israel, both of which it recognized in 1989. Moreover, in the late 1980s the Soviet Union also liberalized many of its own foreign policy positions in an effort to resolve a number of disagreements with Western countries and to seek help for its ailing economy. As part of this approach, Moscow allowed its East European allies much more leeway in foreign policy than it had in the past. Hungary managed to take great advantage of this new Soviet approach.

One of the most significant foreign policy events of the late 1980s was the visit of United States president George Bush to Hungary from July 11 to 13, 1989. President Bush gave moral and material support to Hungary's reform efforts. Four agreements resulted from Bush's visit: the Hungarian airline MALEV won approval to fly into and out of Los Angeles and Chicago; Hungary gained permission to open a consular office on the West Coast of the United States; the two countries signed an agreement on agricultural cooperation; and the two countries signed an agreement for a US$750,000 study by the University of Pittsburgh of the financial operations of Borsod-Abaúj-Zemplén County and its outdated steelworks.

President Bush also agreed to ask other Western countries to help Hungary and to request that the United States Congress make money available to assist the private sector in Hungary. The services of the United States Peace Corps were also to be made available to Hungary. Perhaps most important for Budapest, President Bush said he would ask Congress to give most-favored-nation status to Hungary on a permanent rather than on a yearly basis. On October 27, the president announced that Hungary would be perpetually granted most-favored-nation status.

Relations with the Soviet Union continued to prosper, as they had since Mikhail S. Gorbachev became Soviet leader in March 1985. Significantly, in 1989 Budapest and Moscow agreed to switch to dollar-accounted trade beginning in 1991. Hungary was to pay the Soviet Union for its energy and raw materials using dollars and applying current Western price rates. Hungary was to receive hard currency for its manufactures sold to the Soviet Union. Hungary would have to compete with Western firms for the Soviet market, but Hungary's leaders believed that such competition would help bring their country's industry up to world standards.

The move to trade in hard currency with the Soviet Union was expected to resolve the problem of Hungary's huge trade surplus with that country. In the first half of 1989, the surplus amounted to 800 million rubles. These rubles were not a convertible currency and therefore were of little use to Hungary. The surplus amounted to an interest-free loan to the Soviet Union, and the Hungarian economy could not afford this burden.

Hungary had more serious problems with three other Warsaw Pact allies—East Germany, Czechoslovakia, and Romania. East Germans traveling or vacationing in Hungary used Hungary's open border with Austria to flee to that country en route to West Germany. East Berlin had vociferously protested the Hungarian decision to allow the East Germans to leave for Austria. The official East German news agency called the decision "an organized trade in humans under the pretense of humanitarian considerations." However, after the emergence of a reform government in East Germany and the opening of the Berlin Wall in early November 1989, relations between the two countries warmed considerably.

Relations with Czechoslovakia became problematic when Hungary suspended work on the Gabčíkovo-Nagymaros Dam project on May 13. The Hungarian government took this action in response to public protests over the environmental damage caused by the project and in light of a recommendation by a panel of experts that the project be abandoned. In turn, Czechoslovakia charged that Hungary's suspension of the project was politically motivated and a violation of international law. On November 15, Hungary announced that the Nagymaros section of the dam "will not be built." The new reform government that took power in Czechoslovakia in late 1989 was drafting plans to suspend and halt its part of the project, which had also raised environmental concerns in that country.

Until the overthrow of Romanian leader Nicolae Ceauşescu in late December 1989, Hungary's relations with Romania had progressively worsened over the course of the year. The number of refugees from Romania who settled in Hungary steadily increased in 1989, and, significantly, the number of ethnic Romanians among the refugees rose to about 20 percent of the total.

In an attempt to resolve outstanding problems between the two countries, Rezső Nyers, together with Foreign Minister Gyula Horn and Prime Minister Miklós Németh, met Ceauşescu in Bucharest on July 8. The Hungarians sought a radical improvement in the treatment of ethnic Hungarians in Romania—the most important source of friction between Budapest and Bucharest. The Hungarians rejected Ceauşescu's claim that the nationality issue was strictly Romania's internal affair. The Hungarian delegation also called for easing travel restrictions between the two countries and appealed for a halt to Ceauşescu's plan to raze 7,000 to 8,000 villages and relocate their inhabitants in large apartment complexes. The meeting produced no result, as Ceauşescu again expressed the view that he had "solved" all nationality problems in his country.

The Romanian government's threats to the lives of László Tőkés, an ethnic Hungarian Reformed minister in Timişoara, Romania, and his family initiated the revolution in Romania that brought Ceauşescu's ouster and execution in December 1989. In response to the violence perpetrated by the Ceauşescu regime on its citizens in an effort to stem the popular revolt, the Hungarian government took several measures. Hungary called on the United Nations Security Council to involve itself in the Romanian affair. Hungary canceled the 1948 Treaty of Friendship and Cooperation between the two countries. Hungary also closed the border between Hungary and Romania and formally protested the events in Romania to Romanian representatives in Hungary.

As fighting broke out between the Romanian army, which was supporting the revolutionary Council of National Salvation Front, and Ceauşescu's secret police organization—the Securitate—Hungary extended support to the new regime in Romania. Hungary was the first foreign government to recognize the Council of National Salvation Front as the legitimate government of Romania. The Hungarian army maintained constant contact with the Romanian army. The radio locator units of the Hungarian army established the locations of several secret Securitate radio transmitters and relayed that information to the Romanian military leadership. The Hungarians offered ammunition to the Romanian army, but that offer was turned down. Finally, both the Hungarian government and private citizens and political parties proffered food and medical aid to the beleaguered Romanians.

The revolution in Romania promised an immediate improvement in relations between Budapest and Bucharest. The new Romanian government ended the Ceauşescu regime's harsh measures against its population, including the notorious resettlement program. The two governments agreed to reopen consulates in the Romanian city of Cluj and the Hungarian city of Debrecen and to open cultural institutes in Budapest and Bucharest.

As this account shows, in 1989 and early 1990 Hungary had experienced a dizzying series of political changes. Noncommunist political parties were poised to assume political power. A number of significant steps had been taken to establish the rule of law in Hungary, although the opposition parties made it clear that this process had only just begun. The communist party—in whatever acronymic guise—was dwindling in importance. Soviet troops were beginning their withdrawal from Hungary. The government was pressing toward Hungary's opening to the noncommunist world with vigor and determination. Hungary was indeed in the throes of a revolution, albeit a peaceful one, accompanied by its Central European neighbors on the road to a new political future.

March 13, 1990

* * *

On March 25, 1990, round one of the first free parliamentary elections in forty-three years took place in Hungary. In the 152 district elections, only five candidates succeeded in winning a majority. Among the winners was former Prime Minister Miklós Németh, who ran as an independent. Runoff elections on April 8 were to decide the outcome of the other 147 district races.

In balloting for the county-level lists, the Hungarian Democratic Forum gained 24.7 percent of the vote, which translated into 40 seats in the National Assembly. The Alliance of Free Democrats won 21.39 percent of the vote for thirty-four seats, and the Independent Smallholders' Party 11.73 percent for sixteen seats. Other parties winning the necessary 4 percent threshold for representation in the National Assembly were the Hungarian Socialist Party with 10.89 percent of the vote, the Federation of Young Democrats with 8.95 percent of the vote, and the Christian Democratic People's Party with 6.46 percent of the vote. Among the many parties failing to reach the required threshold were the Social Democratic Party and the Hungarian Socialist Workers' Party.

The Hungarian Democratic Forum emerged as the clear winner after the second round of elections held on April 8 in those electoral districts where no candidate gained a majority in the first round of voting. The forum gained a total of 164 seats in the National Assembly in the two rounds of voting. Second was the Alliance of Free Democrats with ninety-two seats. The Hungarian Democratic Forum chose to form a government together with the Independent Smallholders' Party, which won forty-four seats, and the Christian Democratic People's Party, which won twenty-one seats. Hence, the governing coalition held 229 seats at about 60 percent of the 394 total. (On March 1, the National Assembly had added 8 seats to its previous total of 386, 1 each for the country's Gypsy, Croatian, Serbian, Romanian, Slovak, Slovenian, German, and Jewish minorities. Nominations for these seats were to be prepared by an interparty committee within the National Assembly or by the National Assembly as a whole.)

The new National Assembly convened for the first time on May 2, 1990. At that meeting, it elected Árpád Göncz, a writer jailed for six years following the Revolution of 1956, as president of the National Assembly, which made him interim president of the republic. Göncz was actually a founder of the Alliance of Free Democrats. In return for the Hungarian Democratic Forum's support for Göncz, the Alliance of Free Democrats agreed to support a series of amendments to the Constitution that were to secure the establishment of "an independent democratic constitutional state" in Hungary and provide the legal basis for a market economy. Another amendment agreed to by the two parties would require only a simple majority in the National Assembly to approve legislation for all matters except those of the highest political importance (such matters included a law on referendums, a nationalities law, a citizenship law, legal provisions concerning the freedom of conscience and religion, and other issues). The two parties also agreed to an amendment according to which the president would be elected to a four-year term by the National Assembly rather than be elected by the population as a whole. Yet another amendment would change the method for the representation of national minorities in the government and in the National Assembly.

On May 23, 1990, József Antall of the Hungarian Democratic Forum became the prime minister. Other government ministers included Balázs Horváth of the Hungarian Democratic Forum, who became minister of the interior; Ferenc József Nagy of the Independent Smallholders' Party, who became minister of agriculture; Lajos Für of the Hungarian Democratic Forum, who became minister of defense; Géza Jeszenszky of the Hungarian Democratic Forum, who became minister of foreign affairs; and Peter Akos Bod of the Hungarian Democratic Forum, who became minister of trade and industry.

The elections and the formation of a new noncommunist government took place against the backdrop of crisis situations in the economy and in foreign relations with Romania. In January 1990, prices of meat, poultry, flour, milk and other dairy products, and cooking fat and oil rose an average of 32 percent; car prices rose 25 percent; and prices of beer, cigarettes, and gasoline also rose. On February 1, rents for state-owned apartments increased an average of 35 percent, while bus and train fares rose 45 percent, and railroad fares rose 20 percent. The drastic price increases resulted from a reduction in government spending to reduce the budget deficit from 50 billion forints in 1989 to 10 billion forints in 1990. To meet this objective, the government cut many price subsidies and decontrolled most producer prices.

On March 18 and 19, severe anti-Hungarian violence erupted in the Romanian town of Tîrgu Mureş. In the clashes between

1

Romanians and Hungarians, 3 people died and 269 were injured. This violence led to a rapid deterioration of relations between Hungary and Romania. Prime Minister Miklós Németh addressed a note of protest to Romanian Prime Minister Petre Roman. Hungarian Foreign Minister Gyula Horn addressed a letter to United Nations Secretary General Xavier Peres de Cuellar and to Jan Martenson, head of the UN Human Rights Committee, asking that the committee mediate the dispute without delay. For its part, the Romanian government responded by holding the Hungarian government responsible for the bloodshed in Tîrgu Mureş, and called upon Hungary to refrain from interfering in Romania's internal affairs. In response to these charges, the Hungarian government stated that accusations of Hungarian interference were unfounded, and that the source of the tragic events lay in the Romanian government's hesitancy to take resolute action to stem the rise of national chauvinism in Romania. The Hungarian government called for talks between the two governments on all issues as a means to reduce tension.

May 25, 1990   Stephen R. Burant

Chapter 1. Historical Setting

Refugee writing a letter, Esztergom, 1916

THE HUNGARIAN PEOPLE'S REPUBLIC emerged in 1949 after the Hungarian Workers' Party eliminated its rivals and assumed control of the state. Soviet control of Eastern Europe after World War II had enabled a minuscule communist party lacking popular support to gain power in the country and gradually eliminate its political rivals. Under Mátyás Rákosi, the party consolidated its control and radically transformed the country economically, socially, and politically.

In the mid-1950s, after the Soviet Union had somewhat relaxed its control of Eastern Europe, Hungarian society began to mobilize against the regime, culminating in the Revolution of 1956. Soviet troops crushed the rebellion, leaving power in the hands of János Kádár. After consolidating his authority, Kádár embarked on a program of economic reform in the mid-1960s.

Like other countries of Eastern Europe, Hungary has a history of class, religious, and ethnic conflicts that were intensified and sometimes decided by the actions of larger, more powerful neighbors. Beginning in the tenth century, German and Bohemian missionaries converted the Magyars. In the early eleventh century, Bavarian knights helped Stephen I eliminate rivals and quash peasant revolts. Süleyman the Magnificent's Ottoman armies conquered and partitioned the country with the Habsburgs in the sixteenth century, expediting the spread of Protestant faiths. Habsburg rulers colonized Hungary with non-Magyars, repressed its Protestants, stifled its economic development, and attempted to Germanize its people. The Entente powers carved up Hungary after World War I and distributed most of the land to new nation-states. Finally, dictator Joseph Stalin enforced Soviet domination over postwar Hungary.

Despite internal divisions, strong foreign influence, and outright attempts to force the Hungarians to assimilate into other cultures, Hungarian nationalism has thrived throughout the nineteenth and twentieth centuries. Nationalism drove Hungary to ally itself with Nazi Germany to regain territories lost after World War I. Nationalism also inspired Hungarians to revolt against the Stalinist political order in October 1956.

Early History

The Hungarian nation traces its history to the Magyars, a pagan Finno-Ugric tribe that arose in central Russia and spoke a language

3

that evolved into modern Hungarian. Historians dispute the exact location of the early Magyars' original homeland, but it is likely to be an area between the Volga River and the Ural Mountains. In ancient times, the Magyars probably lived as nomadic tent-dwelling hunters and fishers. Some scholars argue that they engaged in agriculture beginning in the second millennium B.C.

Before the fifth century A.D., the Magyars' ancestors gradually migrated southward onto the Russian steppes, where they wandered into the lands near the Volga River bend, at present-day Kazan', as nomadic herders. Later, probably under pressure from hostile tribes to the east, they migrated to the area between the Don and lower Dnepr rivers. There they lived close to, and perhaps were dominated by, the Bulgar-Turks from about the fifth to the seventh century. During this period, the Magyars became a semi-sedentary people who lived by raising cattle and sheep, planting crops, and fishing. The Bulgar-Turkish influence on the Magyars was significant, especially in agriculture. Most Hungarian words dealing with agriculture and animal husbandry have Turkic roots. By contrast, the etymology of the word *Hungary* has been traced to a Slavicized form of the Turkic words *on ogur,* meaning "ten arrows," which may have referred to the number of Magyar tribes.

The Magyars lived on lands controlled by the Khazars (a Turkish people whose realm stretched from the lower Volga and the lower Don rivers to the Caucasus) from about the seventh to the ninth century, when they freed themselves from Khazar rule. The Khazars attempted to reconquer the Magyars both by themselves and with the help of the Pechenegs, another Turkish tribe. This tribe drove the Magyars from their homes westward to lands between the Dnepr and lower Danube rivers in 889. In 895 the Magyars joined Byzantine armies under Emperor Leo VI in a war against the Bulgars. However, the Bulgars emerged victorious. Their allies, the Pechenegs, attacked the weakened Magyars and forced them westward yet again in 895 or 896. This migration took the Magyars over the Carpathian Mountains and into the basin drained by the Danube and Tisza rivers, a region that corresponds roughly to present-day Hungary. Romans, Goths, Huns, Slavs, and other peoples had previously occupied the region, but at the time of the Magyar migration, the land was inhabited only by a sparse population of Slavs, numbering about 200,000.

Tradition holds that the Magyar clan chiefs chose a chieftain named Árpád to lead the migration and that they swore by sipping from a cup of their commingled blood to accept Árpád's male descendants as the Magyars' hereditary chieftains. The Magyars probably knew of the lands in the Carpathian Basin because from

892 to 894 Magyar mercenaries had fought there for King Arnulph of East Francia in a struggle with the king of Moravia. Estimates are that about 400,000 people made up the exodus, in seven Magyar, one Kabar, and other smaller tribes.

The Carpathian Basin and parts of Transylvania south-southwest of the basin had been settled for thousands of years before the Magyars' arrival. A rich Bronze Age culture thrived there until horsemen from the steppes destroyed it in the middle of the thirteenth century B.C. Celts later occupied parts of the land, and in the first century A.D. the Romans conquered and divided it between the imperial provinces of Pannonia and Dacia. In the fourth century, the Goths ousted the Romans, and Attila the Hun later made the Carpathian Basin the hub of his short-lived empire. Thereafter, Avars, Bulgars, Germans, and Slavs settled the region. In the late ninth century A.D., only scattered settlements of Slavs occupied the Carpathian Basin. The Magyar forces, light cavalrymen who used Central Asian-style bows, quickly conquered the Slavs, whom they either assimilated or enslaved.

Romanian and Hungarian historians disagree about the ethnicity of Transylvania's population before the Magyars' arrival. The Romanians establish their claims to Transylvania by arguing that their Latin ancestors inhabited Transylvania and survived there through the Dark Ages. The Hungarians, by contrast, maintain that Transylvania was inhabited not by the ancestors of the Romanians but by Slavs and point out that the first mention of the Romanians' ancestors in Hungarian records, which appeared in the thirteenth century, described them as drifting herders.

Medieval Period

In the four centuries after their migration into the Carpathian Basin, the Magyars gradually developed from a loose confederation of pagan marauders into a recognized kingdom. This kingdom, which became known as Hungary, was led by the Árpád Dynasty and was firmly allied to the Christian West. Eventually the Árpád line died out, however, and Hungary again descended into anarchy, with the most powerful nobles vying for control.

Christianization of the Magyars

The bonds linking the seven Magyar tribes grew frail soon after the migration into the Carpathian Basin. At that time, Europe was weak and disunited, and for more than half a century Magyar bands raided Bavaria, Moravia, Italy, Constantinople, and lands as far away as the Pyrenees. Sometimes fighting as mercenaries and sometimes lured by spoils alone, the Magyar bands looted towns and

5

took captives for labor, ransom, or sale on the slave market. The Byzantine emperor and European princes paid the Magyars annual tribute. In 955, however, German and Czech armies under the Holy Roman Empire's King Otto I destroyed a Magyar force near Augsburg. The defeat effectively ended Magyar raids on the West, and in 970 the Byzantines halted Magyar incursions toward the East.

Fearing a war of extermination, Chieftain Géza (972–97), Árpád's great-grandson, assured Otto II that the Magyars had ceased their raids and asked him to send missionaries. Otto complied, and in 975 Géza and a few of his kinsmen were baptized into the Roman Catholic Church. Géza consented to baptism more out of political necessity than conviction. He continued to offer sacrifices to the pagan gods and reportedly bragged that he "was rich enough for two gods." From this time, however, missionaries began the gradual process of converting and simultaneously westernizing the Magyar tribes. Géza used German knights and his position as chief of the Magyars' largest clan to restore strong central authority over the other clans. Hungary's ties with the West were strengthened in 996 when Géza's son, Stephen, who was baptized as a child and educated by Saint Adalbert of Prague, married Gisela, a Bavarian princess and sister of Emperor Henry II.

Stephen I

Stephen (997–1038) became chieftain when Géza died, and he consolidated his rule by ousting rival clan chiefs and confiscating their lands. Stephen then asked Pope Sylvester II to recognize him as king of Hungary. The pope agreed, and legend says Stephen was crowned on Christmas Day in the year 1000. The crowning legitimized Hungary as a Western kingdom independent of the Holy Roman and Byzantine empires. It also gave Stephen virtually absolute power, which he used to strengthen the Roman Catholic Church and Hungary. Stephen ordered the people to pay tithes and required every tenth village to construct a church and support a priest. Stephen donated land to support bishoprics and monasteries, required all persons except the clergy to marry, and barred marriages between Christians and pagans. Foreign monks worked as teachers and introduced Western agricultural methods. A Latin alphabet was devised for the Magyar (Hungarian) language.

Stephen administered his kingdom through a system of counties, each governed by an *ispán*, or magistrate, appointed by the king. In Stephen's time, Magyar society had two classes: the freemen nobles and the unfree. The nobles were descended in the male

St. Stephen
Courtesy Sam and Sarah Stulberg

line from the Magyars who had either migrated into the Carpathian Basin or had received their title of nobility from the king. Only nobles could hold office or present grievances to the king. They paid tithes and owed the crown military service but were exempt from taxes. The unfree—who had no political voice—were slaves, freed slaves, immigrants, or nobles stripped of their privileges. Most were serfs who paid taxes to the king and a part of each harvest to their lord for use of his land. The king had direct control of the unfree, thus checking the nobles' power.

Clan lands, crown lands, and former crown lands made up the realm. Clan lands belonged to nobles, who could will the lands to family members or the church; if a noble died without an heir, his land reverted to his clan. Crown lands consisted of Stephen's patrimony, lands seized from disloyal nobles, conquered lands, and unoccupied parts of the kingdom. Former crown lands were properties granted by the king to the church or to individuals.

Politics and Society under Stephen's Successors

Stephen died in 1038 and was canonized in 1083. Despite pagan revolts and a series of succession struggles after his death, Hungary grew stronger and expanded (see fig. 2). Transylvania was conquered and colonized with Magyars, Szekels (a tribe related to the Magyars), and German Saxons in the eleventh and twelfth centuries. In 1090 László I (1077–95) occupied Slavonia, and in 1103 Kálmán I (1095–1116) assumed the title of king of Croatia. Croatia was never assimilated into Hungary; rather, it became an associate kingdom administered by a *bán,* or civil governor.

The eleventh and twelfth centuries were relatively peaceful, and Hungary slowly developed a feudal economy. Crop production gradually supplemented stock breeding, but until the twelfth century planting methods remained crude because tillers farmed each plot until it was exhausted, then moved on to fresh land. Gold, silver, and salt mining boosted the king's revenues. Despite the minting of coins, cattle remained the principal medium of exchange. Towns began developing when an improvement in agricultural methods and the clearing of additional land produced enough surplus to support a class of full-time craftsmen. By the reign of Béla III (1173–96), Hungary was one of the leading powers in southeastern Europe, and in the thirteenth century Hungary's nobles were trading gold, silver, copper, and iron with western Europe for luxury goods.

Until the end of the twelfth century, the king's power remained paramount in Hungary. He was the largest landowner, and income from the crown lands nearly equaled the revenues generated from mines, customs, tolls, and the mint. In the thirteenth century, however, the social structure changed, and the crown's absolute power began to wane. As the crown lands became a less important source of royal revenues, the king found it expedient to make land grants to nobles to ensure their loyalty. King Andrew II (1205–35), a profligate spender on foreign military adventures and domestic luxury, made huge land grants to nobles who fought for him. These nobles, many of whom were foreign knights, soon made up a class of magnates whose wealth and power far outstripped that of the more numerous, and predominantly Magyar, lesser nobles. When Andrew tried to meet burgeoning expenses by raising the serfs' taxes, thereby indirectly slashing the lesser nobles' incomes, the lesser nobles rebelled. In 1222 they forced Andrew to sign the Golden Bull, which limited the king's power, declared the lesser nobles (all free men not included among the great Barons or magnates) legally equal to the magnates, and gave them the right to resist the king's illegal acts. The lesser nobles also began to present Andrew with grievances, a practice that evolved into the institution of the parliament, or Diet.

Andrew II's son Béla IV (1235–79) tried with little success to reestablish royal preeminence by reacquiring lost crown lands. His efforts, however, created a deep rift between the crown and the magnates just as the Mongols were sweeping westward across Russia toward Europe. Aware of the danger, Béla ordered the magnates and lesser nobles to mobilize. Few responded, and the Mongols routed Béla's army at Mohi on April 11, 1241. Béla fled first to Austria, where Duke Frederick of Babenberg held him for ransom, then to Dalmatia. The Mongols reduced Hungary's towns and villages to ashes and slaughtered half the population before news arrived in 1242 that the Great Khan Ogotai had died in Karakorum. The Mongols withdrew, sparing Béla and what remained of his kingdom.

Reconstruction

Béla realized that reconstruction would require the magnates' support, so he abandoned his attempts to recover former crown lands. Instead, he granted crown lands to his supporters, reorganized the army by replacing light archers with heavy cavalry, and granted the magnates concessions to redevelop their lands and construct stone-and-mortar castles that would withstand enemy sieges. Béla repopulated the country with a wave of immigrants, transforming royal castles into towns and populating them with Germans, Italians, and Jews. Mining began anew, farming methods improved, and crafts and commerce developed in the towns. After

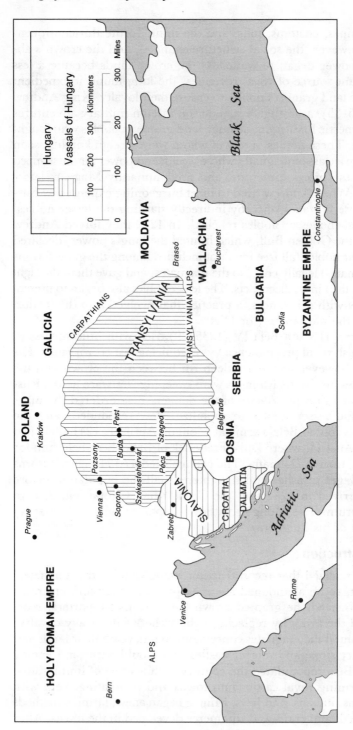

Source: Based on information from C.A. Macartney, *Hungary: A Short History*, Chicago, 1962, 24.

Figure 2. Hungary in A.D. 1200

Béla's reconstruction program, the magnates, with their new fortifications, emerged as Hungary's most powerful political force. However, by the end of the thirteenth century, they were fighting each other and carving out petty principalities.

King Béla IV died in 1270, and the Árpád line expired in 1301 when Andrew III, who strove with some success to limit the magnates' power, unexpectedly died without a male heir. Anarchy characterized Hungary as factions of magnates vied for control.

Renaissance and Reformation

After the Árpád Dynasty ended, Hungary's nobles chose a series of foreign kings who reestablished strong royal authority. Hungary and the adjacent countries prospered for several centuries as Central Europe experienced an era of peace interrupted only by succession struggles. But over time, the onslaughts of the Turks and the strife of the Reformation weakened Hungary, and the country was eventually partitioned by the Turks and the Habsburgs.

Golden Era

Hungary's first two foreign kings, Charles Robert and Louis I of the House of Anjou, ruled during one of the most glorious periods in the country's history. Central Europe was at peace, and Hungary and its neighbors prospered. Charles Robert (1308–42) won the protracted succession struggle after Andrew III's death. An Árpád descendant in the female line, Charles Robert was crowned as a child and raised in Hungary. He reestablished the crown's authority by ousting disloyal magnates and distributing their estates to his supporters. Charles Robert then ordered the magnates to recruit and equip small private armies called *banderia.* Charles Robert ruled by decree and convened the Diet only to announce his decisions. Dynastic marriages linked his family with the ruling families of Naples and Poland and heightened Hungary's standing abroad. Under Charles Robert, the crown regained control of Hungary's mines, and in the next two centuries the mines produced more than a third of Europe's gold and a quarter of its silver. Charles Robert also introduced tax reforms and a stable currency. Charles Robert's son and successor Louis I (1342–82) maintained the strong central authority Charles Robert had amassed. In 1351 Louis issued a decree that reconfirmed the Golden Bull, erased all legal distinctions between the lesser nobles and the magnates, standardized the serfs' obligations, and barred the serfs from leaving the lesser nobles' farms to seek better opportunities on the magnates' estates. The decree also established the entail system (see Glossary). Hungary's economy continued to flourish during Louis's reign. Gold and other precious metals poured from the country's mines and enriched the royal treasury, foreign trade increased, new towns and villages arose, and craftsmen formed guilds. The prosperity fueled a surge in cultural activity, and Louis promoted the illumination of manuscripts and in 1367 founded Hungary's first university. Abroad, however, Louis fought several costly wars and wasted time, funds, and lives in failed attempts to gain for his nephew the throne of Naples. While Louis was engaged in these activities, the Turks made their initial inroads into the Balkans. Louis became king of Poland in 1370 and ruled the two countries for twelve years.

Sigismund (1387–1437), Louis's son-in-law, won a bitter struggle for the throne after Louis died in 1382. Under Sigismund, Hungary's fortunes began to decline. Many Hungarian nobles despised Sigismund for his cruelty during the succession struggle, his long absences, and his costly foreign wars. In 1401 disgruntled nobles temporarily imprisoned the king. In 1403 another group crowned an anti-king, who failed to solidify his power but succeeded in selling Dalmatia to Venice. Sigismund failed to reclaim the territory. Sigismund became the Holy Roman Emperor in 1410 and king of Bohemia in 1419, thus requiring him to spend long periods abroad and enabling Hungary's magnates to acquire unprecedented power. In response, Sigismund created the office of palatine (see Glossary) to rule the country in his stead. Like earlier Hungarian kings, Sigismund elevated his supporters to magnate status and sold off crown lands to meet burgeoning expenses. Although Hungary's economy continued to flourish, Sigismund's expenses outstripped his income. He bolstered royal revenues by increasing the serfs' taxes and requiring cash payment. Social turmoil erupted late in Sigismund's reign as a result of the heavier taxes and renewed magnate pressure on the lesser nobles. Hungary's first peasant revolt erupted when a Transylvanian bishop ordered peasants to pay tithes in coin rather than in kind. The revolt was quickly checked, but it prompted Transylvania's Szekel, Magyar, and German nobles to form the Union of Three Nations, which was an effort to defend their privileges against any power except that of the king.

Additional turmoil erupted when the Ottoman Turks expanded their empire into the Balkans. They crossed the Bosporus Straits in 1352, subdued Bulgaria in 1388, and defeated the Serbs at Kosovo Polje in 1389. Sigismund led a crusade against them in 1396, but the Ottomans routed his forces at Nicopolis, and he barely escaped with his life. Tamerlane's invasion of Anatolia in 1402–03 slowed the Turks' progress for several decades, but in 1437 Sultan Murad prepared to invade Hungary. Sigismund died the same year,

Mátyás Corvinus
Courtesy Kenneth Nyirády

and Hungary's next two kings, Albrecht V of Austria (1437–39) and Wladyslaw III of Poland (1439–44), who was known in Hungary as Ulászló I, both died during campaigns against the Turks.

After Ulászló, Hungary's nobles chose an infant king, László V, and a regent, János Hunyadi, to rule the country until László V came of age. The son of a lesser nobleman of the Vlach tribe, Hunyadi rose to become a general, Transylvania's military governor, one of Hungary's largest landowners, and a war hero. He used his personal wealth and the support of the lesser nobles to win the regency and overcome the opposition of the magnates. Hunyadi then established a mercenary army funded by the first tax ever imposed on Hungary's nobles. He defeated the Ottoman forces in Transylvania in 1442 and broke their hold on Serbia in 1443, only to be routed at Varna (where László V himself perished) a year later. In 1456, when the Turkish army besieged Belgrade, Hunyadi defeated it in his greatest and final victory. Hunyadi died of the plague soon after.

Some magnates resented Hunyadi for his popularity as well as for the taxes he imposed, and they feared that his sons might seize the throne from László. They coaxed the sons to return to László's court, where Hunyadi's elder son was beheaded. His younger son, Mátyás, was imprisoned in Bohemia. However, lesser nobles loyal to Mátyás soon expelled László. After László's death abroad, they paid ransom for Mátyás, met him on the frozen Danube River,

13

and proclaimed him king. Known as Mátyás Corvinus (1458–90), he was, with one possible exception (János Zápolyai), the last Hungarian king to rule the country.

Although Mátyás regularly convened the Diet and expanded the lesser nobles' powers in the counties, he exercised absolute rule over Hungary by means of a secular bureaucracy. Mátyás enlisted 30,000 foreign mercenaries in his standing army and built a network of fortresses along Hungary's southern frontier, but he did not pursue his father's aggressive anti-Turkish policy. Instead, Mátyás launched unpopular attacks on Bohemia, Poland, and Austria, pursuing an ambition to become Holy Roman Emperor and arguing that he was trying to forge a unified Western alliance strong enough to expel the Turks from Europe. He eliminated tax exemptions and raised the serfs' obligations to the crown to fund his court and the military. The magnates complained that these measures reduced their incomes, but despite the stiffer obligations, the serfs considered Mátyás a just ruler because he protected them from excessive demands and other abuses by the magnates. He also reformed Hungary's legal system and promoted the growth of Hungary's towns. Mátyás was a true renaissance man and made his court a center of humanist culture; under his rule, Hungary's first books were printed and its second university was established. Mátyás's library, the Corvina, was famous throughout Europe. In his quest for the imperial throne, Mátyás eventually moved to Vienna, where he died in 1490.

Reign of Ulászló II and Louis II

Mátyás's reforms did not survive the turbulent decades that followed his reign. An oligarchy of quarrelsome magnates gained control of Hungary. They crowned a docile king, Vladislav Jagiello (the Jagiellonian king of Bohemia, who was known in Hungary as Ulászló II, 1490–1516), only on condition that he abolish the taxes that had supported Mátyás's mercenary army. As a result, the king's army dispersed just as the Turks were threatening Hungary. The magnates also dismantled Mátyás's administration and antagonized the lesser nobles. In 1492 the Diet limited the serfs' freedom of movement and expanded their obligations. Rural discontent boiled over in 1514 when well-armed peasants under György Dózsa rose up and attacked estates across Hungary. United by a common threat, the magnates and lesser nobles eventually crushed the rebels. Dózsa and other rebel leaders were executed in a most brutal manner.

Shocked by the peasant revolt, the Diet of 1514 passed laws that condemned the serfs to eternal bondage and increased their work obligations. Corporal punishment became widespread, and one noble even branded his serfs like livestock. The legal scholar Stephen Werböczy included the new laws in his Tripartitum of 1514, which made up Hungary's legal corpus until the revolution of 1848. The Tripartitum gave Hungary's king and nobles, or magnates, equal shares of power: the nobles recognized the king as superior, but in turn the nobles had the power to elect the king. The Tripartitum also freed the nobles from taxation, obligated them to serve in the military only in a defensive war, and made them immune from arbitrary arrest. The new laws weakened Hungary by deepening the rift between the nobles and the peasantry just as the Turks prepared to invade the country.

When Ulászló II died in 1516, his ten-year-old son Louis II (1516–26) became king, but a royal council appointed by the Diet ruled the country. Hungary was in a state of near anarchy under the magnates' rule. The king's finances were a shambles; he borrowed to meet his household expenses despite the fact that they totaled about one-third of the national income. The country's defenses sagged as border guards went unpaid, fortresses fell into disrepair, and initiatives to increase taxes to reinforce defenses were stifled. In 1521 Sultan Süleyman the Magnificent recognized Hungary's weakness and seized Belgrade in preparation for an attack on Hungary. In August 1526, he marched more than 100,000 troops into Hungary's heartland, and at Mohács they cut down all but several hundred of the 25,000 ill-equipped soldiers whom Louis II had been able to muster for the country's defense. Louis himself died, thrown from a horse into a bog.

After Louis's death, rival factions of Hungarian nobles simultaneously elected two kings, János Zápolyai (1526–40) and Ferdinand (1526–64). Each claimed sovereignty over the entire country but lacked sufficient forces to eliminate his rival. Zápolyai, a Hungarian and the military governor of Transylvania, was recognized by the sultan and was supported mostly by lesser nobles opposed to new foreign kings. Ferdinand, the first Habsburg to occupy the Hungarian throne, drew support from magnates in western Hungary who hoped he could convince his brother, Holy Roman Emperor Charles V, to expel the Turks. In 1538 George Martinuzzi, Zápolyai's adviser, arranged a treaty between the rivals that would have made Ferdinand sole monarch upon the death of the then-childless Zápolyai. The deal collapsed when Zápolyai married and fathered a son. Violence erupted, and the Turks seized the opportunity, conquering the city of Buda and then partitioning the country in 1541.

Partition of Hungary

The partition of Hungary between the Ottoman and Habsburg empires lasted more than 150 years. Habsburg Austria controlled Royal Hungary, which consisted of counties along the Austrian border and some of northwestern Croatia (see fig. 3). The Ottomans annexed central and southern Hungary. Transylvania became an Ottoman vassal state, where native princes, who paid the Turks tribute, ruled with considerable autonomy. After the Hungarian defeat at Mohács, the Protestant Reformation took hold in Hungary. Initially, German burghers in Transylvania and Royal Hungary adopted Lutheranism; later, John Calvin's works converted many Magyars in Transylvania and central Hungary. The Reformation spread quickly, and by the early seventeenth century hardly any noble families remained Catholic. Archbishop Peter Pázmány reorganized Royal Hungary's Roman Catholic Church and led a Counter-Reformation that reversed the Protestants' gains in Royal Hungary, using persuasion rather than intimidation. Transylvania, however, remained a Protestant stronghold. The Reformation caused rifts between Catholic Magyars, who often sided with the Habsburgs, and Protestant Magyars, who developed a strong national identity and became rebels in Austrian eyes. Chasms also developed between Royal Hungary and Transylvania and between the mostly Catholic magnates and the mainly Protestant lesser nobles.

Royal Hungary

Royal Hungary became a small part of the Habsburg Empire and enjoyed little influence in Vienna. The Habsburg king directly controlled Royal Hungary's financial, military, and foreign affairs, and imperial troops guarded its borders. The Habsburgs avoided filling the office of palatine to prevent the holder's amassing too much power. In addition, the so-called Turkish question divided the Habsburgs and the Hungarians: Vienna wanted to maintain peace with the Turks; the Hungarians wanted the Ottomans ousted. As the Hungarians recognized the weakness of their position, many became anti-Habsburg. They complained about foreign rule, the behavior of foreign garrisons, and the Habsburgs' recognition of Turkish sovereignty in Transylvania. Protestants, who were persecuted in Royal Hungary, considered the Counter-Reformation a greater menace than the Turks, however.

Ottoman Hungary

Central Hungary became a province of the Ottoman Empire ruled by pashas living in Buda. The Turks' only interest was to secure their hold on the territory. The Sublime Porte (a term used to designate the Ottoman rulers) became the sole landowner and managed about 20 percent of the land for its own benefit, apportioning the rest among soldiers and civil servants. The new landlords were interested mainly in squeezing as much wealth from the land as quickly as possible. Wars, slave-taking, and the emigration of nobles who lost their land depopulated much of the countryside. However, the Turks practiced religious tolerance and allowed the Hungarians living within the empire significant autonomy in internal affairs. Towns maintained some self-government, and a prosperous middle class developed through artisanry and trade.

Transylvania

Transylvania, an Ottoman vassal state, functioned for many years as an independent country. In 1542 Martinuzzi revived the 1437 Union of Three Nations to govern the land, and the Transylvanian nobles regularly met in their own Diet. In 1572 the Diet created freedom of worship and equal political rights for members of Transylvania's four "established" religions: Roman Catholic, Lutheran, Unitarian, and Calvinist. The Eastern Orthodox Romanian serfs were permitted to worship, but the Orthodox Church was not recognized as an "established" religion, and the Romanians did not share political equality.

In 1591 the Habsburgs invaded Transylvania under George Basta, who persecuted Protestants and expropriated estates illegally until István Bocskay, a former Habsburg supporter, mustered an army that expelled Basta's forces in 1604–05. In 1606 Bocskay concluded the Peace of Vienna with the Habsburgs and the Peace of Zsitvatorok with the Turks. The treaties secured his position as prince of Transylvania, guaranteed rights for Royal Hungary's Protestants, broadened Transylvania's independence, and freed the emperor of his obligation to pay tribute to the Ottomans. After Bocskay's death, the Ottomans compelled the Transylvanians to accept Gábor Bethlen as prince. Transylvania prospered under Bethlen's enlightened despotism. He stimulated agriculture, trade, and industry; sank new mines; sent students to Protestant universities abroad; and prohibited landlords from barring children of serfs from an education. Unfortunately, when Bethlen died in 1629, the Transylvanian Diet abolished most of his reforms. After a short succession struggle, György Rákóczi I (1648–60) became prince. Under Rákóczi, Transylvania fought with the Protestants in the Thirty Years' War (1618–48) and was mentioned as a sovereign state in the Peace of Westphalia. Transylvania's golden age ended

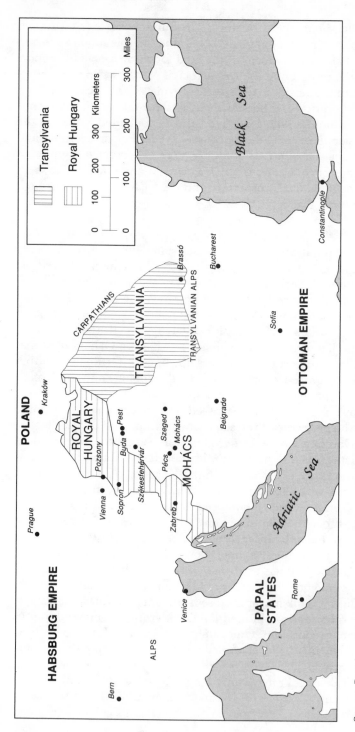

Source: Based on information from C.A. Macartney, *Hungary: A Short History*, Chicago, 1962, 64.

Figure 3. Hungary During the Period of Partition, 1541–1699

after György Rákóczi II (1648–60) launched an attack on Poland without the prior approval of the Ottomans or Transylvania's Diet. The campaign was a disaster, and the Turks used the opportunity to rout Rákóczi's army and take control of Transylvania.

End of the Partition

The Ottoman Empire gradually weakened after Süleyman's death in 1559. The Ottoman occupation of Hungary continued, however, not so much because of the Turks' strength but because of the West's disunity and lack of resolve. Hungarian nobles grew impatient with the Habsburgs' persecution of Protestants and reluctance to take steps to drive out the Turks. Their discontent exploded after the Habsburg imperial army routed a Turkish force at St. Gotthard in 1664. Instead of pressing for concessions, Emperor Leopold I (1657–1705) concluded the Treaty of Vasvár in which he conceded to the Turks more Hungarian territory than they had ever possessed. After Vasvár, even many Catholic magnates turned against the Habsburgs.

After a failed Hungarian plot to throw off Habsburg rule, Leopold suppressed the Hungarian constitution, subjected Royal Hungary to direct absolute rule from Vienna, and harshly repressed Hungarian Protestants, handing over Protestant ministers who refused to deny their faith to work as galley slaves. Hungarian discontent deepened. In 1681 Imre Thököly, a Transylvanian nobleman, led a rebellion against the Habsburgs and forced Leopold I to convoke the Diet and restore Hungary's constitution and the office of palatine. Sensing weakness, the Turks made their strike against Austria, but Polish forces routed them near Vienna in 1683. A Western campaign then gradually drove the Turks from Hungary, and the sultan surrendered almost all of his Hungarian and Croatian possessions in the Peace of Karlowitz in 1699.

Hungary under the Habsburgs

The Habsburgs ruled autocratically on almost all questions except taxation and relegated Hungary to the status of a colony, a factor that, together with other factors, stifled economic development. After more than a century of stagnation, the lesser nobles, under increasing economic pressure and prompted by nascent Hungarian nationalism, pressed for reform. The crescendo of discontent climaxed in the March 1848 revolution. Russian troops quashed the rebellion, enabling Austrian emperor Franz Joseph to impose absolute control for almost two decades.

Reign of Leopold II

As the Habsburgs gained control of the country, the ministers of Leopold I argued that he should rule Hungary as conquered territory. One even said Vienna should first make the Hungarians beggars, then Catholics, and then Germans. At the Diet of Pressburg in 1687, the emperor promised to observe all of Hungary's laws and privileges. Hereditary succession of the Habsburgs was recognized, however, and the nobles' right of resistance was abrogated. In 1690 Leopold began redistributing lands freed from the Turks. Protestant nobles and all other Hungarians thought disloyal by the Habsburgs lost their estates, which were given to foreigners. Vienna controlled Hungary's foreign affairs, defense, tariffs, and other functions, and it separated Transylvania from Hungary, treating it as a separate imperial territory.

The repression of Protestants and the land seizures embittered the Hungarians, and in 1703 a peasant uprising sparked an eight-year national rebellion aimed at casting off the Habsburg yoke. Disgruntled Protestants, peasants, and soldiers united under Ferenc Rákóczi, a Roman Catholic magnate who could hardly speak Hungarian. Most of Hungary soon supported Rákóczi, and the joint Hungarian-Transylvanian Diet voted to annul the Habsburgs' right to the throne. Fortunes turned against the rebels, however, when the Habsburgs made peace in the West and turned their full force against Hungary. The rebellion ended in 1711, when moderate rebel leaders concluded the Treaty of Szatmár, in which the Hungarians gained little except the emperor's agreement to reconvene the Diet and to grant an amnesty for the rebels.

Reign of Charles VI and Maria Theresa

Leopold's successor, Charles VI (1711–40), began building a workable relationship with Hungary after the Treaty of Szatmár. Charles needed the Hungarian Diet's approval for the Pragmatic Sanction, under which the Habsburg monarch was to rule Hungary not as emperor but as a king subject to the restraints of Hungary's constitution and laws. He hoped that the Pragmatic Sanction would keep the Habsburg Empire intact if his daughter, Maria Theresa, succeeded him. The Diet approved the Pragmatic Sanction in 1723, and Hungary thus agreed to became a hereditary monarchy under the Habsburgs for as long as their dynasty existed. In practice, however, Charles and his successors governed almost autocratically, controlling Hungary's foreign affairs, defense, and finance but lacking the power to tax the nobles without their approval. The Habsburgs also maintained Transylvania's separation from Hungary.

Charles organized Hungary's first modern, centralized administration and in 1715 established a standing army under his command, which was entirely funded and manned by the nonnoble population. This policy reduced the nobles' military obligation without abrogating their exemption from taxation. Charles also banned conversion to Protestantism, required civil servants to profess Catholicism, and forbade Protestant students to study abroad.

Maria Theresa (1740–80) faced an immediate challenge from Prussia's Frederick II when she became head of the House of Habsburg. In 1741 she appeared before the Hungarian Diet holding her newborn son and entreated Hungary's nobles to support her. They stood behind her and helped secure her rule. Maria Theresa later took measures to reinforce links with Hungary's magnates. She established special schools to attract Hungarian nobles to Vienna. During her reign, the members of the magnate class lost their Hungarian national identity, including their knowledge of the Hungarian language.

Under Charles and Maria Theresa, Hungary experienced further economic decline. Centuries of Ottoman occupation, rebellion, and war had reduced Hungary's population drastically, and large parts of the country's southern half were almost deserted. A labor shortage developed as landowners restored their estates. In response, the Habsburgs began to colonize Hungary with large numbers of peasants from all over Europe, especially Slovaks, Serbs, Croatians, and Germans. Many Jews also immigrated from Vienna and the empire's Polish lands near the end of the century. Hungary's population more than tripled to 8 million between 1720 and 1787. However, only 39 percent of its people were Magyars, who lived mainly in the center of the country.

A complex patchwork of minority peoples emerged in the lands along Hungary's periphery. Droves of Romanians entered Transylvania during the same period. The Protestant and Catholic Hungarians and Germans who had been there for years had considered the Orthodox Romanians inferior and relegated them to serfdom. In the eighteenth century, leaders of the Orthodox Church began arguing that Romanians were descendants of the Roman Dacians and thus Transylvania's original inhabitants. The Orthodox leaders demanded, without success, that the Romanians be recognized as Transylvania's fourth "nation" and the Orthodox Church as its fifth "established" religion.

In the early to mid-eighteenth century, Hungary had a primitive agricultural economy that employed 90 percent of the population. The nobles failed to use fertilizers, roads were poor and rivers blocked, and crude storage methods caused huge losses of grain. Barter had replaced money transactions, and little trade existed between towns and the serfs. After 1760 a labor surplus developed. The serf population grew, pressure on the land increased, and the serfs' standard of living declined. Landowners began making greater demands on new tenants and began violating existing agreements. In response, Maria Theresa issued her Urbarium of 1767 to protect the serfs by restoring their freedom of movement and limiting the corvée (see Glossary). Despite her efforts and several periods of strong demand for grain, the situation worsened. Between 1767 and 1848, many serfs left their holdings. Most became landless farm workers because a lack of industrial development meant few opportunities for work in the towns.

Enlightened Absolutism

Joseph II (1780–90), a dynamic leader strongly influenced by the Enlightenment, shook Hungary from its malaise when he inherited the throne from his mother, Maria Theresa. Joseph sought to centralize control of the empire and to rule it by decree as an enlightened despot. He refused to take the Hungarian coronation oath to avoid being constrained by Hungary's constitution. In 1781 Joseph issued the Patent of Toleration, which granted Protestants and Orthodox Christians full civil rights and Jews freedom of worship. He decreed that German replace Latin as the empire's official language and granted the peasants the freedom to leave their holdings, to marry, and to place their children in trades. Hungary, Croatia, and Transylvania became a single imperial territory under one administration. When the Hungarian nobles again refused to waive their exemption from taxation, Joseph banned imports of Hungarian manufactured goods into Austria and began a survey to prepare for imposition of a general land tax.

Joseph's reforms outraged Hungary's nobles and clergy, and the country's peasants grew dissatisfied with taxes, conscription, and requisitions of supplies. Hungarians perceived Joseph's language reform as German cultural hegemony, and they reacted by insisting on the right to use their own tongue. As a result, Hungarian lesser nobles sparked a renaissance of the Magyar language and culture, and a cult of national dance and costume flourished. The lesser nobles questioned the loyalty of the magnates, of whom less than half were ethnic Magyars, and even those had become French- and German-speaking courtiers. The Magyar national reawakening subsequently triggered national revivals among the Slovak, Romanian, Serbian, and Croatian minorities within Hungary and Transylvania who felt threatened by both German and Magyar cultural hegemony. These national revivals later blossomed into the nationalist movements of the nineteenth and twentieth centuries that contributed to the empire's ultimate collapse.

Late in his reign, Joseph led a costly, ill-fated campaign against the Turks that weakened his empire. On January 28, 1790, three weeks before his death, the emperor issued a decree canceling all of his reforms except the Patent of Toleration, peasant reforms, and abolition of the religious orders.

Joseph's successor, Leopold II (1790–92), recognized Hungary again as a separate country under a Habsburg king and reestablished Croatia and Transylvania as separate territorial entities. In 1791 the Diet passed Law X, which stressed Hungary's status as an independent kingdom ruled only by a king legally crowned according to Hungarian laws. Law X became the basis for demands by Hungarian reformers for statehood in the period from 1825 to 1849. New laws again required approval of both the Habsburg king and the Diet, and Latin was restored as the official language. The peasant reforms remained in effect, however, and Protestants remained equal before the law. Leopold died in March 1792 just as the French Revolution was about to degenerate into the Reign of Terror and send shock waves through the royal houses of Europe.

Enlightened absolutism ended in Hungary under Leopold's successor, Francis I (1792–1835), who developed an almost abnormal aversion to change, bringing Hungary decades of political stagnation. In 1795 the Hungarian police arrested an abbot and several of the country's leading thinkers for plotting a Jacobin kind of revolution to install a radical democratic, egalitarian political system in Hungary. Thereafter, Francis resolved to extinguish any spark of reform that might ignite revolution. The execution of the alleged plotters silenced any reform advocates among the nobles, and for about three decades reform ideas remained confined to poetry and philosophy. The magnates, who also feared that the influx of revolutionary ideas might precipitate a popular uprising, became a tool of the crown and seized the chance to further burden the peasants.

Economic and Social Developments

By the turn of the nineteenth century, the aim of Hungary's agricultural producers had shifted from subsistence farming and small-scale production for local trade to cash-generating, large-scale production for a wider market. Road and waterway improvements cut transportation costs, while urbanization in Austria, Bohemia, and Moravia and the need for supplies for the Napoleonic wars boosted demand for foodstuffs and clothing. Hungary became a major grain and wool exporter. New lands were cleared, and yields

23

rose as farming methods improved. Hungary did not reap the full benefit of the boom, however, because most of the profits went to the magnates, who considered them not as capital for investment but as a means of adding luxury to their lives. As expectations rose, goods such as linen and silverware, once considered luxuries, became necessities. The wealthy magnates had little trouble balancing their earnings and expenditures, but many lesser nobles, fearful of losing their social standing, went into debt to finance their spending.

Napoleon's final defeat brought recession. Grain prices collapsed as demand dropped, and debt ensnared much of Hungary's lesser nobility. Poverty forced many lesser nobles to work to earn a livelihood, and their sons entered education institutions to train for civil service or professional careers. The decline of the lesser nobility continued despite the fact that by 1820 Hungary's exports had surpassed wartime levels. As more lesser nobles earned diplomas, the bureaucracy and professions became saturated, leaving a host of disgruntled graduates without jobs. Members of this new intelligentsia quickly became enamored of radical political ideologies emanating from Western Europe and organized themselves to effect changes in Hungary's political system.

Francis rarely called the Diet into session (usually only to request men and supplies for war) without hearing complaints. Economic hardship brought the lesser nobles' discontent to a head by 1825, when Francis finally convoked the Diet after a fourteen-year hiatus. Grievances were voiced, and open calls for reform were made, including demands for less royal interference in the nobles' affairs and for wider use of the Hungarian language.

The first great figure of the reform era came to the fore during the 1825 convocation of the Diet. Count István Széchenyi, a magnate from one of Hungary's most powerful families, shocked the Diet when he delivered the first speech in Hungarian ever uttered in the upper chamber and backed a proposal for the creation of a Hungarian academy of arts and sciences by pledging a year's income to support it. In 1831 angry nobles burned Széchenyi's book *Hitel* (Credit), in which he argued that the nobles' privileges were both morally indefensible and economically detrimental to the nobles themselves. Széchenyi called for an economic revolution and argued that only the magnates were capable of implementing reforms. Széchenyi favored a strong link with the Habsburg Empire and called for abolition of entail and serfdom, taxation of landowners, financing of development with foreign capital, establishment of a national bank, and introduction of wage labor. He inspired such projects as the construction of the suspension bridge

linking Buda and Pest. Széchenyi's reform initiatives ultimately failed because they were targeted at the magnates, who were not inclined to support change, and because the pace of his program was too slow to attract disgruntled lesser nobles.

The most popular of Hungary's great reform leaders, Lajos Kossuth, addressed passionate calls for change to the lesser nobles. Kossuth was the son of a landless, lesser nobleman of Protestant background. He practiced law with his father before moving to Pest. There he published commentaries on the Diet's activities, which made him popular with young, reform-minded people. Kossuth was imprisoned in 1836 for treason. After his release in 1840, he gained quick notoriety as the editor of a liberal party newspaper. Kossuth argued that only political and economic separation from Austria would improve Hungary's plight. He called for broader parliamentary democracy, industrialization, general taxation, economic expansion through exports, and abolition of privileges and serfdom. But Kossuth was also a Magyar chauvinist whose rhetoric provoked the strong resentment of Hungary's minority ethnic groups. Kossuth gained support among liberal lesser nobles, who constituted an opposition minority in the Diet. They sought reforms with increasing success after Francis's death in 1835 and the succession of Ferdinand V (1835–48). In 1843 a law was enacted making Hungarian the country's official language over the strong objections of the Croats, Slovaks, Serbs, and Romanians.

The Revolution of March 1848

In March 1848, revolution erupted in Vienna, forcing Austria's Chancellor Klemens von Metternich to flee the capital. Unrest broke out in Hungary on March 15, when radicals and students stormed the Buda fortress to release political prisoners. A day later, the Diet's liberal-dominated lower house demanded establishment of a national government responsible to an elected parliament, and on March 22 a new national cabinet took power with Count Louis Batthyány as chairman, Kossuth as minister of finance, and Széchenyi as minister of public works. Under duress, the Diet's upper house approved a sweeping reform package, signed by Ferdinand, that altered almost every aspect of Hungary's economic, social, and political life. These so-called April Laws created independent Hungarian ministries of defense and finance, and the new government claimed the right to issue currency through its own central bank. Guilds lost their privileges; the nobles became subject to taxation; entail, tithes, and the corvée were abolished; some peasants became freehold proprietors of the land they worked; freedom of the press and assembly were created; a Hungarian national guard was established; and Transylvania was brought under Hungarian rule.

The non-Magyar ethnic groups in Hungary feared the nationalism of the new Hungarian government, and Transylvanian Germans and Romanians opposed the incorporation of Transylvania into Hungary. The Vienna government enlisted the minorities in the first attempt to overthrow the Hungarian government. Josip Jelačić—a fanatic anti-Hungarian—became governor of Croatia on March 22 and severed relations with the Hungarian government a month later. By summer the revolution's momentum began to wane. The Austrians ordered the Hungarian Diet to dissolve, but the order went unheeded. In September Jelačić led an army into Hungary. Batthyány resigned, and a mob lynched the imperial commander in Pest. A committee of national defense under Kossuth took control, authorized the establishment of a Hungarian army, and issued paper money to fund it. On October 30, 1848, imperial troops entered Vienna and suppressed a workers' uprising, effectively ending the revolution everywhere in the empire except Hungary, where Kossuth's army had overcome Jelačić's forces. In December Ferdinand abdicated in favor of Franz Joseph (1848–1916), who claimed more freedom of action because, unlike

Ferdinand, he had given no pledge to respect the April Laws. The Magyars, however, refused to recognize him as their king because he was never crowned.

The imperial army captured Pest early in 1849, but the revolutionary government remained entrenched in Debrecen. In April a "rump" Diet deposed the Habsburg Dynasty in Hungary, proclaimed Hungary a republic, and named Kossuth governor with dictatorial powers. After the declaration, Austrian reinforcements were transferred to Hungary, and in June, at Franz Joseph's request, Russian troops attacked from the east and overwhelmed the Hungarians. The Hungarian army surrendered on August 13, and Kossuth escaped to the Ottoman Empire. A period of harsh repression followed. Batthyány and about 100 others were shot, several society women were publicly whipped, and the government outlawed public gatherings, theater performances, display of the national colors, and wearing of national costumes and Kossuth-style beards.

Aftermath of the Revolution

After the revolution, the emperor revoked Hungary's constitution and assumed absolute control. Franz Joseph divided the country into four distinct territories: Hungary, Transylvania, Croatia-Slavonia, and Vojvodina. German and Bohemian administrators managed the government, and German became the language of administration and higher education. The non-Magyar minorities of Hungary received little for their support of Austria during the turmoil. A Croat reportedly told a Hungarian: "We received as a reward what the Magyars got as a punishment."

Hungarian public opinion split over the country's relations with Austria. Some Hungarians held out hope for full separation from Austria; others wanted an accommodation with the Habsburgs, provided that they respected Hungary's constitution and laws. Ferencz Deák became the main advocate for accommodation. Deák upheld the legality of the April Laws and argued that their amendment required the Hungarian Diet's consent. He also held that the dethronement of the Habsburgs was invalid. As long as Austria ruled absolutely, Deák argued, Hungarians should do no more than passively resist illegal demands.

The first crack in Franz Joseph's neo-absolutist rule developed in 1859, when the forces of Sardinia and France defeated Austria at Solferno. The defeat convinced Franz Joseph that national and social opposition to his government was too strong to be managed by decree from Vienna. Gradually he recognized the necessity of concessions toward Hungary, and Austria and Hungary thus moved toward a compromise. In 1866 the Prussians defeated the Austrians, further underscoring the weakness of the Habsburg Empire. Negotiations between the emperor and the Hungarian leaders were intensified and finally resulted in the Compromise of 1867, which created the Dual Monarchy of Austria-Hungary, also known as the Austro-Hungarian Empire.

Dual Monarchy

The Compromise of 1867, which created the Dual Monarchy, gave the Hungarian government more control of its domestic affairs than it had possessed at any time since the Battle of Mohács (see fig. 4). However, the new government faced severe economic problems and the growing restiveness of ethnic minorities. World War I led to the disintegration of Austria-Hungary, and in the aftermath of the war, a series of governments—including a communist regime—assumed power in Budapest (in 1872 the cities of Buda and Pest united to become Budapest).

Constitutional and Legal Framework

Once again a Habsburg emperor became king of Hungary, but the compromise strictly limited his power over the country's internal affairs, and the Hungarian government assumed control over its domestic affairs. The Hungarian government consisted of a prime minister and cabinet appointed by the emperor but responsible to a bicameral parliament elected by a narrow franchise. Joint Austro-Hungarian affairs were managed through "common" ministries of foreign affairs, defense, and finance. The respective ministers were responsible to delegations representing separate Austrian and Hungarian parliaments. Although the "common" ministry of defense administered the imperial and royal armies, the emperor acted as their commander in chief, and German remained the language of command in the military as a whole. The compromise determined that commercial and monetary policy, tariffs, the railroad, and indirect taxation were "common" concerns to be negotiated every ten years. The compromise also returned Transylvania, Vojvodina, and the military frontier to Hungary's jurisdiction.

At Franz Joseph's insistence, Hungary and Croatia reached a similar compromise in 1868, giving the Croats a special status in Hungary. The agreement granted the Croats autonomy over their internal affairs. The Croatian *bán* would now be nominated by the Hungarian prime minister and appointed by the king. Areas of "common" concern to Hungarians and Croats included finance, currency matters, commercial policy, the post office, and the railroad.

Croatian became the official language of Croatia's government, and Croatian representatives discussing "common" affairs before the Hungarian Diet were permitted to speak Croatian.

The Nationalities Law enacted in 1868 defined Hungary as a single nation comprising different nationalities whose members enjoyed equal rights in all areas except language. Although non-Hungarian languages could be used in local government, churches, and schools, Hungarian became the official language of the central government and universities. Many Hungarians thought the act too generous, while minority-group leaders rejected it as inadequate. Slovaks in northern Hungary, Romanians in Transylvania, and Serbs in Vojvodina all wanted more autonomy, and unrest followed the act's passage. The government took no further action concerning nationalities, and discontent rose.

Anti-Semitism appeared in Hungary early in the century as a result of fear of economic competition. In 1840 a partial emancipation of the Jews allowed them to live anywhere except certain depressed mining cities. The Jewish Emancipation Act of 1868 gave Jews equality before the law and effectively eliminated all bars to their participation in the economy; nevertheless, informal barriers kept Jews from careers in politics and public life.

Rise of the Liberal Party

Franz Joseph appointed Gyula Andrássy—a member of Deák's party—prime minister in 1867. His government strongly favored the Compromise of 1867 and followed a laissez-faire economic policy. Guilds were abolished, workers were permitted to bargain for wages, and the government attempted to improve education and construct roads and railroads. Between 1850 and 1875, Hungary's farms prospered: grain prices were high, and exports tripled. But Hungary's economy accumulated capital too slowly, and the government relied heavily on foreign credits. In addition, the national and local bureaucracies began to grow immediately after the compromise became effective. Soon the cost of the bureaucracy outpaced the country's tax revenues, and the national debt soared. After an economic downturn in the mid-1870s, Deák's party succumbed to charges of financial mismanagement and scandal.

As a result of these economic problems, Kálmán Tisza's Liberal Party, created in 1875, gained power that same year. Tisza assembled a bureaucratic political machine that maintained control through corruption and manipulation of a woefully unrepresentative electoral system. In addition, Tisza's government had to withstand both dissatisfied nationalities and Hungarians who thought Tisza too submissive to the Austrians. The Liberals argued

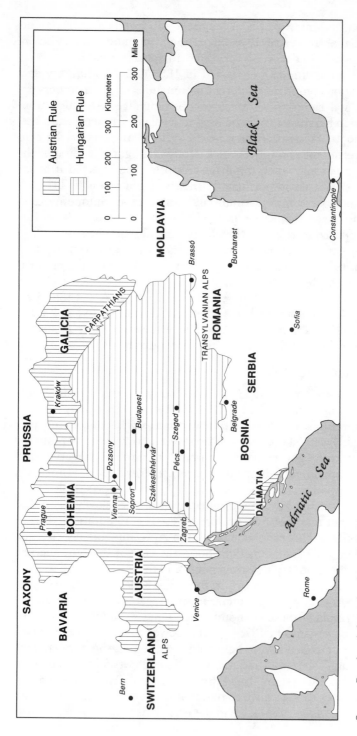

Source: Based on information from C.A. Macartney, *Hungary: A Short History*, Chicago, 1962, 172.

Figure 4. The Dual Monarchy of Austria-Hungary, 1867–1918

that the Dual Monarchy improved Hungary's economic position and enhanced its influence in European politics.

Tisza's government raised taxes, balanced the budget within several years of coming to power, and completed large road, railroad, and waterway projects. Commerce and industry expanded quickly. After 1880 the government abandoned its laissez-faire economic policies and encouraged industry with loans, subsidies, government contracts, tax exemptions, and other measures. The number of Hungarians who earned their living in industry doubled to 24.2 percent of the population between 1890 and 1910, while the number dependent on agriculture dropped from 82 to 62 percent. However, the 1880s and 1890s were depression years for the peasantry. Rail and steamship transport gave North American farmers access to European markets, and Europe's grain prices fell by 50 percent. Large landowners fought the downturn by seeking trade protection and other political remedies; the lesser nobles, whose farms failed in great numbers, sought positions in the still-burgeoning bureaucracy. By contrast, the peasantry resorted to subsistence farming and worked as laborers to earn money.

Social Changes

Hungary's population rose from 13 million to 20 million between 1850 and 1910. After 1867 Hungary's feudal society gave way to a more complex society that included the magnates, lesser nobles, middle class, working class, and peasantry. However, the magnates continued to wield great influence through several conservative parties because of their massive wealth and dominant position in the upper chamber of the parliament. They fought modernization and sought both closer ties with Vienna and a restoration of Hungary's traditional social structure and institutions, arguing that agriculture should remain the mission of the nobility. They won protection from the market by reestablishment of a system of entail and also pushed for restriction of middle-class profiteering and restoration of corporal punishment. The Roman Catholic Church was a major ally of the magnates.

Some lesser-noble landowners survived the agrarian depression of the late nineteenth century and continued farming. Many others turned to the bureaucracy or to the professions.

In the mid-1800s, Hungary's middle class consisted of a small number of German and Jewish merchants and workshop owners who employed a few craftsmen. By the turn of the century, however, the middle class had grown in size and complexity and had become predominantly Jewish. In fact, Jews created the modern economy that supported Tisza's bureaucratic machine. In return, Tisza not only denounced anti-Semitism but also used his political machine to check the growth of an anti-Semitic party. In 1896 his successors passed legislation securing the Jews' final emancipation. By 1910 about 900,000 Jews made up approximately 5 percent of the population and about 23 percent of Budapest's citizenry. Jews accounted for 54 percent of commercial business owners, 85 percent of financial institution directors and owners, and 62 percent of all employees in commerce.

The rise of a working class came naturally with industrial development. By 1900 Hungary's mines and industries employed nearly 1.2 million people, representing 13 percent of the population. The government favored low wages to keep Hungarian products competitive on foreign markets and to prevent impoverished peasants from flocking to the city to find work. The government recognized the right to strike in 1884, but labor came under strong political pressure. In 1890 the Social Democratic Party was established and secretly formed alliances with the trade unions. The party soon enlisted one-third of Budapest's workers. By 1900 the party and union rolls listed more than 200,000 hard-core members, making it the largest secular organization the country had ever known. The Diet passed laws to improve the lives of industrial workers, including providing medical and accident insurance, but it refused to extend them voting rights, arguing that broadening the franchise would give too many non-Hungarians the vote and threaten Hungarian domination. After the Compromise of 1867, the Hungarian government also launched an education reform in an effort to create a skilled, literate labor force. As a result, the literacy rate had climbed to 80 percent by 1910. Literacy raised the expectations of workers in agriculture and industry and made them ripe for participation in movements for political and social change.

The plight of the peasantry worsened drastically during the depression at the end of the nineteenth century. The rural population grew, and the size of the peasants' farm plots shrank as land was divided up by successive generations. By 1900 almost half of the country's landowners were scratching out a living from plots too small to meet basic needs, and many farm workers had no land at all. Many peasants chose to emigrate, and their departure rate reached approximately 50,000 annually in the 1870s and about 200,000 annually by 1907. The peasantry's share of the population dropped from 72.5 percent in 1890 to 68.4 percent in 1900. The countryside also was characterized by unrest, to which the government reacted by sending in troops, banning all farm-labor organizations, and passing other repressive legislation.

The 1896 Millennial Monument in Budapest
Courtesy Robert Lisbeth

In the late nineteenth century, the Liberal Party passed laws that enhanced the government's power at the expense of the Roman Catholic Church. The parliament won the right to veto clerical appointments, and it reduced the church's nearly total domination of Hungary's education institutions. Additional laws eliminated the church's authority over a number of civil matters and, in the process, introduced civil marriage and divorce procedures.

The Liberal Party also worked with some success to create a unified, Magyarized state. Ignoring the Nationalities Law, it enacted laws that required the Hungarian language to be used in local government and increased the number of school subjects taught in that language. After 1890 the government succeeded in Magyarizing educated Slovaks, Germans, Croats, and Romanians and co-opting them into the bureaucracy, thus robbing the minority nationalities of an educated elite. Most minorities never learned to speak Hungarian, but the education system made them aware of their political rights, and their discontent with Magyarization mounted. Bureaucratic pressures and heightened fears of territorial claims against Hungary after the creation of new nation-states in the Balkans forced Tisza to outlaw "national agitation" and to use electoral legerdemain to deprive the minorities of representation. Nevertheless, in 1901 Romanian and Slovak national parties emerged undaunted by incidents of electoral violence and police repression.

Political and Economic Life, 1905-19

Tisza directed the Liberal government until 1890, and for fourteen years thereafter a number of Liberal prime ministers held office. Agricultural decline continued, and the bureaucracy could no longer absorb all of the pauperized lesser nobles and educated people who could not find work elsewhere. This group gave its political support to the Party of Independence and the Party of Forty-Eight, which became part of the "national" opposition that forced a coalition with the Liberals in 1905. The Party of Independence resigned itself to the existence of the Dual Monarchy and sought to enhance Hungary's position within it; the Party of Forty-Eight, however, deplored the Compromise of 1867, argued that Hungary remained an Austrian colony, and pushed for formation of a Hungarian national bank and an independent customs zone.

Franz Joseph refused to appoint members of the coalition to the government until they renounced their demands for concessions from Austria concerning the military. When the coalition finally gained power in 1906, the leaders retreated from their opposition to the Compromise of 1867 and followed the Liberal Party's economic policies. István Tisza—Kálmán Tisza's son and prime minister from 1903 to 1905—formed the new Party of Work, which in 1910 won a large majority in the parliament. Tisza became prime minister for a second time in 1912 after labor strife erupted over an unsuccessful attempt to expand voting rights.

World War I

On June 28, 1914, a Bosnian Serb assassinated Archduke Franz Ferdinand, heir to the Austrian throne. Within days Austria-Hungary presented Serbia with an ultimatum that made war inevitable. Tisza initially opposed the ultimatum but changed his mind when Germany supported Austria-Hungary. By late August, all the great European powers were at war. Bands playing military music and patriotic demonstrators expecting a quick, easy victory took to Budapest's streets after the declaration of war. However, Hungary, was ill prepared to fight. The country's armaments were obsolete, and its industries were not prepared for a war economy.

In 1915 and 1916, Hungary felt the full impact of the war. Inflation ran rampant, wages were frozen, food shortages developed, and the government banned export of grain even to Austria. Franz Joseph died in 1916, and Karl IV (1916-18) became Hungary's new king. Before being crowned, however, Karl insisted that Hungarians have expanded voting rights. Tisza resigned in response. By 1917 the Hungarian government was slowly losing domestic control in the face of mounting popular dissatisfaction caused by the war. Of the 3.6 million soldiers Hungary sent to war, 2.1 million became casualties. By late 1918, Hungary's farms and factories were producing only half of what they did in 1913, and the war-weary people had abandoned hope of victory.

On October 31, 1918, smoldering unrest burst into revolution in Budapest, and roving soldiers assassinated István Tisza. Pressured by the popular uprising and the refusal of Hungarian troops to quell disturbances, King Karl was compelled to appoint the "Red Count," Mihály Károlyi, a pro-Entente liberal and leader of the Party of Independence, to the post of prime minister. Chrysanthemum-waving crowds poured into the streets shouting their approval. Károlyi formed a new cabinet, whose members were drawn from the new National Council, composed of representatives of the Party of Independence, the Social Democratic Party, and a group of bourgeois radicals. After suing for a separate peace, the new government dissolved the parliament, pronounced Hungary an independent republic with Károlyi as provisional president, and proclaimed universal suffrage and freedom of the press and assembly. The government launched preparations for land reform and promised elections, but neither goal was carried out. On November 13, 1918, Karl IV surrendered his powers as king of Hungary; however, he did not abdicate, a technicality that made a return to the throne possible.

The Károlyi government's measures failed to stem popular discontent, especially when the Entente powers began distributing slices of Hungary's traditional territory to Romania, Yugoslavia, and Czechoslovakia. The new government and its supporters had pinned their hopes for maintaining Hungary's territorial integrity on abandoning Austria and Germany, securing a separate peace, and exploiting Károlyi's close connections in France. The Entente, however, chose to consider Hungary a partner in the defeated Dual Monarchy and dashed the Hungarians' hopes with the delivery of each new diplomatic note demanding surrender of more land. On March 19, 1919, the French head of the Entente mission in Budapest handed Károlyi a note delineating final postwar boundaries, which were unacceptable to all Hungarians. Károlyi resigned and turned power over to a coalition of Social Democrats and communists, who promised that Soviet Russia would help Hungary restore its original borders. Although the Social Democrats held a majority in the coalition, the communists under Béla Kun immediately seized control and announced the establishment of the Hungarian Soviet Republic.

Hungarian Soviet Republic

The rise of the Hungarian Communist Party (HCP) to power was swift. The party was organized in a Moscow hotel on November 4, 1918, when a group of Hungarian prisoners of war and communist sympathizers formed a Central Committee and dispatched members to Hungary to recruit new members, propagate the party's ideas, and radicalize Károlyi's government. By February 1919, the party numbered 30,000 to 40,000 members, including many unemployed ex-soldiers, young intellectuals, and Jews. In the same month, Kun was imprisoned for incitement to riot, but his popularity skyrocketed when a journalist reported that he had been beaten by the police. Kun emerged from jail triumphant when the Social Democrats handed power to a government of "People's Commissars," who proclaimed the Hungarian Soviet Republic on March 21, 1919.

The communists wrote a temporary constitution guaranteeing freedom of speech and assembly; free education; language and cultural rights to minorities; and other rights. It also provided for suffrage for people over eighteen years of age except clergy, "former exploiters," and certain others. Single-list elections took place in April, but members of the parliament were selected indirectly by popularly elected committees. On June 25, Kun's government proclaimed a dictatorship of the proletariat, nationalized industrial and commercial enterprises, and socialized housing, transport, banking, medicine, cultural institutions, and all landholdings of more than 40.5 hectares. Kun undertook these measures even though the Hungarian communists were relatively few, and the support they enjoyed was based far more on their program to restore Hungary's borders than on their revolutionary agenda. Kun hoped that the Soviet Russian government would intervene on Hungary's behalf and believed that a worldwide workers' revolution was imminent. In an effort to secure its rule in the interim, the communist government resorted to arbitrary violence. Revolutionary tribunals ordered about 590 executions, including some for "crimes against the revolution." The government also used "red terror" to expropriate grain from peasants. This violence and the regime's moves against the clergy also shocked many Hungarians.

In late May, Kun attempted to fulfill his promise to restore Hungary's borders. The Hungarian Red Army marched northward and reoccupied part of Slovakia. Despite initial military success, however, Kun withdrew his troops about three weeks later when the French threatened to intervene. This concession shook his popular support. Kun then unsuccessfully turned the Hungarian

Red Army on the Romanians, who broke through Hungarian lines on July 30, occupied and looted Budapest, and ousted Kun's Soviet Republic on August 1, 1919. Kun fled first to Vienna and then to Soviet Russia, where he was executed during Stalin's terror against foreign communists in the late 1930s.

Counterrevolution

A militantly anticommunist authoritarian government composed of military officers entered Budapest on the heels of the Romanians. A "white terror" ensued that led to the imprisonment, torture, and execution without trial of communists, socialists, Jews, leftist intellectuals, sympathizers with the Károlyi and Kun regimes, and others who threatened the traditional Hungarian political order that the officers sought to reestablish. Estimates placed the number of executions at approximately 5,000. In addition, about 75,000 people were jailed. In particular, the Hungarian right wing and the Romanian forces targeted Jews for retribution. Ultimately, the white terror forced nearly 100,000 people to leave the country, most of them socialists, intellectuals, and middle-class Jews.

Trianon Hungary

After World War I, a conservative government ruled Hungary and made some progress toward economic modernization. The Great Depression, however, brought economic collapse, and the country's mood shifted to the far right. An alliance with Nazi Germany resulted, and Hungary fought on the Axis side in World War II. Again Hungary experienced defeat, and the country was occupied by the Soviet Red Army.

Postwar Political and Economic Conditions

In 1920 and 1921, internal chaos racked Hungary. The white terror continued to plague Jews and leftists, unemployment and inflation soared, and penniless Hungarian refugees poured across the border from neighboring countries and burdened the floundering economy. The government offered the population little succor. In January 1920, Hungarian men and women cast the first secret ballots in the country's political history and elected a large counterrevolutionary and agrarian majority to a unicameral parliament. Two main political parties emerged: the socially conservative Christian National Union and the Smallholders' Party, which advocated land reform. In March the parliament annulled both the Pragmatic Sanction of 1723 and the Compromise of 1867, and it restored the Hungarian monarchy but postponed electing a king until civil disorder had subsided. Instead, Miklós Horthy

(1920–44)—a former commander in chief of the Austro-Hungarian navy—was elected regent and was empowered, among other things, to appoint Hungary's prime minister, veto legislation, convene or dissolve the parliament, and command the armed forces.

Hungary's signing of the Treaty of Trianon on June 4, 1920, ratified the country's dismemberment, limited the size of its armed forces, and required reparations payments. The territorial provisions of the treaty, which ensured continued discord between Hungary and its neighbors, required the Hungarians to surrender more than two-thirds of their prewar lands (see fig. 5). Romania acquired Transylvania; Yugoslavia gained Croatia, Slavonia, and Vojvodina; Slovakia became a part of Czechoslovakia; and Austria also acquired a small piece of prewar Hungarian territory. Hungary lost about 60 percent of its prewar population, and about one-third of the 10 million ethnic Hungarians found themselves outside the diminished homeland. The country's ethnic composition was left almost homogeneous. Hungarians constituted about 90 percent of the population, Germans made up about 6 to 8 percent, and Slovaks, Croats, Romanians, Jews, and other minorities accounted for the remainder.

New international borders separated Hungary's industrial base from its sources of raw materials and its former markets for agricultural and industrial products. Its new circumstances forced Hungary to become a trading nation. Hungary lost 84 percent of its timber resources, 43 percent of its arable land, and 83 percent of its iron ore. Because most of the country's prewar industry was concentrated near Budapest, Hungary retained about 51 percent of its industrial population, 56 percent of its industry, 82 percent of its heavy industry, and 70 percent of its banks.

Bethlen Government

Horthy appointed Pál Teleki prime minister in July 1920. His right-wing government set quotas effectively limiting admission of Jews to universities, legalized corporal punishment, and, to quiet rural discontent, took initial steps toward fulfilling a promise of major land reform by dividing about 385,000 hectares from the largest estates into smallholdings. Teleki's government resigned, however, after the former emperor, Karl IV, unsuccessfully attempted to retake Hungary's throne in March 1921. King Karl's return marked a split between conservatives who favored a Habsburg restoration and nationalist right-wing radicals who supported election of a Hungarian king. István Bethlen, a nonaffiliated, right-wing member of the parliament, took advantage of this rift by convincing members of the Christian National Union who opposed Karl's reenthronement to merge with the Smallholders' Party and form a new Party of Unity with Bethlen as its leader. Horthy then appointed Bethlen prime minister.

As prime minister, Bethlen dominated Hungarian politics between 1921 and 1931. He fashioned a political machine by amending the electoral law, eliminating peasants from the Party of Unity, providing jobs in the bureaucracy to his supporters, and manipulating elections in rural areas. Bethlen restored order to the country by giving the radical counterrevolutionaries payoffs and government jobs in exchange for ceasing their campaign of terror against Jews and leftists. In 1921 Bethlen made a deal with the Social Democrats and trade unions, agreeing, among other things, to legalize their activities and free political prisoners in return for their pledge to refrain from spreading anti-Hungarian propaganda, calling political strikes, and organizing the peasantry. In May 1922, the Party of Unity captured a large parliamentary majority. Karl IV's death, soon after he failed a second time to reclaim the throne in October 1921, allowed the revision of the Treaty of Trianon to rise to the top of Hungary's political agenda. Bethlen's strategy to win the treaty's revision was first to strengthen his country's economy and then to build relations with stronger nations that could further Hungary's goals. Revision of the treaty had such a broad backing in Hungary that Bethlen used it, at least in part, to deflect criticism of his economic, social, and political policies. However, Bethlen's only foreign policy success was a treaty of friendship with Italy in 1927, which had little immediate impact.

Economic Development

When Bethlen took office, the government was bankrupt. Tax revenues were so paltry that he turned to domestic gold and foreign-currency reserves to meet about half of the 1921-22 budget and almost 80 percent of the 1922-23 budget. To improve his country's economic circumstances, Bethlen undertook development of industry. He imposed tariffs on finished goods and earmarked the revenues to subsidize new industries. Bethlen squeezed the agricultural sector to increase cereal exports, which generated foreign currency to pay for imports critical to the industrial sector. In 1924, after the white terror had waned and Hungary had gained admission to the League of Nations (1922), the Bethlen government secured a US$50 million reconstruction loan from the league, which restored the confidence of foreign creditors. Foreign loans and domestic capital that had been removed from Hungary during the communist revolution flowed back into the country, further fueling industrial development.

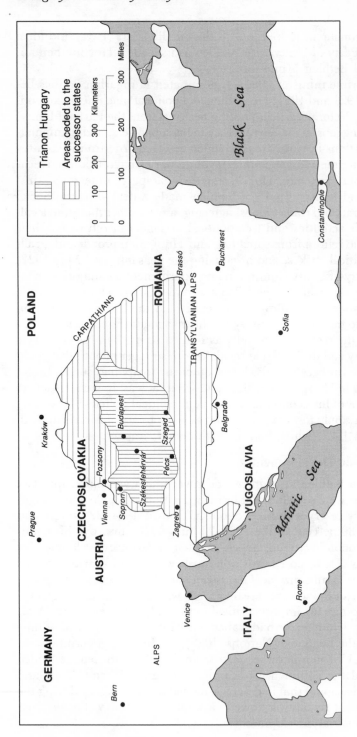

Source: Based on information from C.A. Macartney, *Hungary: A Short History*, Chicago, 1962, 208.

Figure 5. Trianon Hungary, 1920

By the late 1920s, Bethlen's policies had brought order to the economy. The number of factories increased by about 66 percent, inflation subsided, and the national income climbed 20 percent. However, the apparent stability was supported by a rickety framework of constantly revolving foreign credits and high world grain prices; therefore, Hungary remained undeveloped in comparison with the wealthier western European countries.

Despite economic progress, the workers' standard of living remained poor, and consequently the working class never gave Bethlen its political support. The peasants fared worse than the working class (see Interwar Period, ch. 2). In the 1920s, about 60 percent of the peasants were either landless or were cultivating plots too small to provide a decent living. Real wages for agricultural workers remained below prewar levels, and the peasants had practically no political voice. Moreover, once Bethlen had consolidated his power, he ignored calls for land reform. The industrial sector failed to expand fast enough to provide jobs for all the peasants and university graduates seeking work. Most peasants lingered in the villages, and in the 1930s Hungarians in rural areas were extremely dissatisfied. Hungary's foreign debt ballooned as Bethlen expanded the bureaucracy to absorb the university graduates who, if left idle, might have threatened civil order.

The Great Depression

In 1929 the New York Stock Exchange crashed. As a result, world grain prices plummeted, and the framework supporting Hungary's economy buckled. Hungary's earnings from grain exports declined as prices and volume dropped, tax revenues fell, foreign credit sources dried up, and short-term loans were called in. Hungary sought financial relief from the League of Nations, which insisted on a program of rigid fiscal belt-tightening, resulting in increased unemployment. The peasants reverted to subsistence farming. Industrial production rapidly dropped, and businesses went bankrupt as domestic and foreign demand evaporated. Government workers lost their jobs or suffered severe pay cuts. By 1933 about 18 percent of Budapest's citizens lived in poverty. Unemployment leaped from 5 percent in 1928 to almost 36 percent by 1933.

As the standard of living dropped, the political mood of the country shifted further toward the right. Bethlen resigned without warning amid national turmoil in August 1931. His successor, Gyula Károlyi, failed to quell the crisis. Horthy then appointed a reactionary demagogue, Gyula Gömbös, but only after Gömbös agreed to maintain the existing political system, to refrain from calling elections before the parliament's term had expired, and to appoint several Bethlen supporters to head key ministries. Gömbös publicly renounced the vehement anti-Semitism he had espoused earlier, and his party and government included some Jews.

Radical Right in Power

Gömbös's appointment marked the beginning of the radical right's ascendancy in Hungarian politics, which lasted with few interruptions until 1945. The radical right garnered its support from medium and small farmers, former refugees from Hungary's lost territories, and unemployed civil servants, army officers, and university graduates. Gömbös advocated a one-party government, revision of the Treaty of Trianon, withdrawal from the League of Nations, anti-intellectualism, and social reform. He assembled a political machine, but his efforts to fashion a one-party state and fulfill his reform platform were frustrated by a parliament composed mostly of Bethlen's supporters and by Hungary's creditors, who forced Gömbös to follow conventional policies in dealing with the economic and financial crisis. The 1935 elections gave Gömbös more solid support in the parliament, and he succeeded in gaining control of the ministries of finance, industry, and defense and in replacing several key military officers with his supporters. In September 1936, Gömbös informed German officials that he would establish a Nazi-like, one-party government in Hungary within two years, but he died in October without realizing this goal.

In foreign affairs, Gömbös led Hungary toward close relations with Italy and Germany; in fact, Gömbös coined the term *Axis*, which was later adopted by the German-Italian military alliance. Soon after his appointment, Gömbös visited Italian dictator Benito Mussolini and gained his support for revision of the Treaty of Trianon. Later, Gömbös became the first foreign head of government to visit German chancellor Adolf Hitler. For a time, Hungary profited handsomely, as Gömbös signed a trade agreement with Germany that drew Hungary's economy out of depression but made Hungary dependent on the German economy for both raw materials and markets. In 1928 Germany had accounted for 19.5 percent of Hungary's imports and 11.7 percent of its exports; by 1939 the figures were 52.5 percent and 52.2 percent, respectively. Hungary's annual rate of economic growth from 1934 to 1940 averaged 10.8 percent. The number of workers in industry doubled in the ten years after 1933, and the number of agricultural workers dropped below 50 percent for the first time in the country's history. Hungary also used its relationship with Germany to chip away at the Treaty of Trianon. In 1938 Hungary openly repudiated the treaty's restrictions on its armed forces. With German help, Hungary

Drumming on Saint Stephen's Day in Borsod County,
1929 [Sándor Gönyey; Ethnographic Museum, Budapest]
Courtesy Harriet Gerber

extended its territory four times and doubled in size from 1938 to
1941. It regained parts of southern Slovakia in 1938, Carpatho-
Ukraine in 1939, northern Transylvania in 1940, and parts of
Vojvodina in 1941.

Hitler's assistance did not come without a price. After 1938 the
Führer used promises of additional territories, economic pressure,
and threats of military intervention to pressure the Hungarians into
supporting his policies, including those related to Europe's Jews,
which encouraged Hungary's anti-Semites. The percentage of Jews
in business, finance, and the professions far exceeded the percentage of Jews in the overall population. The 1930 census showed
that Jews made up only 5.1 percent of the population but provided
54.5 percent of its physicians, 31.7 percent of its journalists, and
49.2 percent of its lawyers. Jews controlled an estimated 19.5 percent to 33 percent of the national income, four of the five leading
banks, and 80 percent of Hungary's industry. After the depression struck, anti-Semites made the Jews scapegoats for Hungary's
economic plight.

Hungary's Jews suffered the first blows of this renewed anti-
Semitism during the government of Gömbös's successor, Kálmán
Darányi, who fashioned a coalition of conservatives and reactionaries

and dismantled Gömbös's political machine. After Horthy publicly dashed hopes of land reform, discontented right-wingers took to the streets denouncing the government and baiting the Jews. Darányi's government attempted to appease the anti-Semites and the Nazis by proposing and passing the first so-called Jewish Law, which set quotas limiting Jews to 20 percent of the positions in certain businesses and professions. The law failed to satisfy Hungary's anti-Semitic radicals, however, and when Darányi tried to appease them again, Horthy unseated him in 1938. The regent then appointed the ill-starred Béla Imrédy, who drafted a second, harsher Jewish Law before political opponents forced his resignation in February 1939 by presenting documents showing that Imrédy's own grandfather was a Jew.

Imrédy's downfall led to Pál Teleki's return to the prime minister's office. Teleki dissolved some of the fascist parties but did not alter the fundamental policies of his predecessors. He undertook a bureaucratic reform and launched cultural and educational programs to help the rural poor. Illiteracy dropped to about 7 percent by 1941. But Teleki also oversaw passage of the second Jewish Law, which broadened the definition of "Jewishness," cut the quotas on Jews permitted in the professions and in business, and required that the quotas be attained by the hiring of Gentiles or the firing of Jews. By the June 1939 elections, Hungarian public opinion had shifted so far to the right that voters gave the Arrow Cross Party—Hungary's equivalent of Germany's National Socialist German Workers' Party (the Nazi Party)—the second highest number of votes. In September 1940, the Hungarian government allowed German troops to transit the country on their way to Romania, and on November 20, 1940, Hungary signed the Tripartite Pact, which allied Germany, Italy, and Japan.

World War II

In December 1940, Teleki signed a short-lived Treaty of Eternal Friendship with Yugoslavia. The Yugoslav government, however, was overthrown on March 27, 1941, two days after it succumbed to German and Italian pressure and joined the pact. Hitler considered the overthrow a hostile act and grounds to invade. Again promising territory in exchange for cooperation, he asked Hungary to join the invasion by contributing troops and allowing the Wehrmacht (German armed forces) to march through its territory. Unable to prevent the invasion, Teleki committed suicide on April 3. Three days later, the Luftwaffe mercilessly bombed Belgrade without warning, and German troops invaded. Shortly thereafter, Horthy dispatched Hungarian military forces to occupy former Hungarian lands in Yugoslavia, and Hungary eventually annexed sections of Vojvodina.

Horthy named the right-wing radical László Bárdossy to succeed Teleki. Bárdossy was convinced that Germany would win the war and sought to maintain Hungary's independence by appeasing Hitler. Hitler tricked Horthy into committing Hungary to join his invasion of the Soviet Union in June 1941, and Hungary entered the war against the Western Allies the following December. In July 1941, the government deported the first 40,000 Jews from Hungary, and six months later Hungarian troops, in reprisal for resistance activities, murdered 3,000 Serbian and Jewish hostages near Novi Sad in Yugoslavia. By the winter of 1941–42, German hopes of a quick victory over the Soviet Union had faded. In January the German foreign minister visited Budapest asking for additional mobilization of Hungarian forces for a planned spring offensive and promising in return to hand Hungary some territory in Transylvania. Bárdossy agreed and committed one-third of Hungary's military forces.

Horthy grew dissatisfied with Bárdossy, who resigned in March 1942, and named Miklós Kállay, a conservative veteran of Bethlen's government, who aimed to free Hungary from the Nazis' grip. Kállay faced a terrible dilemma: if he broke with Hitler and negotiated a separate peace, the Germans would occupy Hungary immediately; but if he supported the Germans, he would encourage further pro-Nazi excesses. Kállay chose duplicity. In 1942 and 1943, pro-Western Hungarian government officials promised British and American diplomats that the Hungarians would not fire on their aircraft, sparing for a time Hungarian cities from bombardment.

In January 1943, the Soviet Red Army annihilated Hungary's Second Army during the massive counterattack on the Axis troops besieging Stalingrad. In the fighting, Soviet troops killed an estimated 40,000 Hungarians and wounded 70,000. As anti-Axis pressure in Hungary mounted, Kállay withdrew the remnants of the force into Hungary in April 1943, and only a nominal number of poorly armed troops remained of the country's military contribution to the Axis Powers. Aware of Kállay's deceit and fearing that Hungary might conclude a separate peace, Hitler ordered Nazi troops to occupy Hungary and force its government to increase its contribution to the war effort. Kállay took asylum in the Turkish legation. Döme Sztójay, a supporter of the Nazis, became the new prime minister. His government jailed political leaders, dissolved the labor unions, and resumed the deportation of Hungary's Jews.

While Kállay was prime minister, the Jews endured economic and political repression, but the government protected them from the "final solution." The government expropriated Jewish property; banned the purchase of real estate by Jews; barred Jews from working as publishers, theater directors, and editors of journals; proscribed sexual relations between Jews and non-Jews; and outlawed conversion to Judaism. But when the Nazis occupied Hungary in March 1944, the deportation of the Jews to the death camps in Poland began. Horthy used the confusion after the July 20, 1944, attempt to assassinate Hitler to replace Sztójay in August 1944 with General Géza Lakatos and halt the deportation of Jews from Budapest. Of the approximately 725,000 Jews residing within Hungary's expanded borders of 1941, only about 260,500, mostly from Budapest, survived.

In September, Soviet forces crossed the border, and on October 15 Horthy announced that Hungary had signed an armistice with the Soviet Union. However, the Germans abducted the regent and forced him to abrogate the armistice, depose the Lakatos government, and name Ferenc Szálasi—the leader of the Arrow Cross Party—prime minister. Horthy abdicated, and soon the country became a battlefield. Hungary was sacked first by the retreating Germans, who demolished the rail, road, and communications systems, then by the advancing Soviet Red Army, which found the country in a state of political chaos. Germans held off the Soviet troops near Budapest for seven weeks before the defenses collapsed, and on April 4, 1945, the last German troops were driven out of Hungary.

Postwar Hungary

In the aftermath of World War II, a victorious Soviet Union succeeded in forcing its political, social, and economic system on Eastern Europe, including Hungary. But the Hungarians never reconciled themselves to Soviet hegemony over their country and rebelled against the Soviet Union and its Hungarian vassals in 1956. That revolution was crushed by Soviet tanks, but it brought to power János Kádár, who then attempted to institute a milder form of communist rule.

Coalition Government and Communist Takeover

The Hungarian Communist Party (HCP) enjoyed scant popular support after the toppling of Béla Kun's short-lived Hungarian Soviet Republic in 1919 and the subsequent white terror. During World War II, a communist cell headed by László Rajk, a veteran of the Spanish Civil War (1936–39) and a former communist student leader, operated underground within the country. Mátyás Rákosi led a second, Moscow-based group whose members were later called the "Muscovites." After the Soviet Red Army invaded Hungary in September 1944, Rajk's organization emerged from hiding, and the Muscovites returned to their homeland. Rákosi's close ties with the Soviet occupiers enhanced his influence within the party, and a rivalry developed between the Muscovites and Rajk's followers. Between the invasion and the end of the war, party membership rose significantly. Although party rolls listed only about 3,000 names in November 1944, membership had swelled to about 500,000 by October 1945.

Hungary's postwar political order began to take shape even before Germany's surrender. In October 1944, Britain's Prime Minister Winston Churchill and Foreign Minister Anthony Eden agreed with Stalin that after the war the Soviet Union would enjoy a 75 percent to 80 percent influence in Hungary, Bulgaria, and Romania, while the British would have a 20 percent to 25 percent share. On December 22, 1944, a provisional government emerged in Debrecen that was made up of the Provisional National Assembly, in which communist representatives outnumbered those of the other "antifascist" parties, and a cabinet, whose members included a general and two other military officers of the old regime, two communists, two Social Democrats, two members of the Smallholders' Party, one member of the National Peasant Party, and one unaffiliated member. The provisional government concluded an armistice with the Soviet Union on January 20, 1945, while fighting still raged in the western part of the country. The armistice established the Allied Control Commission, with Soviet, American, and British representatives, which held complete sovereignty over the country. The commission's chairman, Marshal Kliment Voroshilov, a member of Stalin's inner circle, exercised absolute control.

Stalin decided against an immediate communist seizure of power in Hungary; rather, he instructed HCP leaders to take a gradualist approach and share power with other parties in freely elected coalition governments. Stalin informed Rákosi that a communist takeover would be delayed ten to fifteen years in order to deflect Western criticism of rapid communist takeovers in Poland, Bulgaria, Romania, and the Soviet zone of Germany. Stalin desired a quick return to normal economic activity to rebuild the Soviet Union and sought to avoid a confrontation with the Allies, who still had troops in Europe. The members of the HCP who had worked underground during the war opposed Stalin's gradualist approach and argued for immediate establishment of a dictator-ship of the proletariat.

In April 1945, after Soviet troops had rid Hungary of the Nazis, the government moved from Debrecen to Budapest, and a second, expanded Provisional National Assembly was chosen. With the sup-port of representatives of the trade unions and the Social Democratic Party, the HCP enjoyed an absolute majority of the assembly's 495 seats. The provisional government remained in power until November 15, 1945, when voters dealt the HCP an unexpected setback in a free election. The Smallholders' Party won 245 seats in the National Assembly; the HCP, 70; the Social Democratic Party, 69; the National Peasant Party, 21; and the Civic Democratic Party, 2. The National Assembly proclaimed the Hungarian Republic on February 1, 1946, and two Smallholder-led coalitions under Zoltán Tildy and Ferenc Nagy governed the country until May 1947.

The HCP soon formed a leftist alliance with the Social Democra-tic Party and the National Peasant Party and gained control of sev-eral key offices, including the leadership of the security police and the army general staff. Voroshilov vetoed an agreement reached by the coalition members to name a member of the Smallholders' Party to head the Ministry of Interior. A National Peasant Party member loyal to the HCP won the post and made the police a powerful tool of the communists. The National Assembly under-mined freedoms guaranteed in Hungary's constitution when it banned statements that could be interpreted as hostile to the democratic order or the country's international esteem. Later, as Hungary's democratic order became identified with HCP policies, the law was used to silence legitimate opponents.

In the immediate postwar period, the government pursued eco-nomic reconstruction and land reform (see Postwar Societal Trans-formation, ch. 2). Hungary had been devastated in the last years of World War II. About 24 percent of its industrial base was de-stroyed. Many of the large landowners and industrialists fled Hun-gary in advance of the Soviet Red Army. Reconstruction proceeded rapidly, expedited by gradual nationalization of mines, electric plants, the four largest concerns in heavy industry, and the ten largest banks. In 1945 the government also carried out a radical land reform, expropriating all holdings larger than fifty-seven hec-tares and distributing them to the country's poorest peasants. Nevertheless, the peasants received portions barely large enough for self-sufficiency. Finally, the government introduced a new currency—the forint—to help curb high inflation.

Using methods Rákosi later called "salami tactics," the HCP strengthened its position in the coalition by discrediting leaders of rival parties as "reactionaries" or "antidemocratic," forcing their resignation from the government and sometimes prompting their arrest. In 1945 ex-members of Horthy's regime lost their positions. A year later, members of the Smallholders' Party and the Social Democratic Party were ousted from power. In late 1946, leaders of the Smallholders' Party were arrested. In 1947 the Soviet Union ordered the arrest of Béla Kovács, the secretary general of the Smallholders' Party, on the false charge of plotting to overthrow the government. The Smallholders' Party was dissolved after Ferenc Nagy resigned his position as prime minister. The leftist bloc gained a small lead over its rivals in the 1947 general elections. The HCP tallied only 22 percent of the vote, but fraud tainted the election, and suspicions arose that the party actually enjoyed less support.

The Treaty of Paris, signed on February 10, 1947, required Hungary to pay US$200 million in reparations to the Soviet Union, US$50 million to Czechoslovakia, and US$50 million to Yugoslavia. Hungary also had to transfer a piece of territory to Czechoslovakia, leaving Hungary with slightly less territory than it had had after the Treaty of Trianon. Stalin had already returned Transylvania to the Romanians to reinforce the position of the procommunist Prime Minister Petru Groza. Thereafter, the Romanians' treatment of the Hungarian minority in Transylvania became an irritant in relations between the two countries (see Relations with Other Communist Neighbors, ch. 4).

Rákosi's Rule

In 1947 the postwar cooperation between the Soviet Union and the West collapsed, marking the beginning of the Cold War and the beginning of the end for Hungary's democratic coalition government. Having seen communist parties seize power in Poland, Romania, Bulgaria, and Yugoslavia and a communist insurgency threaten Greece, the Western powers dedicated themselves to containing Soviet influence. In May communists were expelled from the governments of Italy and France, and a month later the United States promulgated the Marshall Plan for the economic reconstruction of Europe, which was appealing to the East European governments.

Stalin feared a weakening of the Soviet Union's grip on Eastern Europe. Anticommunist forces in the region remained potent, and most of the communist governments were unpopular. In addition, East European parties began taking positions independent of Moscow; for example, communists in the Polish and Czechoslovak governments favored participation in the Marshall Plan, and Yugoslavia and Bulgaria broached the idea of a Balkan confederation. By September Stalin had abandoned gradualism and reversed his earlier advocacy of independent, "national roads to socialism." He now pushed for tighter adherence to Moscow's line and rapid establishment of Soviet-dominated communist states in Hungary and elsewhere. The policy shift was indicated in September 1947 at the founding meeting of the Cominform, an organization linking the Soviet communist party with the communist parties of Eastern Europe, France, and Italy.

The HCP proceeded swiftly to assume full control of the government. First Secretary Rákosi became the country's most powerful official and dictated major political and economic changes. In October 1947, noncommunist political figures were told to cooperate with a new coalition government or leave the country. In June 1948, the Social Democratic Party merged with the HCP, forming the Hungarian Workers' Party (HWP). In 1949 the regime held a single-list election, and on August 20 of that year the government ratified a Soviet-style constitution (see Constitution of 1949, ch. 4). The official name of the country became the Hungarian People's Republic, and the HWP's control of the government was assured. In 1952 Rákosi also became prime minister.

In 1948 Yugoslavia was expelled from the Cominform, and the Soviet-Yugoslav rift broke into the open. Almost overnight it became treasonous for communists to display any approval of Yugoslav leader Josip Broz Tito or to advocate national roads to socialism. Beginning in 1949, the Soviet Union unleashed a four-year reign of terror against "Titoists" in Eastern Europe. Rákosi purged members of the party's wartime underground, potential rivals, and hundreds of others. Rajk, who continued to support a Hungarian road to socialism, "confessed" to being a Titoist and a fascist spy and was hanged in 1950. Another victim was future party chief János Kádár, who was jailed and tortured for three years.

Between 1948 and 1953, the Hungarian economy was reorganized according to the Soviet model (see Economic Policy and Performance, 1945–85, ch. 3). In a campaign reminiscent of the Soviet Union's forced collectivization of agriculture in the 1930s, the regime compelled most peasants to join collective farms and required them to make deliveries to the government at prices lower than the cost of production. The regime accelerated nationalization of banking, trade, and industry, and by December 1949 nearly 99 percent of the country's workers had become state employees. The trade unions lost their independence, and the government introduced Soviet-style central planning. Planners neglected the production of consumer goods to focus on investment in heavy industry, especially steel production, and economic self-sufficiency. In January 1949, Hungary joined the Council for Mutual Economic Assistance (Comecon—see Glossary), an organization designed to further economic cooperation among the Soviet Union's satellites. The authorities also agreed to form joint-stock companies with the Soviet Union. These companies allowed the Soviet Union to dominate Hungary's air and river transportation, as well as its bauxite, crude oil, and refining industries and other sectors.

With the opposition parties disbanded and the trade unions collared, the churches became the communists' main source of opposition. The government had expropriated the churches' property with the land reform, and in July 1948 it nationalized church schools. Protestant church leaders reached a compromise with the government, but the head of the Roman Catholic Church—Cardinal József Mindszenty—resisted. The government arrested him in December 1948 and sentenced him to life imprisonment. Shortly thereafter, the regime disbanded most Catholic religious orders, and it secularized Catholic schools (see Religion and Religious Organizations, ch. 2).

Stalin died in March 1953. The new Soviet leadership soon permitted a more flexible policy in Eastern Europe known as the New Course. In June, Rákosi and other party leaders—among them Imre Nagy—were summoned to Moscow, where Soviet leaders harshly criticized them for Hungary's dismal economic performance. Soviet communist party Presidium member Lavrenti Beria reportedly upbraided Rákosi for naming Jews to Hungary's top party positions and accused him of seeking to make himself the "Jewish King of Hungary." (Communists of Jewish origin had dominated the party leadership and the secret police for a decade after the war, and every party leader from Béla Kun to Ernő Gerő had Jewish roots.) Rákosi retained his position as party chief, but the Soviet leaders forced the appointment of Nagy as prime minister. He quickly won the support of the government ministries and the intelligentsia. Nagy also ended the purges and began freeing political prisoners. In his first address to the National Assembly as prime minister, Nagy attacked Rákosi for his use of terror, and the speech was printed in the party newspaper.

Nagy charted his New Course for Hungary's drifting economy in a speech before the Central Committee, which gave the plan unanimous approval (see Party Structure, ch. 4). Hungary ceased collectivization of agriculture, allowed peasants to leave the collective farms, canceled the collective farms' compulsory production quotas, and raised government prices for deliveries. Government financial support and guarantees were extended to private producers, investment in the farm sector jumped 20 percent in the 1953–54 period, and peasants were able to increase the size of their private plots. The number of peasants on collective farms thus shrank by half between October and December 1953. Nagy also slashed investment in heavy industry by 41.1 percent in 1953–54 and shifted resources to light industry and the production of consumer goods. However, Nagy failed to fundamentally alter the planning system and neglected to introduce incentives to replace compulsory plan targets, resulting in a poorer record of plan fulfillment after 1953 than before. Rákosi used his influence to disrupt Nagy's reforms and erode his political position. In 1954 Soviet leaders who favored economic policies akin to Nagy's lost a Kremlin power struggle. Rákosi seized the opportunity to attack Nagy as a right-wing deviationist and to criticize shortcomings in the economy. Nagy was forced to resign from the government in April 1955 and was later expelled from the Politburo, Central Committee, and finally the party itself. Thus, the Central Committee that had lauded the New Course in June 1953 unanimously condemned its architect less than two years later.

After Nagy's fall, collectivization and development of heavy industry again became the prime focus of Hungary's economy. The purges did not resume, however, as Rákosi did not enjoy the same amount of power or Soviet support that he did while Stalin was alive. Moreover, he now had to contend with many outspoken opponents within the party, including numerous victims of the purges who had been readmitted to the HWP on Moscow's orders. A schism soon split the party leadership from the rank and file, and the party organization within the Writers' Association became a forum for intraparty opposition. In 1955 a rapprochement between the Soviet Union and Yugoslavia produced the Belgrade Declaration, in which Moscow confirmed that each nation had the right to follow its own road to socialism. One year later, Soviet leader Nikita S. Khrushchev denounced Stalin in his "secret speech" before the Twentieth Party Congress of the Soviet communist party. These external events shook Rákosi, who was a strong opponent of Titoism and the instigator of Hungary's purges.

HWP members opposed to Rákosi compelled him to admit that the purges involved abuse of power and that Rajk and others had been its innocent victims. Rákosi ordered an investigation, but it cleared him and blamed the state security police instead. This result not only inflamed the party opposition but also alienated Rákosi from the police. In June 1956, Rákosi's position became untenable.

The party press printed open attacks. The Writers' Association, the newly created Petőfi Circle (see Glossary), and student organizations clamored for Rákosi's ouster and arrest. On June 30, the Central Committee dissolved the Petőfi Circle and expelled intellectuals from the party. By mid-July, however, Soviet leaders began to fear outright revolution and called for Rákosi to step down. He resigned after a meeting of the Central Committee on July 17. Gerő, Rákosi's deputy, was appointed first secretary. Moscow hoped to introduce a slow liberalization, but Gerő was too closely identified with Rákosi, and party discipline subsequently broke down completely.

Revolution of 1956

On October 23, a Budapest student rally in support of Polish efforts to win autonomy from the Soviet Union sparked mass demonstrations. The police attacked, and the demonstrators fought back, tearing down symbols of Soviet domination and HWP rule, sacking the party newspaper's offices and shouting in favor of free elections, national independence, and the return of Imre Nagy to power. Gerő called out the army, but many soldiers handed their weapons to the demonstrators and joined the uprising (see Historical Background and Traditions, ch. 5). Soviet officials in Budapest summoned Nagy to speak to the crowd, but the violence continued. At Gerő's request, Soviet troops entered Budapest on October 24. The presence of these troops further enraged the Hungarians, who battled the troops and state security police. Crowds emptied the prisons, freed Cardinal Mindszenty, sacked police stations, and summarily hanged some members of the secret police. The Central Committee named Nagy prime minister on October 25 and selected a new Politburo and Secretariat; one day later, János Kádár replaced Gerő as party first secretary.

Nagy enjoyed vast support. He formed a new government consisting of both communists and noncommunists, dissolved the state security police, abolished the one-party system, and promised free elections and an end to collectivization, all with Kádár's support. But Nagy failed to harness the popular revolt. Workers' councils threatened a general strike to back demands for removal of Soviet troops, elimination of party interference in economic affairs, and renegotiation of economic treaties with the Soviet Union. On October 30, Nagy called for the formation of a new democratic, multiparty system. Noncommunist parties that had been suppressed almost a decade before began to reorganize. A coalition government emerged that included members of the Smallholders' Party, Social Democratic Party, National Peasant Party, and other parties, as well as the HWP. After negotiations, Soviet officials agreed to remove their troops at the discretion of the Hungarian government, and Soviet troops began to leave Budapest. Nagy soon learned, however, that new Soviet armored divisions had crossed into Hungary.

In response, on November 1 Nagy announced Hungary's decision to withdraw from the Warsaw Pact (see Glossary) and to declare Hungary neutral. He then appealed to the United Nations and Western governments for protection of Hungary's neutrality. The Western powers, which were involved in the Suez crisis and were without contingency plans to deal with a revolution in Eastern Europe, did not respond.

The Soviet military reacted to Hungarian events with a quick strike. On November 3, Soviet troops surrounded Budapest and closed the country's borders. Overnight they entered the capital and occupied the National Assembly building. Kádár, who had fled to the Soviet Union on November 2, assembled a Temporary Revolutionary Government of Hungary on Soviet soil just across the Hungarian border. On November 4, the formation of the new government was announced in a radio broadcast. Kádár returned to Budapest in a Soviet armored car; by then, Nagy had fled to the Yugoslav embassy, Cardinal Mindszenty had taken refuge in the United States embassy, Rákosi was safely across the Soviet border, and about 200,000 Hungarians had escaped to the West.

With Soviet support, Kádár struck almost immediately against participants in the revolution. Over the next five years, about 2,000 individuals were executed and about 25,000 imprisoned. Kádár also reneged on a guarantee of safe conduct granted to Nagy, who was arrested on November 23 and deported to Romania. In June 1958, the Hungarian government announced that Nagy and other government officials who had played key roles in the revolution had been secretly tried and executed.

Kádár's Reforms

The Revolution of 1956 discredited Hungary's Stalinist political and economic system and sent a clear warning to the leadership that popular tolerance for its policies had limits, and that if these limits were exceeded, popular reaction could threaten communist control. In response, regime leaders decided to formulate economic policies leading to an improvement of the population's standard of living. Pragmatism and reform gradually became the watchwords in economic policy-making, especially after 1960, and policymakers began relying on economists and other specialists rather than ideologists in the formation of economic policies. The result was a series of reforms that modified Hungary's rigid, centrally planned economy and eventually introduced elements of a free market, creating a concoction sometimes called "goulash communism" (see Economic Policy and Performance, 1945–85, ch. 3).

In late 1956, the party named a committee of mostly reform-minded experts to examine Hungary's economic system and make proposals for its revision. The committee's report marked the first step on Hungary's road to economic reform. Its proposals presaged many of the changes implemented a decade later, including elimination of administrative direction of the economy, introduction of greater enterprise autonomy, cooperation between private and collective sectors in agriculture, economic regulation using price and credit policies, and central planning focused only on long-term objectives. However, the committee's proposals were never really implemented. Some observers suggested that the party had solidified its power so quickly that it no longer needed to enact such drastic measures; others claimed that Soviet leaders opposed such reform until they ensured that the party (on November 1, 1956, renamed the Hungarian Socialist Workers' Party—HSWP) had consolidated its power and demonstrated a clear need for a fundamental economic change. During the chaos of the revolution, Hungary's collective farms lost about two-thirds of their members. Many left to become private farmers. In July 1957, Kádár appeased hard-liners in Hungary and abroad by agreeing to recollectivize agriculture, and in early 1959 the drive began in earnest. The regime combined force and economic coercion with persuasion and incentives to drive peasants back to the collective farms (see Agricultural Organization, ch. 3). The government abolished compulsory production quotas and delivery obligations and substituted voluntary contracts at good prices. It also permitted profit-sharing schemes and programs to promote technical innovation. The regime allowed peasants to retain sizable private plots and ample livestock and to choose between collective or cooperative farms. The farms also received substantial government investments. As a result, Hungary became the only country with a centrally planned economy where crop output increased as a result of collectivization. By 1962 more than 95 percent of all farmland had been collectivized either in the form of state farms or cooperatives. The collectivization drive deflected the hard-liners' criticism of Kádár for his advocacy of reform, and problems with the program's implementation, including excessive coercion of the peasants, later helped Kádár oust the hard-line agriculture minister.

By the early 1960s, Hungary was ripe for a political shake-up. Khrushchev had consolidated his position in the Kremlin and had begun a second wave of de-Stalinization, thus leading Kádár to believe that the Soviet leadership would support political changes in Hungary. Kádár replaced Ferenc Münnich as prime minister (who had served in that position since January 28, 1958), and assumed the top government post, together with the leadership of the HSWP. He then dismissed other hard-line officials. Kádár's consolidation of power led to a more flexible, pragmatic atmosphere in which persuasion took on greater importance than coercion. Kádár relaxed government oppression and released most of those imprisoned for participating in the revolution. Soon Hungary became the leader of the reform movement within the Soviet alliance system. Kádár intended to provide the regime with some legitimacy and political stability based on solid economic performance. The Soviet Union demonstrated its support with its decision to withdraw its advisers to the Hungarian government.

Kádár next sought a modus vivendi with the population, summarizing the new policy with the slogan "He who is not against us is with us." As part of this "alliance policy," in 1961 he denounced the practice of making party membership a prerequisite for jobs demanding specialization and technical expertise. Kádár sought to remove opportunists who had joined the party solely for the status and economic benefits that membership conferred. Rather, Kádár wanted to open the government and economic enterprises to talented people who were prepared to cooperate without adhering to party discipline or compromising their political beliefs.

At the Eighth Party Congress of the HSWP in November 1962, Kádár supporters replaced Stalinists and incompetent officials in leading party positions. The congress also called for higher party recruitment standards, for elimination of political and class considerations in university admissions, and for allowing nonparty members to compete for leading public positions. Although the party still had influential conservative members after 1962, the Eighth Party Congress removed them from the party's policy-making core. As a result of these changes, by 1963 Kádár had acquired genuine popular support.

Plans for reforming the centrally planned economy steadily took shape after the Eighth Party Congress. Central Committee secretary Rezső Nyers, who supported a comprehensive reform rather than continued piecemeal adjustments to the economic system, took charge of economic affairs. The regime also appointed committees to prepare reform proposals. By 1964 the government had identified problems in the economy, including excessive investment, decreases in output and labor shortages in agriculture, misuse of inputs, hoarding of materials, and production of unsalable goods.

Since the Treaty of Trianon, Hungary had depended on foreign trade, and in the early 1960s the government placed top priority on improving trade with the West and the Comecon countries. Despite improving the terms of trade, however, by 1964 Hungary had accumulated a serious trade deficit, and the government could not slow imports without cutting material supplies and personal consumption. Officials realized that because Hungary had to boost exports, it would have to meet the needs, quality standards, and technological requirements of the world economy.

New Economic Mechanism

Khrushchev's ouster in October 1964 failed to weaken Hungary's desire for reform. Kádár responded to the change in the Kremlin by affirming that "the political attitude of the HSWP and the government of the Hungarian People's Republic has not changed one iota, nor will it change." In December 1964, a Central Committee plenum approved the basic concept of economic reform and formed a committee to provide fundamental guidelines.

Economic problems also continued to underscore the need for reform. Agricultural output fell by 5.5 percent. In addition, the government increased production quotas, cut wages, and announced price hikes. Popular discontent rose as a result.

In May 1966, the Central Committee approved a sweeping reform package known as the New Economic Mechanism (NEM). Although many of its elements could be phased in during a preparation period, the central features of the reform could be implemented only with the introduction of a new price system, which was set for January 1, 1968. With the NEM, the government sought to overcome the inefficiencies of central planning, to motivate talented and skilled people to work harder and produce more, to make Hungary's products competitive in foreign markets, especially in the West, and, above all, to create the prosperity that would ensure political stability.

The NEM decentralized decision making and made profit, rather than plan fulfillment, the enterprises' main goal. Instead of setting plan targets and allocating supplies, the government was to influence enterprise activity only through indirect financial, fiscal, and price instruments known as "economic regulators." The NEM introduced a profit tax and allowed enterprises to make their own decisions concerning output, marketing, and sales. Subsidies were eliminated for most goods except basic raw materials. The government decentralized allocation of capital and supply and partially decentralized foreign trade and investment decision making. The economy's focus moved away from heavy industry to light industry and modernization of the infrastructure. Finally, agricultural collectives gained the freedom to make investment decisions. The NEM's initial results were positive. In the 1968–70 period, plan fulfillment was more successful than in previous years. The standard of living rose as production and trade increased. Product variety broadened, sales increased faster than production, inventory backlogs declined, and the trade balance with both East and West improved. In practice, however, the reform was not as sweeping as planned. Enterprises continued to bargain with government authorities for resources from central funds and sought preferential treatment. The reform also failed to dismantle the highly concentrated industrial structure, which was originally established to facilitate central planning and which inhibited competition under the NEM.

The Kádár regime failed to understand that real economic decentralization required political reform to resolve conflicts that naturally arose between different interest groups. The government's problem was to expand "socialist democracy," that is, to build a system that would simultaneously resolve conflicts and maintain the HSWP's political monopoly. In fact, the government attempted some incremental changes. The courts gained greater independence in administering justice, and changes were introduced in parliament as deputies on committees of the National Assembly were instructed to examine and debate legislation more effectively. A 1966 electoral law created single-representative constituencies and contained a provision for elections with multiple candidates. However, the Patriotic People's Front (PPF) retained control of nominations (see Patriotic People's Front, ch. 4). Even after a second electoral law in 1970 made it legal for other groups to nominate individuals, few multiple candidacies actually arose (see Elections to the National Assembly, ch. 4). These minimal changes quickly encountered resistance from entrenched party officials. The 1968 Soviet invasion of Czechoslovakia and suppression of the reform program there had also discouraged the HSWP from pursuing further political changes. However, Kádár was able to work out a modus vivendi with the Soviet leadership. The Soviet Union allowed Kádár leeway to implement economic reforms, develop some economic contacts with the West, and permit Hungarians to travel abroad as long as Budapest accepted Moscow's hegemony in Eastern Europe and adhered to Soviet foreign policy positions.

The Kádár regime gave serious attention to implementing the NEM from 1968 to 1972. In 1971, however, counterreform forces were gathering strength and calling for the return of central controls. The opposition arose from government and party bureaucrats and was supported by large enterprises and some workers. The bureaucrats perceived the NEM as a threat to their privileged positions. The large enterprises saw their income drop after the introduction of the NEM and were troubled by competition for materials and labor from smaller enterprises. Disaffected workers who were on the payrolls of outdated, inefficient industries resented the higher incomes earned by workers in more modern firms. This opposition successfully reversed the reform a few months after Moscow expressed reservations about the NEM and concern about "petit bourgeois tendencies" in Hungary.

In November 1972, the Central Committee introduced a package of extraordinary measures to recentralize part of the economy, but the regime did not formally abandon the NEM. Fifty large enterprises, which produced about 50 percent of Hungary's industrial output and 60 percent of its exports, came under direct ministerial supervision, supported by special subsidies. New restrictions applied to small enterprises and agricultural producers. Wages rose, prices came under central control, and the regime introduced price supports. In the following years, the government also merged many profitable small firms with large enterprises.

The 1973 world oil crisis and the subsequent recession in the West caused a drastic deterioration of Hungary's terms of trade and strengthened opposition to the reform. Inflation threatened, and counterreformers argued for protecting the living standard of the working class from an economic shock in the capitalist world. The government intervened by raising taxes on successful firms and increasing government purchases and subsidies. Consumer prices eventually fell below the level of producer prices, and Hungary accepted credits from Western banks. Centralized material allocation was reintroduced. After the oil crisis arose, ideological opposition to the NEM and to "bourgeois attitudes" emerged as well. A clampdown on intellectuals began, and Nyers lost his Politburo position in 1974.

By 1978 Hungary's dismal economic performance made it clear even to the counterreformers in the leadership that a "reform of the reform" was necessary. Return to central control had only rewarded inefficiency and stifled innovation and initiative. Enterprises ignored market signals, and shortages plagued producers. Large amounts of money were invested in poorly conceived projects, and a trade deficit accumulated. Hungary's hard-currency debt reached US$7.5 billion by 1978 and had jumped to US$9.1 billion by 1980.

In 1978 the government admitted that its attempt to shield Hungary from world economic conditions could not be continued.

Hoping to improve its trade balance with the West and avoid forced rescheduling of its debt, the government announced its intention to boost exports. This policy change marked the beginning of a new wave of reforms. First, the price system was restructured to bring consumer prices gradually in line with world market prices and to ease the burden of subsidies on the state budget. Next, producer prices were reformed to bring about more rational use of energy and raw materials. Finally, the government overhauled exchange-rate and foreign-trade regulations.

In 1979 and 1980, the government implemented a number of institutional reforms. The new reforms abolished branch ministries and replaced them with a single Ministry of Industry intended to act as a policy-formulating body without direct authority over enterprises. Large enterprises were broken up into smaller firms. In 1982 the government legalized the formation of small private firms, including restaurants, small shops, and service companies, and it permitted workers to lease enterprise equipment, use it on their own time, and keep the earnings from their products. In 1984 the regime introduced new forms of enterprise management, including supervisory councils that would include worker-elected representatives. New financial institutions also emerged, and a 1983 government decree allowed enterprises, cooperatives, financial institutions, and local governments to issue bonds.

In the early and mid-1980s, Kádár had encouraged a limited amount of political liberalization. The HSWP maintained its monopoly on political power, but the norms of democratic centralism were looser than in other countries of Eastern Europe (see Democratic Centralism, ch. 4). County party secretaries acquired the freedom to make decisions of local importance, including control of personnel. The government again exhorted delegates of the National Assembly to scrutinize laws and government policies more critically. In 1983 a new electoral law required a minimum of two candidates for each national and local constituency in general elections. Trade unions began to defend workers' interests more energetically. Journalists were urged to expose low- and mid-level corruption and abuse of power, although they could not criticize the regime's basic tenets. The leadership also bolstered economic reforms of the early 1980s with a foreign policy geared to a greater degree than before on trade with the West, and it maintained this course during the deterioration of superpower relations in the early 1980s. Thus, the economic reforms of the late 1960s had also come to provoke a measure of political reform and changes in foreign policy. These new departures were inspired in large measure by Hungarian nationalism, a force that had long encouraged

Hungarians to control their own destiny and to resist the hegemony of their larger, more powerful neighbors.

* * *

Two brief histories of Hungary are Denis Sinor's *History of Hungary* and C.A. Macartney's *Hungary: A Short History*. Robert A. Kann discusses Hungary against the backdrop of the Austrian empire in *A History of the Habsburg Empire, 1526–1918*. Erik Fügedi's *Castle and Society in Medieval Hungary (1000–1437)* provides an intriguing analysis of the impact of castle-building on Hungary's development. For further reading on Hungary in the nineteenth century, George Barany's *Stephen Széchenyi and the Awakening of Hungarian Nationalism, 1791–1841* is an excellent account of the reform leader's early years; Andrew C. Janos's *The Politics of Backwardness in Hungary, 1825–1945* offers a detailed analysis of Hungary's economic, social, and political history; and John Paget's *Hungary and Transylvania* is an interesting travelogue. Paul Kecskemeti's *The Unexpected Revolution* provides a compelling analysis of the Revolution of 1956, and Charles Gati's *Hungary and the Soviet Bloc* describes the communist takeover of Hungary and Hungary's relations with the Soviet Union. Detailed information on the origins and development of Hungary's economic reform programs is found in Judy Batt's *Economic Reform and Political Change in Eastern Europe* and Paul Marer's "Economic Reform in Hungary." (For further information and complete citations, see Bibliography.)

Chapter 2. The Society and Its Environment

A peasant girl, Esztergom, 1918

THE PEOPLE'S REPUBLIC OF HUNGARY lies in the central Danube Basin. With 92,103 square kilometers of territory, it is the sixteenth largest European country. The country's terrain consists largely of plains and hill country and is divided into three major geographic areas: the Great Plain, covering the central part of the country, the Transdanube in the west, and the Northern Hills along the northern border. The climate is mild and continental, although great contrasts in temperatures can occur.

In 1988 the country had about 10.6 million inhabitants. Population had grown slowly since the late 1970s and had begun to decline in 1981. In 1986 about 19.2 percent of the population lived in Budapest, the country's cultural, political, and economic center. Beginning in 1978, for the first time in the country's history, more people lived in urban centers than in rural areas. By 1988 about 62 percent of the populace lived in urban centers with populations exceeding 10,000.

In the late 1980s, more than 96 percent of the people were ethnic Magyars. The minority, or non-Magyar, population was small and included Germans, Slovaks, Serbs, Croats, Slovenes, Romanians, Jews, Gypsies, and Greeks. Most non-Magyars were bilingual, speaking both their own language and Hungarian.

The combined impact of World War II and the communist takeover in 1947 brought about great changes in the social structure. For more than a decade, the new communist government sought to create a classless society through various forms of social engineering. Beginning in the 1960s, these efforts gave way to more indirect methods of social and economic control. The pace of change slowed, and a social structure took shape that once again contained clearly stratified groups. In its new form, society did not display the extremes of wealth and poverty characteristic of the interwar period. However, as the country's economic difficulties increased in the 1980s, tensions appeared to build between the wealthy elites and the sizable disadvantaged groups in society. Public discussion acknowledged these growing tensions and debated methods for overcoming them.

The family remained the basic social unit. The state recognized marriage as a secular institution and held the stability of families to be a desirable social goal. However, observers in the 1980s identified a number of sources of family stress that appeared to contribute to a high rate of divorce.

After the communist assumption of power in the late 1940s, several mass organizations—official trade unions, the National Council of Hungarian Women, and the Communist Youth League—were established to interpret for various segments of the population the social and political goals of the Hungarian Socialist Workers' Party, to mobilize support for it, and to serve as centers of a collective social life. But in the late 1980s, these organizations were losing members, and they faced growing competition from new unofficial groups that emerged in the relaxed political atmosphere.

According to Western estimates, in the late 1980s about 67.5 percent of the population was Roman Catholic, 20 percent was Reformed (Calvinist), 5 percent was Lutheran, and 5 percent was unaffiliated. The country also contained smaller groups of Uniates (Catholics of the Eastern Rite), Greek Orthodox, various small Protestant sects, and Jews. In 1989 the government abolished the State Office for Church Affairs, which had supervised the churches. A proposal for new law submitted for public discussion in 1989 was intended to eliminate almost all restrictions on the churches.

The country's education system provided free, compulsory schooling for young people from six to sixteen years of age. About half of all students attended general schools (also known as elementary schools) for eight years and then completed their education through vocational training. The remainder continued their studies in a four-year gymnasium (a secondary school for university preparation) or trade school. The general schools' curriculum stressed technical and vocational training. In the 1980s, almost 10 percent of the population aged eighteen to twenty-two was enrolled in regular daytime courses of study at institutions of higher learning.

In the late 1980s, the state health care and pension systems were highly centralized. Medical care was free to all citizens. However, many physicians maintained private practices, and people who could afford to receive care on a private basis often preferred to do so. Availability of medical personnel and hospital beds was high by international standards. The country's pension system, although extensive, was the object of considerable criticism in the 1980s because of the low levels of support provided to many retirees.

In the late 1980s, the bounds of permissible expression in Hungary suddenly had become wide by East European standards. Authorities had lifted most traditional prohibitions. Opposition groups were able to function legally. Consequently, the country experienced a quickening and enlivening of cultural and intellectual life.

Physical Environment

With a land area of 92,103 square kilometers, Hungary is roughly the size of the state of Indiana. It measures about 250 kilometers from north to south and 524 kilometers from east to west. It has some 2,258 kilometers of boundaries, shared with Austria to the west, Yugoslavia to the south and southwest, Romania to the southeast, the Soviet Union to the northeast, and Czechoslovakia to the north.

Hungary's modern borders were first established after World War I when, by the terms of the Treaty of Trianon in 1920, it lost more than two-thirds of what had formerly been the Kingdom of Hungary and 58.5 percent of its population (see Trianon Hungary, ch. 1). With the aid of Nazi Germany, the country secured some boundary revisions at the expense of parts of Slovakia in 1938 and Carpatho-Ukraine in 1939 and at the expense of Romania in 1940. However, Hungary lost these territories again with its defeat in World War II. After World War II, the Trianon boundaries were restored with a small revision that benefited Czechoslovakia.

Topography

Most of the country has an elevation of fewer than 200 meters (see fig. 6). Although Hungary has several moderately high ranges of mountains, those reaching heights of 300 meters or more cover less than 2 percent of the country. The highest point in the country is Mount Kékes (1,008 meters) in the Mátra Mountains northeast of Budapest. The lowest spot is 77.6 meters above sea level, located in the Hortobágy.

The major rivers in the country are the Danube and Tisza. About one-third of the total length of the Danube River lies in Hungary; the river also flows through parts of the Federal Republic of Germany (West Germany), Austria, Czechoslovakia, Yugoslavia, and Romania. It is navigable within Hungary for 418 kilometers. The Tisza River is navigable for 444 kilometers in the country. Less important rivers include the Drava along the Yugoslav border, the Rába, the Azamos, the Sió, and the Ipoly along the Czechoslovak border. Hungary has three major lakes. Lake Balaton, the largest, is 78 kilometers long and from 3 to 14 kilometers wide, with an area of 592 square kilometers. Hungarians often refer to it as the Hungarian Sea. It is Central Europe's largest freshwater lake and an important recreation area. Its shallow waters offer good summer swimming, and in winter its frozen surface provides excellent opportunities for winter sports. Smaller bodies of water are Lake

Velence (26 square kilometers) in Fehér County and Lake Fertő (Neusiedlersee—about 82 square kilometers within Hungary).

Hungary has three major geographic regions: the Great Plain (Nagy Alföld), lying east of the Danube River; the Transdanube, a hilly region lying west of the Danube and extending to the foothills of the Austrian Alps; and the Northern Hills, which is a mountainous and hilly country beyond the northern boundary of the Great Plain.

The Great Plain contains the basin of the Tisza River and its branches. It encompasses more than half of the country's territory. Bordered by mountains on all sides, it has a variety of terrains, including regions of fertile soil, sandy areas, wastelands, and swampy areas. Hungarians have inhabited the Great Plain for at least a millennium. Here is found the *puszta,* long an uncultivated expanse (the most famous such area still in existence is the Hortobágy), with which much Hungarian folklore is associated. In earlier centuries, the Great Plain was unsuitable for farming because of frequent flooding. Instead, it was the home of massive herds of cattle and horses. In the last half of the nineteenth century, the government sponsored programs to control the riverways and expedite inland drainage in the Great Plain. With the danger of recurrent flooding largely eliminated, much of the land was placed under cultivation, and herding ceased to be a major contributor to the area's economy.

The Transdanube region lies in the western part of the country, bounded by the Danube River, the Drava River, and the remainder of the country's border with Yugoslavia. It lies south and west of the course of the Danube. It contains Lake Fertő and Lake Balaton. The region consists mostly of rolling foothills of the Austrian Alps. However, several areas of the Transdanube are flat, most notably the Little Plain (Kis Alföld) along the lower course of the Rába River. The Transdanube is primarily an agricultural area, with flourishing crops, livestock, and viticulture. Mineral deposits and oil are found in Zala County close to the border of Yugoslavia.

The Northern Hills lie north of Budapest and run in a northeasterly direction south of the border with Czechoslovakia. The higher ridges, which are mostly forested, have rich coal and iron deposits. Minerals are a major resource of the area and have long been the basis of the industrial economies of cities in the region. Viticulture is also important, producing the famous Tokay wine.

The country's best natural resource is fertile land, although soil quality varies greatly. About 70 percent of the country's total territory is suitable for agriculture; of this portion, 72 percent is arable

land. Hungary lacks extensive domestic sources of the energy and raw materials needed for industrial development (see Resource Base, ch. 3).

Climate

Temperatures in Hungary vary from −28°C to 22°C. Average yearly rainfall is about sixty-four centimeters. Distribution and frequency of rainfall are unpredictable. The western part of the country usually receives more rain than the eastern part, where severe droughts may occur in summertime. Weather conditions in the Great Plain can be especially harsh, with hot summers, cold winters, and scant rainfall.

By the 1980s, the countryside was beginning to show the effects of pollution, both from pesticides used in agriculture and from industrial pollutants. Most noticeable was the gradual contamination of the country's bodies of water, endangering fish and wildlife. Although concern was mounting over these disturbing threats to the environment, no major steps had yet been taken to arrest them (see Environmental Problems, ch. 3).

Population

Since World War II, Hungary has exhibited several population trends that parallel those in other advanced societies. Population leveled off after the war and even began to decline. The birth rate fell, and people flocked from the countryside to the cities, especially to the major urban areas.

Historical Trends

Trianon Hungary emerged from World War I with reduced borders roughly coterminous with Hungary's present-day borders. In 1920 Hungary had about 8 million inhabitants, and by 1941 the population had grown to approximately 9.3 million (see table 2, Appendix). But the country lost about 5 percent of its population in World War II, so as of 1949 the population was only about 8.8 million. Thereafter, the growth rate of the population fluctuated substantially. Until the mid-1950s, high fertility and declining mortality caused rapid population growth. In 1954 the highest postwar live-birth rate was reached, at 23 births per 1,000 population. Subsequently, until the mid-1960s the birth rate declined, but the mortality rate was also low. In the late 1960s and early 1970s, the birth rate again rose, partly because of demographic measures introduced by the government in 1967 and 1973 (see Health and Welfare, this ch.). Because the overall population had begun to age, the mortality rate also increased during this period, but it was counterbalanced by the higher rate of live births.

Structure

Beginning in the late 1970s, the birth rate declined and mortality increased. By the early 1980s, Hungary's growth rate had become one of the lowest in the world. More ominously, beginning in 1981, deaths outnumbered births. Over the 1980s, population decreased absolutely after peaking at a post-World War II high of 10.7 million in 1980. Thus, the 1988 census reported that about 10.6 million people lived in the country.

In 1986 the birth rate was 12.1 per 1,000 population, up slightly from the postwar low of 11.8 per 1,000 in 1984. However, as recently as 1975 the birth rate had been 18.4 per 1,000, and in 1948 the birth rate had been 21 per 1,000. One major reason for the overall decline of the birth rate appeared to be the increasing number of highly educated and economically active women who, as in other countries, tended to have fewer children. Age appeared to play no role in the declining birth rate. In 1986 women married at an average age of 24.6 years, a figure only slightly higher than in 1948, when the average age was 24.5. In the 1980s, the typical family had only two children (reflecting a dramatic decrease from the final decades of the nineteenth century, when the average number of children per family had been five).

Overall, the population of the country was aging. A growing proportion of the population was aged fifty-five or older, increasing from 19.6 percent of the population in 1960 to 24.5 percent in 1988. By contrast, in 1988 the proportion of the population under fifteen was about 21 percent, which reflected a decrease of about 4 percent since 1949 and resulted from the declining birth rate.

Marriage rates fell steadily from the mid-1970s to the mid-1980s (see table 3, Appendix). In 1975 the marriage rate was 9.9 per 1,000. By 1986 that number had declined to 6.8 per 1,000. Moreover, in 1980 for the first time, the number of marriages that ended because of death or divorce outnumbered the number of marriages that took place. In 1980 the number of "marriages ceased" because of death and divorce was 9.2 per 1,000 population. That number rose to 9.3 by 1983, then fell slightly back to 9.2 by 1986.

Death rates were relatively high, and they were rising. In 1986 the death rate was 13.8 per 1,000, as compared with 12.4 per 1,000 in 1975. In 1986 life expectancy averaged sixty-eight years, up from about sixty-six years in 1975. For women in 1986, the average life span was almost seventy-two years; for men, it was just under sixty-five years.

Lake Balaton
Courtesy Scott Edelman

Settlement Patterns

In 1945 only 35 percent of the population lived in urban areas. After 1945 much of the population moved from the country's less developed counties to Budapest and later to its suburbs and to the industrial counties of Hajdú-Bihar and Borsod-Abaúj-Zemplén. The number of urban dwellers grew by more than 50 percent from 1949 to 1984. In 1978, for the first time in the country's history, more people lived in urban centers than in rural areas. In 1949 the population density was about 100 persons per square kilometer. By the 1980s, that figure had climbed to about 117 persons per square kilometer.

In the late 1980s, nine cities had populations greater than 100,000. Budapest, the country's focal point for government, culture, industry, trade, and transport, was by far the largest city, with 2.1 million inhabitants, or 19.2 percent of the country's population. Other major population centers were Debrecen, with 217,000 inhabitants; Miskolc, with 210,000; Szeged, with 188,000; Pécs, with 182,000; Győr, with 131,000; Nyíregyháza, with 119,000; Székesfehérvár, with 113,000; and Kecskemét, with 105,000. In 1988 the country had a total of 143 urban centers with more than

10,000 inhabitants, where about 62 percent of the population lived.

As of 1988, the country had 2,915 settlements with fewer than 10,000 inhabitants, where 38 percent of the people made their homes. Beginning in the 1950s, the smallest villages, or those with fewer than 5,000 inhabitants, tended to lose their residents. However, the number of people leaving the villages decreased every year after 1960. Whereas in 1960 about 259,000 people left the villages permanently, that number declined to about 129,000 in 1986. The number of people leaving the villages exceeded the number coming to the countryside by approximately 52,000 people in 1960. That number had declined to 37,769 in 1980 and 20,814 in 1986.

In the 1980s, a substantial number of persons of Hungarian origin lived outside the country. Many of these lived in neighboring countries (see Relations with Other Communist Neighbors, ch. 4). Others had moved even farther from their homeland. In the three decades before World War I, some 3 million ethnic Hungarian peasants had fled to the United States to escape rural poverty (see Social Changes, ch. 1). During and after the Revolution of 1956, about 250,000 people left the country, traveling first to Austria and Yugoslavia and eventually emigrating to Australia, Britain, Canada, France, Switzerland, the United States, and West Germany. In the late 1980s, about 40 percent of all persons of Hungarian origin were living outside Hungary.

The Hungarian People

As a result of population transfers after World War II, Hungary became one of the most ethnically homogeneous countries in Eastern Europe. Unlike most Europeans, Hungarians trace their lineage to the Finno-Ugric people—an Asiatic tribe. For this reason, Hungarians have long felt themselves to be distinct from the other peoples who live in their midst.

Ethnic discrimination—except toward the Gypsies—was almost nonexistent in Hungary in the 1980s. Particularly after the late 1960s, the government had made great efforts to ensure fair and equal treatment for minority nationalities. Foreign policy considerations partially explained this liberal policy toward minorities. The Romanian and, to a lesser extent, the Czechoslovak governments subjected Hungarians in their countries to many kinds of discrimination. To provide these governments with incentives to relax their pressure against Hungarian minorities, Budapest pursued very liberal policies toward its own national minorities and sought to make its minority policies a model for other countries in Eastern Europe.

Square in downtown Szeged
Courtesy Scott Edelman

Origins and Language

The Hungarian people are thought to have originated in an ancient Finno-Ugric population that originally inhabited the forested area between the Volga River and the Ural Mountains. Sometime between the first and fifth centuries A.D., after the Ugric and Finnic peoples had split, Ugric tribes in the eastern portion of the territory moved farther south, intermingling with nomadic Bulgar-Turkish peoples (see Early History, ch. 1). Some of these tribes settled in the Carpathian Basin in the ninth century A.D. and became the direct ancestors of today's inhabitants of Hungary. The proper name for the largest ethnic group in Hungary is Magyar. The word is a derivative of Megyeri, supposedly the name of one of the original ten Magyar tribes. Magyar refers specifically to both the language and the ethnic group. The words Hungary and Hungarian are derivatives of a Slavicized form of the Turkic words *on ogur,* meaning ''ten arrows,'' which may have referred to the number of Magyar tribes.

Hungarian is the country's only official language. It is a member of the Finno-Ugric family of languages, unrelated to the Indo-European language family, which contains the major European languages. Within Europe, Hungarian is related to Finnish, Estonian, Komi, and several lesser-known languages spoken in parts of the Ural Mountains region in the Soviet Union. It has a heavy admixture of Turkish, Slavic, German, Latin, and French words. Hungarian is written in Latin characters. The various dialects are intelligible to all Hungarians throughout the country.

Minority Groups

In the 1980s, more than 96 percent of the population consisted of ethnic Magyars. Major transfers of population had occurred after World War II. Substantial numbers of Germans, Czechs, and Slovaks were resettled in neighboring countries, and many Hungarians outside the country's borders moved to Hungary. Today Hungary has few ethnic minority inhabitants. In the 1980s, the population included roughly 230,000 Germans; slightly more than 100,000 Slovaks; about 100,000 Serbs, Croats, and Slovenes (often grouped together as South Slavs); and about 30,000 Romanians. In the late 1980s, the Romanian population in the country increased significantly as thousands of Romanians fled conditions in their homeland and sought refuge in Hungary. About one-third of these émigrés were ethnic Romanians, and the remainder were ethnic Hungarians. In addition, about 500,000 Gypsies, 150,000 Jews, and 4,000 Greeks lived in Hungary. The Jewish community was a mere remnant of the Jewish population that had lived in the country before World War II. During the war, as many as 540,000 Jews and 60,000 Gypsies were deported to Nazi extermination camps (see World War II, ch. 1).

Most of the non-Magyar nationalities were bilingual, speaking both their own language and Hungarian. In the 1980 census, less than 1 percent of the population actually registered as members of national minorities, although a far greater number expressed interest in aspects of their ethnic culture. National minorities did not usually form separate communities but lived interspersed among the entire population.

The Constitution, as well as a sizable body of law, guarantees the cultural rights of recognized national minorities. The Constitution promises them equal rights as citizens, protection against discrimination, and access to education in their own language from kindergarten to university level (see Constitutional Development, ch. 4). Minorities have been able to promote their national cultures through freedom of association in federations, ethnic clubs, and artistic endeavors. They have been able to use their own language in official procedures and could publish newspapers and periodicals, and broadcast radio and television programs in their own

Dohány Synagogue in Budapest
Courtesy Sam and Sarah Stulberg

tongue. Actual government policy in the 1980s was fairly consistent with these promises. In 1984 approximately 55,000 minority students were receiving instruction in their mother tongue in elementary and secondary schools, up from 21,615 students in 1968. When ethnic students did not find the requisite opportunities at domestic institutions of higher education, they could study at appropriate foreign universities. All national minorities had weekly newspapers and other publications and sponsored various cultural activities. As public discussion in the late 1980s noted, however, the minorities had not shared equally in the economic advances of recent decades.

Jews and Gypsies were not officially recognized as national minorities, being defined rather as a "religious community" and an "ethnic community," respectively. However, the Jews occupied a more favorable position in Hungary than they did in other states in Eastern Europe. The country's 150,000 Jews formed the third largest Jewish community on the European continent, being smaller than the Jewish communities in the Soviet Union and France. They maintained a high school, library, museum, kosher butcher shops, an orphanage, a home for the elderly, a rabbinical seminary, a factory producing matzo, and about thirty synagogues. Several publications, including newspapers, served the Jewish population.

The situation of the half million Gypsies, traditionally a poor and marginal element in society and subject to discrimination, was far less favorable. In 1987 about 75 percent of the Gypsies were living at or below the poverty level. About half of them lived in settled conditions, holding down jobs. Most spoke Hungarian. The Gypsy population had a birth rate that was more than twice as high as that of the rest of the population. This circumstance, and the fact that the Gypsy crime rate was disproportionately high, contributed to an apparently growing hostility to Gypsies among the Hungarian population. Many citizens perceived the government's special programs for Gypsies as undeserved favoritism that deprived the rest of the population of needed resources.

In the mid-1980s, in contrast to its earlier policy of encouraging cultural assimilation, the government began to foster a Gypsy ethnic and cultural identity and a sense of community and tradition to enhance the self-esteem of the Gypsy population. In mid-1985 the government established the National Gypsy Council to represent Gypsy concerns to the government and to assist in carrying out measures involving the Gypsies. In 1986 the Cultural Association of Gypsies in Hungary was founded to help preserve and foster Gypsy culture. In 1987 a Gypsy newspaper was established. Despite these signs of progress, Gypsies remained particularly vulnerable as the economic climate deteriorated in the 1980s. With minimal skills, education, and training, they were among the first to lose their jobs as unemployment increased. Their health and living standard remained well below the national average.

Social Structure

Before World War II, Hungarian society was characterized by striking inequalities in economic and social status (see Social Changes, ch. 1). Landownership was the principal source of wealth, because the country was still predominantly rural and agricultural. The poverty of millions of landless laborers stood in stark contrast to the wealth of a small elite of landowners, bankers, and prominent businessmen. Early efforts at industrialization provided few alternative employment opportunities for the impoverished agricultural labor force.

The destruction and turmoil of World War II greatly disrupted the traditional social structure. After the communists assumed power in 1947, society was in flux for almost two decades (see Postwar Hungary, ch. 1). The aim of the new government was to replace the old order with a new social structure that was in line with Marxist-Leninist ideology. The pace of change slowed in the early 1960s as the government reduced its efforts at social engineering. By the early 1970s, society had settled into a discernible pattern in which clear-cut social strata were beginning to reemerge. Changes that continued to affect the social system during the 1970s and 1980s resulted largely from economic growth and urbanization rather than from the efforts of communist social planners.

Interwar Period

Until World War II, striking inequalities distinguished the distribution of wealth, power, privilege, and opportunity among social groups. The various social strata had different codes of behavior and distinctive dress, speech, and manners. Respect showed to persons varied according to the source of their wealth. Wealth derived from possession of land was valued more highly than that coming from trade or banking. The country was predominantly rural, and landownership was the central factor in determining the status and prestige of most families. In some of the middle and upper strata of society, noble birth was also an important criterion as was, in some cases, the holding of certain occupations. An intricate system of ranks and titles distinguished the various social stations. Hereditary titles designated the aristocracy and gentry. Persons who had achieved positions of eminence, whether or not they were of noble birth, often received nonhereditary titles from the state. The gradations of rank derived from titles had great significance in social intercourse and in the relations between the individual and the state. Among the rural population, which consisted largely of peasants and which made up the overwhelming majority of the country's people, distinctions derived from such factors as the size of a family's landholding; whether the family owned the land and hired help to work it, owned and worked the land itself, or worked for others; and family reputation. The prestige and respect accompanying landownership were evident in many facets of life in the countryside, from finely shaded modes of polite address, to special church seating, to selection of landed peasants to fill public offices.

On the eve of World War II, about 4 percent of the population owned more than half the country's wealth. Landowners, wealthy bankers, aristocrats and gentry, and various commercial leaders made up the elite. Together, these groups accounted for only 13 percent of the population. Between 10 and 18 percent of the population consisted of the petite bourgeoisie and the petty gentry, various government officials, intellectuals, retail store owners, and well-to-do professionals. More than two-thirds of the remaining population lived in varying degrees of poverty. Their only real chance for upward mobility lay in becoming civil servants, but such advancement was difficult because of the exclusive nature of the education system (see Education, this ch.). The industrial working class was growing, but the largest group remained the peasantry, most of whom had too little land or none at all.

Although the interwar years witnessed considerable cultural and economic progress in the country, the social structure changed little. A great chasm remained between the gentry, both social and intellectual, and the rural "people." Jews held a place of prominence in the country's economic, social, and political life. They constituted the bulk of the middle class. During the first four decades of the twentieth century, Jews made up more than one-fifth of the population of Budapest. They were well assimilated, worked in a variety of professions, and were of various political persuasions.

Postwar Societal Transformation

Even before the communists came to power in 1947, the turbulent years of World War II had weakened or eliminated much of the old stratified society. Devastation from the fighting in 1944 and 1945, land reforms instituted by the government in 1945, and the nationalization of commerce and industry between 1948 and 1953 destroyed the economic base of the old social system. The country lost about 300,000 Jews, including much of the Jewish business community, to various war-related causes—deportation, massacre, disease, and hunger. Only about 260,500, mostly from Budapest, survived (see World War II, ch. 1).

After the communist takeover, the traditional ruling class was virtually eliminated. More extensive land reform undertaken by the new regime eventually collectivized the majority of the peasantry. In the countryside, anti-kulak measures and compulsory deliveries of produce to the state at extremely low prices destroyed the prosperous peasant class. (In 1948 the term *kulak* came to be defined officially as anyone who owned more than seven hectares of land or had a landed income roughly approximating such ownership. Political conditions caused many with less property also to feel threatened.) Rampant inflation disrupted all aspects of economic life.

In keeping with Marxist-Leninist ideology, during the first decade of communist rule the government sought to create a classless society through policies such as equalization of incomes, collectivization of agriculture, expropriation of property, and tight control over educational opportunities (see Rákosi's Rule, ch. 1). On the remaining peasants with average incomes and on prosperous peasants, the government imposed steeply progressive income taxes and requisitioned large amounts of produce. Collectivization in the early 1950s caused many peasants to seek alternatives to agriculture. Many retained their rural residences but commuted daily or weekly to other jobs, leaving part of the family to continue some agricultural work. Others moved to entirely new jobs, as government policies promoted rapid development of heavy industry (see Economic Policy and Performance, 1945–85, ch. 3).

The social and economic changes that took place after World War II promoted social mobility. During the early years of forced industrialization and continuing to a lesser extent until the early 1960s, the prewar worker strata and peasant strata had enhanced opportunities to rise into white-collar positions. Large numbers of peasants entered the industrial labor force, and the bureaucracy, which grew as a result of centralized planning, was open to persons from all social groups.

Some downward mobility also occurred. Disincentives for formerly independent professionals, crafts people, and merchants were overwhelming. Opportunities also dwindled for prewar executives and managers. Members of the old elite lost property and political power and were forced into the middle or lower class. A large percentage of the prewar elite left the country.

Despite such mobility in the early 1950s, an inegalitarian social system remained in place. The new political elite enjoyed material and symbolic privileges, such as access to special stores containing scarce goods or the free use of secluded and well-guarded villas, that separated it from the rest of the population. A second stratum of the elite consisted of valuable persons such as directors of large enterprises and of the best collective farms. They too lived in comparative luxury. The new elite also included intellectuals who endorsed the party and its interests. Their task was to provide legitimacy for the new regime. In return, they enjoyed living standards superior to those of the working class.

In the aftermath of the Revolution of 1956, career restrictions on the prewar middle class and intellectuals began to ease somewhat as the government ceased most of its social engineering efforts (see Revolution of 1956, ch. 1). Among workers and peasants, political loyalty, although important, could no longer serve as a vehicle for upward mobility in the absence of other qualifications; a person also needed to have appropriate educational credentials or skills. However, political considerations remained paramount for persons who wanted to be part of the ruling political elite.

As the economic reforms introduced in the 1960s increasingly affected all aspects of society, stratified social groups again made their appearance. By the mid-1970s, the regime's objective of a classless society appeared to be increasingly unattainable. To reconcile ideology with these realities, ideologists began modifying Marxist theory. The regime all but abandoned the goal of a classless society, ideologists arguing that in a socialist industrial society certain skills and occupations were more necessary than others. Thus, those persons with greater skills and responsibilities should receive more compensation than those making less valuable contributions. Ideologists rationalized society's inequalities by maintaining that socioeconomic distinctions that evolved under a communist system were qualitatively different from those found in capitalist countries.

Social Relations in the 1980s

In the 1980s, society was complex and highly differentiated. Social scientists agreed that the traditional Marxist-Leninist description of the workers, peasants, and intellectuals all cooperating to build socialism did not accurately depict modern society. They actively sought new categories to account for the great diversity of life-styles and income sources but as of the late 1980s had not reached a consensus concerning modifications in traditional theories.

Most sociologists spoke of the existence of three major strata in society: white-collar workers engaged in mental labor; manual laborers; and peasants. The white-collar category comprised everyone not involved in physical labor—party and government leaders, intellectuals, professionals and teachers, collective farm managers, artists, business persons, traders, shop owners, and specialists such as building contractors. This category constituted 30.3 percent of active earners in 1987, with 14.5 percent classified as professionals. The manual labor category encompassed 61.4 percent of the work force and included skilled, semiskilled, and unskilled blue-collar workers of all ranks and degrees of training and prosperity. The peasantry working on both cooperative and state farms made up 8.3 percent of earners. About 4.6 percent of the work force were also "small-scale producers" of various types.

A survey taken in 1981 revealed the surprisingly widespread nature of small-scale agricultural production among virtually all social categories and occupations; 62.7 percent of active earners lived in households that cultivated at least small gardens of fruit trees or vegetables. A smaller but still substantial number of active earners were involved in animal husbandry (see Agricultural Organization, ch. 3). Sociologists were uncertain about whether or not this phenomenon was a temporary phase in industrial development or a new category of agricultural worker.

The Elite

Persons with some claim to elite status made up no more than 15 percent of the population in the early 1980s. The elite consisted of three identifiable groups in the 1980s: political, technocratic, and intellectual. The political elite consisted of top party and government leaders. Although some members of this group flaunted their status and privileges, most were not highly visible and did not advertise their special status. Members appeared to be relatively sensitive to their public image and did not indulge in conspicuous consumption. The technocrats included managers, directors, economists, and researchers who supported the regime. The benefits they derived from the system were more visible, in the form of bonuses and salaries and of the autombiles, villas, apartments, and other special advantages that these financial windfalls made possible. The intellectual elite, composed of academicians, scientists, musicians, artists, writers, journalists, and actors, included many persons who were comfortably placed, although others lived in relatively humble circumstances. They were leaders in setting both social and political trends. Members of these favored groups often possessed, in addition to relative wealth, the important commodity of influence or ''connections.'' This form of influence gave them and their families access to scarce items and limited opportunities, such as quality higher education.

Additional occupations that were likely to be financially rewarding included medicine, engineering, and, in some cases, skilled technicial jobs, such as electrical work, house painting, plumbing, and building contracting. These technicians might have several income sources from their private work in addition to salaried work. Intellectuals who lacked high salaries but supplemented their income through various types of consulting work, such as editing, translating, and so forth, were also financially secure.

Prosperous individuals enjoyed a very comfortable standard of living. Families who could afford private holiday and weekend houses built them on the shores of Lake Balaton, along rivers, and in mountain areas. From 1981 through 1987, a total of 30,397 private ''holiday houses'' were built. As more people owned their own automobiles, weekend trips became increasingly popular. During the 1970s, more people, even those in relatively modest circumstances, began to travel abroad. In 1981 a record 5.5 million Hungarians traveled outside Hungary. Of these, about 477,000 traveled to capitalist countries, in Europe or overseas. As a result of financial constraints, the number of travelers dropped somewhat in the mid-1980s. Regulations concerning the exchange of foreign currency permitted travel to capitalist countries no more than once a year on organized tours or once every three years on an individual basis. If a traveler had access to additional sources of foreign currency, however, he or she could travel more frequently.

The Disadvantaged

To achieve an acceptable living standard or to improve their modest circumstances, most Hungarians had to work hard; often they held more than one job. Continuing inflation in the 1980s created additional pressures on families with moderate income. Although the government introduced the five-day workweek throughout the economy between 1980 and 1985, more persons worked extended workdays to increase household income. It was estimated that three families in four had some source of additional income not resulting from work in state or collective sources. Many families were thus able to achieve a comfortable, if still modest, life-style.

A number of disadvantaged groups also tried to make ends meet. Western analysts estimated that between 25 and 40 percent of the population lived below the poverty level, which, in the mid-1980s, was defined as a monthly income below 5,200 forints (for value of the forint—see Glossary). Average monthly wages (6,000 forints) were only 10 to 15 percent above this level. In 1988, according to data issued by the Central Statistical Office, between 1.5 million and 3 million people qualified as "socially poor" (out of a population of 10.6 million). These figures included 40 to 50 percent of all retired persons on pensions, about half of families with two children, and from 70 to 90 percent of families with three or more children. Other poor groups were low-paid employees of the state and industry, such as postal employees, various semiskilled and unskilled workers, and minor bureaucrats. Some of these people supplemented their income through second jobs. Single heads of households were often poor. In addition, persons working on less productive collective farms and those living on isolated homesteads (*tanyas*) far from rural centers and even villages, were likely to have scanty incomes.

Although Hungary's living standard was higher than that found in neighboring socialist states in the 1980s, the sharp disparities became the subject of investigative reports, letters to newspaper editors, and various radio and television talk shows. Economic problems were clearly causing concern and some demoralization among the people. The government adopted a variety of austerity measures in response to the country's economic stagnation and staggering foreign debt. These measures included increases in the prices of basic items, such as flour, bread, gasoline, and household energy, and various consumer items such as cigarettes. A new value-added tax (see Glossary) on most goods and services and a stricter income tax law were also introduced (see Economic Regulators, ch. 3).

In 1988 official sources reported an inflation rate of 17 percent. Western analysts estimated that the inflation rate could be as high as 25 to 30 percent. By 1989 the average real wage had dropped to its 1973 level.

Since the mid-1970s, considerable tension has emerged between the rich and the poor, partially because of the long-professed egalitarian views of the regime. During the immediate postwar period, the leadership had advocated (although it had never fully practiced) a general egalitarianism that, combined with the prevailing scarcity, led people to elevate self-denial as a socialist virtue. When conditions subsequently improved, the leadership and the population both were confused about what form the proper socialist way of life should take. The younger generation in particular took pleasure in the increasing comforts of life, but some members of the older generation feared a resurgence of a "bourgeois" life-style and "consumerism." Although poverty remained widespread, socialism's sponsorship of rapid economic development had offered many persons a chance to change their way of life and socioeconomic position in a manner that was unimaginable before the war. As living standards improved, the conviction had grown among significant segments of the population that economic growth and rising standards were inevitable and that ongoing problems—poverty and unequal opportunity—were remnants of the old order, certain to be overcome. Then in the mid-1970s, economic growth had slowed. Although inequalities were much reduced from the prewar scale, they still existed. They were less pronounced in salary differences than they were in working conditions, working hours (including their flexibility), housing conditions, possession of durable consumer items, and, most of all, general life-style. Even more troubling was the appearance of new inequalities, with favored groups consolidating their advantageous positions. The regime had few concrete answers for these problems. Leaders could only point out that the country had no models to follow in developing a socialist system to meet its needs.

In the late 1980s, the worsening economic conditions were a disappointing contrast to the successes and significant improvements in living standards achieved in the 1960s and 1970s. In 1987 the official news agency estimated the number of unemployed persons to be 30,000 to 40,000. In 1988 the press began reporting frankly on the noticeable numbers of beggars and homeless persons on the streets of Budapest. The media also noted that squatters were becoming a problem, especially families coming from the countryside seeking employment and moving into vacant apartments.

Social Institutions

In the 1980s, severe social and economic problems took their toll on the family. Harsh economic conditions meant that most women had to work and most men had to hold second and even third jobs. These factors, combined with a housing shortage, subjected the family to considerable stress. Yet the harsh economic conditions also forced many people to turn inward, and they found in their families a refuge from the difficult economic realities.

In the postwar period, the regime had designed its mass organizations to take over some of the traditional socialization functions of the family. Thus, the mass organizations served as "transmission belts," attempting to inculcate regime values, and relaying and interpreting the policies of the Hungarian Socialist Workers' Party (HSWP) to rank-and-file members and to the general public (see Hungarian Socialist Workers' Party, ch. 4). In the late 1980s, some Western observers considered the mass organizations sponsored by the regime to be in a moribund state, hopelessly outclassed by newer, more spontaneous collective efforts (see Dissent and Freedom of Expression, this ch.). In response, some mass organizations liberalized their programs and distanced themselves from the regime.

Early in its history, the communist party considered the churches as competitors for the allegiance of the people. Therefore, the regime actively persecuted the churches, especially the Roman Catholic Church. After the Revolution of 1956, the regime relaxed its pressure on the churches, viewing them more as partners than as adversaries. By the late 1980s, the government allowed the churches wide latitude and eliminated virtually all legal and institutional restrictions on church activities.

The Family

In traditional Hungary, the family served as the basic social unit. It had multiple functions, providing security and identity to individuals and reinforcing social values. In rural areas, it was also the basic economic unit—all members worked together for the material well-being of the whole family. Even before World War II, however, family cohesion began to decrease as members became increasingly mobile. But the process of change quickened after the communist takeover. Intensive industrialization and forced collectivization prompted many of the younger peasants to leave agriculture for industrial work or other jobs in the cities, some commuting long distances between home and work (see Postwar Societal Transformation, this ch.). Patterns of family life changed. A growing number of women worked outside the home, and children spent much of their time in school or in youth organization activities. Family members spent less time together. The emphasis in daily life shifted from the family to the outside world. Most members of the extended family came together only for important ceremonies, such as weddings or funerals, and other special occasions.

Changes in the traditional roles of family members were dramatic. The dominance of the male head of the family diminished. The remaining family members had greater independence. Most notably, the role of women changed. By 1987 about 75 percent of working-age women were gainfully employed. Even peasant women became wage earners on the collective farms. This fact altered women's status in the family and the community. However, most observers agreed that in the 1980s males were still viewed as the head of most households, if only because of their generally higher incomes.

As women increasingly worked outside the home, their husbands and children assumed some domestic functions, helping with household chores more than they had before. Outside institutions such as schools and nurseries also took over tasks formerly carried out by women within the home. Nevertheless, time budget studies indicated that women were still responsible for most of the child rearing and housework despite their employment outside the home. Women usually worked longer hours than men. Working women spent an average of more than four hours each day on household chores, including child care, while men averaged ninety-seven minutes in such activities. However, the time spent by women in outside employment was not correspondingly shorter than that of men, averaging only 1.5 hours less than men. Women devoted less time than men to leisure activities, such as watching television, socializing, and engaging in sports. (According to the same studies, women did read approximately as many books as men but spent much less time on newspapers and periodicals.)

The state viewed marriage as a secular matter, governed by civil law. A civil marriage was mandatory, but couples were allowed to supplement the procedure with a religious ceremony. The greatest number of both men and women married between the ages of twenty and twenty-four (44.6 percent of all men and 41.3 percent of all women for those marrying in 1987). The law assigned equal rights and obligations to both partners in a marriage.

In the 1980s, social analysts considered the family to be an institution under considerable stress. Statistics supported this contention. From 1975 to 1986, the divorce rate increased from 2.5

to 2.8 per 1,000 population. In the 1980s, every third marriage ended in divorce. The rate of remarriage also dropped significantly. In 1987 about 66,000 marriages were performed, and about 95,600 marriages were terminated as a result of death or divorce. Almost 12 percent of all families were headed by a single parent.

A primary source of stress within families, according to many observers, was the scarcity of adequate housing, especially for young families (see Health and Welfare, this ch.). In many families, members faced the pressures and exhaustion of trying to hold down multiple jobs. Another source of tension within families was the prevalence of commuting. Although in 1960 one in every eight workers commuted, in the 1980s one in every four commuted. One million or more villagers commuted to the cities to work. This figure did not include long-distance commuters who lived in temporary quarters near their workplaces and returned home weekly or more infrequently. In 1980 such workers numbered about 270,000, bringing the total number of commuters to about 1.5 million.

Despite the statistics, most observers found that the cohesive force of the family remained relatively strong in the 1980s. For many people, the family continued to be a source of personal comfort and reassurance in the face of worsening economic conditions. The traditional sense of family loyalty and responsibility also seemed to survive. Family members continued to help each other in finding jobs or housing, in gaining admission to schools, and in providing for each other in times of need.

Mass Organizations

Until the late 1980s, the law contained no provision for voluntary, independent associations of people interested in influencing social or political policy. Potential independent groups had no concrete channels by which to gain regime approval. During four decades of communist rule, clear legal status belonged only to such mass organizations as the Communist Youth League, official trade unions, the National Council of Hungarian Women, and a variety of nonpolitical associations catering to narrow, special interests of the population. Until the late 1980s, authorities actively discouraged the formation of unofficial groups.

Trade Unions

In the mid-1980s, official trade unions had almost 4.4 million members, or about 96 percent of all persons living on wages and salaries. The growth of trade unions was mainly a post-World War II phenomenon; before the war, unions had a total membership of only about 100,000 (mostly crafts people). After the communist takeover, the unions were supervised by the National Council of Trade Unions (Szakszervezetek Országos Tanácsa—SZOT), elected by a national congress. SZOT had nineteen officially recognized unions, organized by industrial branch. Trade unions theoretically had great powers, but they traditionally had made little use of them. For example, SZOT had a legal right to veto decisions made by the government concerning the workers. In practice, the unions' historic inability to strike made this authority meaningless. The government specified overall policy concerning work requirements and wages. Most day-to-day decisions about hiring and firing were made by the management staffs of enterprises and collective farms. Unions did have great influence in the use of the social and cultural funds of enterprises and in industrial safety issues. Trade unions also controlled the administration of health care and holiday resorts. However, in the 1980s subsidies from the central government for these purposes were diminishing, so that maintaining even the existing level of services and amenities was difficult.

In 1985, in a move to increase its appeal to the country's youth, SZOT set up its own organization to represent young people, separate from the Communist Youth League. This organization was the first, other than the Communist Youth League itself, to officially represent young people. According to the authorities, the Communist Youth League was to remain the only political mass organization for youth, while the trade union youth would focus on issues of the workplace, social and cultural programs, and other traditional concerns of trade unions. Trade union members under thirty years of age could be members of the unions' new youth sections.

In the late 1980s, Western analysts detected a significant easing of restrictions on trade union activity in general. The official unions became increasingly outspoken, criticizing such practices as the requirement for overtime work and other austerity measures. In public discussions, both critics and union representatives openly admitted that the unions as constituted inspired little confidence in workers. In 1988 the press began reporting some brief strikes among workers in officially recognized unions, revealing that the outcomes of the strikes had been favorable to the workers. At the same time, some professionals and blue-collar workers made efforts to form independent unions that were not subordinate to SZOT. In May 1988, the Democratic Union of Scientific Workers, the first independent trade union established in Eastern Europe since Poland's Solidarity, was founded. Social scientists at research institutes of the Academy of Sciences, the country's premier research organization, were the first members of the new union. The union's program included a call for the end of discrimination against professionals based on their political views. Additional researchers and teachers from other institutions soon joined, raising the number of members to more than 4,000 by December 1988. Several smaller unions also came into existence. Initially, the membership of such independent organizations appeared to be limited to white-collar workers. The success of these fledgling attempts was uncertain, but after initial hostility from authorities, the groups were permitted to function.

Women

In the 1980s, the principal women's organization was the National Council of Hungarian Women. Its official role was to educate women socially and politically and to participate in devising new laws and regulations that affected women. The organization had a network of local and regional committees, whose members engaged in voluntary social work. In 1985 the council had about 32,000 designated female "stewards," and about 160,000 women were said to be active in the organization.

Youth

The Communist Youth League (Kommunista Ifjúsági Szövetség—KISZ) catered to young people. KISZ was the HSWP's official youth organization (see Hungarian Socialist Workers' Party, ch. 4). It claimed to represent all the country's youth and sought to educate young people politically and to supervise political as well as some social activities for them. KISZ was the most important source of new members for the party. Its organizational framework paralleled that of the HSWP and included a congress, central committee, secretariat, and regional and local committees. Membership was open to youth from the ages of fourteen to twenty-six years, but most of the full-time leaders of the organization were well over the age limit. In the 1980s, KISZ had about 800,000 members. Membership was common, if rather pro forma, among university students (96 percent of whom were members) but was lower among young people already working (31 percent).

In the late 1980s, KISZ undertook sweeping reforms of its own organizational structure. In April 1989 delegates to the organization's national congress voted to change the name of the organization to the Democratic Youth Federation. According to declarations adopted by the congress, the newly refashioned federation would be a voluntary league of independent youth organizations and would not accept direction from any single party, including the HSWP.

A separate organization within KISZ, the Association of Young Pioneers, was formed for youngsters in elementary school. Membership was open to children from six to fourteen years of age. The Young Pioneers served many of the same functions as the Boy Scouts and Girl Scouts in the West. The organization also attempted to explain to children the basic tenets of the Marxist-Leninist worldview. Joining the Young Pioneers was a matter of course for most youngsters in elementary school. Most meetings took place in classrooms of primary schools. Bands of Young Pioneers could be seen on many ceremonial occasions, dressed in the organization's characteristic white shirts and red ties. The summer camps sponsored by the organization were a highlight of the year for many children.

Other Popular Groups

In addition to the traditional mass organizations, a myriad of other officially approved clubs and associations focused narrowly on such areas as agriculture, architecture, history, mathematics, music, the sciences, and so forth. A survey in the early 1980s counted 6,570 cultural, professional, and sports associations (63 percent of which had been established after 1945), ..ith a total of 2.3 million members. The largest associations were the Hungarian Autoclub, with about 291,000 members in late 1982, and the National Association of Stamp Collectors, with approximately 157,000 members. Also worthy of note was the Home Defense Sport Federation, which promoted physical fitness for the masses and sponsored premilitary training for young people. Many Hungarians were also avid sports fans and participants. In 1985 more than 1.2 million persons belonged to the country's 3,860 sports clubs. The most popular sport was soccer. Chess was also widely played.

Religion and Religious Organizations

Particularly during the early years of communist rule, the churches had faced extensive harassment and persecution by the regime. Many clergy had been openly hostile to the new government at its inception. The new secular authorities, for their part, denounced such attitudes as traitorous, and they mistrusted the churches as a source of opposition.

The most protracted case of tension and open conflict involved the Roman Catholic Church. In 1945 the church lost its landed property in the first postwar land reform, which occurred before the communist takeover. Most Catholic religious orders (fifty-nine of a total of sixty-three groups) were dissolved in 1948, when religious schools were also taken over by the state. Most Catholic associations and clubs, which numbered about 4,000, were forced to disband. Imprisoned and prosecuted for political resistance to the communist regime were a number of clergy, most notably József Cardinal Mindszenty, primate of the Catholic Church in Hungary (see Postwar Hungary, ch. 1). In 1950 about 2,500 monks and nuns, about one-quarter of the total in Hungary, were deported. Authorities banned sixty-four of sixty-eight functioning religious newspapers and journals. Although in 1950 the Catholic Church accepted an agreement with the state that forced church officials to take a loyalty oath to the Constitution, relations between the church and the state remained strained throughout the decade.

During the 1960s, the two sides gradually reached an accommodation. In 1964 the state concluded a major agreement with the Vatican, the first of its kind involving a communist state. The document ratified certain episcopal appointments already made by the church, although it did not settle Mindszenty's long-standing case. As before, the agreement mandated that certain individuals in positions in the church were obliged to take an oath of allegiance to the Constitution and the laws of the country. But this oath was to be binding only to the extent that the country's laws were not in opposition to the tenets of the Catholic faith. The church conceded the state's right to approve selection of high church officials. Under the agreement, the Hungarian Roman Catholic Church could staff its Papal Institute in Rome with priests endorsed by the government, and each year every diocese in the country would send a priest to Rome to attend the institute. For its part, the government promised not to interfere with the institute's work.

Following the agreement, many vacant church posts were filled. Gradually, the organizational structure of the church was reestablished, and congregations became active again. The church began to take a role in the ceremonial life of the country. Relations between church and state warmed particularly after 1974, when the Vatican removed Mindszenty from his office (in 1971 Mindszenty had received permission to leave the country after spending many years in the American embassy in Budapest, where he had fled to escape detention by the authorities). The new primate, László Cardinal Lékai, who held office from 1976 to 1986, sponsored a policy of "small steps," through which he sought to reconcile differences between church and state and enhance relations between the two through "quiet, peaceful dialogue." He urged Catholics to be loyal citizens of the state and simultaneously to seek personal and communal salvation through the church.

Evidence suggests that a serious falling away from religion among Catholics (especially a drop in attendance at church services) occurred only during the 1960s and 1970s, ironically during the period

Mátyás Templom, Budapest
Courtesy Scott Edelman

when the government no longer energetically persecuted the church. Some observers have suggested that in the 1950s the church earned popularity as an anticommunist institution because of widespread dissatisfaction with material, political, and cultural trends within the country. As conditions improved, the church no longer served as a focal point for the disaffected. Some Catholics, both lay and clerical, felt that Lékai, in his eagerness to smooth relations between church and state, went too far in compromising the church's position.

The Catholic Church of the 1980s had difficulty providing adequate services to all communities. Its clergymen were aging and decreasing in number. Whereas in 1950 the church had had 3,583 priests and 11,538 monks and nuns, in 1986 it had only about 2,600 priests and a mere 250 monks and nuns. It was clear by this time, however, that the church was reaping tangible benefits from its relationship with the state. For example, in the 1980s the Catholic orders of the Benedictines, the Franciscans, the Piarists, and Our Lady's School Sisters were again functioning in limited numbers. A new order of nuns, the Sisters of Our Lady of Hungary, received permission to organize in 1986. In the 1980s, the church had six seminaries for training priests and a theological academy in Budapest.

After the communist takeover, the historic Protestant churches became even more thoroughly integrated into the new state system than did the Catholic Church. They were not a source of organized dissent. The Reformed (Calvinist), Unitarian, and Lutheran churches all reached accommodation with the government in the late 1940s (as did the small Greek Orthodox and Jewish communities). These agreements guaranteed the Protestants the right to worship and brought about some financial support (contingent after 1949 on the loyalty oath). Some Protestant leaders praised the agreements as heralding a new era in which all religions would be treated equally. However, a number of Reformed clergy and followers became active supporters of the Revolution of 1956. After the Revolution failed, many of these people joined "free churches" (including the Baptist, Methodist, and Seventh-Day Adventist churches), which functioned apart from the historic Protestant churches.

In 1986, according to Western estimates, about 67.5 percent of the population was Roman Catholic, 20 percent was Reformed (Calvinist), 5 percent was unaffiliated, and 5 percent was Lutheran (its members were in particular the German and Slovak minorities but also included many ethnic Magyars). Other Christian denominations included Uniates, Orthodox, and various small Protestant groups, such as Baptists, Methodists, Seventh-Day Adventists, and Mormons. Most of these smaller groups were affiliated with the national Council of Free Churches and were dubbed free churches as a group. The country also had 65,000 to 100,000 practicing Jews. The remainder of the population did not subscribe to any religious creed or organization. Nor was any single church or religion particularly associated with the national identity in the popular mind, as was the Catholic Church in Poland.

Western observers concluded that although the country possessed about 5 million practicing believers, religion did not provide a viable alternative value system that could compete with the predominant secularism and materialism promoted both by the government and by trends within an increasingly modern society. Thus, religion was unlikely to become a vehicle for dissent as in Poland or, in a more limited way, in the German Democratic Republic (East Germany).

A noteworthy phenomenon of the early 1980s was the appearance of thousands of intensely active prayer and meditation groups within Catholic and Protestant congregations. Some of these groups came into conflict with the church hierarchies over military service and other aspects of cooperation with the government (see Dissent and Freedom of Expression, this ch.).

The Constitution guarantees freedom of conscience and religion. Until 1989, however, these guarantees were severely circumscribed

Village church in Mindszentpuszta
Courtesy John Tarafas

by the State Office for Church Affairs, which regulated the activities of the churches. On June 15, 1989, the government abolished this office. In its place, the government planned to establish a "National Church Council" that would act as a "consultative organization," not as an instrument for the control of the churches. In addition, the Ministry of Culture assumed responsibility for church affairs. Also in 1989, the government submitted for public debate new "Principles of a Law on Freedom of Conscience, the Right of Free Exercise of Religion, and Church Affairs." The document, prepared by representatives of the churches, banned discrimination against believers, acknowledged the churches as legal entities, and recognized their equality before the law. Yet in the late 1980s, the state's financial support of all major churches continued to give it considerable leverage in influencing church affairs.

Between 1945 and 1986, religious communities erected or repaired 306 Roman Catholic, 46 Calvinist (Reformed), 33 Lutheran, and 23 Uniate churches. Congregations of the free churches built 185 new structures, and the Jewish community built a new synagogue. The various denominations maintained their own modest publishing organs that produced newspapers, periodicals, and books. Occasionally, religious services were broadcast over radio. The various churches and denominations each supported (collectively, in the case of the free churches) at least one theological academy or college for the training of clergy. However, the number of students was small; 75 students graduated out of a total of 648 students enrolled in such institutions in 1987.

Education

Before the communist assumption of power in 1947, religion was the primary influence on education. The Roman Catholic Church sponsored and controlled most schools, although some other religious denominations (Reformed, Lutheran, and Unitarian) as well as the government ran some schools (see Religion and Religious Organizations, this ch.). The social and material status of students strongly influenced the type and extent of schooling they received. Education above the elementary level was generally available only to the social elite of the country. In secondary and higher-level schools, a mere 5 percent of the students came from worker or peasant families. Only about 1 or 2 percent of all students entered higher education.

Before the communist educational reforms, secondary education was traditional. The curriculum stressed the humanities, often at the expense of the sciences. Technical education received relatively little attention, despite the existence of technical and vocational schools.

In 1946 the government established the principle of free education as a right of all citizens, even before the communist assumption of power. In 1948 the new communist government secularized almost all schools and placed them under state control, giving oversight to the Ministry of Education. The churches retained only a few institutions to train their clergy.

The Marxist-Leninist government made major changes in the education system. Its goal was to mold citizens to work for the benefit of society. The reforms stressed technical and vocational training. Political education also became a high priority. Young people were to receive a thoroughly Marxist-Leninist education both within and outside the school framework (see Ideology, ch. 4). Education also sought to promote a thorough understanding of the political system, an understanding fostered also by youth organizations functioning outside the formal educational process. Russian-language study became compulsory from the upper levels of the general school (also known as the elementary school) through the university. Many Soviet professors taught at Hungarian universities, many textbooks were adaptations of the work of Soviet authors, and Russian-language clubs were established.

Marxism-Leninism had become the backbone of the curriculum by the early 1950s. A brief period of liberalization followed the death of Soviet dictator Joseph Stalin in 1953 (see Rákosi's Rule, ch. 1).

After the failure of the Revolution of 1956, authorities reverted to their former emphasis on Marxist-Leninist indoctrination. However, they did modify the earlier policy of Sovietization in favor of a more Hungarian orientation.

The regime's ideology also dictated the need to increase the total number of students enrolled in higher education, primarily through recruitment from the working class and the peasantry. Whereas in 1939 only 13,000 students were enrolled in higher education, by 1970 this number had grown to 86,000. To be sure, some of these students were participating in correspondence or evening courses rather than regular daytime classwork. Adults were encouraged to study through schools at the workplace and correspondence courses. Authorities also tried to expand the proportion of students from lower social strata by setting a worker and peasant quota of about 60 percent at all places available in higher education. Students seeking admission to these institutions were assessed according not only to their abilities but also to their social origins; the children of families belonging to the formerly privileged classes rarely were given the opportunity to study. When students from modest socioeconomic backgrounds lacked the requisite academic training, one-year remedial courses were available to assist them. In 1963 this class-oriented system of recruitment was abandoned. Nevertheless, political considerations continued to play a role in admissions procedures at secondary schools and universities.

In 1986 the country had 3,540 elementary schools, 587 secondary schools, 278 apprentice schools, and 54 institutions of higher education, of which 18 were universities with several faculties and programs extending five or more years. Of the latter, four were general universities, three were technical universities, six were agricultural universities, four were medical universities, and one was a university of economics. The country had five specialized university-level institutes for the arts and physical education.

Attendance at school was mandatory from age six to sixteen. All students attended general schools for at least eight years. Tuition was free for all students from age six up to the university level. Most students actually began their schooling at five years of age; in 1986 approximately 92 percent of all children of kindergarten age attended one of the country's 4,804 kindergartens. By 1980 every town and two-thirds of the villages had kindergartens. Parents paid a fee for preschool services that was based on income, but such institutions were heavily subsidized by the local councils or enterprises that sponsored them.

By 1980 only 29 percent of males aged fifteen years or older and 38 percent of females aged fifteen years and older had not completed eight years of general school, compared with 78 percent of such males and 80 percent of such females in 1949. About half of the students who completed the general schools subsequently completed their education in two years, through vocational and technical training. The remaining students continued their studies in a four-year gymnasium or trade school.

In 1985 about 98,500 undergraduate students attended the country's higher educational institutions. Almost 10 percent of the population aged eighteen to twenty-two was enrolled in regular daytime courses at institutions of higher education. In the 1980s, about 40 percent of regular students came from worker or peasant families. Most of these students either were exempt from tuition payments or, more often, received financial assistance. In the 1980s, applicants outnumbered places available in the colleges and universities. As a result, many persons enrolled in evening and correspondence courses, although these courses were not considered to be equal in quality to regular day instruction.

In the 1985–86 academic year, about 2,500 foreign students studied full time in Hungary. About half were European students; the remainder came from developing countries. In the same year, about 1,300 Hungarian students were studying in foreign institutions of higher education, most of them in neighboring countries.

In the 1980s, the average educational attainments of Hungarians ranked in the middle, in comparison with those of citizens of other European countries. The quality of Hungary's education system was substantially inferior to those of East Germany, Czechoslovakia, and Sweden and was somewhat lower than those of Austria, Belgium, Finland, Norway, Poland, and West Germany. Many Hungarians voiced concerns about the quality of their schools. Critics noted, among other things, that although Switzerland spent 18.8 percent of its national budget on education, Brazil 18.4 percent, and Japan 19.2 percent, Hungary allotted only 6.6 percent of its state budget to education. In the 1980s, the country experienced shortages of both classrooms and teachers, so that primary-school classes sometimes contained up to forty children. In many areas, schools had alternate morning and afternoon school shifts in order to stretch facilities and staff. Moreover, not all teachers received proper training.

At the university level, in the late 1980s some students and faculty were calling for greater autonomy for institutions of higher education and were demanding freedom from ideological control by both the government and the party. They decried the prominence given to the study of Marxism-Leninism and the Russian language in university curricula. The public was also distressed over the fact that, despite the government's remedial measures during previous decades, in the 1980s children of the intelligentsia had a far greater chance of entering institutions of higher learning than did the children of agricultural workers and unskilled industrial workers.

Health and Welfare

After the communist government assumed power in Hungary, it devoted much attention to meeting the specific health care and social security needs of the population. In comparison with prewar standards, the average citizen received far better health care and social assistance as a result of the government's policy. Such improvements did not extend to housing; like other countries in Eastern Europe, Hungary has faced a severe housing shortage since the late 1940s. However, unlike most other countries in Eastern Europe, since the mid-1970s the government has encouraged citizens to build their own housing. This policy has eased the shortage somewhat, but as of 1989 the lack of adequate housing remained a serious problem.

Health

The modern social welfare system was largely a product of the 1970s and 1980s, although setting of goals, initial planning, and more modest coverage for citizens began in previous decades. Amendments to the Constitution in 1972 guaranteed universal assistance for the ill, the aged, and the disabled. The Public Health Act of 1972 specifically guaranteed that beginning in 1975 all persons would have free medical care as a right of citizenship. The Social Insurance Act of 1975 provided that insurance conditions and benefits, which had been different for various occupational groups, become uniformly applied to all citizens. In 1982 even those persons involved in private economic activity became eligible for full social insurance coverage (including generous sickness and disability pay), instead of being limited to pension and accident coverage.

The social welfare system expanded steadily. According to official statistics, the percentage of the population's income represented by social benefits in cash (including social insurance payments) and kind (including free health care) was 17.4 percent in 1960, 22.8 percent in 1970, 27.3 percent in 1975, and 32 percent in 1980.

The state health care system was highly centralized. Increasingly specialized and sophisticated services were available at the level of the district (the country had 4,374 districts in 1984), municipality, county, region, and nation. Each district had a designated physician to whom its inhabitants first turned for care under the public

99

health system. If an ailing person required a specialist, the district physician made the appropriate referral. In the 1980s, the availability of physicians, nurses, and hospital beds was high by international standards. In 1986 the country had 31,154 physicians, or about one physician per 299 inhabitants (up from one physician per 909 inhabitants in 1950, one per 637 inhabitants in 1960, one per 439 inhabitants in 1970, and one per 398 inhabitants in 1974). The country had 100 hospital beds per 10,000 inhabitants (up from 55.8 beds per 10,000 inhabitants in 1950, 71.1 in 1960, and 85.5 in 1974). The country had 3,801 dentists and dental surgeons, 43,579 nurses, 57,277 other health personnel, and 4,506 pharmacists.

Although by the 1980s about 99 percent of the population participated in the social insurance system and could receive free medical services and hospital care, much private practice was allowed. In 1984 more than 3,600 health service doctors engaged in private practice, treating private patients during their free time. Many of them had very lucrative private practices. Many persons in upper-income groups, who could afford the high price of private medical care, chose to use the services of a private physician rather than one assigned to them by the health service. Public opinion considered the care given by private physicians to be of higher quality than that provided by the health service.

In the 1980s, the public engaged in much frank and apparently uncensored discussion about serious shortcomings in health care. Complaints concerned the aging of hospital facilities, the disrepair of their equipment, the shortages of basic medications, and the inadequate training of low-paid medical personnel. Western analysts estimated that Hungary spent only 3.3 percent of its gross national product specifically on health service (the 6 percent figure listed in most statistical data actually included some social services). This percentage was the lowest of any East European country except Romania (in comparison, the United States spent 11 percent of GNP on health care). Critics judged the health system to be substandard, unreliable, and increasingly tainted by the practice of offering gratuities to medical personnel to ensure quality care. They warned that the achievements of past years were jeopardized by the current neglect.

Certain trends in the general health of the population indeed gave health authorities reason for concern in the 1980s. Life expectancy at birth was the lowest among thirty-three developed countries rated by the World Health Organization. In 1986 the infant mortality rate was 19 per 1,000 live births (see table 4, Appendix). This figure showed an improvement over the 1970 rate of

35.9 per 1,000. However, the infant mortality rate remained among the highest for industrialized countries with developed health systems. In 1985, according to Minister of Defense Ferenc Karpati, 10 to 11 percent of young males were unfit for military service, and another 4 to 5 percent could not undergo strenuous physical training. Among conscripts accepted for service, 3 to 4 percent were discharged before the end of their training for health reasons, primarily because of physical or nervous disorders.

Health authorities had other special concerns less directly related to the health care system. One such problem was the country's high suicide rate. In the mid-1980s, the suicide rate was 44 per 100,000 inhabitants, the highest suicide rate in the world. (The country with the second highest suicide rate, Austria, reported 26.9 suicides per 100,000 inhabitants in 1984.) The very high suicide rate had a lengthy history, confirmed by statistics dating back more than a century. Since the late 1960s, however, the rate had risen noticeably. Hungarian experts cited as factors contributing to the troubling situation alcoholism, mental illness, the growing number of elderly people, the disorienting effect of urban life, stress, and the weakening of family and community bonds as a result of rapid modernization. The high suicide rate among people over age sixty was thought to result from the economic stagnation and inflation of the 1980s, which made it difficult for people to subsist on small pensions.

In the mid-1980s, the authorities were also discussing the growing incidence of substance abuse. The incidence of alcoholism had increased during the previous generation, and a high percentage of suicide victims were alcoholics. As of 1986, consumption of alcohol per person per year was 11.7 liters; consumption of hard liquor (4.8 liters per person) was the second highest in the world. Authorities had increased the price of hard liquor five times between 1973 and 1986, but despite these measures, excessive alcohol consumption remained a problem. Although less salient than alcoholism, drug addiction was also becoming a source of some concern and was discussed in the press. Acquired immune deficiency syndrome (AIDS), a serious health threat associated with drug use in many countries, was not a major health concern in Hungary in the late 1980s. According to government statistics released in early 1989, the first AIDS patient entered a Budapest hospital in 1985. During the following four years, the country had twelve AIDS-related deaths.

In the 1980s, another source of anxiety for both health authorities and the general public was the downward trend projected for the country's population (see Structure, this ch.). As early as 1973, concern about the slowdown in population growth had led to the introduction of a comprehensive population policy. Supplemental provisions had broadened the coverage in subsequent years. The policy mandated generous pregnancy and maternity allowances. Working mothers enjoyed a twenty-week maternity leave with full pay. After the twenty weeks had elapsed, the mother could receive an allowance to enable her to raise the child at home until it reached the age of three; the amount of the allowance varied according to the number of children and amounted to about 25 to 40 percent of national average earnings per month. In addition, working mothers had access to unpaid days off (prorated according to the number and ages of the children involved) or other benefits to enable them to take care of a sick child. Additional ongoing family allowances were available for families with two or more children. In spite of this assistance, child rearing was a large expense to families. The various forms of assistance, while clearly beneficial to young families, actually amounted to only 15 to 20 percent of child-rearing costs.

Welfare

In the late 1980s, the country's pension system covered about 85 percent of the population falling within pensionable ages. Male workers could qualify for pensions at the age of sixty, female workers at the age of fifty-five. The number of pensioners had increased rapidly since the end of World War II as people lived longer and as pension coverage expanded to include additional segments of the population. In the early 1950s, the country had had only 12 to 13 pensioners for every 100 active workers. In the late 1980s, however, the country had 50 pensioners for every 100 active workers. This trend placed a heavy burden on the government, the main source of pension funds.

The amount of a person's pension depended upon earnings and number of years of employment. In 1989 the minimum monthly pension was 3,340 forints (about US$54). Yearly cost-of-living increases had failed to keep up with inflation. In 1979 the government introduced major pension increases for the lowest-paid pensioners in an effort to improve the situation. The most vulnerable pensioners tended to be women, whose pensions averaged 25 percent less than men's pensions. More women had small pensions than men because women generally had worked fewer years and earned lower salaries. About 20 percent of all pensioners, or about 400,000 persons, worked to bring in additional income, usually undertaking part-time or seasonal work. In the 1980s, pensioners constituted a significant segment of the country's poor. The

unfortunate circumstances of many elderly citizens and the need to reform the pension system were the subjects of considerable press commentary.

Housing

For many years, the housing conditions in Hungary were only a peripheral concern of the communist regime. The housing that existed before World War II had many shortcomings. Most prewar apartments had only one room and a kitchen area, and these facilities, already overcrowded and expensive, had been heavily damaged during the war. In 1949 the country had 265 inhabitants for every 100 rooms. After 1949 the government confiscated existing housing and redistributed it. The government chose not to invest heavily in housing, although many buildings were reconstructed. The new regime affirmed the right of all inhabitants to decent housing, prohibited evictions, and regulated rents, but these measures did not accelerate construction. During the early years of communist rule, economic planning gave priority to the building of new plants and other industrial installations rather than to new housing. Thus, construction of housing did not keep pace with urban industrial expansion, which had attracted large numbers of workers from the villages into the cities. Not until the Fourth Five-Year Plan (1971–75) did the housing problem receive serious, sustained

103

attention. Progress then became more rapid, and the government experimented with various approaches to the problem. Because of budget constraints, the government abandoned its goal of providing low-rent apartments for all citizens. Instead, it urged people to invest in their own housing and made available low-interest loans for the construction of cooperative apartment buildings and private homes. This policy spurred construction and helped to reduce the overall housing shortage. However, most new housing units were built for the higher-income groups. Families with lower incomes continued to rely on state-financed or industry-financed low-rent housing, which usually had long waiting lists of prospective tenants.

In the 1980s, housing remained a major concern for families at all status and income levels. As the government's direct role in providing housing diminished, many families tried to use any surplus income they had to acquire modern, spacious, well-equipped dwellings. For private individuals wishing to build dwellings, the most important resources were family and friends (for labor) and loans (usually sponsored by the government at 3 percent interest for up to 70 percent of the total construction cost and repayable over a maximum of thirty-five years). As of 1983, only about 22.3 percent of the country's dwellings were state owned, down from 33.9 percent in the first half of the 1970s. The remaining units were privately owned. In 1986 approximately 69,430 dwellings were constructed, 7,620 by the state and 61,800 by private individuals (the vast majority of whom received some state funding). However, despite significant gains, housing was still not sufficient for the country's needs.

Dissent and Freedom of Expression

In the late 1980s, numerous signs pointed to an enlivening of cultural and intellectual life. The bounds of permissible expression became wider as authorities eased restrictions on artistic, intellectual, and political expression.

Until the mid-1980s, outright opposition to the regime and its social, political, and cultural policies was undertaken primarily by intellectuals. However, the relative success of the economy after 1968 made it difficult for dissidents to attract broad followings. The working class was politically quiescent, being the beneficiary of full employment and generous welfare provisions. The government's response to its critics was to acknowledge their existence but also to stress their small numbers and irrelevance. Few official punitive actions such as arrests or trials took place, but the authorities did use low-level police harassment, surveillance, and other forms of indirect pressure. Prominent individuals found their movements watched and occasionally hindered by the police. Less eminent people sometimes received threats to their jobs and careers. Authorities denied some individuals permission to travel abroad or, at the other extreme, urged them to emigrate. The police conducted occasional house searches and levied fines for illicit printing or distribution of unauthorized publications (samizdat). Most dissidents faced only sporadic repression but also minimal public response.

In addition to the continuing efforts of dissident intellectuals, several groups of protesters pursued specific social or political goals in the early 1980s. The law did not recognize conscientious objection and prescribed up to five years' imprisonment as punishment for refusal to perform military service. Beginning in 1977, however, members of certain small Christian sects, such as the Nazarenes, Jehovah's Witnesses, and Seventh-Day Adventists, were allowed to perform unarmed military service (see Conscientious Objection, ch. 5). This privilege was not available to Roman Catholics and members of larger Protestant denominations, whose church hierarchies had a history of supporting the establishment. As of 1986, Amnesty International reported that as many as 150 Hungarian conscientious objectors were in prison, most of them Jehovah's Witnesses who refused to perform even the alternative military service available to them. In the early 1980s, an independent peace movement of significant proportions developed (called Peace Group for Dialogue, or Dialogus), made up primarily of university students and recent university graduates. Facing official hostility and unable to initiate a dialogue with the authorities, the organization disbanded in 1983. Its members and other persons formed other smaller groups and engaged in small-scale independent activity. Under pressure from the authorities, some of these small groups eventually merged with the officially recognized National Peace Council.

In the mid-1980s, the ecology, or "Green," movement was the largest independent movement. Its supporters opposed the joint project of the Czechoslovak and Hungarian governments, financed partially by the Austrian government, to build the Gabčíkovo-Nagymaros Dam at the border where the Danube River crosses from Czechoslovakia to Hungary (see Relations with Other Communist Neighbors, ch. 4). Demonstrations attracted as many as 20,000 people. Several smaller environmental organizations also engaged in small-scale public awareness campaigns. The environmental groups often sought to maintain distance between themselves and dissident political groups, both to legitimize their viewpoint vis-à-vis the government and to attract wider support.

Environmentalists were very cautious in their response to the 1986 accident at the Chernobyl' nuclear power plant in the Soviet Union, which was a politically sensitive issue. The government criticized independent environmental groups, accusing activists of pandering to nationalist sentiments and permitting foreign agitators to intrude. The official press generally ignored the activities and statements of the environmentalists. Occasionally, the police harassed their leaders. Nevertheless, environmental issues appeared to be of great interest to the public, many of whom signed protest petitions and attended meetings in significant numbers.

In the late 1980s, opportunities for self-expression expanded greatly and abruptly. The party itself was planning to establish a limited multiparty political system in the country (see Amendments of 1972, ch. 4). Increasingly, party members acknowledged public criticism of conditions in society and responded to them. And in the late 1980s, for the first time in decades, the authorities occasionally permitted demonstrations calling for changes in policy. However, signals sent by the government to the public were somewhat mixed; occasional arrests and mistreatment of dissidents continued, and police broke up some demonstrations. In the late 1980s, individuals began testing the limits of the government's less restrictive approach. The system of informal self-censorship, which had operated since the 1960s, appeared to be foundering (see Mass Media, ch. 4). Historians called for archival sources on the nation's recent history to be opened and freely examined by impartial scholars. A variety of independent publishers and periodicals appeared, dealing with sensitive issues or publishing the works of authors previously considered taboo. The official press and occasionally even television journalism were becoming more outspoken on virtually all issues, possibly in response to growing competition for the public's attention.

As freedom of association became more extensive (a more permissive law was officially adopted in 1989), a number of groups emerged with interests spanning the entire range of social and political life. The focus of many new associations revealed a growing popular interest in public affairs. The groups ranged in outlook from the neo-Stalinist Ferenc Münnich Society, founded in 1988, to the "Openness Club," also founded in 1988, which sought to promote complete freedom of the press, television, and radio.

Some groups with definite political leanings hoped eventually to function as viable political parties. Others sought merely to represent and publicize the viewpoints of members. Several of the latter received particular attention throughout the country. In September 1987, a group of about 150 intellectuals, including some party members, formed the Hungarian Democratic Forum to sponsor public debates on social and political policy. At first the regime seemed to welcome the Forum, apparently hoping to reap the support of previously disaffected intellectuals. However, the Forum's status later became less clear, as some of the participating party members were expelled from the party. In 1988 a group of students established a new national organization called the Federation of Young Democrats. A politically radical group, it aimed to establish a democratic Hungary, but its leaders denied any plans to form a political party. In 1989, together with five other organizations, the Hungarian Democratic Forum and the Federation of Young Democrats formed what became known as the Opposition Roundtable to discuss a variety of social and political policy options.

In the late 1980s, more than at any time in the previous four decades, the Hungarian people lacked a consensus on the proper social goals of the country. Some observers, both within the country and abroad, feared that if economic conditions worsened as predicted, latent conflicts among social groups would destabilize the country, especially in the absence of strong state and party influence, which was no longer considered legitimate in the eyes of the populace. However, other observers stressed the opportunities for the emergence of new, fresh ideas and the vigorous, healthy debates that were occurring throughout Hungarian society. The latter assessment gave genuine grounds for optimism.

* * *

For a retrospective view of aspects of society's development, Zsuzsa Ferge's *A Society in the Making* is helpful. Both Hungarian and Western ethnographers have shown special interest in Hungarian rural life and its modern evolution. Two valuable studies are Edit Fél's and Tamás Hofer's *Proper Peasants* and Peter D. Bell's *Peasants in Socialist Transition*. *Hungarian Ethnography and Folklore* by Hungarian ethnographers Iván Balassa and Gyula Ortutay contains a wealth of detail as well as illustrations of traditional Hungarian folkways. For the current urban perspective, Peter A. Toma's *Socialist Authority* provides a readable, somewhat journalistic overview. The Hungarian government's Central Statistical Office publishes statistical yearbooks in English that incorporate much information concerning past and present social structure. The Foreign Broadcast Information Service's *Daily Report: East Europe* offers current reporting of major social developments as depicted in the Hungarian media. The reports published by Radio Free Europe contain valuable information and analyses as well. (For further information and complete citations, see Bibliography.)

Chapter 3. The Economy

Large kitchen for farm workers' meals, 1924

DESPITE WAR, DEPRESSION, revolution, foreign occupation, and periods of near chaos, Hungary's economy has advanced in the twentieth century from a near-feudal state to a middle-level stage of industrial development. The economic system has undergone dramatic change since 1968, evolving from a Soviet-type "command" economy, in which government planners in Budapest dictated much of the country's economic behavior, into a hybrid that combined social ownership of the means of production with a stock exchange, central planning with aspects of a free market, and government intervention with a measure of enterprise autonomy and some private enterprise. After Hungary's failed popular revolution against communist rule in 1956, the government opted to foster domestic tranquility and legitimize control by the Hungarian Socialist Workers' Party by steadily improving the Hungarians' standard of living through economic growth.

For several reasons, the Hungarian economy can grow only if its factories and farms become more efficient and competitive. First, except for excess workers in existing enterprises, Hungary no longer has an untapped labor pool, such as the one that existed after World War II in the female and peasant populations. Second, the country has a paucity of natural resources, and imports of raw materials have become more costly for Hungary on both Western and Council for Mutual Economic Assistance markets. Third, Hungary can pay for imports of raw materials and efficiency-improving Western technology only by exporting goods whose quality and price are competitive in the world market.

Since 1968 the government has launched two rounds of economic reform, seeking to boost efficiency and competitiveness. The first was the New Economic Mechanism, introduced in 1968, in which the government abolished universal compulsory planning, granted enterprises greater autonomy, and unleashed some market forces. The program stalled within four years, but a burgeoning balance of trade deficit, slumping performance, deteriorating terms of trade, and other problems prompted the leadership to start the reform process anew in the late 1970s. Since then the government has streamlined its ministries, dismantled some huge enterprises and trusts, stimulated the growth of small and private firms, implemented a competitive pricing system, decentralized foreign trade, created small stock and bond markets, enacted a bankruptcy law, carried

111

out banking reform, and levied value-added (see Glossary) and personal-income taxes.

In the late 1980s, a burdensome foreign debt, inefficient enterprises, raw-material supply problems, and stiffer competition in the world market were just a few of the problems facing the economy. The country's leaders had to improve Hungary's convertible-currency trade balance significantly in order to import the technology and raw materials necessary for further growth. At the same time, they had to maintain or improve domestic living standards and hold down unemployment and domestic inflation. The conjunction of Soviet leader Mikhail S. Gorbachev's program of restructuring in the Soviet Union and János Kádár's replacement as party general secretary by Károly Grósz in Hungary greatly enhanced the chances that the government would try to achieve further economic progress by implementing even more dramatic reforms.

Although Western observers agreed that Hungary had the most accurate and open reporting of economic statistics in the communist world, they warned against accepting those data at face value. Economists in communist and noncommunist countries used different statistical concepts and procedures that produced differing images of Hungary's economic system. Hungarian and foreign analysts also complained that political expedience had sometimes tainted Hungary's official statistics.

Resource Base

Geologically, Hungary is composed primarily of young sedimentary rock that is generally poor in minerals and other raw materials except bauxite, soft coal, and small deposits of uranium, natural gas, oil, iron ore, manganese, and copper. However, Hungary has large tracts of fertile land, a favorable climate, and some forests. The country's general lack of raw materials has necessitated foreign trade, a concern that has dominated the economic policies of Hungarian governments since 1918, when the country lost much of the territory it held prior to World War I (see Trianon Hungary, ch. 1). Raw materials, semifinished products, spare parts, fuels, and electricity accounted for 64.2 percent of imports in 1986 and cost 25.9 percent of Hungary's gross domestic product (GDP—see Glossary). The Soviet Union was Hungary's principal supplier of raw materials (see Foreign Trade, this ch.).

Energy Resources

In the late 1980s, Hungary's coal deposits totaled about 4.5 billion tons and included hard coal (about 15 percent of the total), brown coal (30 percent), and lignite (55 percent). Hungarian coal generally has a low energy content and lies at great depths in thin seams, making mining difficult and costly. Deep mines in the Mecsek Mountains near Pécs and Komló yield dusty hard coal and coal suitable for coking. Thick layers of higher-quality brown coal lie 200 to 300 meters beneath Tatabánya and Dorog, while lower-quality brown coal lies under the Carpathian foothills near Miskolc and in the central Danube Plain. The Várpalota Basin in Veszprem County and the southern slopes of the Mátra Mountains yield lignite. Hungarian experts predict that the country's coal reserves will last about 400 years at the production levels attained in the late 1980s.

Hungary's natural-gas and oil deposits are far smaller than its coal reserves. The country's largest natural-gas deposits are located near Szeged, Hajdúszoboszló, and Miskolc. Geologists hoped to discover additional natural-gas deposits but predicted that natural-gas reserves would run dry in fifteen to twenty years. Small crude-oil deposits lie beneath Szeged, Zala County, and other areas. The Zala crude is highly viscous and difficult to transport. Wells at Lispeszentadorjám, Lovászi, and other sites yield high-quality oil, but in the late 1980s the deposits were almost exhausted. In the late 1970s, drillers struck oil in the mid-Danube-Tisza region (the central part of the country) and near Sárkeresztúr, Endrőd, and Üllés. However, geologists anticipated no new major oil discoveries and expected the wells to run dry by the year 2000.

In the 1950s, Hungary began mining uranium near Pécs with Soviet assistance. In the late 1980s, estimates of the actual size of the country's uranium deposits were unavailable, but official sources indicated that Hungary had uranium reserves sufficient to supply its domestic needs until about the year 2020. In the mid-1980s, the Soviet Union guaranteed Hungary's future nuclear-fuel needs.

Mineral Resources

The Bakony and Vértes mountains contain 10 to 12 percent of the world's known bauxite reserves and deposits of manganese ore, the only alloy necessary for steel production found in Hungary. The only iron-ore mine, located at Rudabánya, produces ankerite and siderite that contain only 24 to 27 percent iron and require lime before smelting. In the late 1980s, the country's limestone and dolomite reserves satisfied the needs of its pig-iron industry. Copper mines at Recsk remained undeveloped in 1987 because of lack of financing and because of copper's low price on world commodity markets.

Land, Climate, and Forests

Arable land, pastures, meadows, vineyards, and gardens occupy 70 percent of the total land area. Hungary has large tracts of fertile

113

black soil, especially in the Great Plain region; although the climate can be harsh, it is favorable for agriculture (see Climate, ch. 2). Concentrated in mountainous areas, the forests occupy about 1.5 million hectares and contain mostly deciduous trees of little value except for holding moisture. The government launched an extensive reforestation effort after World War II, but in the late 1980s domestic timber still supplied only 10 percent of the country's needs.

Environmental Problems

Rapid industrialization and the priority of plan fulfillment over environmental concerns have produced serious air and water pollution problems in Hungary. In the late 1980s, about 38 percent of Hungary's population lived in regions where air pollution exceeded international standards. Electric plants burning high-sulfur coal and automobiles emitted most of the pollutants that fouled Hungary's air. The country's sulfur-dioxide emissions in 1984 totaled 1.8 million tons, an average of 17.6 kilograms per hectare. Prevailing winds from the west and southwest carried 70 percent of Hungary's sulfur-dioxide emissions into neighboring countries, but acid rain had damaged 25 to 30 percent of the country's forests. Government efforts had succeeded in reducing dust pollution.

Pollutants also fouled the rivers and ground water. The Tisza, Danube, Szamos, Sajó, and Zagyva were Hungary's most polluted rivers, and the water supplies of 773 towns and villages were not fit for human consumption. In 1970 Hungary emitted 1.5 million cubic meters of polluted water per day. Industrial waste from chemical, rubber, iron, paper, and food-processing industries accounted for 70 percent of the effluent, of which only 27 percent was treated. Only 46 percent of Hungary's population had an adequate sewage system.

In the 1980s, Hungary annually produced 5 million tons of hazardous waste, and it reportedly imported hazardous waste from Austria, Switzerland, and the Federal Republic of Germany (West Germany) in return for hard currency. After three years of public protest, in the late 1980s Hungary began constructing an incinerator in Dorog capable of burning about 25,000 tons of hazardous waste per year. Hungary operated a nuclear-waste dump between the villages of Kisnémedi and Püspökszilagy, but precise information on the disposal of radioactive waste from the country's nuclear power plant was unavailable.

Hungary signed the United Nations Convention on Long-Range Transboundary Air Pollution in 1979 and the Helsinki protocol on sulfur-dioxide emissions in 1985. In 1987 and 1988, the government passed new pollution regulations and obtained loans from the World Bank (see Glossary) to improve pollution control. Hungary had antipollution agreements with Czechoslovakia and Austria but had no such agreement with Romania and complained about Romania's chronic discharge of phenol, oil, and other pollutants into the Tisza and smaller rivers.

Labor Force

In the late 1980s, active earners made up a large percentage of the working-age population, and many Hungarians supplemented their income by working outside jobs, tilling household plots, or operating private businesses. Unfortunately, many enterprises used labor inefficiently, and the country suffered from underemployment and relatively low labor productivity. The government had enacted measures aimed at forcing enterprises to operate more efficiently. Regrettably, these measures threatened the elimination of many jobs and signaled a significant ideological departure from communism's commitment to full employment. Fear of unemployment influenced government decisions to allow the private sector to grow and to create jobs for laid-off workers. Despite the government's concern, observers expected overall unemployment to remain low by Western standards.

Work Force

In 1987 about 6.1 million of Hungary's 10.6 million people were of working age, and 4.9 million were active earners. The number of active earners was expected to remain between 4.8 and 5.1 million in the 1990s. The state sector employed about 3.5 million persons (70.5 percent of the country's active earners) in 1986; the cooperative sector, approximately 1.2 million (23.8 percent); and the private sector, about 266,000 (5.4 percent). According to foreign observers, official statistics underestimated the size of the private sector because they included only persons who reported their private activity as their primary occupation. In the late 1980s, approximately 75 percent of Hungary's families earned extra incomes working "sideline activities" to supplement the wages and benefits that family members earned in the state and cooperative sectors. These activities, which were mostly agricultural, generated productive man-hours equal to about 20 percent of the man-hours worked each year in the socialist sector (the state and cooperative sectors). While sideline activities contributed to family incomes and the nation's productivity, they also deprived the socialist sector of the energy and attention that workers would otherwise direct to their primary jobs.

In 1987 workers in industry numbered just over 1.5 million, or 31.2 percent of the active earners, including 57,600 in the private sector (see table 5, Appendix). When rapid industrialization began in 1949, only 19.4 percent of the labor force worked in industry. Hungary had about 19.3 percent of its labor force or 890,000 active earners working in the agricultural sector in 1987, including about 846,100 in the socialist sector and 43,900 in the private sector. The number of persons actually engaged in private agriculture was much higher, however, because government statistics counted collective- and state-farm members who worked household plots only as members of the socialist sector. The number of workers in the agricultural sector has steadily declined since the war. In 1949 about 53.8 percent of the labor force worked in agriculture; this figure dropped to 24.4 percent in 1970 and to 19 percent in 1980, but it rebounded slightly to 19.3 in 1987 as agricultural enterprises began employing more workers in nonagricultural activities. The service sector accounted for 21.3 percent of the active work force in 1986; commerce, 10.5 percent; transportation and telecommunications employed 8.3 percent; and construction, 7 percent.

Underemployment and Unemployment

After World War II, Hungary suffered from chronic, widespread underemployment. Until the late 1980s, the leadership stubbornly clung to the principle of full employment, and employment rolls swelled because, as a consequence of low wages, it was more cost effective to employ human labor than install labor-saving equipment or implement other efficiency measures. In addition, an enterprise tax based on average wages encouraged managers to pad their payrolls with low-paid, redundant employees who worked at or near full capacity only during the closing weeks of a plan period when pressure to meet targets was most intense. Underemployment combined with other factors to make the country's labor productivity only 40 to 50 percent of that in Western countries. In the late 1980s, the government shelved the principle of full employment and enacted measures, including new bankruptcy and tax laws, to induce enterprises to use labor and other resources more efficiently (see Economic Regulators, this ch.). Vigorous implementation of these measures will entail layoffs, retraining, and early retirement for many workers.

Hungary was the first member of the Council for Mutual Economic Assistance (Comecon—see Glossary) to acknowledge the existence of unemployment. Marxist-Leninist ideology has always considered socialism and unemployment incompatible, and until 1987 even the word *unemployment* was taboo in Hungary. The ideological implications of this policy shift outweighed the scale of the potential layoffs. The government reported that 30,000 to 40,000 people were unemployed in late 1987, and government officials have estimated that another 100,000 to 150,000 workers might be laid off while Hungary implemented its economic reform. Compared with Western countries, however, Hungary's unemployment problem was relatively small: a 4 percent unemployment rate is generally considered full employment in a free-market economy; in Hungary this percentage would amount to about 240,000 people.

In 1987 Hungary became the first communist state to establish public works programs to provide jobs for the unemployed. In 1988 it created an unemployment relief fund with the capacity to benefit 25,000 people. Nevertheless, critics argued that the government did not allot sufficient funds to these programs to deal with projected layoffs.

Labor Turnover

Before 1968 the labor force was generally tied to the workplace. The government restricted job changes and prohibited moving to a new city without permission. In the 1980s, however, the annual labor turnover rate averaged about 23 percent, or about 1 million job changes each year, mostly in low-paying, seasonal, and unskilled positions. Although the government had lifted legal restrictions, relocation to another city was unusual because Hungary had a housing shortage.

Women in the Work Force and Foreign Workers

Women joined the work force in great numbers after World War II and contributed significantly to the government's industrialization drive in the 1950s and 1960s. Families supported the entry of women into the work force because they could not survive on a single income or they desired a higher living standard. In 1949 about 29.2 percent of active earners were women; by 1987 they accounted for 46 percent. Likewise, whereas 34.5 percent of working-age women were active earners in 1949, about 75 percent were active earners by 1987. About 59 percent of Hungary's working women were manual workers; the remainder worked in white-collar jobs. (About 70 percent of men were manual workers, and 30 percent had white-collar jobs.) Women dominated low-paying jobs in the textile industry, the service sector, canneries, and commerce; in the white-collar area, women dominated in education, health, and low-profile office jobs.

Hungarian enterprises employed about 10,000 foreign workers in 1986, including about 3,000 Polish miners, 1,300 Cubans in various jobs, and some Vietnamese textile workers. After 1983 Hungarian workers with firm job offers were free to accept employment in Western countries for up to five years, but in 1986 only a small number of Hungarians were employed abroad.

Economic System and Control Mechanisms

In the late 1940s, Hungary's Marxist-Leninist leaders imposed a Soviet-style command economy that included rigid central planning, agricultural collectivization, and rapid industrialization (see Postwar Hungary, ch. 1). Faced with the need to improve efficiency in the late 1960s, however, the government undertook economic reforms and in 1968 introduced the New Economic Mechanism (NEM), which eliminated compulsory plan directives, introduced market mechanisms, allowed many enterprises a measure of autonomy, and legalized a narrow range of private economic activity. The reform stalled between 1972 and 1978, but trade imbalances and other problems prompted the government in 1979 to begin implementing a second wave of reforms that included ministerial and industrial restructuring. These reforms to a great degree differentiated the Hungarian economy from a traditional command economy. The Hungarian Socialist Workers' Party (HSWP), however, has retained its monopoly of political power, and a central plan containing broad goals still existed in 1989. After Kádár's resignation as general secretary in May 1988, Hungary entered a new era that may see more energetic implementation of reforms already on the books and the enactment of even more radical reform measures.

Role of Party and Government Bodies

As of mid-1989, the HSWP was the dominant political institution in the government and the ultimate authority on all political, economic, and social issues (see Hungarian Socialist Workers' Party, ch. 4). The party's leading organs passed resolutions that functioned as basic guidelines for government bodies making economic decisions, and party leaders also exercised formidable informal influence. Primary authority lay with the Politburo and the Secretariat (particularly the latter's committee for economic and social welfare policy, the working group for economics, and the department for economic and social welfare policy). In the 1980s, the party assumed a lower profile in economic decision making than it had before the reform, and it consulted more with ministers, enterprises, and other government and economic organizations.

The Council of Ministers was the government's highest administrative decision-making body. Its State Planning Committee concerned itself with long-term economic issues. The council's Economic Committee oversaw the economy's day-to-day operation (see State Apparatus, ch. 4).

The government consolidated the ministerial structure in the late 1970s and 1980s in order to reduce the ministries' influence on managers of enterprises. In 1989 four branch ministries—industry, agriculture and food, construction, and communications—set policy, assisted in allocating resources (especially investments), promoted development, and ensured achievement of export targets. Hungary's functional ministries were the Ministry of Finance and the Ministry of Trade. The Ministry of Finance supervised the banking system and worked out many of the economic regulators that guided the economy. The Ministry of Trade developed and implemented foreign and domestic trade policy, granted export and import licenses and certain subsidies, and controlled the balance of payments.

The National Planning Authority and the National Price Office acted much like functional ministries. As with traditional centrally planned economies, the National Planning Authority was one of the most powerful economic organs in the government. It participated in almost all of the central government's economic decision making, and its chairman presided over the State Planning Committee. After the NEM was instituted, however, the planning authority focused primarily on medium- and long-term planning. Prices were supposed to reflect "justified" costs, and enterprises had to report price increases to the National Price Office, which could intervene formally or informally if it deemed a price increase unjustified. With the Council of Ministers' approval, the National Price Office could issue administrative commands to enterprises in case of actual or possible economic disruptions. However, the National Price Office usually used persuasion or adjusted one of the economic regulators to implement its decisions.

In the late 1980s, to oversee economic policy the National Assembly had committees on planning and finance, industry, agriculture, and commerce (see National Assembly, ch. 4). The assembly's role in economic policy making was growing, but it was still far less important than its Western counterparts.

Ownership

The means of production consist of all the material factors used to produce goods and include land, raw materials, and capital. In a traditional centrally planned economy, the state owns all the significant means of production outside the agricultural sector. The ruling party and the government planning bureaucracy exercise the functions of ownership and ration the means of production. In the agricultural sector, state, cooperative, and private forms of ownership coexist, but the state closely supervises and controls all key aspects of production.

In Hungary state ownership of the means of production still predominated in the late 1980s, although the government had broadened the scope of private and foreign ownership. The state has owned more than 90 percent of Hungary's agricultural land since its second collectivization campaign ended in the early 1960s. In industry, economic reformers wanted the state to delegate ownership functions to enterprises in the socialist sector or to independent holding companies whose only function would be to exercise ownership rights. (These companies would operate much the same way that incorporated companies in capitalist economies operate.) Hungary had abolished the system of formal central allocation of resources for all but a few goods, and enterprises generally had to purchase labor, raw materials, and other inputs to production and sell output on their own. The government began allowing Hungarian enterprises to form joint ventures with foreign firms in 1972. Subsequent laws made joint ventures even more attractive for foreign investors, and in some instances foreign firms could take more than a 50 percent stake.

Planning

Under capitalism the market guides most economic activity. In a traditional command economy, however, a central planning board sits atop a hierarchy of ministries, branches, and enterprises and attempts to direct almost all economic activity. The board develops a national economic plan after bargaining with ministries, enterprises, and others over production targets and resource allocations. The board then presents the plan to the country's highest political authorities for approval. The plan spells out, among other things, what goods will be produced, who will produce them, how much will be produced, and what materials and capital will be available. After the plan is approved, the planning board issues directives to ministries, enterprises, and other economic institutions. The directives, which have the force of law, contain production targets expressed in physical units for some items and in value terms for others. Although all plan targets are compulsory, enforcement is stricter on targets for higher-priority items such as military hardware and producer goods.

Under the NEM, which was instituted in 1968, the government abolished compulsory plan directives for most enterprises, but left its planning institutions intact. In the late 1980s, the plan was considered a framework rather than a law binding managers of enterprises, and plans often stated targets as ranges. The National Planning Authority developed long-, medium-, and short-term plans. Long-term plans reflected the leadership's overall economic objectives for national income, industrial and agricultural production, investment, and other areas. The government used short- and medium-term planning to guide the economy toward the long-term objectives.

In the planning process, the central government provided each enterprise with information about forthcoming plan objectives, and each enterprise in turn furnished the government with a copy of its plan. In developing short- and medium-term plans, the National Planning Authority first projected supply and demand using enterprise production plans. If supply and demand estimates failed to balance or if enterprise production plans did not comply with broader plan goals, the authorities could manipulate any of a number of economic regulators in order to induce the enterprises to revise their production plans. For example, the management of each state and collective farm had to prepare a five-year plan according to instructions from the Ministry of Agriculture and Food. The ministry then aggregated the plans of all the farms. If the sum of the plan targets indicated that the agricultural sector could not achieve national production goals, the central authorities manipulated prices, credits, subsidies, or other economic regulators to induce farm managers to alter their plans toward fulfilling those goals. The party and government supplemented these economic regulators with direct intervention to ensure plan fulfillment in such key areas as defense and energy production, extractive industries, construction of key infrastructure projects, and foreign trade.

Economic Regulators

Instead of issuing compulsory plan targets, the government administratively adjusted economic regulators to induce enterprises and cooperatives to fulfill the regime's macroeconomic plan. The key economic regulators were prices, taxes, enterprise-income regulations, exchange rates, and direct administrative intervention. The government did not apply the regulators uniformly throughout the economy but changed them according to need.

Prices

In a traditional command economy, prices function as political instruments rather than as natural market regulators that respond to supply and demand. Central authorities set producer and consumer prices, which bear little relationship to each other and often remain fixed for many years. Producer prices are those prices that enterprises pay for goods. Planners use producer prices to facilitate target-setting and to determine plan fulfillment. Consumer prices for all items except housing, foodstuffs, and other basic necessities are set at artificially high levels to avoid open inflation. Consumer prices for essential goods are supposed to be set at market-clearing levels, but actual retail prices are often lower, causing persistent shortages and forced savings. Prices for imports and exports are based on current world market prices in trade with the West and on an average of past world market prices for trade with the Comecon countries.

In 1968 the NEM gave enterprises more flexibility to set prices and permitted market forces to influence prices. Subsequent price reforms created a direct link between world market prices and Hungarian producer prices for most items. The government, however, could not allow prices to float freely because key enterprises faced little domestic or import competition and could dictate the prices of essential items in an unrestricted market. Decades of arbitrary price, wage, tax, and subsidy policies also have left many imbalances in the economy that would cause significant dislocations if the authorities arbitrarily introduced a free market in one stroke.

In 1980 the authorities introduced a so-called "competitive price system" for industrial producer prices. The system was designed to simulate what domestic prices would be if enterprises faced significant market competition. The government assigned each enterprise to one of three groups according to a series of factors, including the amount of competition the enterprise faced in the domestic and foreign market. The different groups were subject to progressively less restrictive pricing rules; enterprises facing the stiffest competition were generally subject to the least restrictive rules. A 1984 reform gradually loosened administrative restrictions in order to permit market forces to guide the pricing decisions of a greater number of enterprises. In agriculture, the government set producer prices annually according to average production costs and other factors, and it used cost-plus pricing for most other sectors.

The NEM left consumer prices virtually untouched, and by 1976 the average of consumer prices had fallen below the average of producer prices. The authorities subsequently adjusted consumer prices in order to manage demand, wean enterprises away from reliance on government subsidies, and reestablish a buffer between producer and consumer prices. Over the course of the 1980s, the government attempted to let market forces influence a growing number of consumer prices.

Wages, Salaries, and Incentives

In a traditional command economy, the government regulates each enterprise's wage fund and fixes wage scales for workers in different job classifications. Managers receive bonuses based on their ability to fulfill plan targets. The government regulates farmers' incomes by establishing prices for deliveries to the state; some farmers legally supplement their earnings by selling produce grown on private plots.

In the late 1980s, labor income was composed of wages, salaries, and profit-sharing payments. In addition to levying taxes, the government regulated wages and salaries by setting basic pay brackets depending on skill classifications and working conditions. For unskilled job categories, the highest-paid workers made 50 percent more than the lowest-paid workers; for skilled categories, the highest-paid workers made 100 percent more than the lowest-paid workers in the same category. Other regulations governed profit-sharing distributions. The government used these income regulators to counterbalance forces that tended to force incomes up and thus create inflationary pressures and widen income differentials. These forces resulted from the enterprises' monopoly over the domestic market and enterprise managers' insufficient economic interest in profitability. Wage increases and profit-sharing payments have been linked to enterprise profits since 1968, and in 1985 the government introduced a radical reform of wage and income rules that abandoned the practice of controlling incomes with a check on average wages.

Taxes

In a command economy, the state collects taxes and other charges from enterprises, collectives, cooperatives, and individuals and redistributes the revenue to fund public consumption, new investment, and subsidies for enterprises unable to cover costs. In the late 1980s, Hungary's tax system was very complex. Few tax rules applied uniformly to all enterprises; some tax scales were custom-fit for individual enterprises, sometimes even within the same branch, and the government often granted one-time tax exemptions to financially strapped enterprises. In 1988 Hungary became the first communist country to introduce value-added and personal-income taxes. The government originally intended to use these new taxes to supplant capital, accumulation, wage, and local taxes on enterprises, but it did not abolish all of the existing taxes.

The 1988 tax law for the first time required state enterprises, private businesses, and individuals to account for all business transactions. The government introduced the value-added tax in order to switch its revenue source from the enterprises to consumers; to increase labor expenses in order to improve labor efficiency; to increase prices and enable the government to reduce state subsidies; to raise import, raw-material, and energy prices to encourage their efficient utilization; and to enhance incentives for export production. The government levied the personal income tax in order to minimize net income differentials in the state, cooperative, and private sectors; to stifle the growth of the underground economy; to tap previously unreported private income; and to create a means to adjust taxes for inflation. The levying of a personal-income tax was also intended to help eliminate other kinds of taxes that impeded productivity.

Enterprise Income Regulation

In addition to price and wage regulation and taxation, the Hungarian government controlled enterprise incomes by prescribing the means by which enterprises calculated revenues and expenses and apportioned earnings. Taxes on inputs and profits were levied at several steps in the sequence of computations. In 1985 the authorities abolished rules requiring enterprises to allocate after-tax profits to various wage and development funds, but in the late 1980s the government still used tax rules and other devices to influence enterprise distribution of after-tax profits.

Exchange-Rate Controls

In 1981 Hungary established a unified exchange rate and became the first Comecon country to permit limited convertibility of its currency. At the same time, the Hungarian National Bank began adjusting the exchange rate of the forint (for value of the forint—see Glossary) on a daily basis against a weighted basket of nonconvertible currencies, using a variety of criteria including export and domestic producer prices. The exchange rate functioned as a domestic price-setting guide that to a certain degree reflected world market prices.

Direct Administrative Intervention

In the late 1980s, the government reserved the right to intervene directly in sectors marked by a significant market imbalance and when manipulation of economic regulators proved insufficient to achieve or restore a state of equilibrium. The government also could intervene directly when a Comecon agreement had to be fulfilled. Means of direct government intervention included allocating resources; adjusting imports, exports, or purchases by producers and distributors; forcing enterprises to accept contracts to supply, for example, important investment projects, the health care system, state reserves, and other areas; designating distribution channels; and prescribing inventory levels. Each year the government decided which enterprises were subject to central intervention, and a list of these enterprises became a part of the annual plan. In the late 1980s, government recourse to central allocation or administrative intervention had become an exception to the rule, and when such intervention did take place, it was in a number of cases only temporary.

Finance

In a centrally planned economy, an enterprise has three sources of finance: the state budget, the banks, and the enterprise's own resources. An enterprise cannot, however, use its after-tax profits to increase wages or to undertake new investment without government approval. Credit is necessary to provide enterprises with the financial means needed to pay for planned inventories and to finance operations during the hiatus between delivery and payment; credit also gives the government an additional means of controlling enterprise activity. A single bank performs both central and commercial banking functions.

The reforms of the mid- to late 1980s significantly altered Hungary's financial institutions and practices. A number of new banks were created, and the government permitted foreign investors to participate in the banking system. The credit system was liberalized, although decisions to extend credit remained unrelated to past economic performance. The government also created a series of new investment opportunities for individuals and enterprises. Finally, in 1986 Hungary enacted a bankruptcy law.

Financial Institutions

The economic reforms of the mid- to late 1980s resulted in a restructuring of the country's financial institutions. Up until that time the institutions included the Ministry of Finance; the Hungarian National Bank; five major and several smaller commercial banks, some with foreign partners; the National Savings Bank; small venture-capital institutions; and a nascent insurance industry.

The Ministry of Finance oversaw the financial and banking system and the insurance industry. The ministry also supervised foreign-exchange policy and concluded international financial agreements through the Hungarian National Bank.

In 1987 Hungary unveiled a new, two-tier banking system consisting of banks that were supposed to function as genuine, profit-making credit institutions. Before the reform, the Hungarian National Bank dominated the banking system, functioning as the central bank, the bank of issue, and the main commercial bank. All banks acted as agents of the state, and their lending decisions were based not on profitability but on government guidelines geared toward implementing the economic five-year plan.

The 1987 reform stripped the Hungarian National Bank of its commercial-banking function, but it remained the country's bank of issue and its central bank. In its role as the bank of issue, the Hungarian National Bank established the national payment and accounting system, promulgated rules on money circulation, coordinated Hungary's relations with international financial institutions, and determined foreign-exchange rates. As the central bank, the Hungarian National Bank regulated the money supply using credit policy, interest rates, obligatory reserve requirements, and other means. The Hungarian National Bank was a member of the International Bank for Economic Cooperation and the International Investment Bank, both headquartered in Moscow. It was also a shareholder in the Bank for International Settlements in Basel, Switzerland, and owned the Hungarian International Bank in Britain and the Central Wechsel- und Creditbank A.G. in Austria.

The reform created five major commercial banks: the Hungarian Foreign Trade Bank, the General Banking and Trust Company, the Hungarian Credit Bank, the National Commercial and Credit Bank, and the Credit Bank of Budapest. They were all Hungarian-owned joint-stock companies and were licensed to perform a full range of commercial-banking services and provide short-term credits for technical-development projects and the implementation of new technology. The government did not permit these banks to establish direct foreign banking relations, however, or to offer banking services to individuals. The Hungarian Foreign Trade Bank handled foreign-currency exchange, countertrade, letters of credit, and industrial cooperation deals. In addition, it provided short-term import and export credits and loans for projects geared toward expanding exports. Eleven smaller financial institutions also offered commercial-banking services.

Hungary has joined with foreign investors to form several other commercial banks. The Central-European International Bank (CIB), which had US$436 million in assets in 1986, performed lease financing and prefinancing of export contracts. Founded in 1979, CIB was the first offshore bank (a bank set up in a foreign country to take advantage of the particular regulatory environment of that country) in a Comecon country and the first joint venture in Hungary in which Western partners took a majority stake. The Hungarian National Bank held a 34-percent share, and six Western banks each held 11-percent shares. Another commercial bank, Citibank Budapest, was a joint venture of Citibank Overseas Investment Corporation and the Central Wechsel- und Creditbank A.G. Citibank Budapest was the first Western bank permitted to take direct part in commercial banking activities in Hungary. It was a full-service commercial bank that operated in forints and convertible currencies. Unicbank was a third commercial bank offering equity financing for new and expanding ventures and short-, medium-, and long-term loans to state-owned enterprises, cooperatives, joint ventures, and private businesses. Six Hungarian financial institutions and cooperative banks from Austria and West Germany joined with the International Finance Corporation, a subsidiary of the World Bank, to form Unicbank in 1987.

Other than local savings cooperatives, Hungary's National Savings Bank was the only financial institution permitted to serve individuals in the late 1980s. The National Savings Bank handled savings accounts, made loans to individuals and private businesses, and engaged in foreign currency exchanges through a countrywide network of branches. The bank also handled convertible-currency accounts for Westerners, offering competitive interest rates and protection from Western tax authorities. Other small venture-capital institutions allowed by a 1982 government decree provided either credit or equity to new businesses engaged in innovation, technical development, and the like, that the traditional financial institutions were not equipped or inclined to finance.

In addition to these financial institutions, in the late 1980s Hungary had two separate insurance companies. Spurred by rising inflation in Hungary, the insurance companies had become strong advocates of further economic reform, especially the broadening of laws on equity investment. One of the companies made direct investments in a private hotel and a brewery and planned to invest in the construction of office buildings.

Credit Criteria

After several rounds of reform, credit decisions often remained unrelated to the past profitability or creditworthiness of the potential borrower, and the government often used the credit system to bail out enterprises operating at a loss. In cooperation with other banks and financial institutions, the Hungarian National Bank issued ''Guiding Principles on Credit Policy'' as part of the state five-year plan. Credits were extended under varying conditions, with different interest rates, maturities, and priorities to influence development in harmony with the national plan. The directives of the Hungarian National Bank were binding on all other parts of the banking system.

Financial Instruments

Before reforms were enacted in 1983, enterprises had no options other than depositing their after-tax profits in bank accounts or investing them in their own operations, and individuals had no options other than maintaining savings accounts or investing in housing or real estate. In 1989 enterprises could deposit funds at a number of banks; invest in their own plants; lend money to other enterprises through inter-enterprise loans; and buy, issue, and trade stocks and bonds. Individuals could invest their funds in a savings bank, purchase bonds, lend money to other individuals, or invest in silent partnerships. The government hoped the development of these new investment opportunities would boost enterprise-profit and personal-income incentives, encourage voluntary savings by enterprises and the population, funnel more capital to efficient enterprises and more productive endeavors, and conversely reduce the capital flow to inefficient enterprises and wasteful projects. In 1989 it was still uncertain whether these reforms would produce the desired effects.

The government allowed agricultural cooperatives to issue up to 200,000 forints (approximately US$3,225) in bonds to members as well as nonmembers beginning in 1984, and the authorities later expanded the right to issue bonds to industrial and other enterprises. In 1987 enterprises issued bonds worth about US$354 million, up from US$87.3 million the year before. Bond issuance accounted for about 7 percent of total private savings and about 10 percent of total investment. By early 1988, banks, enterprises, local councils, agricultural and industrial cooperatives, hospitals, and other entities had issued about US$500 million in bonds. About 100,000 individuals owned 60 percent of the bonds; institutions held the remainder. Returns ranged from 9 to 12 percent and were higher than the interest paid on savings accounts. The government taxed interest on bonds issued after January 1, 1988, at a flat rate of 20 percent.

In early 1987, the government legalized the capitalization of enterprises through the sale of stock without prior authorization. By early 1988, investors had purchased about US$555 million worth of stock in sixteen banks and about fifty enterprises and joint ventures. In the same year, about twenty financial and banking institutions founded a small stock exchange. The exchange opened for trading only once every two weeks, but its founders hoped to expand its operation and introduce a fully computerized trading system. Trading was limited because the government, through the Hungarian National Bank, owned most of the shares. By 1989 at least one enterprise had launched an employee stock ownership plan, and the government had proposed a law lifting existing restrictions on employee stockholding in order to tap uninvested individual savings and give employees a sense of common purpose with their enterprises. The opening of stock and bond markets prompted former Ministry of Finance employees to create a private company to perform independent assessments of individual enterprises.

Bankruptcy

In 1986 Hungary became the first communist country to enact a bankruptcy law. The law sought to induce enterprises to become profitable and less reliant on state subsidies, which in 1987 consumed about 23 percent of the national budget. Under the law, creditors, unpaid suppliers, and other enterprises could initiate bankruptcy proceedings against any insolvent or delinquent enterprise except agricultural collectives. The National Reorganization and Liquidation Board, which oversaw the bankruptcy process, attempted arbitration and reorganization before final liquidation. Workers who lost their jobs as a result of liquidation were entitled to unemployment benefits.

Although by 1987 claimants had filed bankruptcy actions against fifty-five enterprises, including one large construction firm, the government had not enforced the bankruptcy law vigorously. Government interference in the market remained so widespread that in bankruptcy proceedings unprofitable enterprises could justifiably argue that their losses were only marginally related to efficiency or managerial decisions. Despite proclamations that profitability was the main standard for judging enterprise performance, the government continued to compensate firms operating at a loss with subsidies, tax breaks, credits, preferential treatment in price setting, and other means. The government extracted the earnings of profit-making enterprises to fund these measures.

Industrial Organization

In a centrally planned economy, only branch ministries and other government bodies can establish production and distribution enterprises, which are usually very large and have a regional or nationwide monopoly in their business activity. Enterprises carry on official economic relations through the ministerial bureaucracy rather than through a market. State organs appoint, evaluate, promote, and dismiss enterprise managers, whose main responsibility is to meet or exceed plan targets.

Industrial organization in Hungary followed the pattern of a command economy until 1968, when the government granted enterprises a modicum of autonomy. Reform advocates were not, however, powerful enough to force a restructuring of Hungary's industrial institutions. In the late 1970s, Hungary had the world's most concentrated industrial organization, with 699 state enterprises employing an average of 1,569 people each. The bureaucracy functioned in many ways as it did before the reform, supervising and directing large enterprises and trusts, thus stifling the development of true enterprise autonomy and a market mechanism.

On several occasions in the 1980s, the government adopted measures to decentralize Hungary's highly concentrated industrial organization in order to promote enterprise independence, flexibility, and efficiency. In 1981 the authorities eased restrictions on creating small- and medium-sized enterprises in the state, collective, and private sectors. The government merged three industrial ministries into the single Ministry of Industry in order to shrink the bureaucracy and cut the informal channels of influence that existed between the ministries and supposedly independent enterprises. Between 1979 and 1984, the authorities broke up 14 of the country's 28 trusts and divided a number of large enterprises into more than 300 smaller entities. However, despite the government's efforts, Hungary's industrial organization remained one of the world's most highly concentrated. This concentration led to the creation of monopolies that suffocated competition in many production areas. In the late 1980s, the central government also continued to expect the Ministry of Industry to ensure supplies, and both the government and the enterprises continued to expect the ministry to intervene to remedy imbalances.

Also in the 1980s, the government took steps to simplify the complicated and time-consuming process of starting a business. A minister, the head of a nationwide government body, or a local council with prior approval from the minister of finance could found a state-owned enterprise. The founder defined the enterprise's initial activity and supervised its operation, but other changes have eroded much of the control that founders once exercised. In 1985 most of Hungary's industrial enterprises introduced "democratic measures," under which the employees elected top managers directly or indirectly. The government also permitted enterprises to change their economic activities without prior consultation, provided that they informed their founder and the appropriate branch ministry of the change. Enterprise councils or collective management were managing 77 percent of the industrial enterprises by 1986, while the Ministry of Industry continued to supervise the remainder. Even under "industrial democracy," an enterprise's founder could veto candidates for director and dismiss elected directors, and ministries still exercised critical influence. As János Kornai, a leading Hungarian economist, has written, despite "industrial democracy" and the authorities' call for profitability and attention to the market, enterprise managers know that their "career, the firm's life and death, taxes, subsidies and credit, prices and wages, all financial 'regulators' affecting the firm's prosperity, depend more on the higher authorities than on market performance."

In 1982 the government provided for the creation of semiprivate and private industrial ventures, including economic work cooperatives (EWCs) and independent contract work associations (ICWAs), to encourage entrepreneurship and competition. EWCs were groups of no more than thirty workers employed by a state-owned enterprise who were allowed to use the enterprise's machinery outside normal working hours to produce goods under special contracts. The workers needed the enterprise's permission to establish an EWC, and the enterprise often entered into contracts with the EWC itself. The workers received far higher wages for this additional work than they did for their regular jobs. In 1982 approximately 25,000 workers participated in 2,775 EWCs; by the end of 1986, approximately 450,000 workers participated in 35,205 EWCs. ICWAs were self-organized and self-capitalized private groups that performed work under contract but had no affiliation to any single state-owned enterprise. About half of an ICWA's members worked for the group full time. In 1982 Hungary had 2,341 ICWAs; by October 1983, that number had climbed to 4,463.

Agricultural Organization

In a traditional centrally planned economy, state and collective farms play the key role in agricultural production; small private-plot farming is tolerated but is expected to "wither away." The state makes production and marketing decisions for the farms, and individual state-farm managers and collective-farm members have little input into decision making.

Hungary collectivized its agricultural sector in two campaigns beginning in 1949 and ending in 1961. In the first campaign, the government coerced peasants to move to state and collective farms, enforced compulsory delivery quotas and high taxes, and set prices artificially low to gain control of agriculture and use it to generate capital needed for industrial development (see Rákosi's Rule, ch. 1). Peasants reacted by slowing production and departing from the collective farms in great numbers, especially during the Revolution of 1956 (see Revolution of 1956, ch. 1). The government changed its tactics in the second campaign, which began in the late 1950s. The authorities relied more on persuasion than coercion and eliminated compulsory deliveries, increased material incentives, furnished loans, offered tax breaks, and provided seed, fertilizers, and farm equipment. By 1960 about 90 percent of Hungary's farmland was collectivized, and in 1961 nearly 94 percent of the agricultural earners worked in the socialist sector.

After the mid-1960s, the agricultural sector often served as a testing ground for reforms later introduced into the overall economic system. In the 1965–67 period, the government eliminated obligatory plan targets, allowed farms to plan production, loosened restrictions on self-financing, and permitted production on private plots. After the NEM was introduced in 1968, cooperative farms gained true autonomy. In the 1980s, agricultural producers could buy inputs from a variety of sources and sell to purchasers of their choice.

Large-Scale Farming

Large-scale farming—made up of state and cooperative farms—focused on such activities as grain and fodder production, which were capital-intensive and in which economies of scale were most significant. A 1985 law transformed state farms from state-administered organizations into self-governing enterprises under the supervision of the Ministry of Agriculture and Food. However, state farms were subject to more state control than cooperatives in such matters as appointment of managers and the use of profits, and state-farm employees were government employees who worked for fixed wages and bonuses.

A cooperative farm was owned and managed by its members, who elected a chairman to manage the farm according to its charter. Although cooperative farms could employ workers, cooperative members were technically not "employees." The cooperative paid employees a set wage; members received a base salary and a year-end dividend based on net profits. Cooperatives were also freer than state farms in deciding how to use their profits, and many cooperatives delegated certain operations to autonomous work teams or individuals who divided the operation's net profits. The cooperative farms owned only about half the land they worked; the state and individuals owned the rest.

In the late 1980s, the government still fixed prices for a large portion of agricultural production, including corn, wheat, and beef

Farm house in Tata
Courtesy Sam and Sarah Stulberg

cattle. In addition, all state and cooperative farms received some form of state subsidy, and about 27 percent received fixed-rate subsidies for farming low-quality land. Hungary's large-scale farming sector has become increasingly concentrated as state and cooperative farms have merged. Between 1960 and 1986, the number of agricultural cooperatives dropped by 72 percent to 1,260. The amount of arable land per cooperative stood at 3,024 hectares in 1986.

Small-Scale Farming

Small-scale producers—individuals or small groups who tilled household plots or operated small farms—concentrated more on labor-intensive output or activities in which the risks of investment were to be assumed by those doing the work. In the late 1980s, Hungary had three types of small-scale farming units: approximately 623,000 household plots of cooperative members, about 792,000 small auxiliary farms of nonagricultural or state-farm employees, and a few private farms. Approximately 63 percent of the population participated in the small-scale agriculture sector. The combined contribution of household plots and auxiliary and private farms to gross agricultural output was 31.5 percent in 1975 and 31.3 percent in 1986. Successful integration of small-scale farming into the agricultural sector kept overall production levels high.

The government imposed few restrictions on the sale of output in the small-scale farming sector, and supply and demand determined prices in a free market. Thus, producers had a strong incentive to work hard and produce more. Before the mid-1980s, cooperatives were hostile to household producers. In the late 1980s, however, officials proclaimed that private household farming was a permanent component of agriculture under socialism. The central government encouraged cooperatives to assist members with household plots to boost production by providing seed, transport, machinery, advice, and marketing assistance. Household producers also qualified for subsidies, tax breaks, loans, and discount prices for machinery and agricultural chemicals. Regulations limited the size of household plots to 0.6 hectares of cropland and 0.23 hectares of vineyard or orchard per worker. The government abandoned earlier limits on livestock. Pensioners, housewives, dependents, and others performed most of the work on household plots and small-scale farms. Their labor amounted to about 2.3 billion man-hours annually and outstripped the total number of man-hours worked in large-scale farming.

Ancillary Activities

The 1968 reform allowed agricultural enterprises to diversify into nonagricultural economic activities. Twenty years later, the government granted cooperatives the right to change their internal structure, to engage in new activities, and to extend their involvement in nonagricultural production without the permission of regulatory bodies. State farms and cooperatives were engaged in food processing, machinery repair, parts production for manufacturing enterprises, construction, trade, and the restaurant business. Several large-scale farms developed ''technically operated production systems'' for crop production, horticulture, and animal husbandry that used state-of-the-art technology. The farms sold these systems, which included input and output programs and consulting services, to other large-scale farms. These systems have accelerated the modernization of the agricultural sector.

The nonagricultural activities of state and cooperative farms have increased profits and tapped manpower once lost during off-seasons. In 1983 nonagricultural activities accounted for 47 percent of state-farm profits and 44 percent of cooperative-farm profits. By 1988 the farms' ancillary activities accounted for more than 7 percent of Hungary's total industrial production.

Private Activity

Perhaps the most significant aspect of the economic reform and the leadership's most striking break with Marxist-Leninist ideology has been the expansion of the private sector. The government decided to allow the emergence of private enterprise because it believed that private entrepreneurs would increase competition in some areas, fill demand for goods and services that state-owned enterprises had been unable or unwilling to meet, and create work for people who would lose their jobs as unprofitable enterprises reorganized to become more efficient. Changes in the Domestic Trade Law in 1986 opened new areas to private entrepreneurs, especially in services. A year later, the government allowed private businesses in a number of categories to employ twenty to thirty workers. A law passed in 1988 allowed the establishment of limited partnerships, which could include an unlimited number of partners and employees and operate in all fields except finance. However, private businesses continued to suffer from restricted access to capital from state-owned banks and thus had to depend on private and extralegal loans that did not carry full legal protection.

Small family-operated businesses remained the rule in the private sector, and in 1987 only about 300 private businesses employed more than six people. Most entrepreneurs ran their businesses as a part-time activity in order to supplement their earnings from a job in the state sector that provided social benefits. In addition to the household plots, private farms, economic work cooperatives, and independent contract work associations, private business people were operating 28,965 retail shops, restaurants, and other businesses in 1986, more than twice the total in 1980. In addition to private restaurants and stores, which accounted for about 7 percent of domestic trade in 1985, entrepreneurs had established computer-software companies, construction firms, service businesses, and a theater. Individuals could also contract to operate state- or cooperative-owned retail stores or restaurants and retain all profits over the contract cost. In 1986 contractors operated about 12 percent of Hungary's shops and 41 percent of its food-service establishments.

Conflict-Resolution Mechanisms

In countries with a command economy, the ruling communist party generally denies the existence of antagonistic conflicts that arise between groups with differing economic interests. The leadership suppresses open expression of these conflicts and resolves them behind closed doors. When authorities reform such an economic system by introducing market mechanisms, they acknowledge that economic, and therefore political, conflict arises between various groups and that the authorities must devise political mechanisms to resolve them. The market mechanism resolves certain conflicts, such as disputes between buyers and sellers or creditors and borrowers, but new conflict-resolution mechanisms are necessary to resolve broader conflicts.

As of the late 1980s, the Hungarian leadership had chosen to tackle this problem by implementing conflict-resolution devices that did not threaten the HSWP's monopoly of power. The government introduced electoral reform, granted the judiciary greater independence to administer justice according to legal criteria, and encouraged trade unions to become more active in defending the interests of the workers against enterprise managers (see State Apparatus, ch. 4). Trade unions obtained the right to call strikes when management decisions disregarded the law or breached a collective contract or "socialist morality"; however, the authorities tolerated no conflict between the unions' goals and those of the regime (see Mass Organizations, ch. 2). The government also encouraged the press to publicize abuses of power by management (see Mass Media, ch. 4).

After the 1968 reform, organizations also emerged to represent economic interest groups, and some of these organizations acquired a growing influence in party and governmental decision making. The government required private and semiprivate entrepreneurs to become members of the Small Craftsmen's National Association, the Small Tradesmen's National Association, or the Industrial Cooperatives' National Council. In 1988, about 900 small entrepreneurs founded the National Association of Entrepreneurs, which worked through Hungary's Chamber of Commerce. In the late 1980s, the National Association of Entrepreneurs actively participated in the debate over a law on business organization.

Economic Sectors

Industry overtook agriculture in the postwar era to become the predominant economic sector. In 1986 industry accounted for 50.7 percent of gross output; agriculture and forestry, 18.2 percent; nonmaterial branches (generally services), 11.3 percent; construction, 6.3 percent; transportation, post, and telecommunications, 5.6 percent; trade, 6.1 percent; and water works supply, 1 percent (see table 6, Appendix). Industry has taken up most of the investment funds since the early 1960s, followed by consumer goods and services (the nonmaterial branches), agriculture, and transportation and communications (see table 7, Appendix). Despite a growing private sector, state-owned enterprises dominated the economy. According to official statistics, state-owned enterprises produced 63.4 percent of national income in 1986; the cooperative sector produced 23 percent; auxiliary farms of private individuals, 6.6 percent; and the private sector, 7 percent (see table 8, Appendix). Economists estimated that the extralegal "third economy" also made up a significant portion of the country's economic life.

Industry

Energy and raw-material extraction accounted for 13.1 percent of gross industrial production in 1986; metallurgy contributed 8.3 percent; engineering, 25.6 percent; chemicals, 19.1 percent; light industry, 12.9 percent; food processing, 16.8 percent; building materials, 3.2 percent; and other miscellaneous industry, 1 percent. As this industrial profile shows, Hungary's industry continued to reflect the Stalinist emphasis on heavy industry inherited from the immediate postwar period.

Energy

Chronic coal-mining problems and shrinking domestic hydrocarbon reserves have plagued the economy since the mid-1970s. The reliance on imported energy increased steadily from 37.2 percent in 1970 to 51.3 percent in 1986. The Soviet Union furnished most of Hungary's energy imports, but Soviet production setbacks and demands for better trade terms complicated Hungary's energy supply problems after the mid-1980s. Analysts expected the Soviet Union to demand more and better-quality goods from Hungary in exchange for its energy exports in the 1990s (see Relations with the Soviet Union, ch. 4).

Hungary slashed investment in coal mining in the late 1960s and 1970s, when Soviet oil and natural gas were less expensive alternate fuels. Consequently, coal's share of domestic energy production dropped from 62.7 percent in 1970 to 36.6 percent in 1986. Coal accounted for about 26 percent of Hungary's energy consumption. In the early 1980s, rising oil and natural gas prices prompted Hungary to reopen the flow of investment into coal mining but the country still suffered from a severe shortage of miners, and its mines were unable to keep pace with rising demand. The government approved substantial pay increases for miners in order to attract new workers. In 1986 Hungary's mines employed 79,566 workers who labored between sixty and seventy hours per week and produced coal worth about US$779 million. Total annual coal output has hovered around 24 million tons since 1975, but hard-coal production actually fell by about 23 percent between 1975 and

1986, and the calorific value of coal output declined by about 18 percent in the same period. Coal, coke, and briquette imports totaled US$268 million in 1986.

Hydrocarbons, including oil, propane, natural gas, and gasoline, accounted for 61 percent of total energy consumption in 1986. Natural-gas production has increased considerably since the mid-1960s, exceeding 7 billion cubic meters in 1986 and 1987. Domestic consumption, however, has far outstripped production since 1970, nearly doubling from 5.9 billion cubic meters in 1975 to 11.5 billion in 1986. Hungary's wells supplied about 94.8 percent of its natural-gas consumption in 1970 but only 66.1 percent in 1986. Natural-gas imports totaled 4.8 billion cubic meters in 1986 and cost about US$366 million. The Soviet Union supplied Hungary with about 90 percent of its natural-gas imports.

Hungarian wells have pumped about 2 million tons of crude oil yearly since 1975, mostly from the Szeged region, but observers expected production to decline after 1990. Oil imports totaled US$1.1 billion in 1986, while exports added up to about US$332 million. Hungary exported oil by reselling Iranian and other Middle Eastern oil acquired in various compensation schemes.

Hungary launched an energy rationalization program in the early 1980s aimed at maintaining levels of domestic oil and gas production attained in the mid-1980s, increasing exploration, and substituting natural gas and other fuels for oil. The conservation program, backed by stiff price hikes, netted positive results. Oil consumption dipped from 12.5 million tons in 1979 to 9.1 million tons in 1985, and Hungary's imports of petroleum and petroleum products dropped from about US$1.3 billion in 1985 to US$1.1 billion in 1986.

Hungary's power plants had a 6.8-billion-kilowatt capacity in 1986 and generated 28 billion kilowatt-hours of electricity, almost double the amount generated in 1970. The increase failed, however, to keep pace with demand as consumption rose from 17.9 billion kilowatt-hours in 1970 to 38.6 billion in 1986. Hungary overcame the 1986 shortfall by importing 11.9 billion kilowatt-hours of electricity. Transmission lines from the Soviet Union carried about one-third of Hungary's imported electricity.

In the late 1980s, thermal power stations generated 70 percent of Hungary's electricity and burned about 65 percent of Hungary's brown coal production and nearly all of its lignite output. Hungary has constructed large thermal power stations in the last 15 years, including a 1.9-million-kilowatt heat and power plant at Százhalombatta in Pest County that generated almost 40 percent of the country's electricity.

Southern Hungary's uranium reserves supplied the 880-million-kilowatt Paks nuclear power plant in Tolna County, the country's only nuclear power facility. The plant's first reactor went on line in 1983, and its second followed a year later. In 1986 the plant generated 7.4 billion kilowatt-hours, or about 26.5 percent of the nation's electricity output and 19.2 percent of its consumption. Hungary and the Soviet Union agreed in 1986 to build four additional 440-megawatt reactors at Paks in the next decade. Officials hoped that the plant would supply about 40 percent of Hungary's electricity by the early 2000s.

In the late 1980s, Hungary's hydroelectric power stations generated less than 1 percent of the country's electricity, but Hungary has joined with Czechoslovakia to build two hydroelectric power stations on the Danube at Gabčíkovo in Czechoslovakia and at Nagymaros in Hungary. The project, which was scheduled for completion by 1993, received Austrian financial assistance (see Relations with Other Communist Neighbors, ch. 4). However, in May 1989 the Hungarian government suspended work on the power station because of public concern over the damage it threatened to cause to the environment. The power stations' total projected capacity was 3.6 billion kilowatt-hours per year, and their estimated cost was US$1.4 billion.

Mineral Mining and Metallurgy

The aluminum industry developed rapidly after World War II and in the late 1980s employed more than 40,000 workers. The production of bauxite (used in making aluminum) more than doubled since the war, reaching more than 3 million tons in 1986, while alumina (aluminum oxide) output totaled 856,000 tons in the same year. Increased bauxite production was depleting deposits near the surface, however, and costly deep mining had become necessary. Conversion of alumina into aluminum is highly energy intensive, and a lack of inexpensive electricity prevented Hungary from converting more than 25 percent of its alumina output. Therefore, Hungary had to import about 65 percent of the aluminum consumed by its factories each year. Under an exchange agreement signed in 1985, Hungary exported 530,000 tons of alumina to the Soviet Union each year for smelting in return for 205,000 tons of aluminum. In the late 1980s, Hungary received significantly less aluminum per unit of alumina than under previous agreements, largely because the price of aluminum had risen against the price of alumina on world markets since the 1960s. In the late 1980s, Hungary's aluminum-fabrication industry concentrated more on manufacturing semifinished and specialized products and less on bulk production of the metal in the unfinished form. The major aluminum processing plant was the Light Metal Works at Székesfehérvár, which had a capacity of approximately 100,000 tons per year in the late 1970s. Hungary exported much of its bauxite, alumina, and aluminum to the Comecon countries.

Soviet technology and raw-material inputs were key factors in the development of Hungary's iron and steel industry in the 1950s. The large steel mills at Dunaújváros in Fehér County, Ozd, Miskolc, and Budapest have used local low-grade iron ore, but more than 80 percent of their raw-material input originated in the Soviet Union. In the late 1980s, the industry suffered from several major problems. First, Hungary's iron and steel mills were less cost effective than West European mills because, among other factors, Hungary had to pay to transport and process Soviet ore that had only a relatively low (45–50 percent) iron content. Second, the prices Hungary received for its iron and steel exports to convertible-currency markets had fallen. These exports generated losses for the industry, but Hungary continued the trade for several reasons: the domestic market could not absorb enough output to maintain satisfactory use of the country's mill capacity, the state subsidized losses on metallurgical exports, and export income provided the industry with the grounds to increase wages. The industry underwent a sweeping reorganization as part of a 1987 restructuring program that included the elimination of 2,400 jobs. Hungary produced no iron ore in 1986, and analysts expected the country to reduce iron and steel output by up to 10 percent in 1988.

Engineering and Chemicals

Throughout the postwar period, the engineering and chemical branches have been the most important in Hungary's industrial sector. The engineering sector employed about 32 percent of Hungary's industrial workers in 1986 and produced 25.5 percent of the country's total industrial output; the chemical sector employed 7.5 percent of the industrial work force and accounted for 19 percent of industrial output.

Hungary's vehicle-manufacturing subbranch emphasized production of buses and axle housing and accounted for about 28 percent of the engineering branch's output in 1986. Comecon assigned production of large buses to Hungary in the 1950s. Hungary's Ikarus bus enterprise became the world's fourth-largest bus producer, accounting for about 20 percent of the world's bus exports in 1980. The engineering branch also produced tractors, diesel locomotives, river vessels, floating cranes, machine tools, passenger elevators, batteries, telephone equipment, lighting equipment, and other products.

The chemical branch grew faster than any of the other branches after the 1960s, and in 1986 the chemical branch's 133 enterprises accounted for 19 percent of industrial output. Its main subbranches produced fertilizers, pharmaceuticals, and petrochemicals. The pharmaceutical industry was more than a century old and accounted for 1.5 percent of world production. Hungary ranked second to Switzerland in per capita pharmaceutical exports and fifth in the world in overall pharmaceutical exports. It was also Comecon's largest pharmaceutical supplier. Pharmaceutical production expanded at a nearly 18 percent annual rate since 1960, satisfying 80 percent of Hungary's market. Western markets purchased 40 percent of Hungary's pharmaceutical exports. In 1986 the pharmaceutical industry's output totaled about US$513 million.

Rapidly rising demand for synthetic materials and a desire to replace imports with domestic production prompted Hungary to begin developing a petrochemical industry on the eve of the 1973 oil crisis. The project, which required significant investment and integration with the Soviet economy, proceeded despite the changes that the oil crisis brought to the market. In 1989 five Hungarian refineries produced petroleum products, but four were too small to take advantage of economies of scale. Analysts expected a large portion of Hungary's refinery capacity to remain underutilized until sometime in the 1990s. The synthetic-fiber, chemical-additive, and phosphorus-fertilizer branches were especially problematic.

Light Industry and Food Processing

The government neglected the consumer-oriented light-industry and food-processing branches of the economy during its push to develop heavy industry in the 1950s. This policy resulted in shortages, poor quality, a narrow product mix, and slow development of new products. Since that time, production of light industrial goods, such as textiles, garments, furniture, pulp, and other products, has improved significantly. In 1985 Hungary exported about 65 percent of its silk fabric production, 50 percent of its clothing and footwear output, and 25 percent of its textiles.

Although Hungary has not had food shortages for years, its food-processing branch has modernized slowly and produces only a limited range of foodstuffs. Given the importance of foodstuffs in Hungary's export profile, the slow growth of the food-processing industry has prevented the country from capturing potential markets. In the late 1980s, the branch's main products included wine, flour, canned goods, sugar, beer, dairy products, and meat products. After 1970 many state and collective farms set up food-processing operations (see Agricultural Organization, this ch.).

High Technology

Hungary has developed a small but viable computer industry since the late 1960s. The Videoton electronics firm, which was one of Eastern Europe's most aggressive computer manufacturers, developed several computer models in the 1970s and has exported its computer products to West Germany, Austria, Finland, and the Comecon countries. Economic reforms in the early 1980s cleared the way for state firms, research institutes, private partnerships, and even individuals to manufacture personal computers. Hungary possessed an impressive software-producing capability, and many Western countries have purchased Hungarian programs or subcontracted with Hungarian designers to develop software. Unfortunately, the microelectronics industry suffered a major blow in 1986 when a fire gutted its most important plant, located in Budapest. In 1986 the high-technology industry produced 5,128 small computers, 145,717 semiconductors, and 20,690 integrated circuits.

Agriculture

The success of the agricultural sector in large part has underpinned the country's high standard of living relative to the other countries of Eastern Europe. Agriculture provided an abundance of food, that, at least until the late 1980s, reinforced social and political stability. Hungary's farms also supplied about 25 percent of the country's convertible-currency exports, which were key because they funded imports of Western technology vital to industrial development. But the agricultural system also faced several nagging problems, including high production costs, difficulties in carving out new markets, and dependence on imported protein feeds, agricultural machinery, nonnitrogenous fertilizers, and other inputs.

In the late 1980s, agricultural output was divided about equally between plant and animal production. The country's main crops were corn, wheat, and sugar beets; its main animal products were poultry, hogs, eggs, and milk (see table 9, Appendix). Hungary had been a net exporter of grain since 1973 and in the late 1980s was Eastern Europe's largest exporter of meat and meat products.

Hungarian agriculture's capital-intensive nature and its scale of production were closer to West European than East European levels. The agricultural sector used fewer but more powerful tractors in 1986 (53,947) than it did in 1970 (67,472). Hungary also reduced the amount of irrigated land and cut fertilizer use. Irrigated lands shrank from an average of 249,100 hectares in the 1971–75 period to 162,600 hectares in 1986. Fertilizer use fell from 224 kilograms per hectare in 1975 to 212 in 1986, while manure use grew slightly.

In 1986 the 129 state farms worked 26.1 percent of the country's cultivated land (2,159 hectares), employed 17.6 percent of the agricultural work force (163,000), and produced 17.6 percent of the country's agricultural gross output (about US$1.2 billion—see table 10, Appendix). Cooperative farming remained the largest social sector in the agricultural sector. In 1986 some 1,260 cooperative farms worked 76 percent of the cultivated land, employed 74.1 percent of the agricultural work force (691,000), and produced 51 percent of the country's agricultural gross output (US$3.4 billion).

In 1986 cooperative-farm members' household plots combined with auxiliary and private farms to produce 31.3 percent of agricultural gross output. These producers also supplied significant portions of specific crop and animal products. For example, in 1986 household plots and private farms produced 76 percent of Hungary's potatoes, 74.7 percent of its vegetables, 58.6 percent of its fruits, 48.8 percent of its wine grapes, 24.1 percent of its cattle, 55.5 percent of its pigs, and 43.1 percent of its poultry.

Construction

In 1986 the construction sector accounted for nearly US$5 billion in production. The sector had 165 state-owned construction enterprises employing an average of 1,223 workers, 531 cooperative construction firms with an average of 123 workers, 460 economic work cooperatives with an average of 11 members, 2,745 private economic partnerships with an average of 8.5 members, and 24,229 private crafts people who mainly worked alone. Housing accounted for 33.8 percent of construction activity in 1986; industrial building construction accounted for 9.5 percent; roadway construction, 6.4 percent; and cultural and educational buildings, 5.1 percent.

Transportation and Telecommunications

The nation's transportation and communications systems were highly centralized because of Budapest's importance as the capital and principal urban center (see fig. 7). Like other East European countries, Hungary redirected much of its transport system after World War II to accommodate a dramatic increase in trade with the Soviet Union. Despite the fact that transportation employed about 14 percent of the total work force in the late 1980s, transportation delays were frequent.

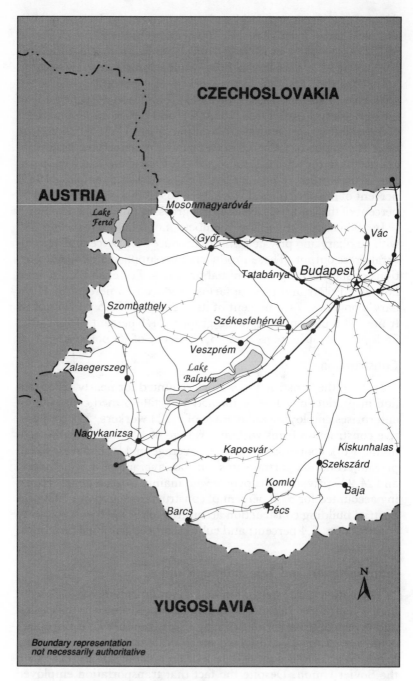

Figure 7. Transportation System, 1989

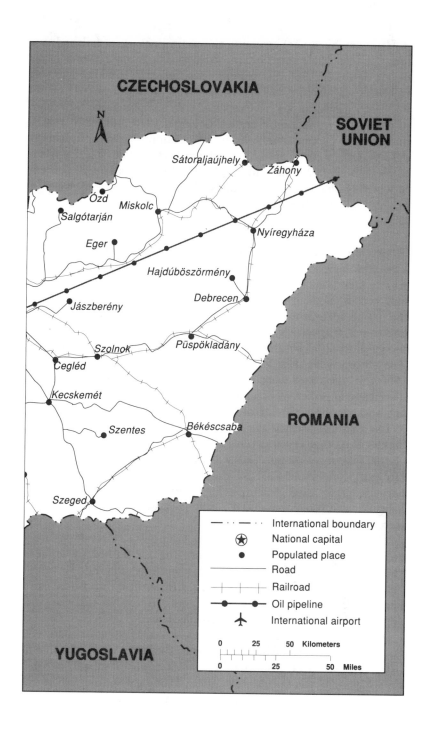

CZECHOSLOVAKIA

SOVIET
UNION

Sátoraljaújhely
Záhony

Ózd
Miskolc
Salgótarján

Eger

Nyíregyháza

Hajdúböszörmény

Debrecen

Jászberény

Szolnok
Püspökladány

Cegléd

Kecskemét

Szentes
Békéscsaba

ROMANIA

Szeged

International boundary
National capital
Populated place
Road
Railroad
Oil pipeline
International airport

0   25   50   Kilometers

0   25   50   Miles

YUGOSLAVIA

145

Hungary began constructing the main lines of its railroad system between 1850 and 1900 in order to link Budapest with other major cities. In 1986 this system consisted of 7,769 kilometers of rail lines, of which 1,128 kilometers were double tracked. Diesel and electric locomotives have replaced steam engines, and the length of electrified track almost tripled between 1970 and 1986, reaching about 25 percent of the system. The country's two rail-transport enterprises employed about 134,000 workers in 1986. The railroads carried about 119 million tons of freight in 1986, about 20 percent of which were coal and other fuels; they also carried 232,920 passengers. The system improved its fuel consumption per ton-kilometer from 1,235 kilojoules in 1970 to 322 in 1986.

In the late 1980s, Hungary's 140,163 kilometers of roadway, 21 percent of which were paved with asphalt or concrete, carried a greater volume of freight than the railroad. The country's sixty-six truck and bus fleets carried 4.5 million passengers and 572 million tons of goods in 1986 and employed 122,000 workers. In 1986 the nation's truck and bus fleets totaled 163,151 and 25,920 trucks and buses, respectively, more than double their size in 1970; passenger automobiles numbered 1,538,900, including 1,500,800 private automobiles. Hungary has modernized its road system since 1950, but the roads were still inadequate to handle the country's increasing number of private automobiles and heavier domestic and international truck traffic.

The Danube formed the largest part of Hungary's 1,622 kilometers of navigable waterway. The principal port was Budapest's Csepel free port. Dunaúváros was also an important port. In 1986 Hungary's fleet included 52 passenger boats, 41 tugboats, 236 barges, and 15 seagoing ships. The river transport system carried 3.4 million tons of cargo and 4.1 million passengers, most of whom were tourists.

The national airline, MALEV, flew twenty-four aircraft on forty-one international routes in 1986, carrying 1.2 million passengers and 16,372 tons of cargo. Hungary discontinued domestic air transport in 1969. Several major Western airlines flew into Budapest's Ferihegy Airport, which in 1986 recorded 18,025 takeoffs and departures and served 2.3 million passengers.

A 5,604-kilometer pipeline network linked Hungary's main oil- and natural gas-producing centers with Budapest and other major cities. The system transported 20.2 million tons of oil and natural gas in 1986. In the mid- to late 1980s, Hungary annually received about 1.2 billion cubic meters of Soviet natural gas through the two Friendship pipelines and an additional 4 billion cubic meters through the Alliance pipeline. In 1986 Hungary and the Soviet Union began

Train station in Csopak
Courtesy Gustav Forster

negotiations on Hungary's participation in the construction of what was to be the longest natural gas pipeline in the world. Planners projected completion by 1990.

In the late 1980s, Hungary continued to suffer from a severe shortage of telephone lines. In 1986 the country had 770,200 telephones, including 524,600 private telephones, which gave it about 145 telephones per 1,000 persons, an increase of 46 percent since 1975. Despite this increase, the average wait for the installation of a telephone was about fifteen years. Telephone possession was one of the clearest indicators of class distinctions in Hungary. A 1983 study showed that only 6 percent of Hungary's unskilled and semiskilled workers had a telephone, while 40 percent of professionals had them. The telephone system did not have the capacity to accommodate computer telecommunications. In the late 1980s, Hungary had two television channels, and it issued more than 2.9 million television licenses in 1986. Licenses to purchase radios were not required after 1980.

Private Sector

Small private enterprises have multiplied rapidly since 1982, when the government eased legal restrictions. But in 1989, the

147

private sector as a whole still made up only a small portion of the economy. The government's tally of persons who reported private economic activity as their primary occupation showed that the private sector accounted for only 5.1 percent of active earners in 1986. The private sector did, however, account for 13.7 percent of the active earners involved in construction, 16.5 percent of those in transport, and 12.6 percent of those in personal- or economic-service businesses. In 1986 Hungary had 150,664 private crafts people, up from 86,303 in 1970 and 111,960 in 1981. Just under 52 percent of the crafts people plied their trade as their principal occupation, about 12 percent were pensioners, and 36 percent were employed full time in other fields.

As officially defined, the private sector's contribution to net material product rose from only 2.6 percent in 1970 to 3.5 percent in 1980 and 7 percent in 1986. Although the private sector's portion of industrial production only increased from 1 percent in 1970 to 1.8 percent in 1986, its share of the construction industry more than doubled from 6.3 percent in 1970 to 14.5 percent in 1986.

The Third Economy

A semilegal or illegal "third economy" operated in Hungary as it did in other communist countries. Activities in the third economy included holding unofficial second jobs, moonlighting on vacations and sick leave, performing outside work during work hours, dealing in illegally imported or pilfered goods, lending money at high rates, renting property illegally, evading taxes, and bribing or "tipping" doctors, lawyers, store clerks, and others. In a 1983 survey, 60 percent of hospital patients admitted they had paid their doctors even though Hungary had free national health care. Many of those active in the third economy had become relatively rich, and tension sometimes arose between the third economy's "haves" and the law-abiding "have-nots." The press attributed the third economy's existence to three main factors: shortages of certain goods and services, an inflation rate that made supplementary income necessary, and the fact that many enterprises possessed monopolies on certain goods and services.

Hungary's Economic Research Institute has estimated that in the early 1980s Hungarians generated the equivalent of about US$2 billion per year in unreported income, which equaled about 20 to 25 percent of their total income and 16 percent of domestic net material product. The newly enacted personal-income and value-added taxes were in part an attempt to tax unreported incomes, and the government created a special office to investigate persons who displayed expensive tastes but reported relatively low incomes

Bus station in Mezőkövesd
Courtesy Sam and Sarah Stulberg

(see Economic Regulators, this ch.). Many pro-reform economists opposed measures to snuff out illegal economic activities, arguing instead for liberalizing private-enterprise laws to include many activities considered illegal.

Foreign Trade

Hungary can compensate for its paucity of natural resources only by engaging in foreign trade, which, in the late 1980s, accounted for about half the country's national income. After the Great Depression, commerce with Germany dominated Hungary's external trade, and agricultural products accounted for most Hungarian exports. After World War II, the communist government limited its economic contacts with the West, and the Soviet Union became the country's principal trading partner. Hungary significantly increased trade with the West after the 1968 economic reforms when its economy could no longer grow without imports of technology and raw materials from the Western nations. It signed the General Agreement on Tariffs and Trade in 1973 and, in the midst of a balance of payments crisis, joined the World Bank and the International Monetary Fund (IMF—see Glossary) in 1982. Although in the late 1980s the Soviet Union remained Hungary's principal trading partner, almost half of Hungary's trade was with Western countries. Production shortfalls had forced the Soviet Union to slow exports

149

of oil and other key raw materials, forcing Hungary to strive to utilize raw materials more efficiently and increase exports to the West to pay for additional raw-material imports. The need to boost efficiency and make Hungarian goods competitive on Western markets also prodded the government to undertake economic reforms.

Ever-worsening terms of trade, increasing Western protectionism, reduced access to foreign credit, interest-rate increases, and the generally slow response of Hungarian enterprises to changing market conditions brought the country serious foreign-trade imbalances after 1987. The net foreign hard currency debt more than doubled from US$7 billion in 1981 to US$15.5 billion in 1987, making its per capita foreign debt the highest among the communist states. Hungary had to spend between 65 and 70 percent of its convertible-currency earnings to service its debt. Despite the fact that the economy did not meet the government's debt-reduction target in 1987, analysts predicted that the convertible-currency debt crisis would recede as a government austerity program began to take hold. The debt and current accounts deficit, which analysts estimated to be US$1.2 billion in 1987, prompted Hungary to conclude a standby credit agreement with the IMF in 1988.

Organization of Foreign Trade

The government maintained a state monopoly on foreign trade until 1988, when it began allowing all but a few production enterprises to participate in foreign trade. In 1989 the country's once-powerful foreign-trade enterprises still existed, but they held exclusive trading rights on only a narrow range of goods. The Ministry of Trade's chief control instrument on foreign trade was the licensing of imports and exports, which the ministry could use to avoid balance of trade and balance of payments disequilibria. For example, the ministry could deny an enterprise a license to export a product to the Comecon market in order to encourage its export to the convertible-currency market. The ministry issued import licenses according to a list of priority items. Highest-priority goods were those necessary to maintain current production, including raw materials, semifinished goods, and spare parts. Second priority went to capital goods and machinery that could quickly boost hard-currency exports. Basic consumer goods and nonessential and luxury items constituted the two lowest categories. The government enacted austerity measures in 1988 that limited imports almost exclusively to the most essential items.

Cooperation Agreements and Joint Ventures

In addition to engaging in direct foreign trade in the late 1980s, enterprises and foreign firms could enter into cooperation agreements or joint ventures that gave Hungary access to Western technology and opened new markets. Cooperation agreements took many forms, including the sale of a plant or production line with partial payment to the seller made from products from the plant or line; the subcontracting of a domestic firm to manufacture products; license agreements under which the foreign partner provided technology to the Hungarian partner to produce a particular product; and production agreements under which the foreign partner provided equipment, expertise, manufacturing processes, and sometimes financing to the domestic enterprise and then purchased all or part of the output. In the late 1980s, the government levied a 40-percent tax on profits from cooperation agreements. The 1988 foreign-trade law gave Hungarian enterprises greater freedom to conclude cooperation agreements. Western companies tended to prefer cooperation agreements to joint ventures because cooperation agreements were more flexible and carried less risk.

The closest cooperation between Hungarian and foreign firms took place through joint ventures, which the government first legalized in 1972. In a joint venture, a foreign firm and a domestic enterprise each put up capital to establish a new company to produce goods or services. Hungarian law required that the Hungarian enterprise hold at least a 51 percent stake, except in such areas as banking and services, in which the Ministry of Finance could authorize the foreign owner to be the majority shareholder. In 1985 a West German cosmetics firm became the first nonbanking Western firm to hold a 51 percent stake in a joint venture with a Hungarian enterprise. The government levied a 20-percent profit tax on joint ventures and permitted the foreign partner to repatriate its share of the earnings in convertible currency. The Hungarian National Bank guaranteed the foreign partner's share of the capital against state takeover subsequent to the agreement. When a joint venture terminated, the foreign firm could repatriate its share of the capital investment. Only three joint ventures were operating in 1977, and in an effort to entice more foreign partners the government broadened the joint-venture law several times and created customs-free zones in 1983. The number of joint ventures rose to 35 in 1984 and to more than 100 in 1988. Most of Hungary's joint ventures involved companies from West Germany, Austria, Switzerland, the United States, and Sweden.

Hungarian enterprises frequently requested foreign partners in joint ventures or cooperation agreements to take payment in kind and then market the goods in the West. Analysts estimated that these and other countertrade arrangements have made up a sizable share of Hungary's trade with the West since the early 1970s, but

151

exact figures were unavailable in mid-1989. The frequency and size of requests for countertrade increased after Hungary began austerity measures to reduce its foreign debt and trade deficit in 1988.

Trade Volume and Structure

Total trade turnover, at 1986 prices, rose from US$13.4 billion in 1981 to US$18.8 billion in 1986. Hungary's exports increased from US$6.5 billion to US$9.2 billion in the same period, while its imports increased from US$6.9 billion to US$9.6 billion.

The principal imports were crude oil, coal, iron ore, copper, raw materials for the plastics industry, chemical fibers, artificial fertilizers, paper, cotton, animal feed, and capital and consumer goods. Raw materials, semifinished goods, and spare parts accounted for 44.8 percent of imports in 1986. Energy imports increased from 6 percent of total imports in 1970 to 19.4 percent in 1986 (see table 11, Appendix).

Hungary's main exports included agricultural products, pharmaceuticals, bauxite, machine tools, buses, telecommunications and electronic equipment, lighting equipment, industrial rubber goods, ball bearings, rolled steel and aluminum, clothing, and footwear. In 1986 raw materials, semifinished goods, and spare parts accounted for 30.2 percent of exports. Exports of machinery, transport equipment, and capital goods increased from 16.7 percent of total exports in 1970 to 30 percent in 1986. Likewise, agricultural exports rose from 7.4 percent of total exports in 1970 to 20.1 percent in 1986. Grain exports increased from an average of about 1 million tons a year from 1976–80 to nearly 2.2 million tons in 1986. Meat exports also rose, from an average of 285,000 tons a year from 1976–80 to 421,000 tons in 1986 (see table 12, Appendix).

Tourism enhanced Hungary's hard-currency balance sheet. The number of foreign tourists visiting Hungary rose from 4 million in 1984 to 10.6 million in 1986, including 2 million from noncommunist countries. Tourist spending netted Hungary about US$371 million in 1986. Most visitors came from Czechoslovakia, Poland, Austria, and Yugoslavia; approximately 117,000 Americans visited the country in 1985. About 6.3 million Hungarians traveled abroad in 1986, mostly in Eastern Europe. In 1988 the government further eased restrictions on its citizens' foreign travel.

Trade Partners

Hungary's foreign trade was about evenly split between the Comecon countries and the West. Trade with the Comecon market accounted for 53.1 percent of its trade turnover in 1986, an increase from 49.3 percent in 1980. Total trade turnover with the

Comecon countries, measured at 1986 prices, increased from about US$6.8 billion in 1981 to US$10 billion in 1986. Exports to the Comecon countries increased from US$3.6 billion to US$5.1 billion in the same period, while its imports from those countries rose from US$3.3 billion to US$4.9 billion.

In 1986 more than 90 percent of the country's energy imports, 42.5 percent of its raw- and basic-materials imports, and more than 60 percent of its capital-goods imports came from the Comecon countries. In addition, 48 percent of exports of raw-materials and semifinished goods, 84.3 percent of its machinery and capital-goods exports, and more than half of the exports of industrial consumer goods and agricultural products went to the Comecon market.

In the late 1980s, the Soviet Union, plus three other Comecon countries—the German Democratic Republic (East Germany), Czechoslovakia, and Poland—made up four of Hungary's six most important trading partners. The Soviet Union was Hungary's main trading partner, accounting for more than 30 percent of Hungary's overall trade and 60 percent of its trade with the Comecon countries (see table 13, Appendix). Raw materials and energy dominated the structure of Soviet-Hungarian trade. Under the Soviet-Hungarian trade agreement for the Seventh Five-Year Plan (1986–90), Hungary agreed to export foodstuffs, computers, telecommunications equipment, buses, and other finished goods to the Soviet Union. In turn, Hungary imported mining equipment, heavy machinery, some consumer goods, and even larger amounts of Soviet raw materials and energy than it did in the preceding plan. East Germany, Hungary's third largest trading partner, Czechoslovakia, and Poland accounted for about 16.5 percent of Hungary's overall trade and 31.1 percent of its trade with the Comecon countries.

About half of Hungary's trade was with Western countries. Trade turnover with the Western world was US$7.9 billion in 1986; imports totaled US$4.2 billion, and exports amounted to US$3.7 billion.

In June 1988, Hungary and the European Economic Community (EEC) signed a ten-year trade agreement, the first of its kind between the EEC and a Comecon country. The agreement provided for a reduction of quotas on about 2,000 items by 1995. Hungarian officials estimated that the trade would boost Hungary's hard-currency exports from US$25 million to US$50 million by 1995. In 1987 the EEC countries accounted for 24.4 percent of Hungary's imports and 19.9 percent of its exports. Hungary accumulated a US$5 billion trade deficit with the EEC countries between 1979 and 1986.

West Germany was Hungary's largest Western trading partner and second largest trading partner overall. Raw materials and semifinished goods made up about 65 percent of the US$1.2 billion of goods that Hungary imported from West Germany in 1986; machinery and equipment made up about another 20 percent. Hungary's exports to West Germany totaled US$771 million and included foodstuffs, live animals, machinery, chemical products, textiles, clothing, pharmaceuticals, and aluminum products. As of 1987, West German banks had furnished Hungary with more than US$16 billion in loans; in the same year, the West German government guaranteed a twelve-year credit for Hungary, marking the first time that the Hungarian government has accepted credits backed by a foreign government. In addition, Hungary and West Germany concluded an investment protection agreement in 1986 under which the Bonn government, based on Hungarian assurances, guaranteed that West German firms with investments in Hungary would be able to repatriate their profits and not be subject to nationalization of their assets. In 1987 West German firms had about 330 cooperation agreements with Hungarian firms; more than half were in engineering and machine industries. Siemens, Krupp, Telefunken, Volkswagen, and smaller West German firms were involved in about thirty joint ventures with Hungarian enterprises (see Relations with the West, ch. 4).

Austria was Hungary's second largest Western trading partner. In 1987 Hungary imported Austrian goods worth US$574 million and exported US$594 million in goods to Austria. In 1987 Austrian and Hungarian firms were engaged in 120 cooperation agreements and fourteen joint ventures.

Hungary and the United States signed their first trade agreement in 1978, and Hungarian goods bound for American ports enjoyed most-favored-nation status. In 1988 ten United States-Hungarian joint ventures operated in Hungary, but, excluding Citibank Budapest's holdings, the total of United States capital invested in Hungary stood at a mere US$58 million. In 1987 bilateral United States-Hungarian trade reached its highest mark ever at more than US$500 million. Exports to the United States, however, accounted for only 2.3 percent of Hungary's exports in 1986, and imports barely exceeded 2 percent of Hungary's total imports.

Trade relations with Japan were growing as Hungary sought Japanese capital and technology and hoped to gain a share of the Japanese market as that country opened its doors to foreign trade. Hungary imported US$142 million worth of Japanese goods in 1986 while exporting only US$42.4 million in goods. Basic materials and semifinished goods accounted for more than half of Hungary's

Japanese imports; machinery and consumer goods accounted for 27 percent and 19 percent, respectively. More than 65 percent of Hungary's exports to Japan were basic materials and semifinished products, including pharmaceuticals, aluminum, and chemical products; foodstuffs accounted for another 16 percent. In addition, Hungary and Japan formed their first joint venture in 1984 to produce polyethylene sheets for insulation.

Hungary's trade with developing countries totaled about US$1.4 billion in 1986 and represented a 7.3 percent share of its total trade, down from 9.5 percent in 1980. Exports to the developing world consisted of machinery, vehicles, industrial consumer goods, and agricultural goods. Hungary imported from the developing countries tropical foods and other agricultural products, petroleum oil, clothing, carpets, electrical appliances, and steel products. In 1985 Hungary joined the International Finance Corporation and the International Development Association, both of which are World Bank affiliates.

Finally, trade with China rose dramatically from about US$112.7 million in 1984 to US$343.9 million in 1986. However, China accounted for less than 2 percent of Hungary's trade in 1986.

Domestic Consumption

Hungary's domestic trade sector differed significantly from the cumbersome rationing system that existed in most centrally planned economies. And since Hungary began implementing economic reforms, the production sectors of the economy funneled through the trade sector a far better supply and variety of goods and services than Hungarians had enjoyed earlier. By the late 1980s, Hungary's economy had largely overcome the supply shortages that tormented both producers and consumers in countries with command economies. Still, many Hungarians lived at or below the officially recognized poverty level (see Social Relations in the 1980s, ch. 2).

Domestic Trade Sector

The domestic trade sector consisted of state- and cooperative-owned wholesale and retail enterprises and privately owned stores and restaurants. The Ministry of Trade oversaw the state-owned trade enterprises, and all state and cooperative commercial enterprises could engage in both wholesale and retail trade. Private merchants were not required to purchase goods from the wholesale dealers, but they were barred from functioning as wholesalers themselves. In 1986 Hungary had 17,222 state retail stores, 20,163 cooperative ones, and 22,230 private ones. Private contractors managed about 12 percent of the total number of state and cooperative-owned shops. About 75 percent of the 445,000 people working in the trade sector were women. Wages in the sector were 10 percent lower than the national average, which may account for the fact that the sector had high employee turnover. In 1985 Hungary had 102 shops that sold imported goods for foreign currency with annual sales topping US$20 million.

The largest retail trade enterprise in Hungary was the Skala-Coop chain, which several cooperative associations founded in 1974. Skala-Coop began purchasing goods directly from manufacturers and used modern marketing techniques, flashy advertising, an aggressive expansion policy, and consumer credit to capture about 13 percent of the country's entire trade by 1986. The chain also became the first large trade enterprise to gain direct foreign-trade rights.

Standard of Living

In 1989 the supply and selection of food and other consumer goods in Hungary exceeded those in most other East European countries, and Hungarians as a whole suffered nothing similar to the hardship that the Romanians and Bulgarians endured in the 1980s as a result of government-ordered energy cutbacks. In 1986 Hungary's per capita meat consumption was the highest in Eastern Europe, while its egg consumption ranked among the highest. Per capita consumption of meat, fish, milk and dairy products, eggs, vegetables, potatoes, coffee, wine, beer, and hard liquor all increased significantly between 1950 and 1984. In 1960 the majority of households had both a bicycle and a radio, 20 percent owned a washing machine, and a few even possessed a television, a refrigerator, or an automobile. By 1984, 96 out of 100 households owned a washing machine, every household owned a refrigerator, and the ratio of television sets to households was 108 to 100. The quality and variety of durable consumer goods on sale had also improved. As in other societies, purchase of luxury items was the prerogative of higher-income groups. For example, in the late 1980s automobiles were owned mostly by upper- and middle-income households. As of 1984, only 34 out of 100 households owned an automobile.

In 1986 the total disposable income of all Hungarians was the equivalent of US$17.2 billion. Hungarians spent 88 percent of that income, saved 6.2 percent, and invested 5.8 percent in building their own housing. Foodstuffs accounted for 27.1 percent of personal spending; services, 26.6 percent; beverages and tobacco, 14.6 percent; other consumer goods, 11.6 percent; clothing, 8.2 percent;

Váci utca, main shopping district, Budapest
Courtesy Scott Edelman

durable goods, 7.9 percent; and heating and energy, 4 percent. The state paid the cost of medical and other social services (see Health, ch. 2).

Official Hungarian sources reported that the average per capita monthly wage was 6,000 forints in 1988, about 14 percent above the officially recognized poverty level of 5,200 forints (US$84). Economists estimated that between 25 and 40 percent of the people lived below the poverty level.

Economic Policy and Performance, 1945–85

After 1949 Hungary's communist government under Mátyás Rákosi applied the Soviet model for economic development (see Postwar Hungary, ch. 1). The government used coercion and brutality to collectivize agriculture, and it squeezed profits from the country's farms to finance rapid expansion of heavy industry, which attracted more than 90 percent of total industrial investment. At first Hungary concentrated on producing primarily the same assortment of goods it had produced before the war, including locomotives and railroad cars. Despite its poor resource base and its favorable opportunities to specialize in other forms of production, Hungary developed new heavy industry in order to bolster further

157

domestic growth and produce exports to pay for raw-material imports (see table 14, Appendix). The Soviet Union became Hungary's principal trade partner, supplying crude oil, iron ore, and much of the capital for Hungary's iron and steel industry. Heavy Soviet demand also led Hungary to develop shipbuilding and textile industries. Trade with the West declined considerably. Soviet pressure, a Western trade embargo, and Hungarian policies favoring domestic and regional autarky combined to reduce the flow of goods between Hungary and the West to a trickle during the Cold War period.

Rákosi's regime also established wage controls and a two-tier price system made up of producer and consumer prices, which the government controlled separately. In the early 1950s, the authorities used these new controls to limit domestic demand and cut relative labor costs by tripling consumer prices and holding back wages. Popular dissatisfaction mounted as the economy suffered from material shortages, export difficulties, and mounting foreign debt. Agricultural growth also stagnated, and the area of cultivated land actually decreased.

During the thaw after Soviet dictator Joseph Stalin died in 1953, Imre Nagy became Hungary's prime minister and, following the Soviet example, implemented an economic policy known as the New Course. Nagy's administration halted the collectivization drive, allowed farmers to leave collective farms, abolished compulsory production quotas, raised procurement prices for farm products, and increased investment in agriculture. Nagy also shifted investment from heavy industry to consumer-goods production. The economic system itself, however, remained unchanged, and plan fulfillment actually worsened after 1953.

Hard-line party members soon undermined Nagy, and Rákosi regained control in 1955. The collectivization drive began anew, and the government redirected investment back to heavy industry before the cataclysmic Revolution of 1956 brought the country's economy to a standstill. According to official statistics, the economy registered an 11-percent negative growth in 1956. After the revolution, János Kádár and others in the new leadership understood that they had to gear their economic policies toward improving the population's living standard, and they recognized that practical considerations had to temper their commitment to the tenets of Marxism-Leninism as defined by the Soviet Union. From 1957 to 1960, consumption grew more rapidly than national income as the government tried to assuage popular discontent. Per capita real income was 54 percent higher in 1960 than it had been in 1950.

In 1959 the Kádár government began a second major collectivization drive. Instead of using coercion, however, the government

Shops in Zalaegerszeg
Courtesy John Tarafas

offered peasants incentives to join cooperative or collective farms. The campaign ended in 1962 after more than 95 percent of agricultural land had come under the socialist sector's control. During the 1960s and 1970s, the Hungarian government made significant investments in agriculture and raised farm prices in an effort to make the sector viable. Agricultural mechanization also expanded by 50 percent.

During the 1960s, the government gave high priority to expanding the industrial sector's engineering and chemical branches. Production of buses, machine tools, precision instruments, and telecommunications equipment received the most attention in the engineering sector. The chemical sector focused on artificial-fertilizer, plastic, and synthetic-fiber production. The Hungarian and Comecon markets were the government's primary targets, and the policies resulted in increased imports of energy, raw materials, and semifinished goods.

By the mid-1960s, the government realized that the policy for industrial expansion it had followed since 1949 was no longer viable. Although the economy was growing steadily and the population's living standard was improving, key factors limited further growth. Returns from mining were diminishing, and Hungary had

159

exhausted previously untapped manpower reserves. The government recognized that the efficiency of Hungary's industries lagged well behind that of Western industries and that its communication and transportation infrastructures were so inadequate that they retarded further economic growth. The Comecon countries were unable to supply Hungary with sufficient energy, raw materials, and technology to achieve further growth, and Hungary's leaders realized that the country would have to seek these critical inputs from the West. The government introduced the NEM in 1968 in order to improve enterprise efficiency and make its goods more competitive on world markets.

From 1968 to 1972, the NEM and a favorable economic environment contributed to good economic performance. The economy grew steadily, neither unemployment nor inflation was apparent; and the country's convertible-currency balance of payments was in equilibrium as exports to Western markets grew more rapidly than its imports. Cooperative farms and factories rapidly increased production of goods and services that were lacking before the reform. By about 1970, Hungary had reached the status of a medium-developed country. Its industry was producing 40 to 50 percent of the gross domestic product, while agriculture was contributing less than 20 percent.

In 1973 and 1974, in the midst of the Fourth Five-Year Plan (1971–75) world oil prices skyrocketed. Hungary's terms of trade, that is, the ratio of the prices Hungary received for its exports to the prices it had to pay for its imports, deteriorated considerably. The leadership responded to the new conditions with several major policy errors, which reversed the changes that had taken place under NEM. First, policy makers assumed world oil prices would soon return to earlier levels and concluded that the economy could be shielded from the capitalist world's crisis. The government did this shielding by subsidizing enterprises hard hit by rising energy costs and taxing the profits of enterprises that benefited from the high world prices. Second, the authorities chose to accelerate economic growth to deal with Hungary's deteriorating terms of trade. The Fifth Five-Year Plan (1976–80) emphasized industrial expansion and modernization and provided for a significant increase in investment. The share of gross investment in the gross domestic product climbed from 34 percent in 1970 to 41 percent in 1978. Third, the government used pre-1974 price and demand figures to justify launching major projects that the economy at that time could not carry out efficiently. Finally, planners earmarked significant investment resources to increase the country's capacity to produce energy, basic materials, and simple semifinished goods in order to meet domestic demand and increase exports to the Comecon markets. However, Hungary's investments did not spawn a modern manufacturing capacity, which is the kind of industrial capacity needed to produce output for sale on the convertible-currency market.

Decision makers discovered to their chagrin that they could not protect the economy from the world price increases. Because the economy depended on energy and raw-material imports, accelerated economic growth required increased imports of raw materials and energy that Hungary could not obtain from the Comecon countries. Thus, Hungary had to turn to the convertible-currency market to obtain a greater proportion of its inputs. In the 1970s, Hungary's spending on consumption and investment outstripped what its economy produced by an annual average of 2.2 percent; in 1978 alone it spent 5 percent more. The export earnings did not cover the cost of imports, convertible-currency trade deficits quickly piled up, and the government used foreign credits to finance the deficits. In addition, the government's efforts to shield the country's enterprises from Western price increases backfired as Hungary's structure of production and investment never adjusted to world demand. Antireform politicians and managers of large enterprises won partial reinstatement of the command economy by the mid-1970s. This recentralization exacerbated Hungary's economic woes by further isolating Hungary's enterprises from market forces and prompting managers to show inadequate concern for efficiency, waste, and the competitiveness of their products on world markets.

Hungary's economic policy makers realized by 1978 that if the economy continued to run trade deficits, the country would soon be unable to honor its debt obligations. In 1978 the HSWP decided to revive the NEM. A year later, the government implemented a stabilization program aimed at, among other things, redirecting the economy away from heavy industry, improving the convertible-currency trade balance, and shrinking the country's foreign debt. The program's architects planned to maintain current levels of material consumption for several years in order to maximize convertible-currency exports; at the same time, they planned to cut spending by reducing investment.

New external shock waves rocked the economy in the late 1970s, further eroding Hungary's terms of trade and undercutting the country's creditworthiness despite the reduction in investment. Oil prices rose dramatically and precipitated a world recession. Soon interest rates rose, and Western banks reduced the flow of credits to the East European countries in 1982 as a result of Poland's debt moratorium, Romania's insolvency, and the economic sanctions levied by the United States against Poland after the declaration of martial law in December 1981. The interest-rate increases helped to increase Hungary's hard-currency debt (see table 15, Appendix). Before the rates rose, Hungary relied heavily on floating-rate, short-term loans whose maturities were poorly staggered. In 1981 more than 80 percent of Hungary's US$8.7 billion convertible-currency debt was due within five years, and debt-servicing costs consumed about 33 percent of Hungary's convertible-currency earnings. In 1982 a liquidity crisis in Hungary shook the confidence of Western bankers, and for several months the country was unable to negotiate new credits from the West.

Eager to avoid debt rescheduling, Hungary joined the IMF and the World Bank in 1982 and received from them about US$2 billion in loans. In addition, Hungary introduced a stricter stabilization program and obtained bridge financing from the Bank for International Settlements. The leadership also renewed its support for economic reforms, which creditors viewed as a positive step toward more efficient use of resources and improvement of the country's balance of payments.

Under the new stabilization program, spending on investment and consumption, which had outstripped the amount the economy had produced by 6.9 percent from 1974 to 1978, fell to 1 percent less than production from 1979 to 1983. By 1985 Hungary had slashed its investment spending to about US$5.2 billion, 21.8 percent less than in 1981. The government also increased prices steeply. Hungary's Sixth Five-Year Plan (1981–85) called for greater austerity, efficiency, and profitability, and it forecast growth of 14 percent to 17 percent over the previous plan period. The economy, however, grew by only 7 percent. Industrial production rose only 12 percent, far below the planned growth of 19 to 22 percent. Agricultural output rose 12 percent over the previous plan period, while the Hungarians' real per capita income increased 7 to 8 percent. Planners targeted exports to increase by 37 to 39 percent and imports by 18 to 19 percent; exports, however, rose only 27 percent, while imports increased merely 6 percent.

The Seventh Five-Year Plan, 1986–90

In the Seventh Five-Year Plan period (1986–90), the leadership expected the economy to supply consumers with a greater assortment of foodstuffs, to improve the country's balance of payments by raising exports, and to increase productivity and profitability. Planners called for the net material product to grow by 15 to 17 percent over the 1985 level. The plan also called for industrial production to rise by 14 to 16 percent over the 1981–85 plan period; agricultural output to rise 7 to 10 percent; domestic consumption, 13 to 16 percent; real per capita income, 9 to 11 percent; and both imports and exports, 16 to 18 percent.

In 1986 Hungary's national income grew by only 0.5 percent, far short of the planned 2.3 to 2.7 percent. Both industrial production, which rose 1.8 percent, and agricultural production, which increased 1 percent, were far short of planned levels. At the same time, domestic consumption jumped 3 percent, consumer prices increased 5.3 percent, and per capita real income rose 0.7 percent. Investment grew by 5.1 percent, the maximum envisaged in the plan. Compared with the previous year, Hungary's imports in 1986 rose by 2.5 percent, while exports fell by 2 percent.

In 1987 national income grew as planned by about 2 percent. Industrial production rose by 3.7 percent, higher than the planned 2 to 2.5 percent, but bad weather caused agricultural output to fall far short of the 1986–90 plan target. In 1987 investment grew by 6 percent, approximately six times the planned amount, while per capita income remained at the 1986 level. The government increased prices on energy and foodstuffs sharply in 1987 and increased prices on 53 percent of the items sold in the country in January 1988. The consumer price index for the first eight months of 1988 was 16 percent higher than for the same period in 1987, while the official inflation rate was 17.7 percent. The government also devalued the forint an average of 13 percent against Western currencies in 1987.

Hungary has enjoyed favorable treatment from international capital markets despite disappointing growth and continued deterioration in external accounts. At least one author has pointed out that Western banks have shown the greatest confidence in countries such as Hungary that have good debt-servicing records, regardless of the countries' economic problems. In the latter half of the 1980s, Japanese banks increased their loan portfolio and sought to make low-risk loans to East European countries, particularly Hungary. Hungary took on loans to restructure its industry, renovate power stations, implement its energy rationalization program, upgrade its telecommunications system, and finance foreign trade.

The current value of Hungarian exports declined between 1984 and 1986, and the country ran a US$548 million trade deficit in 1986 followed by a US$390 million deficit in 1987. As a result of a deteriorating convertible-currency current account, Hungary's debt more than doubled in two years from US$8.6 billion in 1985 to US$18 billion in December 1987, and the country's ratio of debt to convertible-currency exports reached 338 percent by 1986. In

May 1988, the government signed a US$350 million standby credit agreement with the IMF and announced strict austerity measures. In the first nine months of 1988, Hungary's convertible-currency trade netted a US$200 million surplus, rebounding from the US$470 million deficit it showed in the same period in 1987. The surplus marked the first time since 1981 that Hungary's foreign trade with developed countries was balanced.

In 1989 the government sought to achieve large trade surpluses with convertible-currency markets that would enable the country to repay its foreign debt and import raw materials and technology. Hungary could create those surpluses only by importing more raw materials or using existing resources more efficiently. Hungary's major supplier, the Soviet Union, was experiencing shortfalls in oil and other raw-materials production that were forcing it to slow and even reduce exports. Thus, Hungary again was forced to turn to convertible-currency markets to secure additional raw materials. Because neither Hungary nor the Comecon countries generally had the technology and know-how that were necessary to improve efficiency and increase the output of products marketable in the West, Hungary also had to turn to the West for technology. The leadership understood that realizing the benefits of economic relations with the West required significant further improvement of the economic system. At the Thirteenth Party Congress in March 1985, the leadership reaffirmed its commitment to continue economic reforms that promised to improve efficiency and enhance the competitiveness of Hungary's exports. In the last years of the Kádár era, the government had enacted many such reform measures, but the implementation and enforcement of these measures were uneven. With the emergence of a new leadership under Károly Grósz in 1988, Hungary appeared poised to enact and implement more dramatic reforms, including political changes, that could radically alter the country's economic life in the 1990s.

* * *

Hungary's economic reforms proceeded so rapidly in the 1980s that works on the country's economic system have become outdated shortly after appearing in print. The most comprehensive description of Hungary's economic reforms available is Paul Marer's "Economic Reform in Hungary" in *East European Economies: Slow Growth in the 1980s,* a publication of the United States Congress. Marer's *East-West Technology Transfer: Study of Hungary* also examines Hungary's economic reforms and provides detailed analyses of Hungary's major economic sectors and its trade with the Comecon countries and the West. János Kornai's article "The Hungarian Reform Process: Visions, Hopes, and Reality" provides a sober assessment of the reforms by a leading Hungarian economist. Also interesting are Paul Hare's "Industrial Development of Hungary since World War II" and "The Beginnings of Institutional Reform in Hungary." (For further information and complete citations, see Bibliography.)

Chapter 4. Government and Politics

Chapter 4. Government and Politics

A small-town judge, 1916

THE POLITICAL SYSTEM of the Hungarian People's Republic, like others in Eastern Europe, drew heavily upon a model first established in the Soviet Union. The leading political institution in the state was the ruling communist party, in this case the Hungarian Socialist Workers' Party. This monolithic, centralized party determined the basic economic, political, and social policies for the country as a whole, and the government implemented the party's decisions.

The Constitution, ratified in 1949 and amended considerably in 1972, grants political and economic rights to the people, prescribes civic duties, and establishes the institutions of government. According to the Constitution, the National Assembly (the parliament) holds supreme authority in the state. In fact, the Presidential Council, a standing body of the National Assembly that combined legislative and executive functions, assumed most of the duties of the National Assembly and those of a chief of state. The National Assembly, however, did provide a vehicle for expanded political participation. A 1983 amendment to the Constitution mandated multicandidate elections for most seats in the National Assembly. The Council of Ministers—the executive arm of the government—had primary responsibility for the economy. Within the party, the rank-and-file members had virtually no influence over decision making. The permanent party bureaucracy, headed by the Politburo and administered by the Secretariat, exercised supreme power within the party. These organs made policy for the party, enforced discipline, and regulated admissions. Middle-level organs managed policy on the county and district levels. Basic Organizations—on the lowest rung of the party hierarchy—carried out party activities in economic enterprises. The Patriotic People's Front served under the auspices of the party; this mass organization involved the citizenry in carrying out decisions made by the party. The mass media also served as instruments to generate popular support for the party's policies.

In May 1988, Károly Grósz succeeded János Kádár as general secretary of the party. Kádár had been leader of the party since the Soviet invasion of 1956. Mounting economic problems and general dissatisfaction with the pace of political reform led to the ouster of Kádár at the party's Third Party Conference.

Hungary's foreign policy positions generally coincided with those of the Soviet Union. Since 1986 these countries have supported each other's reform efforts. Nevertheless, Hungary displeased the Soviet Union with its efforts to establish an independent role for small- and medium-sized states in international affairs and to obtain Western economic assistance to help modernize its economy. Discord also emerged between Hungary and Romania—ostensibly another fraternal ally—over the latter's oppression of its Hungarian minority.

Constitutional Development

The theoretical foundations of Marxist-Leninist constitutions differ from those underlying Western, democratic constitutions. The latter are fundamentally prescriptive: they define a set of political relations between government and people that ought to exist. By contrast, Marxist-Leninist constitutions attempt to reflect reality by describing an existing set of political relationships. As these political relationships evolve over time, the regime alters the constitution to reflect these changes. The Hungarian Constitution serves several political purposes. It attempts to mobilize the populace in support of the regime's goals. The Preamble of the Constitution formally calls upon the people to promote the construction of socialism and communism. In addition, the Constitution demands that the most loyal sections of the population advance the regime's goals through greater efforts and initiative. The Preamble also offers justifications for the regime's existence by describing the historical past that led to Marxist-Leninist rule.

The Constitution does, however, bear some similarity to democratic constitutions. Like Western constitutions, the Hungarian Constitution establishes the rights and duties of the citizenry, although it devotes more attention to the latter than democratic constitutions. In addition, the Constitution specifies the institutions of government and the relations among them. It is, however, much more detailed in this regard than most democratic constitutions.

The Constitutional Law Council, formed in 1983, had some power to enforce observance of constitutional principles. The council, a fifteen-member body subordinate to the National Assembly, monitored decrees, laws, and resolutions issued by government bodies to ensure their conformity with the Constitution.

Constitution of 1949

In June 1948, the Hungarian Workers' Party (on November 1, 1956, renamed the Hungarian Socialist Workers' Party—HSWP) sought to legitimate the fundamental changes that had taken place in the state, the economy, and the society and directed the government's Council of Ministers to begin work on a constitution. The

Council of Ministers formed a Drafting Committee, which submitted a proposed Constitution on August 5, 1949. The National Assembly ratified the Constitution on August 20, 1949, thus making a new national holiday that coincided with the traditional holiday of the feast of Saint Stephen.

The regime modeled its Constitution on the 1936 "Stalin" constitution of the Soviet Union. As of the late 1980s, its basic features remained in effect, although the regime added important amendments in 1950, 1953, 1954, 1972 and 1983. The 1949 Constitution contained a sociopolitical program dictated by the Soviet Union and listed the achievements of Hungary's "people's democracy" (see Rákosi's Rule, ch. 1). The government, with its ministerial system, collective presidency, and powerless legislature, resembled the Soviet system of the Stalinist period. The Constitution also created the local council system and new kinds of judicial institutions, and it laid the groundwork for the country's system of public prosecutors (see State Apparatus, this ch.). Only Chapter IX, which described the national flag and coat of arms, had a specifically Hungarian character.

Amendments of 1972

To keep pace with the changes that had taken place in Hungary since Kádár became first secretary of the HSWP in 1956, the regime changed every chapter of the Constitution in 1972. According to Hungarian political scientist István Kovács, the 1972 amendments "brought into harmony the wording of the Constitution and the socialist transformation of the country between 1949 and 1972." Thus, the Constitution describes the achievements of the Kádár regime. It also provides a constitutional basis for the regime's efforts to gain the allegiance of all Hungarians by replacing the term *workers,* the only group that the 1949 Constitution entitled to full civil rights, with the term *citizens.* The changes in 1972 signaled a break with Hungary's Stalinist past and the beginning of a new, more benevolent phase in regime-society relations.

The Constitution, as amended in 1972, plays several important roles in Hungarian political life. Most important, the Constitution provides justifications for the emergence and development of the regime itself, as well as for the political forces that shaped its character. The Preamble refers to the Marxist-Leninist regime as the product of more than 1,000 years of Hungarian history, thereby linking it with Hungarian tradition. It also draws on the heritage of the Hungarian Soviet Republic of 1919, thus attempting to create a socialist state tradition in Hungary and link itself to that tradition (see Political and Economic Life, 1905–19, ch. 1).

In justifying the regime, the Constitution attempts to establish the legitimacy of the political system. The Constitution defines the Hungarian People's Republic as a socialist state in which all power belongs to the working people. It labels the Patriotic People's Front (PPF) as a movement uniting all social groups for the resolution of political, economic, and cultural problems. Chapter I, Article 15, establishes the orientation of Hungary's foreign policy by stating that the country forms part of the world socialist system and seeks to develop its friendship with other socialist states. Finally, Chapter IX of the Constitution defines visual symbols for the Hungarian People's Republic by describing the coat of arms and the flag of the state and by locating the country's capital in Budapest.

In establishing the country's political system, the Constitution fixes the HSWP as the leading force in society. Although the Constitution does not formally proscribe other political parties, neither does it provide for their existence. On November 10, 1988, however, the Council of Ministers took the first in a series of steps required to legalize the existence of other parties when it approved draft laws on the rights of assembly and association. The National Assembly approved these new laws on January 11, 1989. According to the new laws, county courts were to register these associations and could not refuse to register them if they met the law's requirements. Thus, private individuals, legal entities, and unofficial groups could set up political parties if their programs observed the law. A separate statute was to deal with matters such as registration, supervision, and dissolution of the parties. A new constitution, which was to be ready for ratification in 1990, would determine the role and status of political parties other than the HSWP in society. Taking advantage of this change in the political atmosphere, other political parties, which had been disbanded in the late 1940s, began to re-emerge in the late 1980s. For example, the Independent Smallholders' Party announced it would resume its activities. The Social Democratic Party and the National Peasant Party also began to reorganize (see Coalition Government and Communist Takeover, ch. 1).

Having provided several kinds of justifications for the regime's existence, the Constitution proceeds to establish the institutions of government. The Constitution delineates the powers of the National Assembly, the Presidential Council, the Council of Ministers, and the local councils. The Constitution establishes a judicial system made up of the Supreme Court and a series of lower courts. The Constitution requires the National Assembly to elect a prosecutor general, who in turn appoints prosecutors at local levels.

Like constitutions in the West, the Hungarian Constitution describes civic and political rights. These rights include the guarantees of equality before the law and the personal freedom and inviolability of the citizenry; liberty of conscience and freedom of worship; freedom of speech, press, and assembly; right of association; and privacy of correspondence and the home. In line with the Marxist-Leninist ideology of the regime, the Constitution also guarantees certain social and economic rights, including the right to leisure time; the right to financial support for old age, disease, and disability; and the right to education.

The Constitution, however, limits citizens' exercise of their political rights. According to Chapter VII, Article 64, the Constitution guarantees the rights of speech, press, and assembly "in a manner conforming to the interests of socialism and the people." This clause allows the government to ban any activities it considers detrimental to its interests. Equally important, Chapter VII, Article 69, states that the "fundamental duty" of the citizenry is to "protect the property of the people, to consolidate social ownership, to increase the economic strength of the Hungarian People's Republic . . . to consolidate the order of society." Although in 1988 the United States Department of State found that Hungarians enjoyed relatively more liberties than their counterparts in other countries of Eastern Europe, duties to the state continued to take precedence over rights contained in the Constitution. The regime did not treat as inalienable the rights held by the people.

Furthermore, socioeconomic rights contained in the Constitution have acted not only as an economic safety net but also as a source of oppression for the people. For example, the right to work not only guaranteed employment but also allowed the regime to enforce compulsory employment for all adult males and all single females because the regime could best exercise power over the populace while they were at work. The right to leisure time allowed the regime to control the forms of entertainment that citizens could enjoy. And the right to primary and secondary education has meant little more than the obligation to listen to regime-sponsored efforts at political indoctrination.

Constitutional Law Council

In 1989 the Constitutional Law Council had the power to monitor constitutional life in Hungary, note possible violations of the Constitution, and initiate procedures to eliminate laws, decrees, and regulations that failed to conform to the Constitution. The National Assembly elected the fifteen members of the Constitutional Law Council, which included National Assembly delegates, the minister of justice, the president of the Supreme Court, the prosecutor general, and the chairman of the People's Control Committee (see State Apparatus, this ch.). The council was subordinate to the National Assembly and, unlike the United States Supreme Court, was not an independent body for judicial review.

In amending the Constitution to establish the Constitutional Law Council in 1983, the regime responded to demands of the public to promote the rule of law and to requests of constitutional lawyers to systematize laws, decrees, and regulations promulgated by the ministries. The council used reports of violations from "reliable entities," which included government agencies, the National Assembly, and the county and district councils. If the Constitutional Law Council found that a law, decree, or regulation violated the Constitution, the council mediated between the body that lodged the complaint and the government organ that issued the law, decree, or regulation. The council could suspend acts it deemed unconstitutional, but it could not repeal them.

Individual citizens lacked direct access to the Constitutional Law Council. In fact, only government organs in a position to violate the Constitution—the National Assembly, the Presidential Council, the ministries, and the county and district councils—had the right to initiate inquiries by this body. If a person submitted a case to the Constitutional Law Council, the council referred that person to the government organ best able to represent the case. However, authorized organs represented only their own viewpoints, not those of individuals. Furthermore, no religious body had access to the council; therefore, issues concerning church-state relations never appeared for review. In effect, the Constitutional Law Council was answerable only to governing organs, not to the Hungarian people.

State Apparatus

The political system of Hungary bore some similarity to a parliamentary form of government. In principle, power in the government emanated from the National Assembly, which elected its own leadership—the Presidential Council and its chairman, who served as chief of state—and the Council of Ministers, which formed the government (see fig. 8). The state apparatus, however, was not the center of political power in Hungary. The government merely executed policies designed by the HSWP. Within the government itself, power resided in the Council of Ministers and the Presidential Council. The National Assembly merely ratified decisions made elsewhere.

Government life centered on the Council of Ministers. The regime established the Council of Ministers in the immediate postwar period using the Soviet Council of Ministers as a model. The primary function of the Council of Ministers was to administer the economy. It also had the power to pass some legislation; the ministries could make laws in their own jurisdictions.

The Presidential Council—the collective chief of state—was modeled after the Soviet Union's Presidium of the Supreme Soviet. The council, headed by its chairman, combined legislative and executive functions. In fact, the Presidential Council passed most of the country's legislation.

The HSWP effectively exercised control over the government. In 1989 all members of the Council of Ministers and most members of the Presidential Council were party members and served on such party bodies as the Central Committee and the Politburo (see Party Structure, this ch.). As party leaders, government officials formulated economic, political, and social policies. These officials were subject to the norms of democratic centralism, which required them to carry out the directives of the HSWP or face party discipline (see Democratic Centralism, this ch.). Equally important, the party exercised control over these governmental institutions through its power of *nomenklatura* (see Glossary), a list of party and government positions for which the party had power to make appointments. The HSWP's Basic Organizations ensured that the staff of each ministry adhered to party policies on a day-to-day basis.

In the 1980s, the regime opened up the political system to a greater degree of popular participation. Although multicandidate elections had been permitted since the late 1960s, a 1983 amendment to the Constitution made mandatory the multicandidate elections for the National Assembly and the local councils. However, these elections took place under the auspices of the PPF, which guaranteed that candidates accepted its program. A national list of candidates to the National Assembly, who ran unopposed, did ensure the election of party and government luminaries, as well as of other figures of national importance. Nevertheless, in the 1985 elections many independent candidates, who were not among the PPF's original slate of nominees, succeeded in gaining seats in the National Assembly and the local councils. Significantly, although the regime structured the elections to favor its candidates, until mid-1989 the Hungarian electoral system was the most democratic in Eastern Europe.

The local councils had very little power. Ironically, their chief importance lay in administering those services, such as education, housing, and food supply, that had the greatest impact on people's lives.

Like other Marxist-Leninist regimes in the late 1980s, Hungary lacked an independent judiciary. The Supreme Court, together with

175

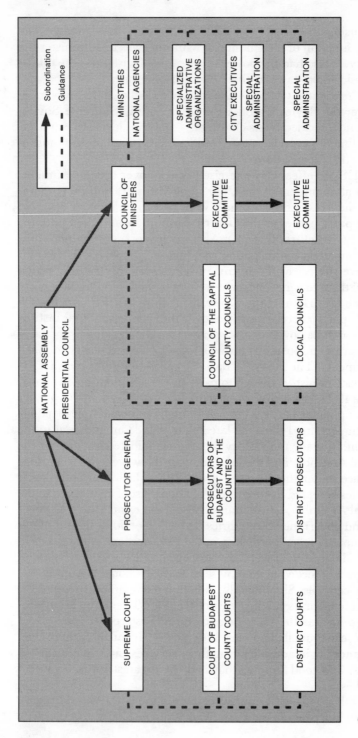

Source: Based on information from Hans-Georg Heinrich, *Hungary: Politics, Economics, and Society,* Boulder, Colorado, 1986, 70.

Figure 8. Government System, 1986

a system of lower courts at the county and district levels, had few duties and little power. The prosecutor general and his subordinates at the local levels represented the state in prosecuting persons accused of a crime. However, the law also obligated these officials to protect the rights of the citizenry and ensure a fair trial for the accused.

Council of Ministers

According to the Constitution, the Council of Ministers guided, influenced, and controlled the entire construction of the economic, political, and social system of socialism. The council had primary authority over economic decision making; it developed and implemented the regime's economic plans. Beginning in 1968 with the introduction of the New Economic Mechanism (NEM), an effort to relax central controls over the economy, the Council of Ministers played a particularly critical role within the political system (see Economic Policy and Performance 1945–85, ch. 3).

In 1989 the Council of Ministers consisted of a chairman (the prime minister), two deputy prime ministers, twelve ministers, the chairman of the National Planning Authority, the chairman of the People's Control Committee, and the chairman of the State Planning Committee. The number of ministries has varied over time. In 1989 they included agriculture and food, culture and education, defense, environmental protection and water management, finance, foreign affairs, health and social affairs, industry, internal affairs, justice, communications, construction, and trade. Other agencies also operated under the auspices of the Council of Ministers and in 1989 included the Central Statistical Office, the Hungarian National Bank, the National Price Office, the State Office for Church Affairs, the State Office for Youth and Sports, the Postal Service, and the State Wage and Labor Office.

Although the Council of Ministers devoted primary attention to the economy, according to the Constitution its first responsibility was to "safeguard and guarantee the political and social order of the state and the rights of the citizens." In 1989 other duties included enforcing laws and decree-laws, supporting scientific and cultural development, establishing a system for social and health services, and concluding and approving international agreements. According to Chapter III, Article 34, of the Constitution, a special act of the National Assembly may assign other duties to the Council of Ministers in addition to those described in the Constitution.

In 1989 ministers had no fixed term of office. Ministers served at the behest of the National Assembly and could, upon recommendation of the party, be recalled at any time.

Hungarian political scientist Mihály Bihari has argued that the Council of Ministers and the ministerial system institutionalized society's economic interests and their representation within the government. The ministerial departments made the most important decisions on the economy because they had the requisite knowledge at their disposal as a result of their day-to-day administration of issues under their jurisdiction. Although the National Assembly and, most often, the Presidential Council issued laws, regulations, and decrees, the ministries developed and selected the suggested proposals. Bargaining among ministries and within the Council of Ministers resolved policy differences on these proposals. All interested ministries had the opportunity to modify these proposals so that it was possible to discern the interests and political demands of the social groupings represented by each ministry.

The People's Control Committee functioned under the direction of the Council of Ministers. The committee supervised a hierarchy of similar committees at the local levels. The Presidential Council appointed members of the People's Control Committee, but volunteers staffed most of the positions at the local levels. The committees oversaw the operations of government organs, social organizations, and economic enterprises to ensure proper management and legality.

Presidential Council

In 1989 the Constitution described the Presidential Council as subordinate to the National Assembly and superordinate to the Council of Ministers. However, the Presidential Council was in fact the highest state organ and, because the National Assembly met so infrequently, it acted as an ersatz parliament. In early 1989, the chairman of the Presidential Council was Bruno F. Straub, at the time the only noncommunist chief of state in Eastern Europe.

The Presidential Council had combined legislative and executive powers. It set the date for elections to the National Assembly, convened the National Assembly, initiated legislation, and decreed national plebiscites. The Presidential Council also contributed to the normal functioning of state life by concluding and ratifying treaties, receiving the credentials of foreign ambassadors, electing professional judges, and conferring awards and titles. The Presidential Council supervised the local councils by setting the date for council elections, ensuring the rights of the councils, and dissolving those councils that infringed on the Constitution. When the National Assembly was not in session, the Presidential Council assumed the powers of a parliament. In fact, the Presidential Council performed most of the government's legislative work. (The

National Assembly usually approved the decree-laws of the Presidential Council at its next session.) In the event of war or threat to the security of the state, the Presidential Council could establish a National Defense Council with extraordinary powers.

In addition to these legislative and executive duties, the members of the Presidential Council undertook a number of other tasks. They participated in the committee work of the National Assembly (see National Assembly, this ch.), held meetings with constituents, and handled complaints about the bureaucracy from the citizenry. Members could represent Hungary abroad and hold meetings with foreign delegations. They also visited county and district governments and participated in awards ceremonies.

In 1989 the secretariat of the Presidential Council consisted of a division for justice, which handled pardons for criminals; a division for civil proceedings; a division for law; and a division for honors and decorations. These divisions had their own organizational statutes. The secretariat lacked a permanent organizational structure because new divisions could be created according to need.

In the late 1980s, the Presidential Council remained a rather secretive body. The media did not publish its discussions and debates. The Presidential Council also did not announce its voting procedures.

In 1989 the Presidential Council consisted of a chairman, two deputy chairmen, a secretary, and seventeen members at large. The National Assembly elected these members from among its own delegates, although the Central Committee of the HSWP actually made the choices. Both party members and nonparty members could be selected for the Presidential Council—including its leadership positions—although party members generally predominated. Three rules seemed to have governed the Central Committee's selections: the council had to be a representative body mirroring the occupational and social structure of the population, it had to contain a number of well-known people in public life, and it had to include several party leaders. The Presidential Council thus was made up of party leaders, as well as representatives of social and political groups, including national minorities, peasants, and women. Church leaders who supported the regime also were selected. A few members were nominated because of their policy expertise in a given field. For example, because the secretary not only supervised the secretariat of the council but also helped to determine its political line and handle its day-to-day affairs, that official usually had had previous experience in the personnel administration of the HSWP.

National Assembly

The Constitution designates the National Assembly as the supreme organ of state power. In reality the parliament played a limited role in the government. Until 1989, the 352-member unicameral National Assembly met only three or four times a year in sessions that lasted no longer than four days each. In addition to electing the membership of state and government bodies nominally subordinate to it, the National Assembly also enacted laws and approved the five-year economic plans. However, from 1980 through 1985 the National Assembly passed only eighteen bills, an insignificant number compared with those passed by the Presidential Council and the Council of Ministers. In the late 1980s, party leaders openly acknowledged that these two bodies made all the important decisions and that the National Assembly was merely a rubber stamp.

Delegates to the National Assembly did play several important roles. They contributed to the plenary discussions of the parliament, acted as members of the county groups, served their constituencies, and participated in the parliament's standing committees. Plenary sessions chiefly concerned local problems and were an attempt to use the parliament's publicity to pressure authorities on the distribution of funds. Delegates elected from each county formed county groups to promote the interests of their region. Because most counties had an urban-rural mix, formation of a common policy outlook was difficult. However, inasmuch as Hungary had more agricultural regions than industrial regions, agriculture enjoyed predominance. As servants of their constituencies, delegates reported on their activities in the National Assembly and attempted to resolve citizens' complaints against the bureaucracy.

The most important duties of the delegates concerned their work on the standing committees of the National Assembly. The National Assembly elected in 1985, in addition to legal, administrative, and judicial committees, had standing committees for construction and transport, culture, industry, trade, foreign affairs, agriculture, social and health affairs, infrastructural development and environmental protection, and planning and budgeting. During the 1980–85 convocation of the National Assembly, 221 out of the 352 delegates served on the standing committees, which met about 50 times a year. The committees discussed draft laws submitted by the Council of Ministers, usually proposing only small changes in the text. The committees did, however, have the power to reject the drafts at this stage. In the 1980s, the committees also actively supervised the implementation of laws. A parliamentary presidency, which consisted of the chairman and two deputy chairmen aided by a small bureau, coordinated the work of the committees.

Elections to the National Assembly

In 1983 the government instituted a new electoral system for the National Assembly and local councils to encourage more popular participation in governmental affairs. Before 1966 Hungary had used an electoral system in which a voter could vote only for or against the official slate of candidates. In 1966 the government initiated election procedures that made the nomination of more than one candidate possible; in the 1971 elections, 49 districts out of 352 nominated two or more candidates. By 1981, however, the number of multicandidate districts declined to fifteen, thus causing concern within the party leadership and eventually triggering reform.

In 1983 the regime instituted a new electoral system for several reasons. British authority Bill Lomax has written that Hungarian leaders "felt sufficient confidence that by granting measured degrees of independence and autonomy to society, they could win not just the passivity but the complicity if not quite the loyalty of major sections of the population." Through its multicandidate elections, the regime attempted to convince the populace that the political system was essentially democratic. The electoral system afforded the government the opportunity to mobilize people in support of a political campaign and thereby increase their political awareness. Finally, the elections provided an occasion for testing the HSWP's organizational and supervisory abilities.

The new rules compelled the nomination of several candidates in single-member districts. Both residents of the district and workers employed in the district but living elsewhere could participate in the nomination meetings. At the meetings, voters could ask questions of the candidates and comment on their programs with support or objections. The PPF organized the meetings and proposed the candidates. Nominations could also be submitted by other social and political organizations or persons in the district. All candidates, however, had to accept the PPF program to be eligible for nomination. Thus the procedure favored regime candidates and minimized the chances for independent candidates. For a candidate to gain nomination, 33.3 percent of the persons present at the meeting had to cast a "yes" vote. If no candidate received the required percentage, another nomination meeting was held. In addition, the rules stipulated that the number of nomination meetings equal the number of candidates, but each parliamentary district had to have at least two candidates and therefore two meetings. All proposals

National Parliament building
Courtesy Gustav Forster

for the nomination of independent candidates had to be resubmitted at the next meeting. The rules also allowed each citizen to vote for several nominees. Because the regime could use the PPF to mobilize large numbers of people against undesirable candidates, this rule discriminated against independent nominees.

The efforts of the dissident László Rajk to gain nomination illustrate the barriers faced by independent nominees. On April 18, 1985, at the first of the two required nomination meetings in the southern constituency of Budapest's fifth district, Rajk gained the support of about 40 percent of the 223 people present. At the second electoral meeting on April 22, the regime attempted to thwart Rajk's nomination. HSWP activists, plainclothes police, and factory workers filled the hall. Rajk's speech raised such controversial issues as conscientious objection to military service, the fate of the environment, and the problem of Hungarian minorities abroad (see Relations with Other Communist Neighbors, this ch.). At the second meeting, only about 27 percent of the 1,388 voters present supported Rajk.

In addition to the obligatory multiple candidacies, the new electoral system called for the establishment of a national list of thirty-five candidates to be elected without opposition. Politburo member Mihály Korom justified the national list by arguing that "important interests demand the representation of leading personalities" from society, culture, science, and the churches. Korom maintained that the "character of their work, the province of their activities go far beyond the boundaries of their electoral districts." The law was successful in promoting multiple candidacies throughout the country. In addition, some independent candidates gained nomination and election. Of the 352 National Assembly constituencies in the 1985 election, 298 had two candidates each, 50 had three candidates each, and 4 had four candidates each. Most of the triple and quadruple candidacies occurred in Borsod-Abaúj-Zemplén, Fejér, and Pest counties and in Budapest. Of the 152 people who were not originally on the PPF list and were nominated from the floor, 78 received the necessary one-third votes at two or more nominating meetings, and 51 of them had been proposed in addition to the 2 nominees successfully nominated by the PPF.

About 1.5 million people, or 20 percent of the country's eligible voters, participated in the nominating meetings for the 1985 elections to the National Assembly and the local councils. Approximately 150,000 people asked to speak out at the meetings in support of the proposed candidates.

In the general election, abstention rates were high by East European standards. Turnout in the whole country was 93.9 percent, down from 97 percent in 1980. The turnout in Budapest was 88.4 percent. The number of valid votes cast (votes submitted according to the rules) was 94.6 percent; in Budapest this figure was 92.3 percent. Negative votes—votes cast against all candidates on the ballot—amounted to 1.2 percent of valid votes.

Of the 352 electoral districts, 42 required runoff elections because no candidate could muster the required 50 percent plus one of the valid votes. Another eighty constituencies had close contests. Of the seventy-eight independents who gained nomination, forty-three won seats after runoff elections. Nevertheless, thirty-three of these forty-three candidates were party members. The proportion of independent candidates was quite low, but, according to American political scientist Barnabas Racz, their nomination marked an unprecedented development in the history of East European elections.

Although the 1985 election was democratic by East European standards, Hungarian dissidents and Western commentators pinpointed several troubling features. In most of the electoral districts, the two PPF candidates were the only nominees. In addition, only the priorities of the candidates differed, not their programs. The regime subjected campaign literature to strict copying regulations, and it took steps to limit publicity for candidates. Dissidents maintained that the procedures favored the big industrial enterprises, which packed nomination meetings with supporters for their preferred candidates. In turn, these candidates, once elected, formed parliamentary lobbies that supported increases in subsidies for the industries to which they owed their nomination.

County and District Government

In 1989 district government resembled that on the national level: a popularly elected local council chose an executive to administer the affairs of its jurisdiction. Communes (*község*), large communes (*nagyközség*), cities, and districts of Budapest elected councils on this level. District councils elected the county-level councils, which also chose an executive.

The councils served as legislatures for their jurisdictions, while a chairman and an executive committee, elected from the ranks, carried out the actual administration of government activities. The executive committee on the county level supervised the work of the executive committee on the district level. In turn, the Council of Ministers directed the work of the county executive committees. The chairmen of the county and district councils sat on the corresponding executive committees of the HSWP (see Party Structure, this ch.).

Executive committees on each level had their own administrative apparatus made up of specialized departments to manage government activities in their jurisdiction. Within their sphere of influence, the executive committees could appoint and remove the directors of branch organizations administering these services. However, these personnel decisions required approval by the executive committee at the county level or by the Council of Ministers. In addition, when the executive committee appointed local officials, it had to take into account the standards established for those positions by the Council of Ministers. The Council of Ministers also had the right to submit its own nominees for positions in the district and county administrations (see Council of Ministers, this ch.).

District and county government dealt with services that had the most immediate impact on the lives of the citizenry: education, housing, day care facilities, and medical care. In the late 1980s, the local government had jurisdiction over 90 percent of the preschool and day care facilities, all general (elementary) schools, most middle schools, 90 percent of government-owned housing, 80 percent of the hospital beds, and 70 percent of the libraries, theaters, and educational centers. The national government had direct control over areas such as railroads, waterways, postal and fire services, and communications. Local councils also had some power in passing a budget for their jurisdiction and to manage its execution.

In the late 1980s, county and district government had relatively large authority in managing the local economy. About 14,000 enterprises and firms meeting the needs of the local population were under their jurisdiction. The law allowed local governments to create these enterprises. The national government also permitted local government to approve the plans of these enterprises, which functioned mainly in the service sector.

Since 1983 multicandidate elections to the district councils have been mandatory. In the 1985 elections, an estimated 88,000 candidates competed for the 42,734 district seats. About 5.4 percent of district constituencies had triple candidacies, and 0.2 percent had quadruple candidacies. Reports of the nomination meetings indicated an average participation of from 200 to 400 people, a very small fraction of the approximately 30,000 people per district. In addition, problems emerged in many districts. In Bács-Kiskun County, the organizers combined the meetings of the twenty-seventh and twenty-eighth council districts and allowed them to vote jointly for each other's nominees. The PPF nullified the results. In Budapest two different constituencies nominated the same

City hall in Győr
Courtesy Gustav Forster

person. In 102 districts, the nominating meetings had to be repeated.

Judicial Organs

The district courts, labor courts, and military courts lay at the bottom of the judicial hierarchy. District courts were the courts of first instance in all disputes. Labor courts operated in Budapest and the counties, hearing cases on appeal from labor affairs arbitration committees and other extrajudicial entities dealing with labor matters. Military courts operated in garrisons and some military units, concerning themselves with military cases and other cases that affected national defense (see Military Justice, ch. 5). The Supreme Court heard appeals directly from the military courts.

County courts served as courts of first appeal for decisions of the district courts and the labor courts. The county courts also acted as courts of first instance in certain cases involving murder, willful homicide, and grave crimes against social property. These courts functioned as courts of first instance in civil suits of a certain magnitude directed against the state, government officials, or socialist enterprises.

The Supreme Court acted as the court of appeal for the county courts and the military courts. One of the judges of the Supreme Court or one of the court's judges working together with lay assessors (non-professional judges) could act as court of first instance for certain important cases. These decisions could then be appealed to a council of the Supreme Court. Councils of the Supreme Court specialized in military, civil, criminal, labor affairs, or economic cases. The Presidential Council of the Supreme Court heard appeals from these councils on points of law.

Professional judges and lay assessors presided over the courts. When courts on any level acted as courts of first instance, they consisted of a professional judge and two lay assessors, although the law provided for some exceptions. Courts hearing appeals consisted of three professional judges, with the exception of the Presidential Council of the Supreme Court, which was led by the council's president.

The Supreme Court could issue "guiding principles or decisions in principle" when guidance was necessary "in the interests of guaranteeing uniformity or on questions of legal interpretation." These decisions were binding on the lower courts. Other decisions of the Supreme Court were not binding, but they influenced the decisions of the lower courts.

The prosecutor general supervised observance of the law. This official, who was appointed by the National Assembly upon recommendation of the party's Central Committee, headed a hierarchy of prosecutorial offices organized on the county and district levels. The prosecutor general undertook criminal investigations and prosecutions and reviewed the legality of actions taken by governmental, social, and economic organs. Only the National Assembly, Presidential Council, and Council of Ministers were excluded from the authority of the prosecutor general.

Hungarian Socialist Workers' Party

The Hungarian Socialist Workers' Party (HSWP) formed the "revolutionary vanguard of the working class" that "organizes and guides the people in their struggle to construct a Socialist society." The ideology, method of decision making, and structure of the HSWP all derived from the Communist Party of the Soviet Union (CPSU). The method of decision making—democratic centralism—stifled intraparty dissent and secured the control of central party organs over the personnel appointments and the activities of lower party organs.

In the late 1980s, the HSWP was a top-down, centralized organization. In theory, representative party bodies such as the party congress held supreme decision-making authority. In practice, bodies such as the party congress and the Central Committee on the national level and the conference on the county and district levels were too large and met too infrequently to exercise decision-making power (see fig. 9). The Politburo and Secretariat centralized power on the national level, and the party bureaus did so on the county and district rungs of the hierarchy. The Basic Organization, the lowest level on the hierarchy, supervised the activities of rank-and-file members in factories, collective farms, and the armed forces.

The party, aiming to be a monolithic organization, enforced strict discipline on the membership for violating the Party Rules (see Glossary) and for infringing on the norms of democratic centralism. The party also attempted to preserve its elite status within society. Therefore, it was very selective in its recruitment policies. Although originally the self-proclaimed party of the working class, in the late 1980s the intelligentsia predominated in its ranks.

The PPF, a mass organization working under the direction of the party, acted as a "transmission belt" for party policies. As of the late 1980s, it had not yet carved out an independent role for itself in Hungarian politics.

Ideology

The HSWP, as a party created under the influence of the CPSU, generally adhered to the Soviet concept of Marxism-Leninism, which regarded the essence of socialism to be state ownership of the means of production, controlled by a dictatorship acting in the name of the working class. Hungarian ideologists echoed their Soviet mentors. For example, György Aczél, until mid-1988 a member of the Politburo, stated that "a society can be called socialist when a new political system and mechanism come into being on the basis of new conditions of ownership."

According to Hungarian Marxist-Leninists, the welfare of the working class constituted the historical goal of the party. However, since 1956 the HSWP has sought to represent the interests of all Hungarians and has devoted greater resources to promoting the spiritual and material progress of the whole society. The party also has come to acknowledge that "a perfect, complete Marxism does not, cannot, and will never exist" and therefore has rejected the notion of a set of eternally valid ideological premises emanating from Moscow. Rather, since the late 1950's the HSWP has sought to adapt general Marxist-Leninist ideas to Hungarian conditions. In the late 1980s, the party considered the country's socialist development to be in transition between the stage of intermediate economic development and the stage of "developed socialism." Developed socialism promised the intensive development of the economy, emphasizing qualitative improvement in working conditions and the standard of living, as well as liberalization of

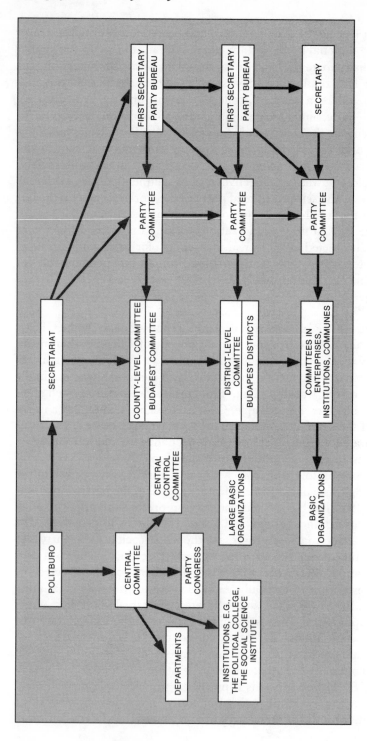

Figure 9. Structure of the Hungarian Socialist Workers' Party, 1988

the political system to encourage incipient pluralism and popular political participation.

Democratic Centralism

According to the Party Rules, the "HSWP is built on the principle of democratic centralism." In theory, democratic centralism calls for the democratic election of all members of leading organs by secret ballot, subordination of lower party organs to higher party organs, and the obligation of the leading organs to report regularly on their activities to their party organization.

In practice, intraparty democracy functioned within narrowly circumscribed limits set by party leaders, who were the only officials able to change party policies. In addition, when the party made a decision, members possessed only the information provided to them by the party hierarchy. Based on that information, the leadership expected the rank and file to endorse its decisions. Delegates sent to meetings at the next highest level were, in fact, chosen by the leaders they ostensibly elected. Moreover, the central party apparatus controlled personnel appointments and ensured that only "trustworthy" members were appointed to positions of authority.

In the late 1980s, party leaders acknowledged problems with this form of decision making. For example, a party document argued that "if democracy is narrowed down, then issues are solved only by the leadership and a group of experts." This document maintained that greater participation of the rank and file would ensure wider responsibility and decisions of higher quality.

Indeed, in 1988 the party loosened some of democratic centralism's traditional precepts. For example, in June 1988 the Budapest party committee chose among two candidates—Mihály Jassó and Pál Iványi—for the position of first secretary of the Budapest party committee. An eight-person nominating committee selected the candidates based on consultations with party committee members, department heads, district first secretaries, and other activists. In the first two votes, neither candidate received the required 50 percent plus one of the valid votes. On the third vote, Jassó received a majority. Later in 1988, the party loosened other strictures, thus allowing party members to join organizations, movements, and associations considered by the party to be its "potential or actual allies."

In July 1988, more evidence appeared that the party was loosening the norms of democratic centralism. The Central Committee approved a resolution reducing the party's *nomenklatura* authority over a number of party, government, and economic positions. In 1973 approximately 1,700 such positions existed, of which more than 800 could be filled by Central Committee secretaries (see Party Structure, this ch.). In 1985 the Central Committee reduced the number of such positions to 1,241. A Central Committee resolution of July 13–14, 1988, further lowered the number of these positions to 435. However, in 1988 István Petrovszki, the head of the Central Committee's Party and Mass Organizations Department, reported that the party would not completely halt the practice of recommending personnel for key positions. When these appointments concerned staff in such bodies as the National Assembly, the PPF, and the National Council of Trade Unions, each of which had the right to nominate and elect its own officials, the party would make recommendations. However, if these organizations selected their own nominees, the party would oppose the selection, according to Petrovszki, only if it questioned the person's "political reliability."

Despite some changes in the procedures of democratic centralism, in the late 1980s participation in decision making remained low in the HSWP. Party studies continued to show that the level of activity and the quality of party work among the rank and file were poor. Individuals or, at most, small committees selected nominees for party offices. Indeed, Sándor Lakos, editor in chief of *Pártélet* (Party Life), wrote in the late 1980s that the most important question facing the party was how to create greater party democracy.

Party Structure

In theory, the party congress formed the highest authority in the HSWP, although, because it met only once every five years, it lacked real power. Its members were appointed by officials of the Central Committee and the Politburo, two organs nominally responsible to the party congress. The Central Committee, which included more than 100 members and usually met once every three months, also was too large to exert much influence. The Central Committee yielded in real power and authority to the Politburo and the Secretariat. Also nominally subordinate to the party congress was the Central Control Committee, which enforced party discipline.

The Politburo and the Secretariat paralleled a set of governmental institutions that included the Council of Ministers and the Presidential Council (see Presidential Council, this ch.). The difference between party and government institutions lay in the distinction between policy formation and policy execution. In general, the party formulated policy and the government carried it out. Since the early postwar period, however, the party has been heavily involved in executing economic, domestic political, and foreign policies. Nevertheless, in the late 1980s party leaders, especially General Secretary Grósz, called upon party organs to withdraw from day-to-day supervision of policy execution and content themselves with establishing broad policy guidelines.

Within the party, the Politburo was responsible for selecting policy alternatives. The Secretariat produced policy alternatives for the Politburo, and, once that body made a decision, the Secretariat carried them out. Of course, in fulfilling its role the Secretariat often made policy decisions itself.

The structure of intermediate party organizations on the county and district levels resembled that of the central institutions. According to the Party Rules, the authoritative body at each level was the conference, which elected a committee that in turn chose a bureau with several members (including a first secretary) and a secretariat. Conferences at the district level elected delegates to the county party conference. However, in the late 1980s the norms of democratic centralism dictated that party leaders at each level approve the composition of the conference that elected them, as well as the composition of party committees, bureaus, and secretariats on the next lowest level.

Basic Organizations made up the lowest rung of the party hierarchy. In contrast to higher rungs on the hierarchy, which were organized on a territorial basis, the Basic Organizations were located at places of work, residences, and armed forces units having more than three party members. The party meeting formed the highest authority at this level. The only full-time, salaried party official in the Basic Organization was the secretary.

Central Institutions

Central party institutions made decisions binding on the party as a whole. In addition, they made policy for every aspect of the country's domestic and foreign policies. Hungary's central party institutions, like those of other Marxist-Leninist parties of Eastern Europe, were modeled on those of the CPSU.

Party Congress

According to the Party Rules, the congress was the "highest organ of the HSWP." The congress had the following powers: it debated reports of the Central Committee and the Central Control Committee, approved the Party Rules, elected the Central Control Committee and the Central Committee, determined the general guidelines of party policy, and determined the most immediate and important tasks of socialist construction. The Central Committee convened a party congress once every five years.

In fact, the party congress usually legitimated policies decided upon elsewhere. The Politburo gave its prior approval to officials elected by the party congress. The congress merely ratified solutions to political, social, and economic problems that had been developed by the Secretariat and approved by the Politburo. Thus, party congresses had mainly a propagandistic character.

The agendas of all party congresses in the postwar period have been similar. The general secretary reads the report of the Central Committee. Debates and approval of the report follow. Speeches are read by leaders of foreign communist party delegations, with the representative of the CPSU going first. The congress also adopts reports of other party organs as well as a party program. Finally, the congress ''elects'' the Central Committee, the Secretariat, and the Central Control Committee.

The Thirteenth Party Congress, held March 25–29, 1985, made no important changes in HSWP policies, continuing the general policy line of the 1960s and 1970s. In contrast to earlier party congresses, however, greater degrees of candor and open criticism characterized the Thirteenth Party Congress. Social problems discussed included the declining birth rate, the poor quality of health services, and the inequalities created by economic reform.

The Thirteenth Party Congress had 935 delegates, or about 1 for every 1,000 party members. The social composition of the delegates mirrored the social composition of the party as a whole (see Social Composition of the Party, this ch.). Workers and peasants made up approximately 30 percent of the delegates. Functionaries in party and social organizations made up 23.1 percent of the delegates, leading executives and administrators 24.9 percent, and employees 8.4 percent. Women comprised about 27 percent of the delegates.

The Central Committee also had the power to convene a party conference at any time during the interval between congresses. The party held its first conference in May 1945 and its second in June 1957. In May 1988, the HSWP leadership convened the Third Party Conference.

The Third Party Conference had 1 delegate for every 1,000 party members, or a total of 859 delegates. In addition, the 106 Central Committee members and 25 members of the Central Control Committee also had the right to vote. The conference had powers similar to a party congress. It approved new directions in economic and social policy, and it ratified important personnel changes in the leadership. Grósz succeeded Kádár as general secretary, and the conference created for Kádár the new, largely honorific position of chairman of the party. In addition, liberal reformers Rezső Nyers and Imre Pozsgay became Politburo members.

Central Committee

Between party congresses, in principle the supreme power in the HSWP rested with the Central Committee. The Central Committee acted on "behalf of the party with respect to state, government, and social organs and in international relations." The Central Committee, according to the Party Rules, held plenums at least once every three months. It had the power to elect department heads of the Central Committee apparatus; direct the operations of the party's central institutions, newspapers, and periodicals; nominate the editorial boards of the central publications; supervise the performance of professional party activists; allocate party funds; control the work of government organs; and approve the economic plan, other economic and social policies, and the national budget for debate and ratification by the National Assembly (see National Assembly, this ch.). The Central Committee also administered leading party education institutions, such as the Political College and the Social Science Institute, and dealt with ideological questions and international affairs. Virtually the whole life of the country fell within the purview of the Central Committee.

The Thirteenth Party Congress elected a 105-member Central Committee. That congress retained seventy-six members elected at the Twelfth Party Congress in 1980 and elected twenty-nine new members. In June 1987, the Central Committee grew to 107 members after the deaths of 5 members and the appointments of 7 others. In April 1988, the Central Committee had 106 members after the death of another member.

Personal merit and institutional affiliation determined who was selected to the Central Committee, with most members selected because of their positions. Members included officials of the central party apparatus, party leaders on the county level, and leading officials of the trade unions, the military, and mass organizations. Some economic officials also gained membership. Other members of the Central Committee worked in the media or were active in the fields of science, culture, or the arts.

Central Control Committee

According to the Party Rules, the Central Control Committee "works to assist the strengthening of the party's ideological, political, [and] organizational unity, and the instruction of party membership; keeps watch over the political behavior, party loyalty, and moral purity of the party membership; [and] fights consistently against all forms of antiparty factional activity.'' This committee conducts disciplinary investigations, hears appeals against decisions of lower party organs, and audits the economic and financial records of party bodies. In 1985 the Thirteenth Party Congress elected twenty-five members to this committee. A chairman and a secretary managed the work of this party organ.

Politburo

The Central Committee nominally elected the membership of the Politburo, which directed party activity between plenums of the Central Committee. The Politburo consisted of the country's most powerful political leaders; its members occupied the most important positions in the party, government, and mass organizations. In early 1989, Politburo membership included Grósz, the general secretary; János Berecz, the party's leading ideologist; István Szabó, an agricultural specialist; Csaba Hámori, the chairman of the Central Committee's Youth Committee; János Lukács, Central Committee secretary for party organization; Pál Iványi, Central Committee secretary for economic policy; Miklós Németh, the chairman of the Council of Ministers; and other government and economic administrators. Each Politburo member had responsibility that often overlapped with an area managed by a government ministry.

The Politburo usually met once a week to address the country's foreign, military, economic, and domestic policies. The Politburo conducted its meetings in secret, although it often invited other members of the party, government, and mass organizations to attend. The general secretary chaired the meeting, and decisions appeared to be reached by consensus. The Politburo informed Central Committee plenums about the issues discussed at these weekly meetings.

Traditionally, succession to the position of general secretary has presented problems for the political elite. No institutionalized procedures governed the transfer of power from one general secretary to the next. And in the late 1980s, the general secretary did not have a set term of office. The general secretary had to secure power by promoting trusted clients to positions of power and influence within other leading party, government, and state institutions. Like other Soviet satellite parties in Eastern Europe, the HSWP Politburo usually gained prior Soviet approval for the appointment of its general secretary. The general secretary also required continued Soviet support to remain in office. Thereafter, the general secretary had to establish his authority by generating successful economic, social, and foreign policies. Kádár accomplished all these objectives, and he remained in the post of general secretary from 1956 to 1988. However, when the leadership deemed Kádár too conservative to push forward further economic and political reforms, it ousted him in favor of Grósz, having gained Soviet approval to do so.

Secretariat

The Secretariat served as the staff of the Politburo, administering a bureaucracy that oversaw all aspects of the party's and the country's activities. The Secretariat, which consisted of five secretaries, prepared decisions for Politburo approval and either implemented these decisions itself or ensured that the responsible government bodies carried them out. In early 1989, four secretaries—Grósz, Berecz, Lukács, and Iványi—also sat on the Politburo and were the most powerful of the five members of the Secretariat.

The general secretary supervised the work of the Secretariat as a whole. In 1989 the five secretaries maintained responsibility for ideology, defense and internal security, party organization, foreign policy, and economic policy. Each secretary worked with a small staff of three to five assistants. The four powerful secretaries—Grósz, Berecz, Lukács, and Iványi—also chaired committees of the Central Committee for international, legal, and state management policy; social policy; party policy; and economic and social welfare policy, respectively. In 1989 working groups of the Central Committee formulated long-term policy recommendations in the areas of party building, economics, educational and cultural policy, science policy, and cooperatives policy.

In the late 1980s, the heads of the five Central Committee departments for social policy, party policy, economic and social welfare policy, international party relations, and management and the head of the Central Committee Office (also considered a Central Committee department) answered to the secretaries. Departments controlled the work of their counterparts on the county and district levels of the party. In addition, they maintained working relations with their counterparts in the CPSU and the relevant departments in the allied communist parties of Eastern Europe. The departments worked closely with their corresponding ministries to ensure that the government properly implemented party policies. In the late 1980s, this task changed, however, as the party leadership sought to lessen the involvement of the party apparatus in the day-to-day administration of the economy. As a result, in late 1988 the

Politburo targeted the 249-member staff of the Central Committee for reductions of 8 to 10 percent.

Intermediate Institutions

Intermediate party institutions embraced organs on the county and district levels. The structure of the party on these levels resembled that on the national level. In principle, at each level the most authoritative body was the conference, which was attended by delegates from lower levels. These conferences took place every two years to review reports, discuss the activities of the government and party bodies under their jurisdiction, and elect a party committee. The conference also elected delegates to the conference at the next highest level. District conferences thus selected delegates to the county party conference, and the county party conference elected delegates to the party congress. If a Basic Organization had more than 1,500 members, it elected delegates directly to the county party conference. In fact, the party leadership at each level nominated the delegates, and the party conferences merely confirmed these nominations.

Between meetings of the conferences, the party committee constituted the highest authority on the district and county levels. The committees on the county level met every three months, and those on the district level met every two months. These committees chose a bureau and a secretariat to manage the affairs of their jurisdictions between committee meetings. Party bureaus consisted of the first secretary, the head of the county or district government, and specialists in industry, economics, agriculture, and youth and ideology. The first secretary at each level was the most powerful official in the jurisdiction.

The secretariat of the county and district party bureaus coordinated and supervised the implementation of party policies in the party bureaucracy and the government (see fig. 10). The secretaries and the bureaus answered to their respective conferences and committees, but they also received directions from the organs above them, particularly the Secretariat of the Central Committee. However, the primary duty of the district-level apparatus was to supervise the Basic Organizations. This apparatus also approved the admission and expulsion of members by the Basic Organizations.

Basic Organizations

A Basic Organization existed in every government institution, production unit, residential unit, and armed forces unit having three or more party members. In 1985 the party had 25,402 Basic

Organizations, of which 37.2 percent were in government institutions or the armed forces, 30.2 percent in industrial enterprises, 15 percent in agricultural enterprises, and the remainder in residences scattered throughout the country.

The membership meeting had the highest authority in the Basic Organization. According to the Party Rules, membership meetings had to be held at least once every two months. The membership meeting elected a secretary, a deputy secretary, and a small bureau to administer the affairs of the Basic Organization. In Basic Organizations of fewer than ten members, the membership meeting elected only a secretary and a deputy secretary. Often the district organization nominated the secretaries as part of its *nomenklatura* authority. In the 1980s, however, competitive elections became more frequent. In 1985 one-third of the newly elected secretaries were newcomers to the position, and, compared with 1980, the number of multiple candidacies rose. Large Basic Organizations were divided into party groups, which elected a steward to direct their affairs. The party groups assessed the work and behavior of their members and the fulfillment of party tasks.

The Basic Organization performed several tasks. Most important, the Basic Organization implemented party decisions in the economic enterprise or other unit under its jurisdiction. The Basic Organization conducted agitation and propaganda to explain party policies to nonparty members, to inspire nonparty members to meet regime goals, and to encourage enthusiasm in the workplace. The Basic Organization admitted new members subject to the approval of the district party organization. The Basic Organization gave informal courses for party and nonparty members on ideology, party history, and current events. The Basic Organization controlled the activity of enterprise management to ensure the fulfillment of its economic plan. Finally, the party expected the Basic Organizations to be vigilant and to report activities within their jurisdiction that could be considered harmful or disloyal.

Discipline

The Party Rules stated that members who violated party norms were subject to punishments ranging from a reprimand to expulsion. In addition, a less formal form of punishment involved the so-called ''exchange of party cards,'' in which the old party cards were replaced for the faithful and the membership of those persons who had broken party discipline was revoked.

The HSWP could take several forms of disciplinary action against its members. Punishments included a reprimand, censure, severe censure, severe censure with final warning, and expulsion. From

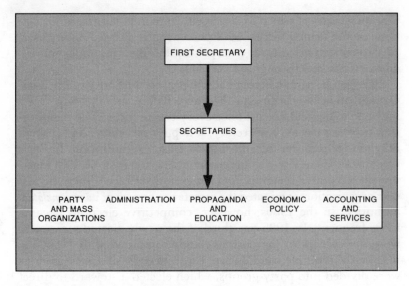

Source: Based on information from Hans-Georg Heinrich, *Hungary: Politics, Economics, and Society,* Boulder, Colorado, 1986, 55.

Figure 10. Structure of the County Committee Apparatus, 1986

1980 through 1985, the HSWP expelled 7,639 members. In addition, the party could suspend members from their office for a specified period of time or could recall party members from public office.

Disciplinary proceedings took place at the membership meetings of the Basic Organization. Higher party organs confirmed or rejected the decision of the Basic Organization. Ultimately, the party's Central Control Committee could also review the decision.

The exchange of party cards took place on a party-wide scale. Between 1945 and 1977, six such exchanges occurred. The HSWP began another exchange of party cards in 1986 to strengthen party discipline and maintain Kádár's control over the party. As of April 1988, approximately 46,000 members left the party as a result of that exchange: 250 were expelled, about 40,000 left voluntarily, 1,500 were advised to leave, and 4,000 were taken off the membership list, probably for failure to pay their membership dues.

Membership

The HSWP placed strict requirements on membership in the party. Members had to work actively on the party's behalf and set a moral and political example for nonparty members.

The HSWP opened membership to persons at least eighteen years of age who accepted Marxist-Leninist ideals, participated in one or more of the party's Basic Organizations, and paid their dues. In addition, the Party Rules obliged members to accept the policies, guidelines, and organizational rules of the HSWP. The Party Rules called upon members to be politically active and morally above reproach, command the respect of others for their work, and "live in a socialist fashion." The party enjoined its members to master the fundamentals of Marxism-Leninism, expand their practical and theoretical knowledge of this ideology, and fight against the remnants of bourgeois ideology and morality. Members had to observe the rules of party discipline and execute the decisions of the party and the government. Members also undertook self-criticism to expose their own shortcomings. Finally, they worked to strengthen and expand the party's links with the masses and to propagate the party's ideals and policies.

Party members enjoyed certain rights. They participated in the discussion of theoretical, political, and organizational issues at party meetings and voted on the adoption of resolutions. Members had the right to vote in party elections and to stand as candidates. Members were able to criticize "in a party-like manner" the work of another party member or party organ at meetings, to present a request or recommendation to the Basic Organization, as well as to higher party bodies including the party congress, and to receive a valid response. However, democratic centralism discouraged such criticism. Any party member who questioned the policies of the leadership would be subject to party discipline.

Social Composition of the Party

In mid-1988 the HSWP had about 817,000 members, or 10.3 percent of Hungary's adult population. Nominally the party of the working class, the HSWP actually was dominated by members of the intelligentsia. Men outnumbered women.

Since 1956 the proportion of workers and peasants in the party has declined. In 1962 industrial and agricultural workers made up 59 percent of the party. This figure dropped to 38 percent in 1970, and by 1985 it had declined to 31.9 percent. By contrast, in 1975 members of the intelligentsia made up 40 percent of the membership, and by 1985 that figure had risen to 42.4 percent.

Other statistics showed that members used their membership to raise their social status. In 1985 about 62 percent of party members originally were workers when they joined the party and 8.9 percent originally were peasants. As a result of the influence that party members held in society and the favors that the regime granted to party members, about 40 percent of the party membership was able to climb into the ranks of the intelligentsia from the working class and the peasantry. Thus, children of workers and peasants used the party as a vehicle of upward mobility. Having joined the "political class," party members, particularly full-time party officials, could pass their new status on to their children.

Statistics on the educational background of party members confirmed the dominance of the intelligentsia. In 1985 approximately 21 percent of party members had received degrees from a higher educational institution. The corresponding figure for the population as a whole was only 6.1 percent. In 1985 about 43.9 percent of the membership had a high school or special secondary school education. The figure for society as a whole was 27.1 percent. Between 1975 and 1985, the proportion of members who had no more than a primary-school education declined from 55.4 to 28.4 percent.

Historically women have formed a minority of the party's membership, although since the 1960s their percentage of the membership has risen. In 1966 women made up 22.9 percent of the HSWP, and by 1970 this figure had risen to 24.4 percent. By mid-1988 women made up approximately 32.1 percent of the party. In the late 1980s, however, women generally had not advanced into positions of power. For example, in the Central Committee elected in 1985, a mere 11 percent of the members were women. In early 1989, only two women sat on the Politburo.

Patriotic People's Front

According to the Constitution, the Patriotic People's Front (PPF) "unites the forces of society for the complete building up of socialism, for the solution of political, economic, and cultural tasks." The Constitution adds that the PPF "cooperates in the election and operation of the organs of popular representation." The PPF facilitated broad mass participation in regime policies and generated mass support for party programs. In 1988, according to Imre Pozsgay, at that time head of the PPF, the tasks of that organization included helping to achieve a new social accord in Hungary, consolidating new public thinking in the public consciousness, and helping citizens to participate in building a socialist society from below.

Approximately 130,000 grass-roots committees elected by local citizens carried out PPF policies on the local level. A congress of the PPF met every four years to elect its National Council and to review the activities of the organization. The National Council elected the National Presidency and the National Secretariat, which managed the PPF and set policy for it.

The PPF undertook a variety of tasks. Perhaps most important, it organized national and local elections (see Elections to the National Assembly; County and District Government, this ch.). The PPF served as an umbrella organization that united such bodies as the National Council of Hungarian Women, the National Gypsy Council, and other bodies representing national minorities in Hungary. The PPF also provided a framework for cooperation among different classes and strata of society, between religious believers and nonbelievers, and between party members and nonparty members. Finally, the PPF attempted to protect citizens' interests by leading the struggle against the corruption and abuse of power.

Mass Media

In Hungary the media served as instruments of regime policy, so their primary task was to promote the party's policies. Although other organizations, such as the PPF, the Communist Youth League, and the trade unions, produced their own publications, the regime controlled their content (see Mass Organizations, ch. 2). In the 1980s, the regime continued to suppress other sources of information, although it made available in hotels some Western periodicals and newspapers. The regime banned private ownership of the media.

In the late 1980s, Hungary had no censorship laws. However, informal censorship occurred in a number of different ways. Both the party and the government had organs for censorship. The party set guidelines, which were transmitted from its Department for Agitation and Propaganda to the lower party organs and to the editors in chief of the media. The Council of Ministers' Information Bureau acted as the government's agency for censorship (see Council of Ministers, this ch.). The Hungarian Telegraph Agency (Magyar Távirati Iroda—MTI) was the primary source of information for the media. Because the news media often lacked other sources of information, they depended on MTI for materials. MTI could thus exercise centralized control over the kinds of information that appeared in print or over the airwaves. The regime carefully selected editors and informed them about party and government censorship standards. Editors could be fired for failure to comply with these standards. For example, in 1983 Ferenc Kulin, editor of *Mozgó Világ* (World In Motion), lost his position for "systematic defiance" of party directives. Editors often exercised informal censorship, rejecting an article, for instance, because they claimed it did not suit the profile of their publication. Editors also exercised censorship when they recommended changes to a work that removed or softened its politically sensitive parts. Paradoxically, the lack of censorship standards encouraged editors to take a conservative approach to censorship to ensure that their publications did not include materials that might offend anyone in authority.

On March 20, 1986, the National Assembly passed a new press law defining the "rights and duties of journalists and the right of the public to fast and timely information." The law compelled government officials to respond to requests for information from reporters. Journalists, however, had to submit a copy of their article to people they had interviewed for it. The law prevented the publication of materials that "would hurt the constitutional order of the People's Republic and its international interests . . . and public morals." Critical pieces of writing could be rejected on that basis. In addition, according to Politburo member and Central Committee secretary Berecz, the law proscribed questioning Hungary's "socialist achievements" and its "national historical and moral values."

Hungary had three major daily newspapers: *Népszabadság* (People's Freedom), the official organ of the HSWP; *Népszava* (People's Voice), the organ of the trade unions; and *Magyar Nemzet* (Hungarian Nation), the organ of the PPF and the most liberal of the three newspapers. *Népszabadság* was the party daily and had a circulation of approximately 467,000 in early 1989. In November 1988, a new daily—*A Nap* (The Sun)—began publication with a circulation of between 80,000 and 100,000 a day. An afternoon paper—*Esti Hírlap* (Evening News)—had a circulation of between 200,000 and 250,000 a day.

The regime also published a number of specialized journals. *Társadalmi Szemle* (Social Review) was the HSWP's ideological monthly; it had a circulation of approximately 41,000. *Pártélet* (Party Life) had a circulation of about 130,000. Other, more obscure journals contained more interesting subject matter by virtue of their lower circulation and more specialized audiences. *Valóság* (Reality) was intellectually the most stimulating journal because it dealt with politically sensitive and highly unorthodox topics.

Most provincial journals treated only topics of regional interest. Nevertheless, *Jelenkor* (Present Age), published in Pécs, and *Forrás* (Source), published in Kecskemét, had wider audiences because they included interviews with national literary figures and scholarly research from Budapest. *Tiszatáj* (Tisza Country), published in Szeged, claimed a wide readership because it published materials on Hungarian national minorities living outside the country. However, in 1986 the government banned *Tiszatáj* because of "publication policy mistakes." The editors were dismissed and subjected to party discipline. The publication reappeared in 1987, and the party rehabilitated the editors in early 1989.

In the late 1980s, television was the most popular form of entertainment. Approximately 95 percent of Hungarian households had a television set. In the early and mid-1980s, Hungarians watched an average of 140 minutes of television programs per day. Programming on the country's two channels ran from mid-afternoon to late at night. In addition, some hotels and local cable and aerial systems had the equipment to receive and transmit Western-relayed satellite programs. Near the country's western border, households with a good roof antenna could receive one Austrian, two Yugoslav, and two Czechoslovak channels.

Hungary's three radio stations broadcast a variety of programming. In addition, Hungary concluded a radio agreement with Austria to establish a joint German-language radio station called Radio Danubius. In May 1986, the station began broadcasting a twelve-hour program. The station eventually was to attain economic self-sufficiency through advertising.

In the late 1980s, videocassette recorders (VCRs) became very popular in Hungary. At the end of 1987, VCRs numbered between 200,000 and 300,000, and an estimated 1 million people had access to a VCR. In 1984 Hungary became the first East European country to have stores renting videotapes, and more than fifty videotape outlets existed in late 1987. The government-operated outlets, however, had only 800 titles and a total of only 15,000 copies. Illegally produced, copied, and distributed cassettes accounted for 80 percent of the videotape market. These tapes treated taboo themes such as religion, anti-Soviet sentiments, sex, and violence. The regime acknowledged that these tapes had spread throughout the country like a ''contagious disease'' and held them responsible for the rise in the crime rate, increased drug use, and the higher suicide rate (see Health, ch. 2).

Foreign Policy

In the 1980s, Hungary attempted to carve out a semi-independent role for itself within the Soviet alliance system in Eastern Europe. The origins of the Hungarian position lay in the regime's efforts to promote economic reform, which required Western involvement and support. The regime also sought to create popular support for itself by providing an abundance of consumer goods supplied by the West. For reasons of history and tradition, Hungary cultivated ties with Austria and the Federal Republic of Germany (West Germany). In the mid- and late 1980s, Hungary also attempted to further relations with Britain and the United States. In addition, as further evidence of its initiative in foreign policy, Hungary developed relations with Israel, China, and the Republic of Korea (South Korea), which had previously been considered "pariah" states by most East European regimes.

Hungary's most important ally was the Soviet Union, with which it has enjoyed particularly good relations since 1986, when Soviet leader Mikhail S. Gorbachev initiated his reform program. In the late 1980s, Hungary strongly supported Soviet foreign policy positions. In return, Hungary received Soviet support for its efforts at domestic reform. Hungary also accepted integration into the alliance system through the Council for Mutual Economic Assistance (Comecon—see Glossary) and the Warsaw Pact (see Glossary).

Relations with its other communist neighbors played a crucial role in Hungarian foreign policy. The state of relations between Hungary and Romania, Czechoslovakia, and Yugoslavia generally depended on how these countries treated their Hungarian minorities. Because Yugoslavia treated its Hungarian minority well, relations between the two countries were excellent. In Czechoslovakia, the relation between Slovaks and ethnic Hungarians were not smooth. Through bilateral contacts, Hungary sought to encourage the Czechoslovak government to improve its treatment of Czechoslovakia's Hungarian minority. However, Romania's treatment of the Hungarian minority in Transylvania received worldwide condemnation. Hungary sought, through a variety of bilateral and multilateral efforts, to encourage more equitable treatment of Hungarians in Romania.

Principles of Foreign Policy

When superpower relations deteriorated in the early to mid-1980s, Hungary defined a role for small- and medium-sized states in maintaining ties between countries of the Warsaw Pact and the North Atlantic Treaty Organization (NATO). The reasons for Hungary's interest in East-West dialogue lay in its relatively liberal domestic policies as well as its foreign economic policies. Following the Revolution of 1956, the leadership determined that a policy of isolation threatened the stability of the Soviet alliance system in general and Hungary in particular. In addition, the leadership believed that without access to the world economy, Hungary's economy would continue to lag behind the economies of the West.

In the late 1970s and early 1980s, the Soviet invasion of Afghanistan, the crackdown on the Solidarity labor union movement in Poland, and the deployment of United States intermediate-range ballistic missiles (IRBMs) in Western Europe led to a deterioration of relations between the superpowers. Hungary resisted this worsening of relations with the West. Thus, the theory that Hungary had won some freedom of action in the domestic sphere by remaining loyal to the Soviet Union in foreign policy lost much of its validity in the mid-1980s.

Several factors led Hungary to push for an independent stance. First, the Kádár regime believed that any return to economic isolation from the West would endanger policies designed to modernize the economy and to promote political liberalization. In turn, these two policies were intended to encourage popular political support for the regime and bolster its legitimacy. Their failure could have led to political catastrophe for the leadership. Second, Romania and the German Democratic Republic (East Germany) were pursuing their own independent initiatives with selected NATO countries. The Hungarians believed that their policy would also find supporters in Bulgaria and Poland, both of which needed help from the West to overcome their economic problems. Third, the Soviet leadership experienced internal differences over the issue of East-West relations. In 1984 some Soviet economists and political commentators positively evaluated the Hungarian reforms. The Kádár regime believed that it had allies in the top Soviet leadership, possibly including then-General Secretary Konstantin U. Chernenko himself.

The Soviet Union used its allies in the Communist Party of Czechoslovakia (CPCz) to reply to Hungary's initiatives. On March 30, 1984, the CPCz daily *Rudé právo* published a scathing critique of Hungary's policy, which it labeled "one-sided particularism." The article maintained that the Hungarian stance would lead to a weakening of the common international strategy and foreign policy of the Warsaw Pact, encourage efforts by capitalist states to gain one-sided advantages by promoting differences among socialist states, and favor a narrow, nationally oriented approach to transitory economic difficulties. The Czechoslovak newspaper also argued that the Hungarians attached importance to distinctions between large and small states rather than to the class structure of these states. Finally, *Rudé právo* complained that national interests were beginning to take precedence over the interests of the Soviet alliance system as a whole. Articles in several Soviet party and government publications echoed the Czechoslovak comments, suggesting that the CPCz and the CPSU coordinated their attacks on Hungary.

Secretary of the Central Committee for Foreign Policy Mátyás Szűrős laid out Hungary's response to the charges of its allies. In 1984 Szűrős began publishing his justifications for Hungary's stance. He later added other arguments to underscore Hungary's stance. Szűrős averred that, although relations between the superpowers might be poor, historical traditions and contemporary geopolitical relations could encourage the development of relations between certain socialist states and certain capitalist states. Particularly the small- and medium-sized states in each alliance system, through dialogue and constructive relations, could improve the international atmosphere and thereby create possibilities for the improvement of relations between the United States and the Soviet Union. In turn, such an improvement could lead to an overall reduction of international tension.

Szűrős believed that national interests had to be given more weight when formulating common Warsaw Pact positions on foreign policy and military issues. A conception of the common goals of socialist states could command the support of the individual socialist countries only if it took national interests into account. Szűrős rejected the notion that, by pursuing its national interests, Hungary sought to gain one-sided advantages from the West. He wrote that as a result of historical and geopolitical factors, capitalist states showed different degrees of interest in developing relations with the various socialist states. Thus Bulgaria carried on intense relations with Greece and Turkey, and Austria and West Germany developed close relations with Hungary.

In 1985 and 1986, Szűrős broadened these considerations when he wrote that the communist movement lacked an organizational and a political center that could enforce prescriptions for behavior. He argued that although a common ideology united the international communist movement, ideology was neither a code of dogma nor a closed system but a body of ideas undergoing constant change. Szűrős therefore advocated the "proper adaptation" of the basic principles of Marxism-Leninism to specific national circumstances. These formulations justified renovations in domestic policy, in turn leading to innovations in foreign policy, including Hungary's opening to the West.

In July 1986, Szűrős went beyond these arguments when he wrote that small- and medium-sized countries had more to lose in the event of a conflict between the superpowers than did the superpowers themselves. Therefore, smaller countries had objective interests in seeking and maintaining détente. Smaller countries also had a special responsibility to contribute to an atmosphere encouraging the reduction of tension, deepening of dialogue, and strengthening of trust. Therefore, claimed Szűrős, small- and medium-sized states had interests of their own, regardless of their class structure.

Relations with the Soviet Union

In the postwar period, several factors contributed to Soviet influence in Hungary. The Soviet Union maintained a large troop presence in Eastern Europe (see Soviet Influence, ch. 5). The structural characteristics of the Warsaw Pact minimized the independence of East European military establishments and the CPSU exercised significant political influence within the HSWP and the government.

Relations between Hungary and the Soviet Union also depended on a series of more personal factors. Thus, before Gorbachev assumed power in the Soviet Union, the conservative Soviet leadership disapproved of Hungarian reform efforts, and relations between the two countries were therefore cool. After Gorbachev became general secretary of the CPSU and initiated his reform program, the leadership of each country found in the other an ally for its program of economic and political change. Consequently, beginning in mid-1986 relations between Hungary and the Soviet Union warmed considerably.

At the Thirteenth Party Congress, the HSWP stressed the decisive importance of relations with the Soviet Union. At this congress, however, Grigorii V. Romanov, then a hard-line member of the CPSU Politburo and Secretariat, criticized Hungary for its relations with the West. Romanov supported "businesslike contacts" with capitalist countries, but he warned that the socialist countries could not "allow the imperialist forces to use economic levers as a means of political pressure and interference in the affairs of socialist states." Romanov advised Hungary not to go too far in increasing trade and cooperation with the West.

The Twenty-Seventh Party Congress of the CPSU in March 1986 marked the beginning of a steady improvement in relations between Hungary and the Soviet Union. Kádár endorsed the Soviet reform program and drew parallels between the CPSU's party congress and the HSWP's Thirteenth Party Congress. Hungary also supported the Soviet Union's foreign policy and disarmament proposals. In June 1986, Gorbachev visited Hungary for talks with Hungarian party and government leaders. According to the joint communiqué, both sides shared "fully identical views" on foreign and security policies. Each side pledged to assist the other in accelerating socioeconomic and scientific development.

In the mid- to late 1980s, the Soviet Union sought to expand bilateral economic relations and scientific-technical relations with Hungary. The Soviet Union needed Hungarian scientific and technical expertise as well as economic assistance to strengthen Soviet economic reform. Hungary, by contrast, sought to devote more resources to its trade with the West and with the newly industrialized countries of the Third World.

Soviet efforts to tie Hungary more closely to the Soviet economy and to Comecon have achieved some success. In 1985 Hungary and the Soviet Union signed a long-range economic and scientific-technical program of cooperation to last until the year 2000. The Kádár-Gorbachev talks in 1985 called for the strengthening of scientific-technical cooperation and the development of new forms of cooperation between each country's research institutes, economic enterprises, and work cooperatives. At a meeting between Grósz and Gorbachev in July 1987, the two countries agreed to expand bilateral trade in the 1986–90 period. The two leaders also commissioned a fifteen- to twenty-year plan for developing economic and scientific-technical cooperation between their two countries.

In 1988 two high-level meetings took place between Soviet and Hungarian leaders. In April, Soviet then-President Andrei A. Gromyko visited Hungary to promote the expansion of bilateral ties in light of the changes taking place in both countries. Gromyko met with Kádár, and they expressed a common interest in implementing reform in their own countries and in establishing new kinds of cooperation. Grósz was the first East European leader to visit the Soviet Union after the CPSU's Nineteenth Party Conference in July, a sign of Hungary's close relations with Moscow. Gorbachev praised the HSWP party conference and drew parallels between the reform efforts of both countries. Grósz called his meeting with Gorbachev "useful and valuable" and said that the two countries had never been more in harmony.

Relations with Other Communist Neighbors

In the mid- to late 1980s, Hungary attached particular importance to relations with Romania, Czechoslovakia, and Yugoslavia, because each of these countries contained rather large Hungarian minorities. A common culture and language, as well as family ties, linked Hungarians in these countries to Hungary. The Romanian government and, to a lesser extent, the Czechoslovak government have subjected their Hungarian minorities to various forms of political and cultural oppression. On the one hand, Hungarian public opinion has pressured the HSWP leadership and the government to work for the amelioration of the harsh circumstances of Hungarians in neighboring countries. The regime, seeking to strengthen its legitimacy within Hungarian society, has taken up the cause of Hungarians living abroad. On the other hand, the prospect of open discord within the Soviet alliance system has restrained Hungarian criticism of Romanian and Czechoslovak nationality policies.

Romania

According to Romanian statistics, 1.7 million Hungarians were living in Romanian Transylvania in the late 1980s. Western experts maintained that at least 2 million Hungarians inhabited this part of Romania, and some estimates put the figure as high as 2.2 million. Although problems existed earlier, in the mid-1980s Romanian treatment of the Hungarian minority became increasingly harsh. For example, the Romanian city of Braşov had no Hungarian-language schools, although the city was home to Transylvania's second-largest Hungarian minority. In 1983 the Romanian government reduced Hungarian-language television broadcasts from two and one-half hours per day to one hour per day. In 1984 it discontinued Hungarian-language programming altogether. The Romanian government allowed the importation of only one periodical—*Sakkalet* (Chess Life)—from Hungary. The Romanian government also attempted to prevent Hungarians from traveling to Romania. During the height of the summer tourist season, Hungarians had to wait up to a whole day while Romanian authorities searched their cars and baggage. Many Hungarians were not allowed to enter Romania after the seizure of books, periodicals, and even HSWP and Hungarian government newspapers.

The Hungarian regime failed to respond quickly to the Romanian actions. As Austrian political commentator Paul Lendvai has noted, because all communist countries are, according to their official definition, brothers, they must bury the differences that frequently appear between noncommunist states. Therefore, until the mid-1980s the regime remained silent about the treatment of Hungarians in neighboring countries. For example, after a high-level Romanian delegation visited Hungary in April 1985, the joint communiqué contained no reference to Romania's nationality problem.

Beginning in 1984, however, Hungarian criticisms of Romania began to surface in the media, and Hungarian leaders began to develop their own position on minority nationalities. In August 1984, the deputy prime minister, Lajos Faluvégi, criticized Romania's treatment of its minorities. In a November 1984 speech to the Thirteenth Party Congress of the Romanian Communist Party (RCP), National Council of Trade Unions secretary Lajos Méhes echoed Faluvégi's comments. The Thirteenth Party Congress of the HSWP in 1985 also addressed this problem. Kádár twice spoke about the need to respect the rights, language, and culture of national minorities and to allow them freedom of movement and contacts with their mother country. Kádár emphasized that national minorities ought to act as a bridge between neighboring countries.

In June 1987, at a meeting with a Romanian delegation headed by Emil Bobu, an RCP Politburo member and Central Committee secretary for party organization, Hungarian officials brought up the problem of Romania's treatment of its Hungarian population. Hungary maintained that Romania's treatment of Hungarians failed to comply with a 1977 agreement between Kádár and Romanian leader Nicolae Ceauşescu to strengthen friendship and cooperation between the two peoples and to develop good relations between the two countries. However, the two sides failed to reach an agreement on the minority problem. Hungary wanted Hungarians in Romania to be loyal citizens of that country but to preserve their language and culture and be considered equals in "building socialism." Hungary agreed that the problem could be settled only by Romania. However, the Romanian report of the meeting failed to mention that the two sides had discussed the problem.

Hungary took the unprecedented step of raising the minority issue at multilateral forums. In October 1985, Hungary addressed this problem at the Cultural Forum of the Conference on Security and Cooperation in Europe (CSCE). A representative of the Hungarian delegation revealed that Hungary, Poland, the Soviet Union, and East Germany prepared a proposal "about the assertion by national minorities of their cultural rights" in which Romania and Czechoslovakia did not participate. More important, on November 15 Márton Klein, a department head in the Ministry of Foreign Affairs, condemned the oppression of 3 million Hungarians in neighboring countries. He called for guarantees of the minorities' civil rights and for granting them specific collective rights to use their language to enable them to preserve and enhance their cultural traditions.

In March 1987, at a closed session of the CSCE review conference in Vienna, the Hungarian delegation supported proposals for protecting minority rights submitted by Yugoslavia and Canada. This action marked the first time a Soviet ally supported a Western proposal at a CSCE review conference. Hungary faced heavy pressure from its allies for this decision. In April, Hungary responded to Romanian criticisms of its "diversionary moves" and "nationalist" and "chauvinist" practices. Rezső Bányász, head of the Council of Ministers' Information Bureau, argued that the Romanian charges lacked foundation and damaged the basic interests of the Romanian and Hungarian peoples.

Relations between Hungary and Romania further deteriorated in 1988. Thousands of ethnic Hungarians (and some ethnic

Romanians) were fleeing from Romania to Hungary to escape Ceauşescu's political oppression. The National Assembly passed a resolution calling Romania's planned destruction of thousands of villages a violation of human rights. The razing of between 7,000 and 8,000 villages and the relocation of their inhabitants were not directed at minorities as such, but the minorities would suffer the most because they would be scattered throughout the country and lose their national identities. In July tens of thousands of Hungarians demonstrated in front of the Romanian embassy in Budapest against the destruction of the villages. In response, Ceauşescu threatened to close the Romanian embassy, closed the Hungarian consulate in Cluj-Napoca, and blamed Hungary for the worsening of relations.

Grósz and Ceauşescu held an impromptu meeting in Arad, Romania, on August 28, 1988, to discuss relations between their countries. The talks lasted eight hours but failed to produce tangible results. The joint communiqué did not mention the nationality issue. Hungary later conceded that the two sides had made no progress on this problem.

On November 14, 1988, relations fell to a new low when Romanian police arrested Károly Györffy, the Hungarian commercial counselor, in Bucharest. The Romanians accused Györffy of using a stolen automobile, causing a serious accident, and distributing leaflets inciting public opinion against the authorities. On November 19, Romania declared Györffy persona non grata and instructed him to leave the country within three days. Hungary rejected all accusations against Györffy and noted that this incident did not mark the first time that Romanian organs had hindered the work of its diplomats. On November 24, Hungary expelled Romania's political counselor.

Czechoslovakia

Since the formation in Slovakia (Czechoslovakia's eastern republic) of a dissident organization for the defense of the rights of Hungarians in 1979 and after frequent arrests of the Hungarian activist Miklós Duray, discrimination against the approximately 600,000 ethnic Hungarians in Czechoslovakia became a problem in the relations between the two communist neighbors. As of 1986, about 100 Hungarian activists had been arrested and imprisoned by Czechoslovak authorities. Other problems included the lack of Hungarian-language books and newspapers in Slovakia, discouragement of Hungarian-language training, and vandalism of Hungarian monuments and cultural offices.

In the late 1980s, as a result of pressure from Hungary, Czechoslovakia attempted to redress some of the Hungarian minority's complaints. In 1986 the two countries concluded an agreement that called for Hungarian construction of a Hungarian cultural center in Bratislava, the capital of Slovakia. In 1987 the Cultural Association of Hungarian Workers in Czechoslovakia was allowed to rejoin the Czechoslovak National Front, from which it had been expelled in 1972. Yet Czechoslovakia attempted to downplay the minority problem. In the communiqué issued following the meeting between Grósz and Czechoslovak prime minister Lubomír Štrougal in August 1987, Štrougal mentioned the minority issue only in passing. By contrast, Grósz noted the role of minorities as a bridge between Hungary and Czechoslovakia and called for greater cultural contacts between the two countries.

Another outstanding issue between Hungary and Czechoslovakia concerned the Gabčíkovo-Nagymaros Dam project. In 1977 the two countries agreed to build this hydroelectric power and navigation system on the Danube River between Bratislava and Budapest. Hungarian public opinion strongly protested the project. Environmental activists in Hungary claimed that the project would severely damage the potable water supply, agriculture, and forests of both countries. Czechoslovakia has pressured the Hungarian government to proceed more quickly with the project.

Yugoslavia

In the late 1980s, approximately 430,000 Hungarians lived in Yugoslavia, primarily in the autonomous province of Vojvodina. In the late 1980s, relations between Hungary and Yugoslavia were good. After a December 1986 visit to Yugoslavia, Hungarian prime minister György Lázár termed ''exemplary'' Yugoslavia's treatment of its Hungarian minority. Yugoslavia provided an adequate number of Hungarian-language schools on all educational levels to this minority. In addition, the Yugoslav government freely permitted the publication and dissemination of periodicals and newspapers in the Hungarian language.

In other areas, bilateral ties developed remarkably well. Since the 1970s, Hungary has maintained governmental relations with the various republics of Yugoslavia. The two countries also undertook a variety of successful economic and scientific-technical ventures. In 1985 Hungary and Yugoslavia signed a trade agreement worth US$4.8 billion. In the late 1980s, each side expressed its readiness to increase cooperation in culture, education, information exchange, and sports.

Relations with the West

In the 1970s and 1980s, the consensus between regime and society in Hungary called for political support for the regime in return for improvements in the standard of living and a loosening of regime controls over society. Hungary needed Western economic support to raise its standard of living. Western economic support also entailed a modicum of political support. Hungary put out feelers to Austria as early as 1964 and sought to use that country—a permanent neutral—as a bridge to the West. Subsequently, the Hungarians turned to West Germany, historically the country's most important trade partner in Central Europe. In the mid- to late 1980s, Hungary has also sought to improve relations with Britain and the United States. In each case, Hungary wanted increased trade and cultural contacts. By contrast, in 1988 Hungary had only begun to cultivate relations with France, and economic and cultural contacts with that country therefore remained at a low level.

Austria

Since the mid-1960s, good relations between Hungary and Austria have resulted from a number of factors. A common water system, including the Danube, the Drava, and the Mur rivers, together with countless smaller rivers and Lake Fertő (Neusiedlersee), meant each country's use of it affected the other country. Means of transportation, including road and railroad connections such as the Rába-Ödenburger railroad line, also drew the countries together. Equally important, in the mid-1960s each country came to accept the permanence of the other's social system and attempted to find common areas of agreement despite political differences. Finally, in 1981 the two countries agreed that the border, which had earlier caused discord, no longer presented a problem.

In the 1980s, economic relations between Hungary and Austria were quite strong. More than 100 cooperation agreements in areas such as machine-building, metallurgy, pharmaceuticals, agriculture, and light industry were in force between the two countries. In 1986 total trade between the two countries amounted to US$1.1 billion. Hungary was Austria's fourth largest trade partner overall, and Austria was Hungary's second largest Western trade partner.

The two countries also cooperated considerably in culture, science and technology, sports, and other fields. The Hungarian Cultural Institute in Vienna organized an average of fifty events per year, and the Austrians operated their own cultural institute in Budapest. In 1987 the Hungarian-Austrian Friends Circle was established to promote common cultural traditions and Hungarian interest in Austrian history and culture. In the late 1980s, the theme that the two countries shared "a special relationship" has recurred in both governments' commentaries on their political relations. The Hungarian media also stressed the Central European identity and interests common to the two countries.

West Germany

Since the early 1970s, when the Four Power Agreement on Berlin and the Basic Treaty between East Germany and West Germany normalized West Germany's relations with the Soviet Union and East Germany, respectively, Hungary has greatly expanded its ties with West Germany. After West German chancellor Helmut Kohl's visit to Hungary in 1984, the Hungarian press stressed the special place of West Germany in Hungary's foreign policy and West Germany's efforts to reduce tension between East and West. *Népszabadság* called Kohl "the patron of East-West relations." Over the course of the 1980s, political contacts and dialogue have been constant and frequent, despite problems in superpower relations.

For Hungary, West Germany has served as an economic gateway to the West. In the late 1980s, West Germany was Hungary's largest Western trading partner. As of 1984, 332 cooperation agreements linked the economies of the two countries. That same year, the two countries extended a ten-year agreement on economic, industrial, and technical cooperation signed in 1974. In 1987 Hungary and West Germany signed a five-year agreement on scientific and technical cooperation.

Cultural relations between the two countries also expanded. In 1987 the two governments agreed to set up cultural and information centers in each other's country and concluded a visa agreement easing restrictions on Hungarians trying to enter West Germany. The West Germans also praised Hungary's treatment of its German minority and its policy of allowing ethnic Germans to resettle in West Germany.

Britain

To diversify support for its economic reforms, in the mid-1980s Hungary began to pursue relations with Britain. In 1984 Britain accounted for 4.3 percent of Hungary's exports to the West and 5.2 percent of its imports from the West. In the mid-1980s, Hungary was able to increase its trade with Britain owing to Britain's recovery from its economic recession, the flexible price policy of Hungarian economic enterprises, and a more favorable international climate.

Crown of Saint Stephen, which the United States returned to Hungary in 1978
Courtesy Gustav Forster

Kádár paid an official visit to Britain in the fall of 1985. According to British prime minister Margaret Thatcher, the two sides shared common ideas "with regard to peace, prosperity, and security." The two governments admitted that differences persisted, although they agreed to play a "useful role" in creating good relations between the Warsaw Pact and NATO.

The good political climate facilitated the expansion of cultural relations. Hungary and Britain carried out bilateral cultural and scientific exchanges within the context of an agreement that was renewed every two years. In 1985 Glasgow held a five-week festival of Hungarian culture. In addition, the British firm Pergamon Press published an English translation of Kádár's speeches and articles.

United States

Relations between Hungary and the United States began to warm in 1978 when the United States returned the Crown of Saint Stephen to Hungary (the crown had fallen into American hands after World War II). High-level political contacts took place rather frequently in the 1980s. Hungary benefited from these contacts because the United States kept it abreast of the course of Soviet-United

States arms control negotiations. In 1986 Secretary of State George Shultz visited Hungary, and in 1987 Central Committee secretary Szűrős visited the United States. In the summer of 1988, General Secretary Grósz paid a ten-day visit to the United States.

Hungary has taken certain steps to improve its relations with the United States. The Department of State has reacted favorably to Hungary's efforts in the area of human rights. United States officials have also praised the introduction of market mechanisms in the Hungarian economy.

In 1986 trade between Hungary and the United States amounted to US$345 million. The Hungarian government sought the renewal of most-favored-nation status on a three-year cycle rather than annually to facilitate planning in the foreign trade sector. During his visit in 1988, Grósz devoted most of his attention to economic matters, seeking to encourage greater and more varied cooperation between the two countries. The United States responded by allowing Hungary to open a trade bureau on the Pacific coast.

Relations with Selected Non-Western Countries

In the mid- to late 1980s, Hungary began to forge new economic and political relations with three countries that had long been ignored by most other countries in Eastern Europe. Hungary had broken off political relations with Israel in 1967, all but cut off relations with China as a result of the Sino-Soviet split, and neglected South Korea for fear of angering the communist Democratic People's Republic of Korea (North Korea). Given the varying circumstances of these countries, Hungary had different reasons for seeking to reopen relations with them, although in the case of all three countries, economic relations figured prominently. The Hungarians sought to develop trade and commercial ties with Israel. Hungary and China shared an interest in economic and political reform. South Korea provided a key to opening Hungarian relations with the newly industrialized countries of the Pacific Basin.

Israel

On September 14, 1987, Israel and Hungary agreed to open interest sections with a maximum of five diplomats in each other's countries. The Hungarian interest section in Tel Aviv was to have been established at the Swedish embassy and the Israeli interest section in Budapest at the Swiss embassy. This low level of diplomatic representation was to facilitate economic, trade, cultural, and humanitarian cooperation between the two countries and to help remove obstacles to consular relations.

In 1988 both Israeli foreign minister Shimon Peres and Israeli prime minister Yitzhak Shamir visited Hungary. Hungary designated Shamir's visit as private to avoid offending Arab states. Hungary sought to use both visits to strengthen trade and cultural relations with Israel. Western observers regarded these high-level contacts as another step toward the reestablishment of full diplomatic relations.

China

In the late 1970s, Hungary began working toward better relations with China. Trade and economic relations began to expand in 1983, followed by the improvement of interstate relations and cultural ties. However, because of ideological differences, Hungarian-Chinese relations focused on economic ties. In 1985 the two countries signed a long-term foreign trade agreement to expand bilateral economic and trade cooperation. The two countries also agreed to exchange information on their economic reform efforts. Imports from China rose from 0.6 percent of Hungary's total in 1984 to 1.8 percent of the total in 1986. Exports to China rose from 0.8 percent of the total to 1.9 percent of the total in that same period. Hungarians participated in several Chinese industrial development and reconstruction programs.

By 1982 both communist parties began to show an interest in resuming political relations. In 1985 the HSWP sent the Chinese Communist Party (CCP) the guidelines for its Thirteenth Party Congress. In return, the CCP sent a message to the "dear comrades" of the HSWP, wishing the Hungarian people success in the building of socialism.

Political relations intensified in 1987. In June Chinese premier and acting general secretary of the CCP Zhao Ziyang visited Hungary. Kádár's visit to China in October 1987 marked the resumption of party-to-party relations. The Chinese praised Hungary's reform program and called Kádár's visit "historic" because it symbolized a new era of friendship and cooperation between the two peoples.

South Korea

In February 1989, Hungary and South Korea agreed to establish full diplomatic relations. Hungary thus became the first communist country to recognize South Korea. South Korea was one of the most developed countries in Asia, and the Hungarians sought South Korea's assistance in developing their economy. In addition, Central Committee secretary Szürös argued that economic ties to South Korea would facilitate the development of ties with other countries of East Asia and the Pacific Basin and the increase of foreign economic assistance to develop Hungary's economy.

Hungary and the Soviet Model

Hungary's interest in economic reform prompted not only political reform but also changes in its foreign policy stance. The regime found that successful economic reform required political reform to encourage greater popular participation in governmental affairs and an increase in regime legitimacy. Thus, the regime took certain steps to expand political participation and to promote more individual freedom. Successful economic reform also necessitated changes in Hungary's relationship to the world economy. Hungary developed and diversified its relations with many Western countries and with several non-Western countries. Political reforms also encouraged Western countries, particularly the United States, to furnish economic assistance to Hungary. Domestic economic reform therefore provided the impetus for Hungary's willingness to emancipate itself, if only to a small degree, from both the Soviet political model and Soviet foreign policy tutelage.

* * *

In 1989 monographs on Hungary's political system and foreign policy remained scarce. Hans-Georg Heinrich's *Hungary: Politics, Economics, and Society* presents an overview of the government, state, and party structures. Baruch Hazan's *The East European Political System,* although a general work, contains some useful information about Hungary. Peter Toma's *Socialist Authority* also provides material on the political system. For most aspects of government and politics, the interested reader is encouraged to turn to more specialized works. István Kovács's "The Development of the Constitution of the Hungarian People's Republic" discusses the Constitution. Heinrich's *Verfassungswirklichkeit in Osteuropa* contains much material on the Presidential Council. Barnabas Racz's "Political Participation and Developed Socialism: The Hungarian Elections of 1985" is the best secondary source on the electoral system. George Schöpflin's *Censorship and Political Communication in Eastern Europe* provides a perspective on the media. The best writings on foreign policy are the reports prepared by analysts at Radio Free Europe, particularly those by Alfred Reisch. In addition, an account of Hungary's attempts to develop a new foreign policy role for itself is found in works by Gyula Józsa. (For further information and complete citations, see Bibliography.)

Chapter 5. National Security

Two soldiers, Esztergom, 1918

THE HUNGARIAN PEOPLE'S ARMY (HPA) of the late 1980s comprised ground and air forces under the supervision of the Ministry of Defense. The ground forces accounted for more than 77 percent of the total strength of the HPA, which in 1989 numbered slightly less than 100,000 troops. The armed forces that constituted the HPA were committed by treaty to the Soviet-East European alliance known as the Warsaw Pact. Another military force, the Border Guard, which patrolled the country's frontiers, was supervised by the Ministry of Interior, as were the National Police and the Security Police. Hungary had no uniformed state security police. The Workers' Guard, a part-time force similar to a national guard was an arm of the Hungarian Socialist Workers' Party. The HPA and the Border Guard obtained manpower through a system of universal male conscription; service in the other organizations was voluntary. A small number of women also served in the armed forces in auxiliary roles but were not subject to conscription.

Political changes in Hungary and the Soviet Union in the late 1980s promised drastic changes in the HPA's relationship to the party and to the Warsaw Pact. Reformers proposed removing the national security forces from tight party control to reduce the likelihood that they would be used for domestic political coercion. The lessening of tensions in Europe had allowed the financially strapped Hungarian government to severely cut its military budget without fearing domestic or international reprisal. Both Soviet and Hungarian officials spoke cautiously of the possibility of a politically and militarily neutral Hungary. In 1989 the Soviet Union had begun withdrawing a small portion of its 65,000 troops stationed in Hungary. Ironically, by the late 1980s many Hungarians viewed this withdrawal with dismay because they had begun to see the Soviet forces in their country as protection against an increasingly militant Romania.

Political liberalization also encouraged changes in the criminal justice system. Regime leaders promised to depoliticize the administration of justice and the police, although as of 1989 the apparatus of repression remained intact. However, harsh measures against dissent and public demonstrations, which had been taken as late as 1986, had stopped by 1989.

Historical and Political Setting

Hungary had a glorious military tradition in the Middle Ages. However, long resistance to the Ottoman Turks left Hungary weak, and the country was eventually partitioned by the Turks and the Habsburgs in 1541. Thereafter—except for the period between World War I and World War II—Hungary's armed forces have been subject to those of an outside power, first the Habsburg imperial army and then, after World War II, the Soviet-dominated Warsaw Pact.

Hungary has played less of a role in the Soviet alliance system than the other Warsaw Pact countries except for Romania. It had the smallest army in the Warsaw Pact (see Glossary). Unlike the German Democratic Republic (East Germany) and Czechoslovakia, which border on the Federal Republic of Germany (West Germany), Hungary does not border on a member of the North Atlantic Treaty Organization (NATO).

Historical Background and Traditions

Since the Magyars' conquest of the Carpathian Basin in 896, Hungarians have had to be concerned about their national security. Twice in Hungary's history, a foreign invader killed nearly half of the country's population, and at other times Hungarians had to endure occupation by a foreign power seeking to destroy their national identity. For this reason, a military leader who delivered the people, however temporarily, from foreign oppression became a hero.

The Medieval Period

Before the Magyar tribes conquered the Carpathian Basin in 896, they lived a seminomadic life on the Russian steppe (see Early History, ch. 1). Their military organization and weaponry resembled those of various Bulgar-Turkish tribes who also inhabited the steppe at that time. Riding on swift steppe ponies, the Magyar horsemen used recurved bows for battle at long distance, and they used sabers, short lances, axes, and clubs for hand-to-hand combat. In the ninth century, Arab historians wrote that the Magyars could muster 20,000 horsemen for battle.

In the mid- to late ninth century, the Magyar tribes inhabited the territory lying to the north of the Black Sea between the lower Don and lower Dnepr rivers. From there they made armed forays against kingdoms to the west, first against the Bulgars on the lower Danube in 839 and then in 862 against Pannonia (see Glossary), which at that time was part of the eastern Frankish Kingdom.

In the last decade of the ninth century, the Magyar tribes engaged in a series of military actions that culminated in their conquest of the Carpathian Basin. From 892 to 894, they raided Moravia (in what is today the central part of Czechoslovakia) and

Pannonia, gaining valuable knowledge about the fortified passes in the Carpathian Mountains, the natural defenses of their future homeland. In 894–95 three Magyar forces were operating in the Danube Basin—one allied with Byzantium against the Bulgars in the south, one allied with the Franks against Moravia in Pannonia, and a third that was invading what is now the Trans-Carpathian oblast in the Soviet Ukraine. With most of their armed men away in battle, the Magyars remaining in the Dnieper-Dnestr region could offer little resistance to the Pechenegs, a steppe people who attacked them from the east. Suffering great material losses, the Magyars on the steppe fled westward, through the Carpathian mountain passes, into their future homeland.

Even though their conquest of the Carpathian Basin was not yet complete, in 899 the Magyars launched their first plundering expedition against the rest of Europe. Terrorizing Europe for more than half a century, the Magyar raiders reached southern Italy, France, Spain, northern Germany, Greece, and even the gates of Constantinople. However, the raids against Western Europe ended when in 955 the Magyars suffered a disastrous defeat near Augsburg (in Bavaria) against a coalition headed by the Holy Roman Emperor, Otto II.

Hungary was one of the strongest military powers in Europe for nearly 250 years following its establishment as a kingdom in A.D. 1000 (see Medieval Period, ch. 1). Engaging in small wars for either territorial or dynastic reasons, the country successfully resisted German and Byzantine attempts to meddle in its internal affairs. However, Hungarian armies could not stop the Mongols, who invaded the country in 1241. Although the attack was expected and the border fortifications reinforced, the Mongols easily swept through the Carpathian passes into the Danube Plain in March 1241. In April the Hungarian army met one of the Mongol armies in the area between present-day Leninváros and Miskolc. The Hungarian force was surrounded and totally annihilated at Mohi, but Hungary's King Béla IV managed to elude the Mongols and escape.

The Mongol occupation was brief but devastating, wiping out at least half the population. The country soon recovered economically but remained militarily weakened until the beginning of the fourteenth century. Charles Robert (1308–42), the first Anjou king of Hungary, required the nobles to maintain small armed units, or *banderia,* which served as a reserve force in addition to the nobility and mercenaries serving in the royal army. This renewed military strength, combined with the fact that Hungary's neighbors were either militarily weak or preoccupied elsewhere, helped create a relatively peaceful Eastern Europe in the fourteenth century. Even the increasing threat from the Ottoman Turks, starting in the 1360s, was successfully resisted during this time.

The Modern Period

In the fifteenth century lived János Hunyadi, perhaps the greatest Hungarian general of all time (see Renaissance and Reformation, ch. 1). Although Hunyadi fought, not always successfully, against the Turks several times in the 1440s, he is best known for his victory against them near Belgrade in 1456. There the Hungarian forces decisively defeated the Turkish army and sent the sultan into flight. However, the Turkish wars, together with the petty struggles on the western borderlands, drained the national treasury, and increasingly heavy taxation and feudal obligations pushed the peasantry into a rebellion that was eventually crushed. The country was economically weakened and racked by political instability, and its military might declined precipitously after the death of King Mátyás Corvinus in 1490.

The Ottoman Turks threatened to invade in the 1520s, but the Hungarian nobility seemed oblivious. The Turks successfully attacked Belgrade in 1521, and on August 29, 1526, met the small, poorly equipped Hungarian army at Mohács. The Hungarian forces were nearly wiped out, and their king, Louis II, died in the rout. The Turks captured Buda in early September but then retreated southward, loaded with captives, and having no intention of permanently occupying Hungary. However, the struggle between the Habsburgs and the Hungarian contenders for the Hungarian throne pulled the Turks deeper into Hungarian politics, leading to their military occupation of Buda in 1541 and the entire Hungarian plain soon afterward. The Habsburg emperor was left with a strip of land in northeastern Hungary (called "Royal Hungary"), while Transylvania remained nominally independent under Turkish suzerainty (see fig. 3). The section of Hungary directly under Ottoman rule became a wasteland, as various Turkish military formations periodically looted and destroyed settlements, killing the inhabitants or selling them into slavery.

In Royal Hungary, the Habsburgs constructed a system of fortifications along the border with Ottoman Hungary during the seventeenth century. Many Hungarian nobles, having fled the Turkish zone of occupation, assumed military leadership of important sectors of this border zone. Their serfs were obliged to work twelve days annually on border fortifications, to perform military service, and to pay a military tax. Several Hungarian military leaders during this time achieved fame for their exploits. Miklós Zrínyi's heroic stand against the Turks in 1564 and István Bocskay's victory over the Habsburgs in Transylvania in 1604–05 were bright spots in the otherwise dismal military history of the Hungarians during the period of Ottoman occupation (see Partition of Hungary, ch. 1).

The failed Turkish attack on Vienna in 1683 began a process of retreat that led to the Ottomans' being driven out of Buda in 1686 and most of Hungary by the end of the century. The subsequent Habsburg rule, however, proved to be just as cruel as that of the Turks, and resulted in an eight-year rebellion led by Ferenc Rákóczi (see Hungary under the Habsburgs, ch. 1). The Treaty of Szatmár (1711) ended this war, during which half a million Hungarians died.

During the eighteenth century, the Habsburg Hofkriegsrat (see Glossary) in Vienna directly controlled the Hungarian army, which was created in 1715. The Palatine (see Glossary) was commander in chief of the armed forces in Hungary, but the Habsburgs deliberately left the office vacant. Responsibility for recruitment and supply was assumed by the Hungarian Viceregal Council, located in Pozsony, the capital of Royal Hungary (present-day Bratislava in Czechoslovakia), until 1785 and then transferred to Buda.

During the first half of the eighteenth century, the Habsburgs established a Hungarian standing army made up of six high commands: one for Hungary proper and the others for Croatia, Slavonia, Transylvania, the Banat (in southern Hungary), and the Military Frontier Zones (located in Croatia). The Hungarian standing army was supported by war taxes paid by the counties and towns. Soldiers were supposed to serve for life but were usually discharged after twenty years of service. This term was reduced to ten years in 1830. Until 1840 soldiers were forced into service by press gangs; later they were selected by lot.

In 1790 the Hungarian nobility revolted against the Habsburgs in an attempt to restore former feudal privileges and Hungarian autonomy. A separate Hungarian army was formed from the *banderia,* but it was dissolved when the Habsburgs managed to avoid war with Prussia and thus were able to redirect their imperial forces toward Hungary.

Hungarian soldiers fought in the Habsburg army during the wars against France from 1792 to 1815. Except for a small battle at Győr in 1808—which the French won—no military action took place on Hungarian soil. Nevertheless, the Hungarian troops suffered more than 150,000 casualties during these wars.

The revolution that broke out in Vienna in 1848—part of a wave of revolts that swept across Europe that year—caused enough disruption in the imperial government to allow the Hungarian nobility to seize more political autonomy for Hungary. After quelling the revolt in other parts of the empire, the Habsburg government in September 1848 sent forces into Hungary under Josip Jelačić, the Habsburg governor of Croatia. Jelačić's army was met by a hastily formed Hungarian army and was driven out of the country. The government in Vienna attacked again in the late fall and even occupied Pest in early December. In the spring, however, these Habsburg forces were driven out by a Hungarian army under a young major, Artur Görgei, while another Hungarian army, under General József Bem, drove the Habsburg forces out of Transylvania. Nevertheless, in June 1849 the Russian army came to the rescue of the Habsburgs and invaded Hungary through the Carpathian Mountains. Outnumbered and outgunned, Bem's small army was defeated in August, and Görgei surrendered his forces to the Russians shortly afterward. The revolt was crushed and its leaders hanged, although Lajos Kossuth, the leader of the revolutionary government, escaped to the Ottoman Empire.

Although the Compromise of 1867 establishing the Dual Monarchy of Austria-Hungary gave each country separate parliaments and separate governments, the Hungarian military forces remained under centralized Habsburg control (see Dual Monarchy, ch. 1). Thus, Hungarian soldiers, together with the other troops of nations under the Habsburg monarchy, found themselves mobilizing for war in the summer of 1914, first against Serbia and then against Serbia's ally, Russia. The largest Hungarian army in history fought under the imperial flag on the side of the Central Powers.

The Military in Trianon Hungary

Hungarian independence came in 1918, when the Habsburg Empire's disintegration gave not only the Hungarians but also the empire's other nationalities the opportunity to establish sovereign states. Hungarian soldiers, scattered among the Habsburg troops at various places within and outside the empire, were ordered home by the government of Mihály Károlyi in the fall of 1918. They found their country racked by political and economic strife. Hungary could not resist the Romanian army's advance to Budapest but did drive the Czechs out of northern Hungary (present-day Slovakia). However, the Treaty of Trianon signed in June 1920 pushed the Hungarian army back close to the present-day boundaries (see Trianon Hungary, ch. 1). Moreover, the Treaty of Trianon limited Hungary's military forces to 35,000 soldiers.

Motivated by a desire to regain lands lost as a result of the Treaty of Trianon, Hungary allied itself with Italy in the late 1920s and with Germany during the 1930s. Diplomacy and alliances, rather

*Liberation Monument on
Gellert Hill in Budapest
Courtesy
Sam and Sarah Stulberg*

than military action, brought about the return of some former Hungarian lands in 1938–39. Hungary participated in the German invasion of the Soviet Union in June 1941 by committing a small force to aid in the German occupation of the Ukraine. After January 1942, however, the Hungarian army was thrown into the front lines with the Germans. Underequipped (one machine gun was allotted for every kilometer of front line) and lacking warm clothing and fuel, this army suffered about 200,000 casualties at the battle of Stalingrad during the winter of 1942–43. This defeat, combined with the Soviet rollback of the German invasion, quickly turned Hungarian public opinion against the war. Many Hungarian prisoners of war fought on the side of their Soviet captors or were sent as partisans behind the Axis lines in southeastern Europe. Tired of the half-hearted Hungarian war effort, the Germans occupied Hungary in March 1943. Admiral Miklós Horthy, the Hungarian regent, attempted to negotiate an armistice with the Allies in the fall of 1944. Horthy was soon arrested by the Germans, but by then the Red Army had already entered eastern Hungary. The Red Army captured Budapest in December and pushed the Germans completely out of Hungary by early April 1945.

Sovietization

By the end of World War II, the public had little respect for the army because the war had been lost and the territory that had been

229

reincorporated after 1938 was given back to Czechoslovakia, Romania, and Yugoslavia. Soviet officers believed Hungarian army officers to be as guilty as their German counterparts and, because of the undistinguished performance of the Hungarian army during the war, the Soviets had no respect for Hungary as a military force. The communists distrusted the former army officers, and these officers hated the communists. After the Hungarian People's Republic was established in 1949, many of these officers were punished and often sent to the harshest labor camps (see Postwar Hungary, ch. 1).

The postwar Hungarian army developed out of divisions put together to fight Germany after Hungary had made peace with the Allies in December 1944. Under Soviet pressure, however, the army was quickly demobilized in 1946, and most officers were removed because of pro-Western or anticommunist sympathies. A new force was then created under an independent command controlled by the Hungarian Communist Party, and a new army—the Hungarian People's Army—officially emerged in 1948. The military clause of the peace treaty that Hungary signed with the Allies permitted it to have an army of 65,000 troops and an air force of 5,000 personnel and ninety aircraft.

According to American expert Iván Völgyes, Mihály Farkas, the minister of defense from 1948 to 1953, served as the chief architect of the new Hungarian People's Army. Following Soviet orders, Farkas, himself an avowed Stalinist, set out to imitate the Soviet army and to Sovietize the Hungarian army. The HPA's organization mirrored that of the Soviet army. Its uniforms, ranks and insignia, decorations, and "general privileges" were all based on the Soviet model, as was the "dual command system," whereby the party attached political commissars to each military commander to ensure the political reliability and ideological commitment of the troops. These political officers were assigned by the Ministry of Defense's Main Political Administration (see Glossary) and were given instructions by the Administrative Department of the Secretariat of the Hungarian Workers' Party (HWP—on November 1, 1956, renamed the Hungarian Socialist Workers' Party— HSWP). Although this dual command system was still in effect in the late 1980s, it placed the most restrictions on military commanders in the period between 1949 and 1955.

Soviet influence further increased when, starting in November 1948, hundreds of Soviet military "advisers" were assigned to the Hungarian army at all command levels down to the regimental one. Although theoretically acting only as advisers, they influenced all important decisions. Beginning in December 1948, thousands

of Hungarians began attending Soviet military and political academies to gain technical expertise and political indoctrination. Hungarian generals were sent to Soviet general staff schools (see Soviet Influence, this ch.).

The regime managed to create a communist officer corps by actively recruiting workers and peasants into the higher ranks of the military. By 1954 a little more than half of the officers were children of manual laborers, while about one-third came from peasant families. The officer corps provided upward mobility for the former "underclass," while providing material benefits in a country where standards of living were low compared with those of Western Europe.

State Security Forces and the Revolution

Ironically, by the time the HPA had become thoroughly Sovietized, the first waves of de-Stalinization rippled through the Hungarian Workers' Party. In 1953 the Stalinist party leader, Mátyás Rákosi, lost his position as prime minister, and the Stalinist minister of defense, Mihály Farkas, fell from power. Professional training for officers was instituted at the military academies. A better educated and increasingly professional officer corps began to question

231

the dogmatic teachings of the party. Tension arose when the "internationalism" (a euphemism for following the Soviet line in foreign and military policy) stressed by the communist state clashed with the latent nationalism of the officers. These officers also resented special privileges bestowed on both the State Security Department (Állámvédelmi Osztály—AVO—the name for the pre-1956 secret police) and the Soviet officers in the country.

Although the HPA did not participate in the Revolution of 1956 as an organized force, its role in that conflict demonstrated its political unreliability to both the regime and the Soviet Union (see Revolution of 1956, ch. 1). Organized military support for the revolution did not occur for two reasons. First, before being sent home on October 28–29, the Soviet military advisers in Hungary ordered various sections of the Hungarian army to disperse. Second, Prime Minister Imre Nagy refused to order the HPA to oppose the final Soviet invasion that took place on November 3. However, not only did conscripts refuse to fire on mass demonstrations that took place on October 23 (although the AVO forces did), but some even went over to the insurgents and supplied them with weapons. Supposedly "politically reliable" cadets from military academies likewise joined the insurgents, as did some military officers. One of the most important military figures to join the revolutionaries was Colonel Pál Maléter, the commander of an armored unit sent to recapture the Kilián barracks in Budapest from the Freedom Fighters. In a parley with the insurgents, Maléter became convinced that they "were loyal sons of the Hungarian people," and he joined them. Maléter eventually became minister of defense in the Nagy government; he was later tried and executed with Nagy in 1958.

The regular police, at least those in Budapest, were likewise sympathetic to the insurgents. On October 24, Sándor Kopácsi, chief of the Budapest police, gave orders to supply the revolutionaries with weapons. Budapest police joined the rebels but did not fight the Soviet army. Police headquarters then became headquarters for revolutionary forces.

Many members of the dreaded AVO, by contrast, fell victim to the public's wrath. During the revolution, AVO recruits deserted, and its professional officers found themselves hunted down by mobs. Some lynchings occurred. The regular police helped disarm the security police, and those security police known to have committed acts of state terror against the citizenry were taken into custody to await trial (some were summarily executed). Most AVO officers were detained by the revolutionary government, which abolished the security police on October 29. At first, Moscow sought to suppress the insurgency with the forces at hand. Soviet armored units began arriving in Budapest in the early morning of October 24. For the next four days, they fought intermittently with the insurgents. They were unable to dislodge Hungarian army units in the Kilián barracks that were under the leadership of Colonel Maléter or the units near the Corvin Cinema. Soviet forces and advisers publicly withdrew from Budapest on October 28. On the surface, it seemed as through the revolt was victorious.

On October 30, the government formed the Revolutionary Committee of the Armed Forces, with representatives from the army, police, and the Freedom Fighters. The following day, the appointment as its head of General Béla K. Király, who had been imprisoned from 1951 to 1956, was announced. On November 1, 1956, Hungary withdrew from the Warsaw Pact and declared political neutrality. This act was in response to reports of the Soviet army's entering the country in force on October 31.

The Soviet army began pouring into Hungary on November 1 and proceeded to occupy airfields and other strategic points in the country. The invasion used 120,000 soldiers taken from eleven fully staffed, "category-one" (forces of three-quarters' to full strength) divisions in Romania and the Ukraine. Völgyes believes that the coordinated nature of the attack and the positions taken by Soviet units suggest that the Soviet Union had planned the invasion far in advance.

The Soviet army returned to Budapest in force on November 4. The HPA, still splintered and riddled with pro-Soviet officers, could not offer organized resistance. The Freedom Fighters had neither the manpower nor the ammunition to oppose the Soviet army for long. After the fighting stopped, the Soviet authorities began to round up suspects, disarm the Hungarian People's Army, and carry out summary executions. In the next few years, the Hungarian courts handed down an estimated 2,000 death sentences, primarily to street fighters.

The Postrevolutionary Period

The HPA underwent a purge after the revolution. Officers were required to sign a declaration condemning the revolution, praising Hungarian-Soviet "friendship," and pledging allegiance to the new government of János Kádár. Nearly 20 percent of the officer corps refused to sign the declaration, even under threats, and were expelled from the army. In the year following the revolution, the army was reorganized under Soviet supervision, with increased power given to the political commanders. However, in order to assuage public opinion, the official mission of the army changed from "defending socialism" to defending Hungary.

The HPA became an integral part of the Warsaw Pact forces in 1957 but did not participate in pact military exercises until 1962. The HPA participated, although reluctantly, in the Soviet-led Warsaw Pact invasion of Czechoslovakia in August 1968. In 1989 the Hungarian government revealed that the HPA participated in the invasion because the Kádár regime feared that failure to do so would have halted Soviet exports of raw materials to Hungary.

Through the late 1980s, the HPA and Soviet troops held joint exercises on Hungarian soil twice a year, and Hungarian forces participated in exercises held on the territory of other Warsaw Pact countries. Rarely, however, did forces from the other Warsaw Pact nations conduct military exercises in Hungary.

Government and Party Control

Ultimate responsibility for defense policy lay with the HSWP Politburo (see Party Structure, ch. 4). The party exercised several channels of control over the armed forces. The party officially controlled the army through the Government Administration and Administration Department of the Secretariat. The head of the Ministry of Defense's Main Political Administration reported to this party body and to the minister of defense. The Main Political Administration, in turn, controlled the political departments at the division level and the political deputies of the commanding officers at the subdivision level. Party cells were subordinated to the deputy commanders for political affairs. The Army Committee of the Central Committee of the HSWP supervised overall political work in the army.

During peacetime the Presidential Council, whose members were subject to the HSWP's *nomenklatura* (see Glossary) authority, oversaw national defense; the defense committee of the National Assembly also worked closely with the Presidential Council (see State Apparatus, ch. 4). At the government level, the Council of Ministers' Committee of Defense supervised the defense committees of Budapest and those of the counties. The minister of defense was a member of the defense committees of both the Council of Ministers and the National Assembly in peacetime. During wartime, the president would transform the Presidential Council into the National Defense Council, with the minister of defense leading the war effort.

In theory the Presidential Council appointed and dismissed officers, but in fact this responsibility was assumed by the minister of defense. The minister of defense had always been a member of the Central Committee of the HSWP, the highest ranking officer, and the commander in chief of the armed forces. He reported to the chairman of the Council of Ministers and to the HSWP Politburo in peacetime. In late 1989, Hungary's minister of defense was Colonel General Ferenc Karpati, who was appointed in December 1985 upon the death of his predecessor, Colonel General István Oláh. Karpati had joined the Hungarian Communist Party in 1945 at age nineteen. His chief of staff was Lieutenant General József Pacsek. At the same time, Brigadier General István Bracsok served as secretary of the HSWP's People's Army Committee, while Lajos Krasznai served as chief of the HPA's Main Political Administration.

Party membership was essential for career advancement in the military; hence, party membership among officers was high; according to Karpati it was 80 percent in 1989. This high level of party membership among officers was another means of party control over the military. The party began recruiting prospective officers in the military academies, where students underwent a screening process to assess their political reliability.

By contrast, party membership among enlisted men and noncommissioned officers (NCOs) was relatively low. Estimates placed party membership at 0.5 to 0.8 percent of those persons drafted, compared with about 4 percent for the general population of the same age. In the late 1980s, however, party membership was seriously declining, and it can safely be assumed that the percentage of HSWP members among the military rank and file was dropping as well.

Expenditures

The military budget underwent a series of reductions in the late 1980s because of the country's worsening economic problems. The 1987 estimated military budget, based on Ministry of Finance information, was US$867 million (40.745 billion forints). The 1989 budget was cut to US$576 million (40.3 billion forints) even before January 1, 1989. The proportion of the military budget devoted to the acquisition of new technology dropped from 32 percent in 1988 to 16 percent in 1989. From 1980 to 1985, this proportion had averaged about 50 percent of the military budget.

In the late 1980s, the Soviet Union and other Warsaw Pact countries expressed displeasure with the relatively low Hungarian defense budget, but this pressure did not induce the Hungarians to increase the percentage of the gross domestic product (GDP—see Glossary) devoted to defense. Only Romania spent a smaller percentage of GDP on national defense than Hungary, but in absolute numbers Hungary's outlay was the smallest in the Warsaw Pact.

By contrast, the funds spent by the government for armed forces subject to the Ministry of Interior and the Workers' Guard increased by nearly 22 percent from 1987 to 1988 and by nearly 24 percent from 1988 to 1989. Much of this increase, however, was expected to be canceled out by inflation and price reform.

The budget for the defense and interior ministries had to be approved by the defense committee of the National Assembly, a body that managed to increase its power during the late 1980s. Nevertheless, in 1989 the committee once again approved the state budgets for the ministries of defense and interior and, for the first time, the Workers' Guard, without inquiring about how the money was to be spent.

Military Industry

In the late 1980s, the government's defense industry produced only a small amount of the HPA's needs. Major weapons were obtained from the Soviet Union. Communications and instrumentation equipment made up about three-quarters of the country's military production, while artillery and infantry weapons and ammunition made up another 12 percent. The production of vehicles and aviation components contributed about 8 percent, while chemicals and light industrial products formed the remaining 5 percent.

In early 1989, military industries anticipated a 31-percent decline in production compared with the previous year because of the slashed military budget and a drop in exports. Factories that produced mostly military equipment were expected to be hard hit. Military orders, mostly long-range microwave equipment and accessories, made up about 80 percent of the production of the Precision Mechanics Enterprise. Military orders for handguns made up 35 percent of the Weapon and Gas Appliance Factory's production and 25 percent of the orders for the Diosgyör Engineering Factory. The Machine Factory at Gödöllő, which produced components for military vehicles and tanks and repaired army equipment, was owned by the Ministry of Defense and operated by soldiers. In January 1989, it was operating at 50 percent of capacity because orders from the other Warsaw Pact countries dropped by 50 percent and a cut in sales to the HPA was anticipated. The military production of the Videoton telecommunications factory, valued at US$132 million in 1988, was expected to fall to US$84.9 million in 1991, and more than 2,000 of its 7,000 workers were expected to be released, resulting in a 40-percent idle manufacturing capacity. The effects of cutbacks in military procurement on the euphemistically named "Lamp Factory" (Lámpagyár), which produced pistols and automatic rifles, and the Danuvia Factory, which manufactured machine guns, was not known.

Soviet Influence

In the late 1980s, Soviet influence on Hungary's HPA was exercised in two ways. Numerous organizational ties linked the Soviet military with Hungary's armed forces. An equally important influence was the fact that a major component of the Warsaw Pact's military forces—the Southern Group of Forces—was stationed in Hungary.

Loyalties and Control

Soviet leader Nikita S. Khrushchev (1953–64) once said that the Soviet government had never trusted the Hungarian army. Despite the training that Hungarian officers had received from the Soviet military since 1948 and the Soviet infiltration of the HPA's top command structure, the Revolution of 1956 confirmed Moscow's apprehensions. The events of 1956 threw the loyalty of even the top Hungarian military elite into question.

In the 1980s, Soviet influence on Hungarian military officers was much greater among the upper-level officers than among lower-level officers, regimental sergeants major, or NCOs (see Uniforms and Rank Insignia, this ch.). The higher-ranking officers saw their careers tied to Hungary's association with the Soviet Union and the Warsaw Pact, while those of lesser ranks saw Soviet troops in Hungary as an army of occupation.

The Soviet Union exerted its military influence within Hungary in a variety of ways. The obvious means were official ministry-to-ministry contacts and the presence of Soviet troops in the country. In addition, the chief Soviet representative of the Warsaw Treaty Organization in Hungary exercised day-to-day control of both the Soviet army and the Hungarian People's Army. Also, the Soviet military attaché and staff in the Soviet embassy maintained a liaison office with the HSWP Central Committee's Government Administration and Administration Department, the Ministry of National Defense's Main Political Administration, and the Central Committee of the HPA's party organization. And, finally, the representative and staff of Soviet military intelligence met frequently with various military and political authorities.

Nevertheless, the HPA was hardly a pawn of the Soviet military establishment. During the 1980–81 crisis in Poland, the Hungarian military leadership received instructions from the HSWP not to intervene in Poland without orders from the party. This order emanated not only from a purportedly sovereign government's desire to retain control over its own military but also from a determination to maintain civilian control over the military.

In the late 1980s, the HPA also pressed for "more democracy" in Warsaw Pact decision making. This term justified requests for giving Hungary and other non-Soviet members a greater voice in decision making within the pact and for rotating the command of the Warsaw Pact forces among all the military leaders of the non-Soviet Warsaw Pact (NSWP) countries.

Soviet Southern Group of Forces in Hungary

Soviet troops have been stationed in Hungary since April 1945, when they pushed the German army completely out of the country. After Hungary signed a peace treaty with the Allies in 1947, Soviet forces remained in order to secure lines of communication with Soviet troops occupying Austria. Soviet forces withdrew from Austria in May 1955 but remained in Hungary at the request of the High Command of the Warsaw Treaty Organization, which was formed one day before the Austrian treaty was signed.

In May 1957, the Soviet-installed government under Kádár signed an agreement with the Soviet Union to legally recognize the Soviet forces that had occupied the country in 1956 (see Revolution of 1956, ch. 1). Called the Decree Having the Force of Law No. 54 of 1957, it justified the Soviet presence as a defense against NATO "aggression" and West German rearmament. The agreement mentioned no specifics, such as the number of Soviet troops, their deployment within Hungary, and the facilities made available to them, although such items may have been written down in a secret protocol. The version of the agreement made public mentioned only that the Soviet troops were to be stationed "indefinitely" and that the compact could be changed only by mutual consent.

Officially called the Southern Group of Forces (SGF), Soviet troops in Hungary numbered 65,000, according to NATO estimates made in November 1988. At that time, the troops were under the command of Lieutenant General Aleksei A. Demidov. The Soviet forces in Hungary corresponded strategically to the Group of Soviet Forces stationed in East Germany, the Northern Group of Forces in Poland, and the Central Group of Forces in Czechoslovakia.

The SGF, headquartered in Budapest, commanded the 13th Guards Tank Division in Veszprém, the 2d Tank Division in Esztergom, the 253d Motor Rifle Division in Székesfehérvár, and the 93d Guards Motor Rifle Division in Kecskemét. These forces were supported by an air assault brigade, five fighter regiments, two fighter-ground attack regiments, several combat helicopter units, and reconnaissance aircraft. In a war against NATO, the SGF and the Hungarian troops would be used as part of the South-western Theater of Military Operations (*teatr voennykh deistvii—* TVD).

In December 1988, Soviet leader Mikhail S. Gorbachev announced that the Soviet Union would unilaterally remove some of its forces from Eastern Europe. This force reduction, which began in April 1989, was to be carried out over a two-year period. It would include the tank division deployed at Veszprém and the surrounding area, an armored training regiment, a paratroop battalion and interceptor squadron based at Tököl airport in Pest County, a chemical defense battalion, and the SGF training school for NCOs in Szolnok. This partial withdrawal would remove 450 tanks; 200 guns, trench mortars, and mine throwers; 3,000 vehicles; and 10,400 of the 65,000 Soviet troops in Hungary. In April 1989, Hungarian foreign minister Gyula Horn said that all Soviet soldiers might be removed from the country in the first half of the 1990s.

The Soviet troops were generally isolated from Hungarian life. They did not interfere in Hungarian affairs and appeared in public usually in small groups and only in certain restricted areas. The Hungarians generally did not like the Soviet soldiers and did not fraternize with them.

External Threats to National Security

In the late 1980s, Hungary's defense policy was in a state of flux. The government no longer stressed the possibility of a NATO attack, nor did it consider likely a Soviet intervention to halt Hungary's march toward reform. In fact, spokesmen for both Hungary and the Soviet Union publicly alluded to a possible withdrawal of Hungary from the Warsaw Pact and the proclamation of neutrality for Hungary such as that enjoyed by Finland and Austria. But both sides spoke cautiously about this possibility, and the Hungarian government stressed that it did not wish to pursue neutrality at the risk of upsetting the balance of power in Europe.

Threat from the North Atlantic Treaty Organization

Traditionally, Hungary's role in the Warsaw Pact had been to follow the Soviet lead on matters of national and bloc defense. But even during the early and middle 1980s, when member countries of the North Atlantic Treaty Organization (NATO) began installing intermediate-range ballistic missiles in Western Europe in response to the installation of Soviet SS–20 missiles in the western portion of the Soviet Union, the attitude of the Hungarian government toward the West was never as rabidly vehement as that displayed by the governments of Czechoslovakia or East Germany (see Principles of Foreign Policy, ch. 4). In fact, the Soviet Union had criticized Hungary for not spending enough on its military and for stressing defense of the country (*hónvédelem*) instead of defense of the countries of the Warsaw Pact.

Western analysts speculated about Hungary's military role in a Warsaw Pact conflict with the West. Hungary does not border any NATO country and therefore was not in the front line of Warsaw Pact troop deployment. It was seen to play a supporting role, primarily by supplying military engineering support and some antiaircraft defense. In a war with NATO, Hungarian forces would either be used in the Warsaw Pact's Western Theater of Military Operations against West Germany or in the Southwestern Theater of Military Operations against NATO's southern flank. In both scenarios, Hungarian forces would have to enter the territory of neutral countries. For instance, Yugoslavia's neutrality might be breached to project Soviet and Warsaw Pact power in the Mediterranean. Hungarian military engineering support would prove crucial in such a campaign.

Threat from Romania

During the 1980s, the Hungarian government broke its silence about Romania's oppression of its Hungarian minority, numbering about 2 million to 2.2 million people (see Relations with Other Communist Neighbors, ch. 4). Under Soviet pressure and for the sake of socialist solidarity, the Hungarian government had refrained from criticizing Romania, but increasing domestic pressure forced it to act.

As the war of words between the two countries heated up, so did the potential for armed conflict. In July 1989, *Der Standard,* published in Vienna, reported that a secret meeting of the Hungarian state and party leadership had taken place in November 1988 in which the military was asked to assess the strategic balance between Hungary and Romania. The resulting report, published in February 1989, revealed Hungary's "striking military inferiority." Hungary had no fortifications on its border with Romania, and in a private meeting Romanian leader Nicolae Ceauşescu allegedly warned Károly Grósz, Hungary's party leader, not to install such defenses. During the summer of 1989, Hungarian diplomats hinted at fear of attack by Romania. *Der Spiegel,* published in Hamburg, reported in July 1989 that Hungary felt threatened by the Condor intermediate-range missiles that Romania had acquired with "German and Argentine help." At a July 1989 Warsaw Pact meeting in Bucharest, Ceauşescu was said to have threatened Hungary with war, although representatives of both countries agreed that steps had to be taken to stem the rising tension. Ironically, by this time the Hungarian opposition had stopped insisting that Soviet troops leave the country because they were seen to be the country's main protection against Romania.

Threat from the Soviet Union

From the mid-1940s through the mid-1980s, the threat of a Soviet invasion prevented the other Warsaw Pact countries from deviating from Moscow's prescribed domestic and foreign policies. The Soviet invasion of Hungary in 1956 demonstrated that Moscow would act if it believed that changes in that country threatened the security of the Warsaw Pact or the leading role of the communist party in Hungary. After economic reforms began in the 1960s, Hungary's government and party leaders were careful to take Soviet sensitivities into account. However, in the late 1980s, Moscow showed that it was sympathetic rather than hostile to reforms within Hungary, thus lessening the chances of a Soviet invasion.

The Hungarian Armed Forces

Compared with the other countries in the Warsaw Pact, in the late 1980s Hungary had the smallest army and air force, as well as the fewest artillery pieces, light armored vehicles, and antiaircraft weapons. It ranked last, along with Bulgaria and Romania, in the number of military helicopters, and only Romania had fewer tanks. In addition to lagging behind its Warsaw Pact allies quantitatively, the quality of its military equipment was decidedly "middle level," according to Völgyes. As of mid-1988, the military did not possess modern Soviet T–84 tanks, MiG–29 fighter aircraft, or the new Soviet 5.48mm infantry weapons. Western analysts have claimed that the Hungarian military forces had the lowest combat readiness in the Warsaw Pact and were one of the non-Soviet Warsaw Pact military forces least trusted by Moscow. The HPA's military construction branch was the only section of the armed forces held in high regard by all observers.

Of approximately 100,000 personnel on active duty in the HPA in 1988, about 64,000 were conscripts. During a national emergency, Hungary could mobilize about 900,000 trained men.

Ground Forces

In 1989 about 77,000 troops served in the ground forces (commonly referred to as the army), and about 45,000 of them were conscripts. As in other Warsaw Pact armed forces, the army was by far the largest service.

The reorganization of the HPA, still under way in 1989, attempted to transform its overall structure from one army and one corps possessing one tank and five motorized rifle divisions into three corps with a combined total of five tank brigades and ten motorized rifle brigades. This reorganization set the HPA apart from the other armies of the Warsaw Pact, which were still primarily divided into divisions and regiments. The leadership of the HPA believed the reorganization would make the armed forces more efficient by reducing the number of commands by about one-third.

In the late 1980s, the central headquarters of the HPA was in Székesfehérvár, with the three corps headquartered in Tata, Kaposvár, and Cegléd, respectively. Each corps consisted of five brigades subdivided into battalions, including an independent artillery battalion and an engineering battalion. The largest corps, centered in Tata, possessed three tank brigades and two motorized rifle brigades. The two other corps each had one tank brigade and four motorized rifle brigades. The corps stationed in Cegléd was a skeleton unit. The three corps together possessed three SA–6 surface-to-air missile (SAM) regiments.

In addition to the three corps and fifteen tank and motorized rifle brigades, the HPA possessed independent artillery and Scud surface-to-surface missile brigades, as well as an airborne battalion (the thirty-seventh, stationed in Szolnok). An antitank regiment, an antiaircraft artillery regiment, and an SA–4 SAM regiment were still likewise army, and not corps, troops. Independent engineering battalions were used for rail and roadway repairs, construction projects, and maintenance and repair of telephone and power lines.

In 1988 the Danube Flotilla, incorporated into the army in 1968, consisted of 700 men and eighty-two vessels, including ten Nestin MSI (riverine) boats. During wartime its chief functions would be to clear the Danube and Tisza rivers of mines and to assist the army and its matériel in river crossings.

In 1988 the army possessed 1,200 T–54 and T–55 battle tanks. The Soviet Union has been producing these tanks since 1945, but some have been built as recently as 1979, and many have been upgraded with infrared night-vision systems and laser range-finders. The HPA also had about 100 T–72s, a model that appeared in Soviet units in the early 1970s and began to be seen in Warsaw Pact armies about 1980. Hungary also possessed about 100 PT–76 light tanks.

The HPA's artillery inventory in 1988 included 225 M–1938 (122mm) and 50 M–1943 or D–1 (152mm) howitzers and 100 D–20 (152mm) gun howitzers. It also included 90 2S1 (122mm) and

20 2S3 (152mm) self-propelled guns and 100 M–43 (120mm) mortars. The HPA had fifty BM–21 (122mm) multiple-rocket launchers and twenty-four Frog-7 and Frog-9 Scud surface-to-surface missile launchers. Antitank defense consisted of 100 AT–3 Sagger (including BRDM–2 self-propelled) and 100 AT–4 Spigot antitank guided weapons, 125 SPG–9 (73mm) recoilless launchers, and 100 D–44 (85mm) and 50 D–12 (100mm) antitank guns. Air defense weaponry consisted of 80 S–60 (57mm) towed antiaircraft guns, 50 ZSU–4 SP (23mm) self-propelled antiaircraft guns; and 30 SA–4, 60 SA–6, 350 SA–7, and 50 SA–9 SAMs.

Reconnaissance units in the HPA possessed an estimated 300 BRDM–2 and 400 Hungarian-produced FUG–65 (OT–65) scout vehicles. Motorized infantry units were equipped with 350 BMP–1 infantry combat vehicles and 1,000 Hungarian-produced PSz-H–IV (FUG–70) armored personnel carriers. The PSz-H–IV had been in service since 1983, but production was discontinued; it was to be replaced by Soviet BMP–1 tracked mechanized infantry combat vehicles.

In the late 1980s, the HPA used as its standard infantry weapon the Kalashnikov 7.62mm AKM assault rifle and its 7.62mm AMD–65 version with a folding stock. The 7.62mm RPK and RPD light machine guns were also in service. As of mid-1988, the armed forces planned to convert to the new standard Soviet 5.45mm weapons, but the actual conversion had not yet begun.

The HPA imported most of its ground forces weaponry from the Soviet Union. Domestic industry supplied only a small portion of the army's needs, such as small-caliber weapons (pistols, rifles, and machine guns), some types of artillery pieces, and ammunition.

In 1988 the HPA's stock of road transport vehicles consisted mostly of Hungarian-produced heavy-duty D–566 trucks, Soviet GAZ–69 and UAZ–69 trucks, and East German Robur LO–1800 trucks. Soviet Ural-355 and ZIL–131 trucks had just been introduced into service.

Engineering equipment included PMP heavy pontoon bridges, GSP ferries, K–61 and PTS amphibious vehicles, T–54 MTUs, MT55s, and TMM truck-mounted bridging units to build shorter spans. Hungary built bridging equipment under license from the Soviet Union, Czechoslovakia, and East Germany. Signal troops used Hungarian-made and Soviet-made equipment.

The HPA's engineering and construction corps were considered top notch among the Warsaw Pact countries for their excellent support of amphibious operations. Even Western analysts have called this contribution Hungary's most important one to Warsaw Pact defense.

If engineering was the strongest component of the HPA, logistics was its weakest. Only the regular army was trained in logistics and provided with means of transportation. In a war, the underequipped units would have few logisticians and an insufficient number of vehicles.

In August 1989, the Ministry of Defense disbanded an armored brigade of about 2,000 officers and enlisted men stationed in Szabadszallas in Bács-Kiskun County as part of a planned 9 percent reduction of troops and arms in the army scheduled for 1989 and 1990. Most of the heavy weaponry at the site was scheduled to be melted down.

Air Force

In 1989 the Hungarian air force was organized into one air division and one air defense division, both headquartered at Veszprém. The air division consisted of three fighter or fighter-bomber regiments of three squadrons each. The air division also possessed one helicopter regiment consisting of three squadrons, one transport regiment consisting of two squadrons, and one reconnaissance squadron. The air defense division, responsible for ground-based air defense, consisted of three SAM regiments. Air force personnel in 1988 numbered approximately 22,000, of whom 8,000 were conscripts. The ratio of career personnel to conscripts was slightly less than two to one.

In 1988 the air force possessed 135 combat aircraft and 40 attack helicopters. The three fighter-bomber squadrons possessed ninety MiG-21F/PF/bis/U and forty-five MiG-23M fighter-ground attack aircraft. The reconnaissance squadron flew ten Su-22 aircraft. The two transport squadrons possessed fifteen An 24/26s and An-2s. The three helicopter squadrons together had forty Mi-24 attack helicopters, twenty-five Mi-8 medium-transport helicopters, twenty-five Ka-26 helicopters for training and civilian duties, and five Mi-2 light transport helicopters. Yak-11s and Yak-18s, L-29s, and MiG-15UTIs were used for training purposes. The air defense system consisted of one division with three SAM regiments possessing some twenty sites and 120 SA-2/3 missiles. In June 1989, Brigadier General István Schmidt, commander of the Hungarian air force, announced that no modernization of the air force would take place in the near future, meaning that Hungary would continue to rely heavily on the units of the Soviet air force stationed in the country.

Manpower

Article 70 of the Constitution states that the ''defense of the country shall be the duty of every citizen of the Hungarian People's Republic. Citizens shall perform military service on the basis of the universal system of the draft.'' Therefore, according to the National Defense Act of 1976, male citizens become eligible for military service after January 1 of the year in which they turn eighteen. In 1988 about 75,300 males turned eighteen, of whom 25 percent— the highest percentage among the Warsaw Pact armies—could be expected to be found unfit for military service because of health problems. More than 32 percent of conscripts were twenty-two years old, showing that many men were able to defer their military service for educational or other reasons.

Young men were liable for national service conscription until age twenty-three and subject to call-up in times of an emergency until age fifty-five. Those whose military service had been interrupted or postponed were liable for conscription until age twenty-eight, although draft evaders were liable for conscription until age forty. Women from ages eighteen to forty-five in medical professions and women professionals within the Ministry of Interior were automatically registered for military service but could serve only in time of war and then only in noncombatant functions.

Before 1980 all recruits served for two years except those who had a completed their higher education; these recruits served for eighteen months. In 1980 the term of conscription was reduced to eighteen months but remained at twenty-four months for those conscripted into the air force. Recruits having children served even less time. In the late 1980s, call-up occurred twice a year, in February and in August.

Reserves consisted of physically fit men who were not currently serving in the armed forces. Men who had never been drafted could be called up for six months of reserve training until age forty. Officers who had served could be called up every five years for a four-month period of refresher training, while NCOs and privates could be so trained for up to three months every five years. All physically fit males could be called up at least once a year for maneuvers lasting no more than twenty days, although legally, if necessary, they could serve for a full year. Conscripts could be kept an additional two months after completing national service.

Conscientious Objection

According to the National Defense Act, those persons who refused military service during peacetime could receive up to five years' imprisonment. Permission was sometimes given, however, to Jehovah's Witnesses, Seventh-Day Adventists, or Nazarenes to serve as noncombatants in military construction units. Government opposition to Catholic conscientious objectors increased after October 1986, when the country's Catholic bishops declared that Catholics could neither refuse nor condemn obligatory military service, although they did urge the state to allow some sort of alternative service. This proclamation was followed by reports of dozens of conscientious objectors' being arrested and sentenced to thirty to thirty-six months' imprisonment by the Budapest Military Tribunal. These so-called "expedited" proceedings were characterized by trials lasting only ten to fifteen minutes. One man so imprisoned, Károly Kiszely, wrote a letter to the Conference on Security and Cooperation in Europe enumerating the ways in which conscientious objectors were harassed: they were physically abused, and their punishments were imposed without court hearings, without regard for judicial processes, and without legal counsel. Those convicted were allowed contact with only two family members, and they were permitted to send or receive only one "heavily censored" letter per month and to receive only one authorized visit by a relative each month. Furthermore, they were crowded together in prison with common criminals.

The government showed signs of softening its position in late 1987, when it reduced the term of military service for future clerics from eighteen to twelve months. And in early 1989, an amendment to the National Defense Act permitting conscientious objection was introduced into the National Assembly. Conscientious objection was to be allowed beginning in the second half of 1989. On March 1, 1989, the government announced that seventy conscientious objectors serving time in prison had been released and that their criminal record would be dropped, pending approval of a new National Defense Act. Noncombatant service was twenty-four months in the army and another twelve months of nonarmed reserve service. Civilian service was initially proposed for thirty-six months at locations to be determined by the government, with labor paid for in wages. In June 1989, the National Assembly voted to lower the duration of civilian service to twenty-eight months and resolved that the noncombatant service and nonarmed reserve service together not exceed twenty-eight months.

Education and Training

Much of the military education system developed since 1949 has been patterned on Soviet models, with the help of Soviet advisers. This pattern was also applied to troop training programs in garrisons and in the field. Yet despite Soviet attempts to make the

HPA more concerned with defense of the Warsaw Pact countries than with national defense, the army remained highly patriotic and nationalistic. Moreover, toward the end of the 1980s attempts were made, despite the HSWP's objections, to partially depoliticize the military.

Conscript Programs

Call-up consisted of three steps: obligatory premilitary training from January 1 of the year in which the future draftee turned seventeen; military registration at the District Military Replacement Center, where the registree received a medical examination and, if disabilities were found, was obliged to correct those disabilities capable of correction and continue premilitary training; and recruitment, at which time questions of medical fitness and service branch and unit assignment were resolved. Recruits underwent basic training for four weeks, then took the oath of allegiance. This process was followed by six months of specialized training for whatever task the recruits were to perform. They were then assigned to units. During all this time, the recruits also underwent ideological training.

Through political indoctrination, the military aimed at inculcating soldiers with a Marxist-Leninist worldview that would enable them to accept party positions and the way these positions related to internal and external events. Soldiers were taught the need for discipline, self-sacrifice, and loyalty to party, country, and the socialist alliance (including the Soviet Union), and were inculcated with a consciousness of their own invincibility. In fact, the HPA required that only 10 percent of a conscript's training time during the first phase of basic training be devoted to strictly political topics, while 70 percent was spent on military subjects. These relative proportions demonstrated that the HPA leadership viewed political indoctrination as secondary to teaching basic soldiering to recruits and persuading the brighter among them to seek a professional military career. Those who showed both desire and ability were given twenty-eight hours of free time each week to prepare to enter university. The HPA also awarded scholarships to some recruits to attend university full time during their service time, plus another twenty-four days of additional annual leave and considerably increased pay and benefits.

The combat training for recruits resembled that of other Warsaw Pact countries. Soldiers were taught proficiency with weapons, weapon systems, battlefield tactics, endurance, and stress prevention. Tactical exercises and maneuvers were often undertaken with Soviet forces in the country. Battle areas in such exercises could be twenty-six to thirty-two kilometers deep, and nuclear strikes were simulated. Soldiers sometimes were electronically monitored for stress.

Housing provided to conscripts was of poor quality. In December 1988, Minister of Defense Ferenc Karpati admitted that 10 percent of the barracks were not fit for habitation because they did not have regular hot water service. In general, most barracks were sixty to eighty years old and badly needed new wiring and plumbing.

Material deprivation aside, most conscripts considered their military training inadequate. As well as spending time in political indoctrination courses, conscripts were obliged to perform a great deal of work in the labor-starved economy (see Labor Force, ch. 3). For example, in 1987 soldiers worked 32,000 man-days in agriculture. Many conscripts, even those assigned to border guard duty, regarded military service as a waste of time.

Specialized-Officer Programs

Despite the benefits, youth in the late 1980s showed little interest in professional military careers. According to the Ministry of Defense, this lack of interest resulted in a pool of applicants smaller than the number needed for a good selection of candidates.

Candidates for officer training were chosen by the ministries of defense, interior, and education, together with the Communist Youth League's central committee (see Mass Organizations, ch. 2). These candidates had to be of "good character," politically reliable, physically fit, single, and not over twenty-one years of age, and they had to demonstrate military aptitude. They were required to take mathematics and physics tests and psychological examinations. Knowledge of Russian was necessary to become an officer in the air force. After such screening, candidates attended a military college for four years as officer cadets. After passing final examinations, they became junior officers (in the army, air force, or border guard) and were obligated to serve fifteen years.

Political officers were trained in military colleges but took different courses. A background in the Communist Youth League and the Hungarian National Defense Association (Magyar hónvédelmi szövetség—MHSz) helped in selection for this career. Older candidates were chosen from the party apparatus or from those with degrees in the "science of Marxism-Leninism." The Ministry of Defense's Main Political Administration oversaw the selection and screening of political officers.

In the late 1980s, the HPA operated schools ranging from secondary schools through colleges for the academic, technical, and political training and advancement of regular personnel. Many senior officers, in addition to successfully completing military schooling at all levels, also were sent to the Soviet Union for courses in that country's military institutions. Such Soviet schools included the Voroshilov General Staff Military Academy in Moscow, the Frunze Military Academy and the Malinovskii Military Academy, the Zhukov Air Defense Academy, and the Moscow Military Academy of the General Staff. Courses of study in the Soviet Union lasted from two to eight years. The Soviet Union also sent lecturers and textbooks to Hungary. Hungarian officers also were trained in Czechoslovakia and Poland.

The military academies were the highest level of military schooling, the most important of which was the Miklós Zrínyi Military Academy in Budapest. Before 1968 its entrance requirements were lenient, but after that time entry was obtained only upon the successful completion of a military college or an officers' training school of equivalent ranking. The course of study took three years, and a variety of subjects were offered. Graduation from the Miklós Zrínyi Military Academy was necessary to attain high-level command positions.

The Lajos Kossuth Military Academy in Szentendre in Pest County also ranked high in the military education system. It was considered to be academically equal to other institutions of higher learning. Graduates were commissioned as army officers. The Lajos Kossuth Military Academy offered specialized training in mechanized infantry, armored troops, surface-to-surface artillery, engineering, military economy and supply, and border guard work. The Kossuth Academy required knowledge of two foreign languages, one of which had to be Russian. The school also offered many courses on various aspects of Marxism-Leninism.

Other high-level military schools included the Máté Zalka Technical Military Academy in Budapest, which specialized in antiaircraft, artillery, radar technology, signaling and telecommunications, and nuclear, biological, and chemical (NBC) defense and warfare; the György Kilián Technical Air Force Academy, which trained ground and air crews and taught aviation and aircraft maintenance; the Honvéd Military College, which offered a three-year course of study for university graduates training to become officers; and the Frigyes Karikas Military College. The HPA also operated specialized military high schools in Eger, Nyíregyháza, and Tata.

Volunteers for military colleges were generally between the ages of eighteen and twenty-one and were drawn from all parts of the country. As a group, their precollege academic performance was not impressive. Nearly three-quarters chose a military career because they liked the military life-style and its contribution to society.

The remainder had motives that the HPA found less than admirable, such as the desire for high pay and fringe benefits, and had goals that have been described as "incoherent" or "selfish," such as a desire for adventure. Some students also came from families with a strong military tradition. In the mid-1970s, about 14 percent of the students at the György Kilián Technical Air Force Academy and 19 percent of those sent to study at Soviet military colleges had at least one parent with a military background.

Warrant officers were selected from career servicemen and conscripts. They could not be older than twenty-three, and they had to have had at least an eight-year general (elementary) school education certificate. Their training took two years, and they could be promoted to the rank of sergeant or staff sergeant. They were obligated to serve at least twelve years.

Officers and regimental sergeants major (sergeant, master sergeant, and sergeant major) in the military were compensated relatively well. Although starting salaries were low, they more than doubled after fifteen to twenty years of service. Officers also received an additional clothing allowance. They could retire at age fifty-five instead of age sixty (the age required for the rest of the population), and their pensions totaled 60 to 90 percent of the average of their last five years' salaries. They also received from twenty-five to thirty-seven days of vacation a year.

However, the professional military life also had its disadvantages. Officers could not engage in the second, unofficial economy and were thus required to live solely off their salaries, a difficult situation in Hungary (see Domestic Consumption, ch. 3). The housing provided by the military was both cramped and substandard. A professional soldier could be assigned to four or five different garrisons during his career, requiring moves by the entire family. In some locations, wives could not easily find suitable employment, essential foods, and social services. Military authorities were very concerned about the increasing alienation and materialism and the resulting high rates of alcoholism, suicide, and divorce among officers of the HPA.

Premilitary Programs

Hungarian schools required some military education for all students from the seventh grade through secondary school and higher education. The regime saw military education as an integral part of general education, a way by which young people could acquire the skills they would need when serving in the army and a means to increase the defense capability of the country. Such training included weapons maintenance and use, radio communications, electronic and mechanical engineering, aircraft piloting, parachute training, and scuba diving.

Actual premilitary training was optional but was advised before age seventeen and obligatory from age seventeen to call-up, up to age twenty-three. No more than two years of such training could be required. This training could assume different forms, including a camp setting. In 1984 the MHSz and the Pioneer youth organization established such a camp for premilitary training on Szentendre Island in the Danube, north of Budapest. In 1987 nearly 150 secondary students attended, half the number that applied. The boys were placed in radio communications and shooting groups, while both girls and boys participated in sports. Various programs included military theory and practice, computer games, movies, "patrol competitions," sports, and excursions. Soldiers supervised some activities, and the HPA provided the meals.

Paramilitary Programs

In the late 1980s, the MHSz gave lessons and courses related to defense and civil defense, and it aided in the premilitary training of young people and in military training for reservists. The MHSz resembled the Soviet Voluntary Society for the Promotion of the Army, Air Force, and Navy (Vsesoiuznoe Dobrovol'noe Obshchestvo Sodeistviia Armii, Aviatsii, i Flotu—DOSAAF).

In small villages, men were required to take part in weapons training, using air guns, at least once a year. All adults were also obliged to participate in civil defense drills, using as masks.

In the cities, workers in large organizations formed "civil defense chains," a system of notifying co-workers to meet at a prearranged place during a civil emergency. Every year each workplace held at least one civil defense drill.

Uniforms and Rank Insignia

In 1989 the army had approximately the same number of ranks found in other typical military organizations, but these ranks were grouped into six classifications, the names of which did not always translate readily to those used by other military organizations. Commissioned officer ranks, however, were standard and ranged from second lieutenant to general. They included four general officer ranks: brigadier general, lieutenant general, colonel general, and army general. Field grades were major, lieutenant colonel, and colonel. Junior officer ranks began with sublieutenant and advanced through second lieutenant and first lieutenant to captain.

Enlisted grade nomenclature differed from that used by most of the world's armies. The three lowest grades—private first class, corporal, and lance sergeant—were called noncommissioned officers. The next four grades—staff sergeant, sergeant first class, master sergeant, and command sergeant major—were called regimental sergeants major; in the armies of most countries these ranks would also be included among the NCO grades. Above the regimental sergeants major but below the lowest commissioned officer ranks were two grades that were translated as ensigns, which were the equivalent of warrant officers in other armies.

Rank insignia consisted of shoulder boards for officers, ensigns, and higher-grade enlisted men (see fig. 11). Lower grades wore patches on shirt or blouse collars. Rank was indicated by the amount of ornamentation and the number of stars on the shoulder board. Officers had gold piping around the edges of the boards; ensigns and enlisted men had silver. Generals' stars were placed upon a solid gold braid background. Junior officers' boards did not have braiding; officers of field grades had boards that were partly braided. Except for the outer braiding, boards of the higher-grade enlisted men resembled those of junior officers. Background colors and bronze devices identified service branches. Uniforms were brownish-olive drab. Enlisted men wore heavy wool in winter and a lighter colored cotton in the warmer seasons. Officers wore the same colors, but the materials were worsted wool for winter and either cotton or tropical-weight worsted wool for summer. The most frequently seen uniforms were the service, dress, and field uniforms. The service uniform was worn for most light-duty work, recreation, and informal social occasions. It consisted of a comfortably fitting "blouse," long trousers, and low shoes. In summer a lighter-weight, light-colored shirt was worn instead of the blouse. The dress uniform consisted of the same blouse and trousers but had extra ornamentation, and the trousers were tucked into high boots. Officers wore a Sam Browne belt (a belt with a strap over the right shoulder) and, for the most formal occasions, a sword. Field uniforms included high boots into which the trousers were tucked. In summer the officers' field uniforms included a short jacket, Sam Browne belt, and sidearm; enlisted men's uniforms had a cotton shirt, which could be worn with the sleeves rolled up. A heavy overcoat was added in the winter.

Twelve decorations were still being awarded in the late 1980s for extraordinary achievement, special merit, or outstanding performance. Another twenty-four were authorized to be worn but were no longer awarded. A few of those had been discontinued, but most of them were applicable to earlier service, such as during World War II or the communist takeover after the war.

The highest-ranking decoration was the Hero of Socialist Labor. It was followed in order by the Medal of the Hungarian People's Republic, the Red Banner Order of Merit, and the Red Star Order of Merit. Some of these decorations were awarded in two or more degrees, in which the first degree was the highest class. The Order of Merit for Outstanding Service was frequently awarded to higher-ranking military personnel. Although it ranked twenty-fourth in the list of thirty-six decorations, it was one of the few that was accompanied by a monetary award. A substantial pension supplement accompanied three or four of the more important decorations.

Internal Security and Public Order

In 1989 the Ministry of Interior was responsible for public order, public safety, internal security, and, since the beginning of 1988, public administration. The ministry controlled the armed security organizations in the country—the National Police, the Security Police, and the Border Guard—but not the Workers' Guard, which was subject directly to the HSWP. The ministry was also responsible for such diverse tasks as fire prevention and passport control.

In the late 1980s, the government attempted to limit the ministry's arbitrary use of power or at least tried to clean up its public image. In an interview in June 1989, Minister of Interior István Horváth suggested that the ministry ought to transfer its control of the Security Police to the local governments.

National Police

The public police forces performed routine police duties throughout the country. Although they operated within local jurisdictions, they were centrally organized and controlled by the Ministry of Interior.

To become a public police officer, a candidate had to have finished general elementary school and, in theory, to have completed two ten-month training periods. However, most officers serving in 1989, according to the Ministry of Interior, did not have this kind of education. In the late 1980s, morale problems affected the police. Inflation had eaten away their salaries, and the crime increases had overburdened their work loads (see Incidence of Crime, this ch.). In addition, policemen could not travel to the West. On July 5, 1989, policemen founded the Independent Policemen's Trade Union to protect their interests.

As Hungary inched toward democracy during the late 1980s the populace felt freer to criticize the police. The Ministry of Interior, in turn, felt obliged to publicize reforms. For example, in April 1989, the Federation of Young Democrats staged a sit-in in front

COMMISSIONED OFFICERS

HUNGARIAN RANK	ALHADNAGY	HADNAGY	FOHADNAGY	SZAZADOS	ORNAGY	ALEZREDES	EZREDES	VEZER-ORNAGY	AL-TABORNAGY	VEZER-EZREDES	HADSEREG-TABORNOK
ARMY AND AIR FORCE											
U.S. ARMY AND AIR FORCE RANK TITLES	2D LIEUTENANT		1ST LIEUTENANT	CAPTAIN	MAJOR	LIEUTENANT COLONEL	COLONEL	BRIGADIER GENERAL	MAJOR GENERAL	LIEUTENANT GENERAL	GENERAL

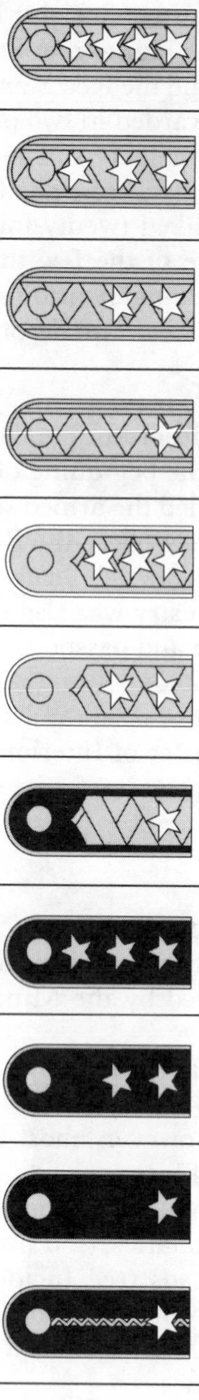

WARRANT OFFICERS AND ENLISTED PERSONNEL

HUNGARIAN RANK	HONVED	ORVEZETO		TIZEDES		SZAKASZ-VEZETO	ORMESTER	TORZS-ORMESTER	FOTORZS-ORMESTER	ZASZLOS	TORZS-ZASZLOS
ARMY AND AIR FORCE											
U.S. ARMY RANK TITLES	BASIC PRIVATE	PRIVATE	PRIVATE 1ST CLASS	CORPORAL	SERGEANT	STAFF SERGEANT	SERGEANT 1ST CLASS	MASTER SERGEANT	COMMAND SERGEANT MAJOR	WARRANT OFFICER W-1	CHIEF WARRANT OFFICER W-2
U.S. AIR FORCE RANK TITLES	AIRMAN BASIC	AIRMAN	AIRMAN 1ST CLASS	SERGEANT	STAFF SERGEANT	TECHNICAL SERGEANT	MASTER SERGEANT	SENIOR MASTER SERGEANT	CHIEF MASTER SERGEANT	NO RANK	NO RANK

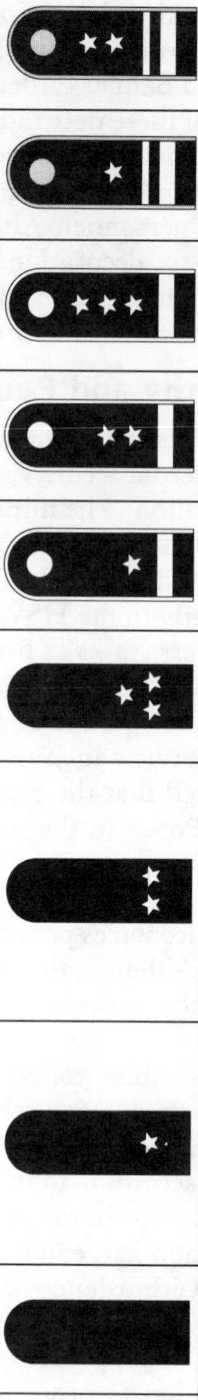

NOTE--Hungary has no navy. The highest air force rank is altabornagy.

Figure 11. Military Ranks and Insignia, 1989

of the headquarters of the Ministry of Interior. This organization was protesting the lenient sentences given by military courts to policemen who committed brutality. Federation members demanded that the minister of interior resign and that the ministry be removed from party control.

More surprising was the ministry's reaction to this criticism. In a press conference, a ministry spokesperson claimed that the "direct supervision" of the ministry had indeed been transferred to the government. During the same month, a ministry spokesperson condemned the acts of some police officers who had abused their authority and engaged in "impermissible activities." In the late 1980s, the ministry appeared to be concerned with its public image and claimed to be investigating "all allegations" of unlawful or improper activities by its agents. In a rather euphemistic but telling statement, Minister of Interior Horváth proclaimed in August 1989 that "protection of the public order [must] be provided according to European standards in the late 20th century."

Security Police

In the late 1980s, Hungary's 15,000 member Security Police was controlled by the Ministry of Interior. However, unique among Warsaw Pact countries, Hungary lacked a uniformed security police force. Such a force—the AVO—had existed but was disbanded in October 1956 (see Background and Traditions, this ch.). Given the vehemence with which the public hated the AVO and associated it with the Stalinist terror, the Kádár regime saw fit not to revive it, even under a different name. Nevertheless, until the late 1980s the Security Police continued to harass and arrest those persons deemed to be political enemies.

The reform of the political system during the second half of the 1980s appeared to have also affected the Security Police. In an interview on Hungarian television in July 1989, Minister of Interior Horváth claimed that the Security Police no longer viewed the domestic opposition as political enemies, an image that had become "obsolete" in a multiparty system. He condemned previous Security Police actions, such as harassing and detaining known dissidents before national holidays as "a bad reflex action of a different type of power structure." Horváth stressed that the Security Police did have a legitimate intelligence and counterintelligence function but was not an organization "placed above the citizens."

Border Guard

In 1989 Hungary's Border Guard numbered 16,000, operating in eleven districts. Conscripts totaled 11,000, or nearly 70 percent of the total. Although nominally controlled by the HPA, the Border Guard Headquarters of the Ministry of Interior took orders from both the party Basic Organization in the ministry and the Government Administration and Administrative Department of the HSWP's Secretariat (see Party Structure, ch. 4). The Border Guard Command was established in 1946 and reorganized in 1950. Its tasks were governed by Decree Number 40/1974, which brought border regulations into conformity with those of other Warsaw Pact countries. The exact level of party and Communist Young League membership among the Border Guard was unknown, but it was certainly higher than that of the army. For this reason, Völgyes argued that the regime may have considered this organization to be more reliable than the army as a whole, although the high percentage of conscripts left this contention open to question.

Border Guard work in Hungary required a high level of education, political training, good health, "good appearance," and even a knowledge of the foreign languages necessary for work at border crossing stations. Statistics from 1987 showed that 40 percent of guards at border crossing points had finished secondary school or university. In 1986 border guards checked the documents of 50 million people visiting or transiting Hungary through sixty-six highway, rail, river, and air border crossing points.

In the late 1980s, a permit was nominally required to enter a narrow zone along the western and southern borders, but according to Major General János Székely, chief of the Border Guard Headquarters, "anyone who applies to the proper agency for a permit usually gets it." An estimated 900 voluntary Border Guard auxiliary groups aided in the arrest of about 20 percent of border violators.

During the late 1980s, Hungary's borders with two countries received international attention. On May 3, 1989, Hungarian soldiers began removing the barbed wire fence on the border with Austria. Calling the fence "outdated" and superfluous, given the existence of Hungary's new (1988) liberal passport law, the Hungarian government publicly stated that all sections of the fence would be removed by the end of 1990. Although the Austrian government publicly welcomed this development, it privately feared that other East Europeans, especially Romanians, would travel to Hungary in order to escape into Austria.

It was not Romanians but East Germans touring Hungary in the summer of 1989 who took advantage of the newly opened border to flee to Austria. The Hungarian Border Guard interfered only sporadically with this flight, and eventually the Hungarian government allowed the East Germans to leave through Hungarian border checkpoints. In September 1989, the government announced that it would allow all the East Germans in the country wishing to emigrate to the West to leave Hungary. By the beginning of October, more than 35,000 had left the country to go to West Germany. The East German government protested that Hungary had reneged on its border agreements with the other members of the Warsaw Pact, but the Hungarian government claimed that it was merely following the spirit of the Helsinki Accords that were signed as part of the Conference on Security and Cooperation in Europe in 1975 and the border remained open.

Workers' Guard

The Workers' Guard, a paramilitary organization directly controlled by the HSWP, claimed to have 60,000 members in 1988. Possessing only small arms, its mission was officially limited to protecting the population and state property in times of war or unrest. In fact, the Workers' Guard assisted the National Police and army during events that required crowd control. The guard wore its own distinctive gray uniform.

Directly controlled by a permanent department of the HSWP's Central Committee, the Workers' Guard was, in effect, the party's private army, and the overwhelming majority of the guard were party members. Founded in 1957 shortly after the revolution, this organization became the chief protector of the newly formed Kádár regime.

In June 1989, the government announced that in the future it, not the party, would have control over the Workers' Guard and that many of the functions of this paramilitary organization would be eliminated. An interministerial committee of the government was formed to examine the mission and activities of the guard and perhaps even to rename it.

Criminal Justice System

Like other criminal justice systems in Marxist-Leninist countries, Hungary's criminal justice system was, until the late 1980s, heavily politicized. The system, like other aspects of the political system, was subject not to the rule of law but rather to the whims of the party. As part of its efforts at democratization in the late 1980s, the government began an effort to create an independent judicial system.

Incidence of Crime

Crimes against both people and property soared during the 1980s. Violent crime, which also increased dramatically, was disproportionately committed by Gypsies (see Minority Groups, ch. 2).

Gypsies made up about 4.7 percent of the population, but they numbered 54 percent of those persons convicted of murder and rape and 49 percent of those convicted of robbery.

Criminal offenses against the state and private individuals cost the economy nearly US$50 million in 1988, or 0.5 percent of the country's annual budget. Losses from criminal offenses against private property doubled from 1987 to 1988. White-collar crime, especially bribery of office executives, also rose, and the country's efforts to increase the role of private enterprise led to a new type of criminal activity—money laundering.

By contrast, certain other types of activities formerly considered illegal by the state had become legal under new, more tolerant laws. Thus, in the late 1980s liberalized passport and customs regulations reduced currency crimes by 25 percent and smuggling cases by 20 percent.

In the 1980s, the level of alcoholism in Hungary grew at the fastest rate in the world. In the 1950s, the communist regime considered alcoholism to be a "remnant of the past," but the increase in alcoholism over the years had forced the government to pay attention to this problem. The rapidly rising rate of alcohol consumption was fueled by an increasing number of women and youth with drinking problems. About 120,000 children lived in families in which one or both parents were heavy drinkers, and reports surfaced of youth gangs drinking in Budapest subway stations.

However, the government's data showed that at least in the workplace the problem of alcoholism was diminishing, rather than increasing. Surveys taken between 1985 and 1987 showed that drunkenness in the workplace dropped each year: from 9.1 percent in 1985, to 3.7 percent in 1986, and to 2.2 percent in 1987. Nevertheless, alcohol, rather than controlled substances, was related to virtually all of the crimes committed under the influence of any type of drug. In the first eight months of 1988, more than 18,500 crimes were committed under the influence of alcohol, while 37 crimes were committed under the influence of hard drugs (heroin and cocaine) and 84 under the influence of drug substitutes.

According to the Ministry of Interior, although hard drugs were shipped through Hungary, they did not appear to be a serious problem for Hungarian society. In the late 1980s, Ministry of Interior statistics cited only forty-five to fifty prosecutions per year for narcotics violations. Nevertheless, the use of hard drugs did appear to be rising.

The use of drug substitutes or the abuse of prescription drugs, however, caused the government serious concern. Abusers obtained opium-based and other drugs from hospitals, pharmacies, and drug factories by stealing, by forging prescriptions, or by buying drugs from staff looking for extra money. Glue sniffing was also a problem, especially for children aged seven to fifteen. In the late 1980s, the press admitted that the country possibly had 50,000 drug addicts but did not mention the drugs responsible for addiction.

Before 1984 the government had denied the existence of a drug problem, but since then the subject has received wide public discussion. In the late 1980s, laws against the use of controlled substances were flexible and gave judges the ability to adjust sentences according to the quantity of the drug involved and the age of the seller. Those persons in possession of "excessive amounts" could receive up to an eight-year prison term.

Penal Code and Criminal Procedure

Hungary's legal system has been influenced by Roman law. The country's first written law code, compiled by Stephen Werböczy in 1514, codified the unwritten laws and customs that had existed up to that time. The Tripartitum, as this codification was called, was modified over the following centuries, but a written, formal law code was not officially published until 1878. This publication formed the basis of the Penal Code appearing in the early 1950s, but many articles remained unchanged until the entire code was republished in 1961.

The Penal Code and a decree on criminal procedures that appeared in 1972 incorporated constitutional revisions made at that time (see Amendments of 1972, ch. 4). Both the code and the decree reflected the subordination of the legal system to the state, and harsher penalties were meted out for crimes against the state and state property than for crimes against the person and private property. The Penal Code was revised in late 1978 and again in September 1989. The latest revision, which still required the approval of the National Assembly as of September 1989, abolished the use of the death penalty for crimes against the state.

Hungary's system of justice did not subscribe to the adversary system; neither did it recognize common law or precedent (see Judicial Organs, ch. 4). The prosecutor in a Hungarian court was responsible for presenting all the evidence, both for and against the defendant. Defendants had the right to legal counsel, who attempted to ensure that the prosecutor's presentation of the case was unbiased. Judges were bound by the law as written, not by the decisions of other judges. The judge's interpretation applied only to the specific case; it set no precedent for other cases.

Military Justice

Military tribunals were part of Hungary's judicial system and were responsible to the minister of justice and to the minister of defense. A military council of the Supreme Court reviewed cases from lower military tribunals or tried the most serious cases.

Military court jurisdiction was usually limited to cases involving military personnel, cases involving civilians on military installations, or cases involving an aspect of the country's defense. Military courts had a judge and two lay assessors (non-professional judges), whose functions were similar to their equivalents in civilian courts. Military judges were commissioned professional officers with law degrees. Lay assessors were chosen from all ranks, at respective meetings of officers, regimental sergeants major, and enlisted personnel. Members of the court had to have a rank at least equal to that of the accused.

Penal System

From 1949 to 1961, the penal system consisted of labor or internment camps and prisons with three types of disciplinary regimes. By 1961 the regime claimed it had abolished the labor camps. A law eliminated these different regimes, but a new system containing four regimes has been instituted since. Confinement to penitentiaries was the most severe regime under the new system, while local jails provided the lightest. Prisoners sentenced to the two intermediate regimes were assigned to one of two different types of prisons. In 1975 the government introduced an additional regime for convicts who committed for the fourth time a violent crime carrying a sentence of more than one year.

In July 1989, a prisoner in the Vác Prison north of Budapest committed self-immolation, and several hundred of his fellow prisoners went on a hunger strike to protest the harshest possible regime. The government immediately promised to abolish this regime, thus affecting 282 male and 14 female prisoners.

In the late 1980s, the HPA possessed just one penal battalion, located in Nagyatad in Somogy County. Soldiers who had received seven-month to two-year sentences were sent there to perform manual labor, primarily for the HPA but often for the national economy. Alcohol played a part in two-thirds of crimes committed by soldiers. At least one-third of these crimes involved violence against superiors, insubordination, or draft dodging.

Reaction to Political Dissent

As with the constitutions of the other Warsaw Pact countries, Hungary's Constitution grants rights to citizens but qualifies these rights so that they are meaningless (see Constitutional Development, ch. 4). For example, Chapter VII, Article 64 of the

Constitution gives citizens freedom of speech, press, and assembly, yet Section 54 states that citizens' rights "shall be exercised in accordance with the interests of socialism and the people" and that these rights "shall be inseparable from the fulfillment of the duties of citizens."

Nevertheless, from the 1970s well into the 1980s Hungarians had a wider latitude to criticize their government than did other East Europeans. But most Hungarians developed a "self-censorship" in which they avoided publicly discussing such sensitive topics as one-party rule and Hungary's relations with the Soviet Union and the other Warsaw Pact countries. Hungarians thus generally avoided problems with the state, while the state gave the appearance of tolerating dissent.

The development of samizdat in the early 1980s provoked a severe government reaction. In June 1982, several samizdat editors were subjected to police surveillance, and later in the year one was fined 4,000 forints (for value of the forint—see Glossary), about the average wage for one month at that time, for publishing without official permission. In the following months, the police began to subject others associated with samizdat to both "light" measures (denial of permission to travel abroad, periodic house searches, detention, fines, or employment difficulties) to those of outright oppression (beatings or imprisonment). The regime even used psychiatric methods such as closed wards and electric shock therapy against dissidents. In 1987 dissidents were still subject to house searches, and in 1988 they were still denied passports.

To stop the tide of unofficial publishing, the government passed Decree 49/1984 (XI.21), which required that all duplicating machines and photocopiers be registered with the state, and Decree 4/1985 (VII20), which allowed police surveillance and even expulsion from the country for those persons whose political beliefs the government considered a danger to the Hungarian People's Republic, its social order, or public security. The authorities also punished official publishers when magazines touched upon taboo subjects. For example, in 1983 the editor of *Mozgó Világ* (World in Motion) lost his job for defying party directives. In 1986 the editors of *Tiszatáj* (Tisza Country) were ordered to resign because of articles in their journal describing the horrible situation of Hungarians living in Romania (see Mass Media, ch. 4).

Rock musicians also felt the state's wrath when their music did not meet official approval. During the mid-1980s, the Committee of Hungarian Radio censored records and songs because they were not "optimistic enough" or because they referred to drugs or to "red, white, and green" (the colors of the precommunist Hungarian flag).

Unauthorized street demonstrations were also harshly punished in the mid-1980s. In 1986 the police brutally broke up a demonstration held on March 15 to commemorate Hungary's declaration of independence from the Habsburg Empire in 1848. Unofficial peace and environmental groups were also harassed when attempting to meet publicly.

However, political reforms of the late 1980s softened the government's view of dissent, although its behavior remained ambiguous. In October 1988, street demonstrations commemorating the revolution were tolerated, and a relatively free press arose. The government spoke openly about liberalizing its passport law. Yet a Miskolc court in 1988 handed an elderly, disabled pensioner a one-and-a-half-year suspended sentence for writing an open letter to the HSWP in which he criticized "domestic conditions and certain leaders." Legal sanctions resulting from involvement in the Revolution of 1956 were lifted for twelve people but remained for another fifty-four.

Hence, as of 1989 the government's record on dissent, as with other aspects of the reform of the national security system, was mixed. To be sure, regime leaders repeatedly announced their intent to reform, and, indeed, many important steps were taken in that direction. But as Hungarian dissident Miklós Haraszti reminded his audience in 1989, Hungary was still "a country with powerful bureaucrats, with the same armed forces, and with a political police."

* * *

Unfortunately, few English-language sources deal with the past and present Hungarian military. English-language sources for Hungarian military history are almost nonexistent outside of the few standard surveys of Hungarian history, such as Denis Sinor's *History of Hungary*. A notable exception is Béla K. Király's *Hungary in the Late Eighteenth Century,* which sets forth detailed information about the Hungarian-Habsburg military structure of that time. Peter Weiss's "The Hungarian Armed Forces Today" provided the most current information at the time of this writing. An excellent overview of the HPA since World War II is given by Iván Völgyes in his article "Hungary." F. Rubin's "The Hungarian People's Army" is also useful but dated. For information about the HPA's force strengths and weaponry, no source is better than the International Institute for Strategic Studies' annual *The Military Balance.*

Radio Free Europe occasionally produces articles that treat Hungarian military matters. Some translations produced by the Joint Publications Research Service and the Foreign Broadcast Information Service concern questions of Hungary's national security. (For further information and complete citations, see Bibliography.)

Appendix

Table 1. Metric Conversion Coefficients and Factors

When you know	Multiply by	To find
Millimeters	0.04	inches
Centimeters	0.39	inches
Meters	3.3	feet
Kilometers	0.62	miles
Hectares (10,000 m²)	2.47	acres
Square kilometers	0.39	square miles
Cubic meters	35.3	cubic feet
Liters	0.26	gallons
Kilograms	2.2	pounds
Metric tons	0.98	long tons
....	1.1	short tons
....	2,204	pounds
Degrees Celsius	9	degrees Fahrenheit
(Centigrade)	divide by 5 and add 32	

Table 2. Population, Selected Years, 1920–87
(in thousands)

Year	Females	Males	Total
1920	4,112.8	3,874.1	7,986.9
1930	4,436.7	4,248.4	8,685.1
1941	4,755.2	4,560.9	9,316.1
1949	4,781.4	4,423.4	9,204.8
1960	5,157.0	4,804.0	9,961.0
1970	5,318.4	5,003.7	10,322.1
1980	5,520.8	5,188.7	10,709.5
1985	5,508.1	5,149.3	10,657.4
1986	5,501.9	5,138.1	10,640.0
1987	5,494.5	5,126.6	10,621.1

Source: Based on information from Hungary, Central Statistical Office, *Statistical Yearbook, 1986,* Budapest, 1988, 39.

267

Table 3. Marriages and Divorces, Selected Years, 1921–86
(per thousand population)

Year	Marriages	Divorces
1921	11.6	0.8
1930	9.0	0.6
1938	8.1	0.6
1948	10.7	1.2
1960	8.9	1.7
1970	9.3	2.2
1975	9.9	2.5
1980	7.5	2.6
1985	6.9	2.8
1986	6.8	2.8

Source: Based on information from Hungary, Central Statistical Office, *Statistical Yearbook, 1986*, Budapest, 1988, 48.

Table 4. Infant Mortality, Selected Years, 1921–86
(per thousand live births)

Year	Total	Year	Total
1921	192.7	1980	23.2
1930	152.5	1981	20.8
1938	131.4	1982	20.0
1948	94.1	1983	19.0
1960	47.6	1984	20.4
1970	35.9	1985	20.4
1975	32.8	1986	19.0

Source: Based on information from Hungary, Central Statistical Office, *Statistical Yearbook, 1986*, Budapest, 1988, 61.

Table 5. Active Earners by Sector, Selected Years, 1949–87
(in percentages)

Sector	1949	1960	1970	1980	1987
Industry	19.4	27.9	36.3	33.9	31.2
Construction	2.2	6.1	7.4	8.2	7.0
Agriculture and forestry	53.8	38.5	24.4	19.0	19.3
Waterworks and supply	0.1	0.2	1.2	1.5	1.6
Transportation and telecommunications	4.4	6.5	7.3	8.1	8.3
Trade	5.3	6.3	7.9	9.8	10.5
Other material activity	n.a.	n.a.	n.a.	0.9	1.0
Personal and economic services	3.5	2.5	2.8	3.1	3.7
Sanitary, social, and cultural services	3.8	5.6	7.7	10.4	12.5
Public administration and other services	7.5	6.4	5.0	5.1	4.9
TOTAL	100.0	100.0	100.0	100.0	100.0
Percentage of women	29.2	35.5	41.2	43.4	46.0

n.a.—not available.

Source: Based on information from Hungary, Central Statistical Office, *Statistical Yearbook, 1986*, Budapest, 1988, 27, 28, 39.

Table 6. *Gross Output and Net National Product by*
Sector, 1970, 1980, and 1986
(in percentages, at constant prices)

Sector	Gross Output			Net National Product		
	1970	1980	1986	1970	1980	1986
Industry	50.2	51.8	50.7	36.2	36.9	36.0
Construction	8.2	7.5	6.3	9.1	8.8	7.4
Agriculture and forestry	17.8	17.4	18.2	22.3	19.6	21.5
Transportation, post, and						
telecommunications	5.6	5.4	5.6	7.7	7.9	7.8
Wholesale and retail trade	7.2	5.9	6.1	11.8	11.0	10.6
Water works and supply	1.0	1.0	1.1	0.9	1.2	0.9
Other material activities	n.a.	0.5	0.7	n.a.	0.7	1.2
Nonmaterial branches and price						
differences	10.0	10.5	11.3	12.0	13.9	14.6
TOTAL	100.0	100.0	100.0	100.0	100.0	100.0

n.a.—not available.

Source: Based on information from Hungary, Central Statistical Office, *Statistical Yearbook,*
1986, Budapest, 1988, 30.

Table 7. *Average Investment by Sector, 1961–70, 1971–80, and 1981–86*
(in percentages, at current prices)

Sector	1961–70	1971–80	1981–86
Industry	38.2	34.6	31.4
Construction	2.5	2.6	1.4
Agriculture	16.6	13.8	12.8
Transportation and communications	12.9	12.0	11.3
Trade	3.1	4.2	4.3
Waterworks and supply	2.9	5.1	6.1
Other material activities	n.a.	n.a.	0.5
Nonmaterial branches	23.8	27.7	32.2
TOTAL	100.0	100.0	100.0

n.a.—not available.

Source: Based on information from Hungary, Central Statistical Office, *Statistical Yearbook,*
1986, Budapest, 1988, 30.

Table 8. Share of Social Sectors in Employment and National Income, 1970, 1980, and 1986 (in percentages)

Sector	Distribution of Active Earners			Contribution to National Income		
	1970	1980	1986	1970	1980	1986
State sector	67.7	71.1	70.5	70.7	69.8	63.4
Cooperative sector	28.1	25.5	24.4	23.6	23.0	23.0
Auxiliary farms of persons employed outside agriculture .	n.a.	n.a.	n.a.	3.1	3.7	6.6
Private sector	4.2	3.4	5.1	2.6	3.5	7.0
TOTAL	100.0	100.0	100.0	100.0	100.0	100.0

n.a.—not available.

Source: Based on information from Hungary, Central Statistical Office, *Statistical Yearbook, 1986,* Budapest, 1988, 30; and János Kornai, "The Hungarian Reform Process: Visions, Hopes, and Reality," *Journal of Economic Literature,* 24, December 1986, 1692.

Table 9. Output of Selected Agricultural Products, 1976–87

Product	1976–80 [1]	1981–85 [1]	1986	1987
Wheat [2]	5,186	6,066	5,740	5,674
Corn [2]	6,374	6,977	7,029	6,987
Potatoes [2]	1,567	1,446	1,264	1,270
Sugarbeets [2]	3,979	4,461	3,760	4,224
Sunflower seed [2]	300	615	857	787
Cattle [3]	1,926	1,919	1,766	1,725
Hogs [3]	7,805	8,953	8,280	8,687
Poultry [3]	63,002	65,082	61,570	67,010
Sheep [3]	2,560	3,044	2,465	2,337
Beef and Veal [3]	203	204	196	200
Pork [3]	922	1,097	1,048	1,038
Poultry Meat [3]	328	320	440	470
Milk [3]	2,283	2,752	2,778	2,786
Eggs [4]	4,475	4,351	4,290	4,120

[1] Average.
[2] By 1,000 tons.
[3] By 1,000 head.
[4] By million pieces.

Source: Based on information from Hungary, Central Statistical Office, *Statistical Yearbook, 1986,* Budapest, 1988, 181, 187, 188; and Nancy J. Cochrane and Miles J. Lampert, *Agricultural Performance in Eastern Europe, 1987,* Washington, 1988, 19–20.

Table 10. *Contribution to Agricultural Gross Output*
by Type of Farm, Selected Years, 1966–86
(in percentages)

Type of Farm	1966	1975	1980	1986
State farms	16.4	18.0	16.8	17.6
Cooperative farms	48.4	50.5	50.4	51.0
Household plots	23.7	19.0	18.5	16.4
Auxiliary and private farms	11.5	12.5	14.3	14.9
TOTAL	100.0	100.0	100.0	99.9 *

* Figures do not add up to 100 percent because of rounding.

Source: Based on information from János Kornai, "The Hungarian Reform Process: Visions, Hopes, and Reality," *Journal of Economic Literature*, 24, 1986, 1701; and Hungary, Central Statistical Office, *Statistical Yearbook, 1986,* Budapest, 1988, 174.

Table 11. *Structure of Imports and Exports, 1986*
(in percentages)

Commodity Group	Imports	Exports
Fuel and electricity	19.4	3.5
Raw materials, semifinished goods, and spare parts	44.8	30.2
Machinery and capital goods	16.7	30.0
Industrial consumer goods	11.7	16.2
Agricultural goods	7.4	20.1
TOTAL	100.0	100.0

Source: Based on information from Hungary, Central Statistical Office, *Statistical Yearbook, 1986,* Budapest, 1988, 272.

Table 12. *Agricultural Imports and Exports, 1976–86*
(in thousands of tons) *

Product	Average 1976–80 Imports	Average 1976–80 Exports	Average 1981–85 Imports	Average 1981–85 Exports	1986 Imports	1986 Exports
Grain						
Wheat	8	682	26	1,363	n.a.	1,669
Corn	116	330	23	250	23	478
Other	167	23	49	32	118	27
Total grain	291	1,035	98	1,645	141	2,174
Oilseed Meal	614	5	679	32	566	31
Meat Products	13	285	14	423	19	421
Sugar	84	31	28	43	n.a.	5

n.a.—not available.
* No information reported on amounts less than 1,000 tons.

Source: Based on information from Nancy J. Cochrane and Miles J. Lampert, *Agricultural Performance in Eastern Europe, 1987,* Washington, 1988, 13–14, 17–18.

Table 13. *Rank Order of Hungary's Principal Trading*
Partners, 1984, 1985, and 1986 *
(in percentages)

Country	1984		1985		1986	
	Imports	Exports	Imports	Exports	Imports	Exports
Soviet Union	29.1	30.1	30.0	33.6	30.9	33.9
West Germany	10.7	7.4	11.4	7.8	12.4	8.4
East Germany	6.4	5.9	6.5	6.1	6.7	6.4
Austria	5.1	5.3	6.4	5.3	6.2	5.3
Czechoslovakia	5.0	5.2	5.0	5.7	5.2	5.9
Poland	4.4	4.2	4.7	3.8	4.7	4.2
Italy	2.4	3.3	2.8	2.9	2.7	3.2
Yugoslavia	3.9	3.4	3.5	3.6	2.7	3.1
United States	2.5	2.7	3.0	2.3	2.0	2.3
Switzerland	2.0	2.2	2.0	2.0	2.1	1.9
Romania	1.8	1.5	1.8	1.7	1.9	2.0
China	0.6	0.8	0.9	1.3	1.8	1.9
France	1.7	1.7	1.8	1.4	1.9	1.5
Britain	1.8	1.5	1.9	1.5	1.8	1.3
Bulgaria	1.4	1.5	1.5	1.4	1.4	1.6
Netherlands	1.3	1.1	1.3	0.9	1.4	1.1
Japan	1.1	0.4	1.7	3.4	1.5	0.5
Belgium	1.0	0.5	1.1	3.8	1.3	0.7
Sweden	1.0	0.7	1.1	0.7	1.1	0.8
Brazil	3.1	n.a.	1.7	0.3	1.2	0.5
Others	13.7	20.6	9.9	10.5	9.1	13.5
TOTAL	100.0	100.0	100.0	100.0	100.0	100.0

n.a.—not available.
* Percentages of imports and exports for each year, ranked according to the total for 1986.

Source: Based on information from "Hungary," *The Europa Yearbook 1988,* London, 1988,
1309; and Hungary, Central Statistical Office, *Statistical Yearbook, 1986,* Budapest,
1988, 276–77.

Table 14. National Economic Indicators, Selected Years, 1950–86
(1950 = 100)

Indicator	1950	1960	1970	1980	1986
National income	100	177	300	467	501
National income in industry (percentage of total)	27	37	46	48	46
National income in agriculture (percentage of total)	48	31	22	16	19
Industrial output	100	228	456	804	919
Agricultural output	100	106	103	115	124
Investment (excluding private)	100	197	448	708	618
Investment in industry (percentage of total investment)	n.a.	41	34	31	29
Production per person in state industry ..	100	148	226	381	462
Agricultural hauling power (in thousands of kilowatts)	302	1,325	3,824	7,461	8,509
Fertilizer per hectare (in thousands of kilograms)	5	23	122	211	212

* n.a.—not available.

Source: Based on information from Hungary, Central Statistical Office, *Statistical Yearbook, 1986*, 1988, 7–9, 15, 79; and Diane Flaherty, "Regional Policy and the Reform of Central Planning: An Assessment of the GDR, Hungarian, and Yugoslav Approaches," *Contributions to Political Economy*, 3, March 1984, 42.

Table 15. Foreign Trade and Current Account Balance, 1981–87

	1981	1982	1983	1984	1985	1986	1987
Current account balance [1]	−730	−64	298	338	−459	−1440	−945
Trade account balance [1]	−83	459	533	608	112	−440	−20
Gross hard-currency debt [2]	8.7	7.7	8.3	8.8	11.8	15.1	7.7
Net hard-currency debt [2]	7.0	6.6	6.8	6.7	8.6	12.0	5.5

[1] In millions of United States dollars.
[2] In billions of United States dollars.

Source: Based on information from Przemyslaw T. Gajdeczka, "International Market Perceptions and Economic Performance: Lending to Eastern Europe," *Eastern European Politics and Societies*, 2, No. 3, Fall 1988, 10; and Nancy J. Cochrane and Miles J. Lampert, *Agricultural Performance in Eastern Europe, 1987*, Washington, 1988, 566–67.

Bibliography

Chapter 1

Barany, George. *Stephen Széchenyi and the Awakening of Hungarian Nationalism, 1791-1841.* Princeton: Princeton University Press, 1968.

Bartha, Antal. *Hungarian Society in the 9th and 10th Centuries.* Budapest: Akadémiai Kiadó, 1975.

Batt, Judy. *Economic Reform and Political Change in Eastern Europe.* New York: St. Martin's Press, 1988.

Bayerle, Gustav. *Ottoman Diplomacy in Hungary.* Bloomington: Indiana University Press, 1972.

Birkbeck, A.M. *Rural and Historical Gleanings from Eastern Europe.* London: Parton, 1854.

Brabourne, Cecil Marcus Knatchbull-Hugessen. *The Political Evolution of the Hungarian Nation.* London: National Review Office, 1908.

Crankshaw, Edward. *Khrushchev: A Career.* New York: Viking Press, 1966.

Deák, István. "The Decline and Fall of Habsburg Hungary." Pages 10-30 in Iván Völgyes (ed.), *Hungary in Revolution, 1918-19.* Lincoln: University of Nebraska Press, 1971.

Deutscher, Isaac. *Stalin.* New York: Oxford University Press, 1967.

Dvornik, Francis. *The Making of Central and Eastern Europe.* Gulf Breeze, Florida: Academic International Press, 1974.

Fejtö, F. *A History of the People's Democracies: Eastern Europe since Stalin.* Harmondsworth, United Kingdom: Penguin, 1974.

Fischer, Rolf. *Entwicklungsstufen des Antisemitismus in Ungarn, 1867-1939.* Munich: Oldenbourg Verlag, 1988.

Fügedi, Erik. *Castle and Society in Medieval Hungary, 1000-1437.* Budapest: Akadémiai Kiadó, 1986.

Gati, Charles. *Hungary and the Soviet Bloc.* Durham, North Carolina: Duke University Press, 1986.

Hare, Paul G. "The Beginnings of Institutional Reform in Hungary," *Soviet Studies* [Glasgow], 35, No. 3, July 1983, 313-30.

_____. "Industrial Development of Hungary since World War II," *Eastern European Politics and Societies,* 2, No. 1, Winter 1988, 115-51.

Heinrich, Hans-Georg. *Hungary: Politics, Economics, and Society.* Boulder, Colorado: Lynne Rienner, 1986.

Held, Joseph. *Hunyadi: Legend and Reality*. Boulder, Colorado: East European Monographs, 1985.

Helmreich, Ernest C. (ed.). *Hungary*. New York: Praeger, 1957.

Hengelmuller, Ladislas. *Hungary's Fight for National Existence*. London: Macmillan, 1913.

Hoensch, Jörg K. *A History of Modern Hungary, 1867–1986*. London: Longman, 1988.

Ignotus, Paul. *Hungary*. New York: Praeger, 1972.

Janos, Andrew C. *The Politics of Backwardness in Hungary, 1825–1945*. Princeton: Princeton University Press, 1982.

Jászi, Oszkár. *The Dissolution of the Habsburg Monarchy*. (2d ed.) Chicago: University of Chicago Press, 1961.

Kann, Robert A. *A History of the Habsburg Empire, 1526–1918*. Berkeley: University of California Press, 1974.

Kecskemeti, Paul. *The Unexpected Revolution*. Stanford, California: Stanford University Press, 1961.

Kennan, George F. *Russia and the West under Lenin and Stalin*. New York: Mentor, 1961.

Kertesz, Stephen. *Between Russia and the West*. Notre Dame, Indiana: University of Notre Dame Press, 1984.

Király, Béla. *Hungary in the Late Eighteenth Century: The Decline of Enlightened Despotism*. New York: Columbia University Press, 1969.

Király, Béla, and Paul Jonas. *The Hungarian Revolution of 1956 in Retrospect*. (East European Monographs, No. 40.) New York: Columbia University Press, 1978.

Kosáry, Domokas. *A History of Hungary*. New York: Arno Press and New York Times, 1971.

Kovrig, Bennett. *Communism in Hungary from Kun to Kadar*. Stanford, California: Hoover Institution Press, 1979.

Le Clerc, Jean. *Memoirs of Emeric Count Teckely*. London: T. Goodwin, 1693.

Lukinich, Imre. *A History of Hungary in Biographical Sketches*. Freeport, New York: Books for Libraries Press, 1968.

Macartney, Carlile Alymer. *A History of Hungary*. New York: Praeger, 1956.

_____. *Hungary: A Short History*. Chicago: Aldine, 1962.

_____. *The Magyars in the Ninth Century*. Cambridge: Cambridge University Press, 1968.

_____. *October Fifteenth: A History of Modern Hungary, 1929–1945*. Edinburgh: University Press, 1961.

Marczali, Henrik. *Hungary in the Eighteenth Century*. Cambridge: Cambridge University Press, 1910.

Mičunović, Veljko. *Moskovske godine, 1956–1958.* Beograd: Jugoslovenska Revija, 1984.

Paget, John. *Hungary and Transylvania.* London: John Murray, 1839.

Pamlényi, Ervin (ed.). *History of Hungary.* London: Collet's, 1975.

The Present State of Hungary or, A Geographical and Historical Description of That Kingdom. London: Henry Rhodes, 1687.

Pryce-Jones, David. *The Hungarian Revolution.* New York: Horizon Press, 1970.

Rothschild, Joseph. *East Central Europe Between the Two World Wars.* Seattle: University of Washington Press, 1974.

Rusinow, Dennison. *The Yugoslav Experiment, 1948–1974.* Berkeley: University of California Press, 1978.

Scenes of the Civil War in Hungary in 1848 and 1849. Philadelphia: E.H. Butler, 1850.

Schöpflin, George. *Hungary Between Prosperity and Crisis.* London: Institute for the Study of Conflict, 1981.

Schöpflin, George (ed.). *The Soviet Union and Eastern Europe.* New York: Facts on File, 1986.

The Seat of the War in Hungary, Between the Emperor and the Turks. London: A. Bettesworth, 1717.

Seton-Watson, Hugh. *Eastern Europe Between the Wars, 1918–1941.* Cambridge: Cambridge University Press, 1945.

Seton-Watson, Robert W. *Racial Problems in Hungary.* London: S. Constable, 1908.

Sinor, Denis. *History of Hungary.* New York: Praeger, 1959.

Spira, György. *A Hungarian Count in the Revolution of 1848.* Budapest: Akadémiai Kiadó, 1974.

Stroup, Edsel Walter. *Hungary in Early 1848.* Buffalo: Hungarian Cultural Foundation, 1977.

Talbott, Strobe (ed.). *Khrushchev Remembers.* Boston: Little, Brown, 1970.

Thurston, Herbert S.J., and Donald Attwater. *Butler's Lives of the Saints.* New York: P.J. Kenedy and Sons, 1956.

Tőkés, Rudolf L. *Bela Kun and the Hungarian Soviet Republic.* New York: Praeger, 1967.

Toma, Peter A., and Iván Völgyes. *Politics in Hungary.* San Francisco: W. H. Freeman, 1975.

A True and Exact Relation of the Imperial Expedition in Hungaria in the Year 1684. London: R. Taylor, 1685.

United States. Congress. 99th, 2d Session. Joint Economic Committee. *East European Economies: Slow Growth in the 1980s,* 3. (Country Studies on Eastern Europe and Yugoslavia.) Washington: GPO, March 28, 1986.

Várdy, S.B., Géza Grosschmid, and Leslie S. Domonkos. *Louis the Great.* Boulder, Colorado: East European Monographs, 1986.

Verdery, Katherine. "On the Nationality Problem in Transylvania until World War I," *East European Quarterly,* 19, Spring 1985, 15–30.

_____. *Transylvanian Villagers.* Berkeley: University of California Press, 1983.

West, Rebecca. *Black Lamb and Grey Falcon.* Middlesex, United Kingdom: Penguin, 1986.

Zarek, Otto. *The History of Hungary.* London: Selwyn and Blount, 1934.

_____. *Kossuth.* Port Washington, New York: Kennikat Press, 1970.

Chapter 2

"AIDS Specialist on Disease in Republic," MTI [Budapest], January 28, 1989. Foreign Broadcast Information Service, *Daily Report: East Europe.* (FBIS–EEU–89–020.) February 1, 1989, 34.

Ambrus, János. "Unions and Democracy," *Hungarian Observer* [Budapest], 1988, 34–35.

_____. "The Unions Shuffle Their Scripts," *Hungarian Observer* [Budapest], 1, 1989, 9–11.

Andorka, Rudolf, István Harcsa, and Márta Gyenei. "First Results of a Survey of Social Stratification." Pages 15–50 in Rudolf Andorka and Tamás Kolosi (eds.), *Stratification and Inequalities.* Budapest: Institute of Social Sciences, 1984.

Andorka, Rudolf, and Tamás Kolosi. "Introduction." Pages 7–14 in Rudolf Andorka and Tamás Kolosi (eds.), *Stratification and Inequalities.* Budapest: Institute of Social Sciences, 1984.

Ash, Timothy Garton. "Refolution: The Springtime of Two Nations," *New York Review of Books,* 36, No. 10, June 15, 1989, 3–4, 6, 8, 10.

Balassa, Bela. "Reforming the New Economic Mechanism in Hungary," *Journal of Comparative Economics,* 7, No. 3, September 1983, 253–76.

Balassa, Iván, and Gyula Ortutay. *Hungarian Ethnography and Folklore.* (Text trans., Maria Bales and Kenneth Bales; poems trans., Laszlo T. Andras.) Budapest: Corvina, 1984.

Barta, Barnabás, András Klinger, Károly Miltényi, and György Vukovich. *Fertility, Female Employment, and Policy Measures in Hungary.* (Women, Work, and Development, No. 6.) Geneva: International Labour Organisation, 1984.

Bauer, Tamás. "The Hungarian Alternative to Soviet-Type Planning," *Journal of Comparative Economics,* 7, No. 3, September 1983, 304–16.

Bell, Peter D. *Peasants in Socialist Transition: Life in a Collectivized Hungarian Village.* Berkeley: University of California Press, 1984.

Böhm, Antal. "Changes in the Situation of Commuters." Pages 287–98 in Rudolf Andorka and Tamás Kolosi (eds.), *Stratification and Inequalities.* Budapest: Institute of Social Sciences, 1984.

_____. "Industry's Stepchildren: The Commuters," *Hungarian Observer* [Budapest], 1, 1989, 33.

Comisso, Ellen, and Paul Marer. "The Economics and Politics of Reform in Hungary," *International Organization,* 40, No. 2, Spring 1986, 421–54.

Connor, Walter D. *Socialism's Dilemmas: State and Society in the Soviet Bloc.* New York: Columbia University Press, 1988.

_____. "Varieties of East European Dissent," *Studies in Comparative Communism* [Guilford, Surrey, United Kingdom], 15, No. 4, Winter 1982, 396–412.

Countries of the World and Their Leaders Yearbook. Detroit: Gale Research, 1986.

Csaba, Csaki. "Economic Management and Organization of Hungarian Agriculture," *Journal of Comparative Economics,* 7, No. 3, September 1983, 317–28.

de Fontenay, Patrick, Gérard Bélanger, Emine Gürgen, Alexander Mountford, and Subhash Thakur. *Hungary: An Economic Survey.* Washington: International Monetary Fund, 1982.

"DEMISZ Congress Adopts Program," MTI [Budapest], April 22, 1989. Foreign Broadcast Information Service, *Daily Report: East Europe.* (FBIS-EEU-89-079.) April 26, 1989, 36.

"DEMISZ Holds 1st Congress," Budapest Domestic Service [Budapest], April 23, 1989. Foreign Broadcast Information Service, *Daily Report: East Europe.* (FBIS-EEU-89-079.) April 26, 1989, 36.

"Democratic Forum Leader on Power Sharing," MTI [Budapest], May 11, 1989. Foreign Broadcast Information Service, *Daily Report: East Europe.* (FBIS-EEU-89-073.) April 18, 1989, 32.

"Demonstration Protests Russian Language Courses," MTI [Budapest], April 14, 1989. Foreign Broadcast Information Service, *Daily Report: East Europe.* (FBIS-EEU-89-091.) May 12, 1989, 37.

Endrst, Jaroslav. "Tradition in Hungary Said to Be Women's Enemy," *Radio Free Europe Research* [Munich], March 30, 1988, 41–42.

Fél, Edit, and Tamás Hofer. *Proper Peasants: Traditional Life in a Hungarian Village.* Chicago: Aldine, 1969.

Ferge, Zsuzsa. "The Dynamics of the Reproduction of Social Relations." Pages 193–222 in Rudolf Andorka and Tamás Kolosi (eds.), *Stratification and Inequalities.* Budapest: Institute of Social Sciences, 1984.

––––––. *A Society in the Making: Hungarian Social and Societal Policy, 1945–75.* White Plains, New York: M.E. Sharpe, 1979.

Flakierski, Henryk. *Economic Reform and Income Distribution.* Armonk, New York: M.E. Sharpe, 1986.

Forray, Katalin R. *Die Bildungswege der Frauen in Ungarn: Neue Tendenzen in der Ausbildung und Beschäftigung aus soziologischem Aspekt.* (Forschungen zum Bildungspolitik, 97.) März, Austria: Institut für Bildungsforschung, 1985.

From Below: Independent Peace and Environmental Movements in Eastern Europe and the USSR. (A Helsinki Watch Report.) New York: Helsinki Watch, 1987.

" 'Glasnost Club' to Study Post-1945 History," MTI [Budapest], May 6, 1989. Foreign Broadcast Information Service, *Daily Report: East Europe.* (FBIS–EEU–89–087.) May 8, 1989, 27.

"Government Releases AIDS Statistics," MTI [Budapest], April 24, 1989. Foreign Broadcast Information Service, *Daily Report: East Europe.* (FBIS–EEU–89–083.) May 2, 1989, 16.

Gutman, Judith Mara. "Fresh Breezes in Budapest," *Washington Post Book World,* May 7, 1989, 15.

Halász, Gábor. "A New Education Act," *New Hungarian Quarterly* [Budapest], 28, No. 106, Summer 1987, 49–56.

Hankiss, Elemér. "Demobilization, Self-Mobilization, and Quasi-Mobilization in Hungary, 1948–1987," *Eastern European Politics and Societies,* 3, No. 1, Winter 1989, 105–51.

Hewett, Ed A. "Introduction," *Journal of Comparative Economics,* 7, No. 3, September 1983, 209–10.

"Hungarian Real Wages Sink to 1973 Level," *Washington Post,* January 4, 1989, A15.

"Hungarian Revolt Reclassified as 'Popular Uprising'," *Washington Post,* January 1, 1989, A35.

"Hungarians Back Creating More Parties," *Washington Post,* February 13, 1989, A1, A20.

"Hungary Aims to Emulate W. Europe," *Washington Post,* February 19, 1989, A39, A49.

Hungary. Central Statistical Office. *Education and Cultural Conditions in Hungary, 1960–1984.* Budapest: 1985.

––––––. Central Statistical Office. *Hungary Today.* Budapest: 1985.

_____. Central Statistical Office. *Statistical Pocket Book of Hungary 1987.* Budapest: 1988.

_____. Central Statistical Office. *Statistical Yearbook, 1986.* Budapest: 1988.

_____. *Dynamics of Public Health in Hungary, 1986.* Budapest: Ministry of Health, 1986.

_____. Ministry of Finance. Secretariat. *The Social Insurance System.* Budapest: 1982.

Hungary: Economic Developments and Reforms. (A World Bank Country Study.) Washington: World Bank, 1984.

Kamm, Henry. "Hungarians Move to Limit Dissent," *New York Times,* March 13, 1987, A13.

_____. "Hungary in a Sour Mood as Leadership Shifts," *New York Times,* December 25, 1987, A24.

_____. "Hungary Seeks Way to Cut High Suicide Rate," *New York Times,* July 30, 1987, A14.

_____. "Hungary Tries Letting Its Unions Be Unions," *New York Times,* September 11, 1985, A15.

_____. "In Hungary, Students Call for Freedom," *New York Times,* November 9, 1988, A7.

_____. "Lean Times in Hungary: The Land of Good Living Is Looking a Bit Wan," *New York Times,* August 5, 1987, A3.

_____. "Protesters March to Remember Nagy," *New York Times,* June 17, 1988, A5.

Katzner, Kenneth. *The Languages of the World.* New York: Funk and Wagnalls, 1975.

Kemény, István. "Trade Unions and Workers' Interests in Hungary." Pages 173–90 in Alex Pravda and Blair A. Ruble (eds.), *Trade Unions in Communist States.* Boston: Allen and Unwin, 1986.

"KISZ Renamed Democratic Youth Federation," MTI [Budapest], April 22, 1989. Foreign Broadcast Information Service, *Daily Report: East Europe.* (FBIS–EEU–89–079.) April 26, 1989, 36.

Kolosi, Tamás, and Edmund Wnuk-Lipinski. "Impact on Social Structure." Pages 32–49 in Tamás Kolosi and Edmund Wnuk-Lipinski (eds.), *Equality and Inequality under Socialism: Poland and Hungary Compared.* London: International Sociological Association, 1983.

Koppany, Steven. "Frank Radio Debate about Causes of Inequality in Hungary," *Radio Free Europe Research* [Munich], February 25, 1986, 9–12.

Kornai, János. "Comments on the Present State and the Prospects of the Hungarian Economic Reform," *Journal of Comparative Economics,* 7, No. 3, September 1983, 225–52.

Kovács, Ferenc. "Industrialization." Pages 13–31 in Tamás Kolosi and Edmund Wnuk-Lipinski (eds.), *Equality and Inequality under Socialism: Poland and Hungary Compared.* London: International Sociological Association, 1983.

Kovács, Mária M., and Antal Örkény. "Promoted Cadres and Professionals in Post-War Hungary." Pages 139–52 in Rudolf Andorka and László Bertalan (eds.), *Economy and Society in Hungary.* Budapest: Department of Sociology, Karl Marx University of Economic Sciences, 1986.

Kronstein, Gábor. "Being Hungarian in Eastern Europe," *Hungarian Observer* [Budapest], 1, 1989, 4–7.

_____. "Dam and Nation," *Hungarian Observer* [Budapest], 1, 1988, 20–23.

Kulcsár, Kálmán. *Social Changes and Modernization in Hungary.* (Underdevelopment and Modernization Working Papers.) Budapest: Hungarian Academy of Sciences, 1983.

Kusin, Vladimir V., and Judith Pataki. "A Federation Replaces the Communist Youth League," *Radio Free Europe Research* [Munich], May 9, 1989, 27–29.

Lengyel, Eva. "The Unresolved Plight of Pensioners," *Radio Free Europe Research* [Munich], June 8, 1985, 29–35.

Lovenduski, Joni, and Jean Woodall. *Politics and Society in Eastern Europe.* Bloomington: Indiana University Press, 1987.

Markos, Edith. "Escalation of Drug Abuse Admitted," *Radio Free Europe Research* [Munich], December 6, 1985, 33–39.

_____. "Fast-Growing Gypsy Minority and Its Problems," *Radio Free Europe Research* [Munich], June 15, 1987, 13–16.

_____. "First Independent Hungarian Labor Union Established," *Radio Free Europe Research* [Munich], May 19, 1988, 17–19.

_____. "Hungary's First Independent Trade Union Holds Its Founding Congress," *Radio Free Europe Research* [Munich], January 12, 1989, 27–30.

_____. "Lawyers Set Up Independent Organizations to Promote Reform of the Law," *Radio Free Europe Research* [Munich], February 8, 1989, 17–20.

_____. "More Latitude for the Churches?" *Radio Free Europe Research* [Munich], March 30, 1988, 21–24.

_____. "New Organizations to Help the Communist Youth League," *Radio Free Europe Research* [Munich], January 3, 1986, 35–39.

_____. "Poverty Spreading in Hungary," *Radio Free Europe Research* [Munich], August 12, 1988, 37–40.

_____. "Suicide: A Hungarian Tragedy," *Radio Free Europe Research* [Munich], September 19, 1987, 19–22.

Marrese, Michael. "Agricultural Policy and Performance in Hungary," *Journal of Comparative Economics,* 7, No. 3, September 1983, 329–45.

Miklós, Imre. "Church Policy in Hungary," *New Hungarian Quarterly* [Budapest], 29, No. 110, Summer 1988, 57–69.

Noti, Stephen. "The Shifting Position of Hungarian Trade Unions Amidst Social and Economic Reforms," *Soviet Studies* [Glasgow], 39, No. 1, January 1987, 63–87.

Nyers, Rezső. "Interrelations Between Policy and the Economic Reform in Hungary," *Journal of Comparative Economics,* 7, No. 2, September 1983, 211–24.

Okolicsanyi, Karoly. "Does the Future Lie in a Grand Coalition?" *Radio Free Europe Research* [Munich], May 9, 1989, 31–34.

_____. "Massive Price Hikes Polarize Trade Unions and Government," *Radio Free Europe Research* [Munich], February 8, 1989, 21–26.

_____. "National Assembly Restores National Holiday and Approves Government Reorganization," *Radio Free Europe Research* [Munich], February 8, 1989, 3–6.

_____. "The 1987 Economic Results: Stagnation Continues," *Radio Free Europe Research* [Munich], March 30, 1988, 25–30.

_____. "Small Reduction in the 1989 State Budget," *Radio Free Europe Research* [Munich], January 12, 1989, 17–22.

_____. "Startling Changes in the Press," *Radio Free Europe Research* [Munich], February 8, 1989, 31–36.

_____. "Wage Ceilings for 1989 Lifted," *Radio Free Europe Research* [Munich], January 12, 1989, 23–26.

Pataki, Judith. "Children in Eastern Europe: Hungary," *Radio Free Europe Research* [Munich], October 26, 1987.

_____. "The Cost of 'Free' Health Care," *Radio Free Europe Research* [Munich], June 8, 1985, 23–27.

_____. "The Institutionalized Perils of Hungarian Hospitals," *Radio Free Europe Research* [Munich], June 15, 1987, 39–43.

_____. "New Pension Proposals Highlight Problems of the Elderly," *Radio Free Europe Research* [Munich], July 22, 1987, 21–24.

_____. "The Rebirth of Political Parties," *Radio Free Europe Research* [Munich], January 12, 1989, 3–8.

Petrik, Ferenc. "The Family and Family Law," *New Hungarian Quarterly* [Budapest], 28, No. 106, Summer 1987, 36–48.

"Plea Made to Koch by Jews in Hungary for Help from U.S." *New York Times,* January 30, 1987, B2.

Polinszky, K., and É. Széchy. *Higher Education in Hungary.* (Monographs on Higher Education.) Bucharest: United Nations Educational, Scientific and Cultural Organization, 1985.

Potsubay, Melinda. "Hungary's Latter-Day Saints," *Hungarian Observer* [Budapest], 1, 1989, 27.

"Refugees Continue to Arrive from Romania," *Nepszabadsag* [Budapest], May 5, 1989. Foreign Broadcast Information Service, *Daily Report: East Europe.* (FBIS-EEU-89-088.) May 9, 1989, 37.

Reisch, Alfred. "The HSWP CC Grapples with the Implications of Political Pluralism," *Radio Free Europe Research* [Munich], January 12, 1989, 9–14.

_____. "Hungary," *Radio Free Europe Research* [Munich] December 30, 1988.

_____. "National Assembly Passes Landmark Laws on Rights of Association and Assembly," *Radio Free Europe Research* [Munich], February 8, 1989, 7–12.

Révész, László. *Staat und Kirche im 'realen' Sozialismus: Recht und Wirklichkeit.* Bern: Schweizerisches Ost-Institut, 1986.

"Romanian Refugees Stage Rally in Budapest," Vienna Television Service [Vienna], May 7, 1989. Foreign Broadcast Information Service, *Daily Report: East Europe.* (FBIS-EEU-89-087.) May 8, 1989, 29.

Rothschild, Joseph. *Return to Diversity: A Political History of East Central Europe since World War II.* New York: Oxford University Press, 1989.

Rugg, Dean S. *Eastern Europe.* (The World's Landscapes Series.) New York: Longman, 1985.

Schöpflin, George. *Hungary Between Prosperity and Crisis.* London: Institute for the Study of Conflict, 1981.

_____. "Opposition in Hungary: 1956 and Beyond." Pages 69–81 in Jane Leftwich Curry (ed.), *Dissent in Eastern Europe,* New York: Praeger, 1983.

Schöpflin, George, Rudolf Tőkés, and Iván Völgyes. "Leadership Change and Crisis in Hungary," *Problems of Communism,* 37, No. 5, September–October 1988, 23–46.

Székely, András Bertalan. "Access to Culture for National Minorities," *New Hungarian Quarterly* [Budapest], 29, No. 110, Summer 1988, 106–15.

Tagliabue, John. "Hungary Hardens Its Line Against Internal Critics," *New York Times,* May 1, 1988, A24.

_____. "Independents Pose Problem for Budapest," *New York Times,* December 19, 1988, A9.

_____. "Rumanians Choose Life in Hungary," *New York Times,* April 4, 1988, A3.

Tardos, Márton. "The Increasing Role and Ambivalent Reception of Small Enterprises in Hungary," *Journal of Comparative Economics,* 7, No. 3, September 1983, 277-87.

"10,000 Crying 'Democracy' March in Budapest," *New York Times,* March 16, 1988, A5.

Tőkés, Rudolf L. "The Science of Politics in Hungary in the 1980s: People, Ideas, and Contradictions," *Südosteuropa: Zeitschrift für Gegenwartsforschung* [Munich], 37, No. 1, 1988, 8-32.

Toma, Peter A. *Socialist Authority: The Hungarian Experience.* New York: Praeger, 1988.

Tyson, Laura D'Andrea. "Investment Allocation: A Comparison of the Reform Experience of Hungary and Yugoslavia," *Journal of Comparative Economics,* 7, No. 3, September 1983, 288-303.

"U.S. Support for FIDESZ Questioned," *Pravda* [Bratislava], April 8, 1989. Foreign Broadcast Information Service, *Daily Report: East Europe.* (FBIS-EEU-89-070.) April 13, 1989, 24.

Völgyes, Iván. *Hungary: A Nation of Contradictions.* (Westview Profiles Nations of Contemporary Eastern Europe Series.) Boulder, Colorado: Westview Press, 1982.

Warren, Clay. "Communication Theory and Practice Behind the See-Through Iron Curtain of Hungary," *East European Quarterly,* 23, No. 1, March 1989, 85-98.

_____. "Hungary." Pages 127-36 in Moshe Y. Sachs (ed.), *Worldmark Encyclopedia of the Nations,* 5. New York: Wiley, 1988.

Chapter 3

Adam, Jan. "The Hungarian Economic Reform of the 1980s," *Soviet Studies* [Glasgow], 29, No. 4, October 1987, 610-27.

_____. "Regulation of Labor Supply in Poland, Czechoslovakia, and Hungary," *Soviet Studies* [Glasgow], 36, No. 1, January 1984, 69-86.

Alisov, N.V., and E.B. Valev. *Economic Geography of the Socialist Countries of Europe.* Moscow: Progress, 1985.

Batt, Judy. *Economic Reform and Political Change in Eastern Europe.* New York: St. Martin's Press, 1988.

Bauer, Tamás. "Hungarian Economic Reform in East European Perspective," *Eastern European Politics and Societies,* 2, No. 3, Fall 1988, 418-32.

Berend, Ivan T., and György Ránki. *The Hungarian Economy in the Twentieth Century.* London: Croom Helm, 1985.

Bigler, Robert M. "The Role of Bureaucracies and Experts in the Planning and Implementation of Hungary's New Economic Mechanism," *East European Quarterly*, 18, No. 1, March 1984, 93–112.

Brada, Josef C., and Istvan Dobozi (eds.). *The Hungarian Economy in the 1980s.* Greenwich, Connecticut: JAI Press, 1988.

Buzescu, Petru. "Joint Ventures in Eastern Europe," *American Journal of Comparative Law*, 32, Summer 1984, 407–47.

Cochrane, Nancy J., and Miles J. Lambert. *Agricultural Performance in Eastern Europe, 1987.* (Staff Report AGES 881025.) Washington: Economic Research Service, United States Department of Agriculture, 1988.

de Bueky, Barnabas. "Price Increases in Eastern Europe with Special Regard to Hungary," *Radio Free Europe Research* [Munich], May 16, 1984.

———. "What Would Convertibility for the Hungarian Forint Mean?" *Radio Free Europe Research* [Munich], August 2, 1985.

"Economic Results for January–August Announced," *Nepszabadsag* [Budapest], October 12, 1988. Foreign Broadcast Information Service, *Daily Report: East Europe.* (FBIS–EEU–88–201.) October 18, 1988, 32–34.

"The Environment in Eastern Europe," *Radio Free Europe Research* [Munich], March 20, 1987.

Enyedi, Gyorgy. *Hungary: An Economic Geography.* Boulder, Colorado: Westview Press, 1976.

———. "Planning for Purposeful Use of the Environment: A Hungarian Viewpoint." Pages 123–29 in Iván Völgyes (ed.), *Environmental Deterioration in the Soviet Union and Eastern Europe.* New York: Praeger, 1974.

Flaherty, Diane. "Regional Policy and the Reform of Central Planning: An Assessment of the GDR, Hungarian, and Yugoslav Approaches," *Contributions to Political Economy*, 3, March 1984, 39–63.

French, Hilary F. "Industrial Wasteland," *Worldwatch* [London], 1, No. 6, November–December 1988, 21–30.

Gajdeczka, Przemyslaw. "International Market Perceptions and Economic Performance: Lending to Eastern Europe," *Eastern European Politics and Societies*, 2, No. 3, Fall 1988, 558–76.

Glenny, Misha. "Muddy Danube," *Technology Review*, No. 5, July 1986, 14–15.

Hare, Paul. "The Beginnings of Institutional Reform in Hungary," *Soviet Studies* [Glasgow], 35, No. 3, July 1983, 313–30.

———. "Industrial Development in Hungary since World War II," *Eastern European Politics and Societies*, 2, No. 1, Winter 1988, 115–51.

Hartford, Kathleen. "Hungarian Agriculture: A Model for the Socialist World?" *World Development,* 13, No. 1, 1985, 123–50.

Heinrich, Hans-George. *Hungary: Politics, Economics, and Society.* Boulder, Colorado: Lynne Rienner, 1986.

Hungary. Central Statistical Office. *Statistical Yearbook, 1986.* Budapest: 1988.

"Hungary." Pages 1301–22 in *The Europa Year Book.* London: Europa, 1988.

"January–September. Trade Registers Surplus," MTI [Budapest], October 27, 1988. Foreign Broadcast Information Service, *Daily Report: East Europe.* (FBIS-EEU-88-211.) November 1, 1988, 37.

Jerome, Robert T. "Sources of Economic Growth in Hungary, 1950–1985," *East European Quarterly,* 22, No. 1, March 1988, 107–18.

Koppany, Steven. "A Chronology of Recent Soviet-Hungarian Trade Negotiations and Agreements," *Radio Free Europe Research* [Munich], February 25, 1986, 25–29.

———. "Hungary Already Concerned about Prospects for Its 1986–1990 Plan," *Radio Free Europe Research* [Munich], April 24, 1986.

———. "Hungary's First Nuclear Power Plant," *Radio Free Europe Research* [Munich], March 25, 1986, 19–23.

———. "Hungary's Oil and Natural Gas Reserves: Going After Every Last Drop," *Radio Free Europe Research* [Munich], January 3, 1986, 13–22.

Kornai, János. "The Hungarian Reform Process: Visions, Hopes, and Reality," *Journal of Economic Literature,* 24, December 1986, 1687–1737.

"Main Statistical Data on Economic Situation—Economic Performance for January–August 1988." *Nepszabadsag* [Budapest], October 12, 1988. Foreign Broadcast Information Service, *Daily Report: East Europe.* (FBIS-EEU-88-201.) October 18, 1988, 32–34.

Marer, Paul. *East-West Technology Transfer: Study of Hungary.* Paris: Organization for Economic Cooperation and Development, 1986.

Markos, Edith. "Hungary and Austria to Pursue Cordial Relations," *Radio Free Europe Research* [Munich], October 30, 1987, 25–28.

———. "Invisible Incomes," *Radio Free Europe Research* [Munich], August 11, 1987, 17–19.

———. "Public Works Introduced to Reduce Unemployment," *Radio Free Europe Research* [Munich], October 3, 1987, 15–19.

———. "The Third Economy," *Radio Free Europe Research* [Munich], April 6, 1985, 29–32.

Naray, Petar. "Hungarian Foreign Trade Reform," *Journal of World Trade Law* [Twickenham, Middlesex, United Kingdom], 20, May–June 1986, 274–86.

Okolicsanyi, Karoly. "Attempt to Freeze Wages in Response to Worsening Economic Conditions," *Radio Free Europe Research* [Munich], December 23, 1986, 19–24.

_____. "An Austere State Budget for 1988," *Radio Free Europe Research* [Munich], January 11, 1988, 19–23.

_____. "The Bank Reforms: A Balance Sheet for the First Six Months," *Radio Free Europe Research* [Munich], September 19, 1987, 13–17.

_____. "Bankruptcy," *Radio Free Europe Research* [Munich], May 18, 1987, 19–22.

_____. "CC Endorses Drastic Economic Proposals," *Radio Free Europe Research* [Munich], August 5, 1988, 3–7.

_____. "Corporate Socialism: Hungary Prepares to Promote Stock Ownership," *Radio Free Europe Research* [Munich], June 10, 1988, 19–22.

_____. "Domestic Trade and the New Trade Law," *Radio Free Europe Research* [Munich], December 23, 1986, 31–36.

_____. "Drastic Price Increases," *Radio Free Europe Research* [Munich], February 15, 1988, 19–22.

_____. "Easing of Constraints on Agricultural Cooperatives," *Radio Free Europe Research* [Munich], May 2, 1988, 29–31.

_____. "Economic Aspects," *Radio Free Europe Research* [Munich], July 8, 1988, 47–49.

_____. "Expanding Economic Relations with the FRG," *Radio Free Europe Research* [Munich], October 30, 1987, 13–23.

_____. "The Heat Is on Large Unprofitable Enterprises," *Radio Free Europe Research* [Munich], January 11, 1988, 25–29.

_____. "HSWP Announces Tough New Economic Stabilization Program," *Radio Free Europe Research* [Munich], July 22, 1987, 13–16.

_____. "The Hungarian Insurance Industry: A Case Study of Economic Reform," *Radio Free Europe Research* [Munich], August 18, 1988, 3–4.

_____. "Hungary Cuts State Subsidies for CMEA Trade," *Radio Free Europe Research* [Munich], August 18, 1988, 5–10.

_____. "Hungary Reaches Trade Agreement with the EEC," *Radio Free Europe Research* [Munich], August 12, 1988, 27–30.

_____. "Inflation and Monetary Policy," *Radio Free Europe Research* [Munich], June 15, 1987, 17–21.

_____. "Layoffs Started in Earnest," *Radio Free Europe Research* [Munich], June 30, 1987, 17–20.

_____. "Major Economic Report Published in a Revised Form," *Radio Free Europe Research* [Munich], August 10, 1987.

_____. "New Bankruptcy Law," *Radio Free Europe Research* [Munich], September 30, 1986, 3-6.

_____. "New Legislation to Encourage Private Enterprise," *Radio Free Europe Research* [Munich], October 5, 1988, 9-14.

_____. "The New Reform Program: Where and What Is It?" *Radio Free Europe Research* [Munich], September 19, 1987, 7-11.

_____. "The 1987 Budget," *Radio Free Europe Research* [Munich], January 31, 1987, 7-10.

_____. "The Pain of Change: The First Effects of the New Tax System," *Radio Free Europe Research* [Munich], June 10, 1988, 13-17.

_____. "Plans for Value-Added Tax," *Radio Free Europe Research* [Munich], June 15, 1987, 29-32.

_____. "Plans to Introduce Personal Income Tax," *Radio Free Europe Research* [Munich], June 15, 1987, 23-27.

_____. "Poor Foreign Trade," *Radio Free Europe Research* [Munich], December 23, 1986, 25-29.

_____. "Press Comments about the Latest Price Increases," *Radio Free Europe Research* [Munich], August 11, 1987, 9-11.

_____. "Price Increases: Old Problems and Old Solutions," *Radio Free Europe Research* [Munich], July 22, 1987, 17-19.

_____. "Private Enterprise: Slowdown or Further Expansion," *Radio Free Europe Research* [Munich], May 2, 1988, 23-27.

_____. "The Specter of Unemployment Becomes a Reality," *Radio Free Europe Research* [Munich], February 15, 1988, 23-27.

_____. "Stock Exchange Opened," *Radio Free Europe Research* [Munich], March 30, 1988, 31-35.

_____. "A Survey of United States-Hungarian Trade," *Radio Free Europe Research* [Munich], August 12, 1988, 21-25.

_____. "Tax Legislation Approved By National Assembly," *Radio Free Europe Research* [Munich], October 30, 1987, 15-19.

_____. "What to Do about the Worsening Economy," *Radio Free Europe Research* [Munich], December 23, 1986, 7-11.

O'Relley, Z. Edward. "The Changing Status of Collectivized and Private Agriculture under Central Planning," *American Journal of Economics and Sociology*, 45, No. 1, January 1986, 9-16.

Pataki, Judith. "Buying Fever," *Radio Free Europe Research* [Munich], November 28, 1987, 41-45.

_____. "Investment Protection Agreement," *Radio Free Europe Research* [Munich], July 11, 1986, 31-35.

Pissula, Petra. "The IMF and the Countries of Eastern Europe: Rumania, Hungary, and Poland," *Intereconomics* [Hamburg], No. 2, March–April 1984, 65-70.

Rasko, Laszlo. "Hungarian Agriculture in 1984," *Radio Free Europe Research* [Munich], December 29, 1984, 23–25.

———. "Joint Ventures in Eastern Europe," *Radio Free Europe Research* [Munich], April 19, 1985, 9–10.

———. "More State Subsidies for Agriculture," *Radio Free Europe Research* [Munich], October 14, 1985, 23–33.

———. "National Bank Monopoly," *Radio Free Europe Research* [Munich], February 25, 1986, 35–38.

Reisch, Alfred. "Coal Mining Industry in Dire Straits," *Radio Free Europe Research* [Munich], January 3, 1986, 23–34.

———. "EEC Ban on Food Imports," *Radio Free Europe Research* [Munich], May 27, 1986, 9–15.

———. "Hungarian-Japanese Trade and Economic Cooperation," *Radio Free Europe Research* [Munich], October 14, 1985, 17–22.

———. "Hungary Joins Two World Bank Affiliates," *Radio Free Europe Research* [Munich], May 16, 1985, 33–34.

Richet, Xavier. *The Hungarian Model: Markets and Planning in a Socialist Economy.* Cambridge: Cambridge University Press, 1989.

Schöpflin, George, Rudolf Tőkés, and Iván Völgyes. "Leadership Change and Crisis in Hungary," *Problems of Communism,* 37, No. 5, September–October 1988, 23–46.

The Statesman's Year-Book, 1988–1989. New York: St. Martin's Press, 1988.

Steblez, Walter G. "The Mineral Industry of Hungary." Pages 393–404 in United States, Department of the Interior, Bureau of Mines, *Minerals Yearbook, 1985,* Washington: GPO, 1987.

Swain, Nigel. "Hungarian Agriculture in the Early 1980s: Retrenchment Followed by Reform," *Soviet Studies* [Glasgow], 29, No. 1, January 1987, 24–39.

Tőkés, Rudolf L. "Hungarian Reform Imperatives," *Problems of Communism,* 34, No. 5, September–October 1984, 1–23.

United Nations. Conference on Trade and Development. *Manual on Trading with the Socialist Countries of Eastern Europe.* New York: 1987.

United States. Congress. 99th, 2d Session. Joint Economic Committee. *East European Economics: Slow Growth in 1980s,* 3. (Country Studies on Eastern Europe and Yugoslavia.) Washington: GPO, March 28, 1986.

Völgyes, Iván. "The Burden of Equality: Kadar's Hungary Today," *Radio Free Europe Research* [Munich], November 23, 1984.

Wilczynski, Jan. *The Economics of Socialism.* London: Allen and Unwin, 1982.

Chapter 4

Asmus, Ronald D. *East Berlin and Moscow: The Documentation of a Dispute.* (Radio Free Europe Occasional Papers, No. 1.) Munich: Radio Free Europe, 1985.

Barany, Zoltan. "An Assessment of Grosz's Visit to the USA," *Radio Free Europe Research* [Munich], August 12, 1988, 7-12.

_____. "Grosz's Visit to Moscow Demonstrates Close Relations with Gorbachev," *Radio Free Europe Research* [Munich], August 12, 1988, 3-6.

_____. "Political Reform: Revising the Constitution," *Radio Free Europe Research* [Munich], July 8, 1985, 41-45.

Bihari, Mihály. "The Political System and the Representation of Interests." Pages 287-312 in Rudolph Andorka and László Bertalan (eds.), *Economy and Society in Hungary.* Budapest: Department of Sociology, Karl Marx University of Economic Sciences, 1986.

_____. "Reform und Demokratie," *Europäische Rundschau* [Vienna], 16, No. 3, 1988, 85-94.

Bruk, S.I. *Naselenie mira.* Moscow: Nauka, 1986.

"Communique on Central Committee Meeting Issued," *Nepszabadsag* [Budapest], December 19, 1988. Foreign Broadcast Information Service, *Daily Report: East Europe.* (FBIS-EEU-88-224.) December 20, 1988, 39-42.

The Constitution of the Hungarian People's Republic. Budapest: Athenaeum, 1980.

"East European Leadership List," *Radio Free Europe Research* [Munich], September 9, 1988.

Fehér, Ferenc, Agnes Heller, and György Markus. *Dictatorship over Needs.* New York: St. Martin's Press, 1983.

Felkay, Andrew. *Hungary and the USSR, 1956-1988.* New York: Greenwood Press, 1988.

"Foreign Ministry Reacts," Budapest Domestic Service [Budapest], November 21, 1988. Foreign Broadcast Information Service, *Daily Report: East Europe.* (FBIS-EEU-88-224.) November 21, 1988, 27.

Haraszti, Miklos. *The Velvet Prison. Artists under State Socialism.* New York: Basic Books, 1987.

Hazan, Baruch. *The East European Political System.* Boulder, Colorado: Westview Press, 1985.

Heinrich, Hans-Georg. *Hungary: Politics, Economics, and Society.* Boulder, Colorado: Lynne Rienner, 1986.

_____. *Verfassungswirklichkeit in Osteuropa.* Vienna: Springer-Verlag, 1980.

Hungary. Central Statistical Office. *Statistical Yearbook, 1986.* Budapest: 1988.

Józsa, Gyula. *Ungarn im Kreuzfeuer der Kritik aus Prag und Moskau, Teil I: Aussenministerkonferenz der WP-Staaten (April 1984) und die Polemik zwischen Prag und Budapest.* Cologne: Bundesinstitut für ostwissenschaftliche und internationale Studien, 1985.

————. *Ungarn im Kreuzfeuer der Kritik aus Prag und Moskau. Teil II: Moskauer Regie und Hintergründe der Polemik gegen Ungarns Positionen.* Cologne: Bundesinstitut für ostwissenschaftliche und internationale Studien, 1985.

"Kadar Admits Shortcomings and the Need for a Program of Action," *Radio Free Europe Research* [Munich], April 27, 1985, 3–8.

Koppany, Steven. "Election Results and Assessment," *Radio Free Europe Research* [Munich], June 21, 1985, 9–19.

————. "Importance of National Interests in Interparty Relations Reasserted," *Radio Free Europe Research* [Munich], December 6, 1985, 3–7.

————. "Kadar in Britain: The Dialogue Continues," *Radio Free Europe Research* [Munich], December 6, 1985, 9–15.

————. "Nomination of Candidates for Hungarian Elections Completed," *Radio Free Europe Research* [Munich], June 28, 1985.

————. "Shultz Pleased to Have Met 'Wise Man' of Hungary," *Radio Free Europe Research* [Munich], February 3, 1986, 3–10.

————. "Unprepared Regime Scrambles to Meet Challenges of the Video Era," *Radio Free Europe Research* [Munich], September 4, 1985, 17–24.

Kovács, István. "The Development of the Constitution of the Hungarian People's Republic." Pages 3–69 in György Szoboszlai (ed.), *Politics and Public Administration in Hungary.* Budapest: Akadémiai Kiadó, 1985.

Kovrig, Bennett. *Communism in Hungary from Kun to Kadar.* Stanford, California: Hoover Institution Press, 1979.

Kusin, Vladimir. "Satellite Television for Eastern Europe: Signposts in a Changing Landscape," *Radio Free Europe Research* [Munich], May 26, 1988.

Lahav, Yehuda. *Der Weg der kommunistischen Partei Ungarns zur Macht.* Munich: Ungarischen Institut, 1986.

Lendvai, Paul. *Das eigenwillige Ungarn.* Zürich: Edition Interfrom, 1986.

Lomax, Bill. "Hungary—The Quest for Legitimacy." Pages 68–110 in Paul G. Lewis (ed.), *Eastern Europe: Political Crisis and Legitimation.* New York: St. Martin's Press, 1984.

Lovas, Istvan, and Ken Anderson. "State Terrorism in Hungary: The Case of Friendly Repression," *Telos,* No. 54, Winter 1982–83, 77–86.

Mandel, Stefan. "Filling the Vacuum," *Index on Censorship* [London], 7, No. 2, March–April 1978, 40–41.

Markos, Edith. "CC Secretary Matyas Szuros's Visit to the USA," *Radio Free Europe Research* [Munich], May 18, 1987, 9–13.

_____. "The Gabcikovo-Nagymaros Dam Project," *Radio Free Europe Research* [Munich], September 4, 1985, 3–10.

_____. "The Hungarian and Czechoslovak Prime Ministers' Meeting," *Radio Free Europe Research* [Munich], September 19, 1987, 3–6.

_____. "Hungary and Austria to Pursue Cordial Relations," *Radio Free Europe Research* [Munich], October 30, 1987, 25–28.

_____. "Official and Dissident Views on the Magyar Minority in Slovakia," *Radio Free Europe Research* [Munich], June 15, 1987, 9–12.

Mlynar, Zdenek (ed.). *Die Beziehungen zwischen Österreich und Ungarn: Sonderfall oder Modell?* Vienna: Universitäts-Verlagsbuchhandlung, 1985.

"New Tabloid to Be Launched in November," MTI [Budapest], November 15, 1988. Foreign Broadcast Information Service, *Daily Report: East Europe.* (FBIS–EEU–88–225.) November 22, 1988, 23–24.

Pataki, Judith. "CC Secretary Claims Special Role for Small Nations," *Radio Free Europe Research* [Munich], July 31, 1986, 27–31.

_____. "Chinese Foreign Minister Visits Hungary," *Radio Free Europe Research* [Munich], July 11, 1986, 15–20.

_____. "Diplomatic Relations with Israel Restored at Low Level," *Radio Free Europe Research* [Munich], October 30, 1987, 31–34.

_____. "Dispute Between Hungary and Romania Continues," *Radio Free Europe Research* [Munich], July 8, 1988, 15–19.

_____. "Four Prominent Intellectuals Expelled from Party," *Radio Free Europe Research* [Munich], May 2, 1988, 15–18.

_____. *"Frank Official Reporting on Magyar Minority in Romania," Radio Free Europe Research* [Munich], March 21, 1988, 25–29.

_____. "Massive Rally in Budapest Protests Romanian Plan to Raze Villages," *Radio Free Europe Research* [Munich], July 8, 1988, 9–13.

_____. "New Press Law Approved by National Assembly," *Radio Free Europe Research* [Munich], April 28, 1986, 7–11.

_____. "Shamir's Visit: Hungary and Israel Closer to Resuming Diplomatic Relations," *Radio Free Europe Research* [Munich], October 5, 1988, 15–17.

Piroschka, Farkas. "Information statt Befehl," *Frankfurter Allgemeine Zeitung* [Frankfurt], August 4, 1988, 19.

Pokol, Béla. "Changes in the System of Political Representation in Hungary." Pages 267–86 in Rudolph Andorka and László Bertalan (eds.), *Economy and Society in Hungary*. Budapest: Department of Sociology, Karl Marx University of Economic Sciences, 1986.

Racz, Barnabas. "Political Participation and Developed Socialism: The Hungarian Elections of 1985," *Soviet Studies* [Glasgow], 39, No. 1, January 1987, 40–62.

Reisch, Alfred. "The Battle for the Post of Budapest Party First Secretary," *Radio Free Europe Research* [Munich], August 5, 1988, 15–19.

_____. "CC Adopts Draft Position Paper for National Party Conference," *Radio Free Europe Research* [Munich], March 30, 1988, 3–8.

_____. "CC Secretary Matyas Szuros on Diversity and Unity," *Radio Free Europe Research* [Munich], July 11, 1986, 21–24.

_____. "Central Committee Approves Organizational Changes and Referendum Law Guidelines," *Radio Free Europe Research* [Munich], December 15, 1988, 3–8.

_____. "CPSU Formally to Endorse Hungary's Economic Reform," *Radio Free Europe Research* [Munich], April 27, 1985, 3–10.

_____. "Ethnic Minority Issue Still Clouds Hungarian-Romanian Relations," *Radio Free Europe Research* [Munich], November 27, 1985.

_____. "First Step Toward Resurrecting a Multiparty System," *Radio Free Europe Research* [Munich], November 17, 1988, 3–6.

_____. "Gorbachev in Hungary," *Radio Free Europe Research* [Munich], July 11, 1986, 3–6.

_____. "Gromyko's Visit and Soviet-Hungarian Relations," *Radio Free Europe Research* [Munich], March 21, 1988, 13–18.

_____. "Grosz's Successful Visit Opens New Phase in Relations with the FRG," *Radio Free Europe Research* [Munich], October 30, 1987, 3–8.

_____. "Growing Hungarian-British Economic and Cultural Ties," *Radio Free Europe Research* [Munich], December 6, 1985, 17–23.

_____. "The HSWP Prepares for Its 13th Congress," *Radio Free Europe Research* [Munich], April 6, 1985, 3–8.

_____. "HSWP to Hold Conference in 1988," *Radio Free Europe Research* [Munich], January 11, 1988, 3–6.

_____. "Hungarian CC Keeps to Reform Course Amid Conservative Fears and Rumblings," *Radio Free Europe Research* [Munich], October 28, 1988, 41–46.

_____. "Hungarian Party Congress Guidelines Stress Continuity and Improvements," *Radio Free Europe Research* [Munich], January 7, 1985.

_____. "Hungarian-Romanian Party Talks Fail to Yield Results," *Radio Free Europe Research* [Munich], June 15, 1987, 3-7.

_____. "Hungarian-Yugoslav Friendship Confirmed," *Radio Free Europe Research* [Munich], February 25, 1986, 19-24.

_____. "Hungary Seeks to Make Minority Rights an International Issue," *Radio Free Europe Research* [Munich], April 3, 1987, 11-17.

_____. "Kadar Returns to China to Seal Restoration of Party Relations," *Radio Free Europe Research* [Munich], October 30, 1987, 29-34.

_____. "Long-Term Trade Agreement with China," *Radio Free Europe Research* [Munich], August 7, 1985, 29-33.

_____. "The Minority Issue: Hungary Rebuts Romanian Charges," *Radio Free Europe Research* [Munich], May 18, 1987, 27-32.

_____. "The New HSWP Leadership," *Radio Free Europe Research* [Munich], April 27, 1985, 39-46.

_____. "Nonparty Academician Elected Head of State," *Radio Free Europe Research* [Munich], August 5, 1988, 27-29.

_____. "Officials Qualify Reactions to the Hungarian Democratic Forum," *Radio Free Europe Research* [Munich], October 28, 1988, 25-29.

_____. "Romanian Prime Minister in Budapest," *Radio Free Europe Research* [Munich], May 16, 1985, 21-29.

_____. "Satisfaction with and Optimism about Soviet Party Congress Program," *Radio Free Europe Research* [Munich], March 25, 1986, 7-12.

_____. "Senior HSWP Official Visits the USA," *Radio Free Europe Research* [Munich], February 15, 1985, 3-7.

_____. "Some Preliminary Facts and Figures," *Radio Free Europe Research* [Munich], May 19, 1988, 7-9.

Rumyantsev, Oleg. "Perestroika in Hungary," *International Affairs* [Moscow], No. 9, September 1988, 49-56.

Schmidt, Josef. *Interessen in der ungarischer Gesellschaft: Theoretische und politische Aspekte.* Cologne: Bundesinstitut für ostwissenschaftliche und internationale Studien, 1979.

Schöpflin, George. *Hungary Between Prosperity and Crisis.* London: Institute for the Study of Conflict, 1981.

Schöpflin, George (ed.). *Censorship and Political Communication in Eastern Europe.* New York: St. Martin's Press, 1983.

Schöpflin, George, Rudolf Tőkés, and Iván Völgyes. "Leadership Change and Crisis in Hungary," *Problems of Communism*, 37, No. 5, September–October 1988, 23–46.

Singer, Ladislaus. *Der ungarische Weg*. Stuttgart: Seewald-Verlag, 1979.

Socor, Vladimir. "Eastern Europe Inching Toward Resumption of Relations with Israel," *Radio Free Europe Research* [Munich], September 16, 1987.

_____. "Summit Meeting Between Hungarian and Romanian Leaders," *Radio Free Europe Research* [Munich], September 16, 1988, 21–26.

"Szuros Gives News Conference," Budapest Domestic Service [Budapest], September 27, 1988. Foreign Broadcast Information Service, *Daily Report: East Europe*. (FBIS–EEU–88–188.) September 28, 1988, 23–24.

Tőkés, Rudolph L. "Intellectuals and Their Discontent in Hungary: Class Power or Marginality?" Pages 160–89 in Michael J. Sodaro and Sharon L. Wolchik (eds.), *Foreign and Domestic Policy in Eastern Europe in the 1980s*. New York: St. Martin's Press, 1983.

Toma, Peter A. *Socialist Authority: The Hungarian Experience*. New York: Praeger, 1988.

United States. Department of State. Bureau of Public Affairs. *Implementation of Helsinki Final Act, October 1, 1987–April 1, 1988*. Washington: 1988.

"The Video Revolution in Eastern Europe," *Radio Free Europe Research* [Munich], December 18, 1987.

Völgyes, Iván. *Politics in Eastern Europe*. Chicago: Dorsey Press, 1986.

Wettig, Gerhard. *Die kleineren Warschauer-Pakt-Staaten in den Ost-West-Beziehungen*. Cologne: Bundesinstitut für ostwissenschaftliche und internationale Studien, 1979.

White, Stephen, John Gardner, and George Schöpflin. *Communist Political Systems*. New York: St. Martin's Press, 1987.

Zawadzka, Barbara (ed.). *System terenowych organów wladzy i administracji państwowej w europejskich państwach socjalistycznych*. Warsaw: Ossolineum, 1985.

Chapter 5

"Alcohol Consumption, On-the-Job Drunkenness Down in 1987," *Nepszava* [Budapest], April 10, 1987. Joint Publications Research

Service, *East Europe Report*. (JPRS-EER-87-119.) August 3, 1987, 103-4.

"Alternative Military Service Proposed," MTI [Budapest], February 14, 1989. Foreign Broadcast Information Service, *Daily Report: East Europe*. (FBIS-EEU-89-030.) February 15, 1989, 23.

"Amends Penal Code," MTI [Budapest], June 1, 1989. Foreign Broadcast Information Service, *Daily Report: East Europe*. (FBIS-EEU-89-106.) June 5, 1989, 15.

"Armored Brigade Disbanded in Szabadszallas," MTI [Budapest], August 11, 1989. Foreign Broadcast Information Service, *Daily Report: East Europe*. (FBIS-EEU-89-155.) August 14, 1989, 28.

"Army Officer Discusses Belt-Tightening Problems of Military," *Nepszabadsag* [Budapest], July 19, 1988. Joint Publications Research Service, *East Europe Report*. (JPRS-EER-88-082.) September 30, 1988, 30-32.

Az MSZMP Honvédelmi Politikájárol 1956 November-1973 (Dokumentum-, beszéd és cikkgyüjtemény). Budapest: Zrínyi Katonai, 1974.

"Children Attend Military Training Camps," *Nephadsereg* [Budapest], June 27, 1987. Joint Publications Research Service, *East Europe Report*. (JPRS-EER-87-142.) September 29, 1987, 21-22.

Clarke, Douglas. "The USSR Cannot Expect Greater Military Efforts from Hungary," *Radio Free Europe Research* [Munich], January 27, 1989.

"Conscientious Objectors Released from Prison," Budapest Domestic Service [Budapest], March 1, 1989. Foreign Broadcast Information Service, *Daily Report: East Europe*. (FBIS-EEU-89-041.) March 3, 1989, 40.

"Contingency Plan on Possible Romanian Attack," *Der Standard* [Vienna], July 31, 1989. Foreign Broadcast Information Service, *Daily Report: East Europe*. (FBIS-EEU-89-141.) July 31, 1989, 15-16.

"Defense Minister Details Soviet Troop Pullout," *Magyar Hirlap* [Budapest], January 26, 1989. Foreign Broadcast Information Service, *Daily Report: East Europe*. (FBIS-EEU-89-022.) February 3, 1989, 15.

"Defense Minister Gives 'Exclusive' Interview," *Danas* [Zagreb], July 12, 1988. Foreign Broadcast Information Service, *Daily Report: East Europe*. (FBIS-EEU-89-137.) July 18, 1988, 19-23.

"Defense Ministry Tries to Offset Budget Cuts: Options Described," *Figyelo* [Budapest], April 13, 1989. Joint Publications Research Service, *East Europe Report*. (JPRS-EER-89-061.) May 25, 1989, 39-43.

"Deputy Defense Ministers Relieved of Posts," MTI [Budapest], December 2, 1988. Foreign Broadcast Information Service, *Daily Report: East Europe*. (FBIS-EEU-88-223.) December 5, 1988, 29.

"Dissidents Go on Hunger Strike in Budapest," APF [Paris], July 20, 1988. Foreign Broadcast Information Service, *Daily Report: East Europe.* (FBIS-EEU-88-139.) July 20, 1988, 34.

"Ecological Aspects of Gabcikovo-Nagymaros Viewed," *Rude Pravo* [Prague], June 16, 1989. Foreign Broadcast Information Service, Daily *Report: East Europe.* (FBIS-EEU-89-112.) June 27, 1989, 28-30.

Erdély története. (3 vols.) Budapest: Akadémiai Kiadó, 1986.

"German Editorial Examines Prospect of Soviet Troop Withdrawal from Hungary," *Frankfurter Allgemeine Zeitung* [Frankfurt], July 14, 1988. Joint Publications Research Service, *East Europe Report.* (JPRS-EER-88-065.) August 10, 1988, 29-30.

"Grosz Envisions Continued Political Role for Armed Forces," *Nepszabadsag* [Budapest], May 19, 1989. Joint Publications Research Service, *East Europe Report.* (JPRS-EER-89-074.) June 9, 1989, 34.

"Grosz Visits Defense Ministry 22 Mar." MTI [Budapest], March 22, 1989. Foreign Broadcast Information Service, *Daily Report: East Europe.* (FBIS-EEU-89-055.) March 23, 1989, 34.

Györffy, György. *The Original Landtaking of the Hungarians.* Budapest: Hungarian National Museum, 1975.

Harden, Blaine, and Mary Battiata. "East Germany Lets Refugees Leave, Bars Free Travel to Czechoslovakia," *Washington Post,* October 4, 1989, A1, A34.

Hóman, Bálint, and Gyula Szekfű. *Magyar történet.* (5 vols.) Budapest: Királyi Magyar Egyetemi Nyomda, 1935-36.

Honvédelemről, nevelőknek. Budapest: Zrínyi Katonai, 1975.

"Horn Cited on Romanian Missile Purchase, Tension," *Der Spiegel* [Hamburg], July 24, 1989. Foreign Broadcast Information Service, *Daily Report: East Europe.* (FBIS-EEU-89-141.) July 25, 1989, 20.

"Interior Minister Horvath Comments on New Tasks," *Magyar Hirlap* [Budapest], June 9, 1989. Foreign Broadcast Information Service, *Daily Report: East Europe.* (FBIS-EEU-89-114.) June 15, 1989, 52.

"Interior Minister Says Police Force Intimidated, Very Tense," *Magyarorszag* [Budapest], June 9, 1989. Joint Publications Research Service, *East Europe Report.* (JPRS-EER-89-071.) June 22, 1989, 3-5.

"Interior Ministry Apologizes for Police Brutality," *Nepszava* [Budapest], April 19, 1989. Joint Publications Research Service, *East Europe Report.* (JPRS-EER-89-056.) May 15, 1989, 1.

"Interior Ministry Seeks to Change Police Image," *Magyar Hirlap* [Budapest], June 5, 1989. Joint Publications Research Service,

East Europe Report. (JPRS-EER-89-092.) August 17, 1989, 9-10.

International Institute for Strategic Studies. *The Military Balance, 1988-1989.* London: 1988.

Joes, Anthony James. "Armed Forces and Revolutions: Some Practical Considerations," *Journal of Defense and Diplomacy,* 6, February 1988, 52-55.

Jones, Christopher D. *Soviet Influence in Eastern Europe.* New York: Praeger, 1981.

Karacs, Imre. "Hungary Allows Thousands of East Germans to Flee to West," *Washington Post,* September 11, 1989, A1, A18.

Király, Béla K. *Hungary in the Late Eighteenth Century: The Decline of Enlightened Despotism.* New York: Columbia University Press, 1969.

Kopácsi, Sándor. *In the Name of the Working Class.* New York: Grove Press, 1986.

"Kristaly Case: Article Questions Legal Bases of Sentencing," *Otlet* [Budapest], September 15, 1988. Joint Publications Research Service, *East Europe Report.* (JPRS-EER-88-099.) November 2, 1988, 2.

"Legitimacy of Soviet Troops in Hungary Disputed," *Heti Vilaggazdasag* [Budapest], April 29, 1989. Joint Publications Research Service, *East Europe Report.* (JPRS-EER-89-068.) June 14, 1989, 17-19.

"Life in Prison Camp for Soldiers Described," *Magyar Hirlap* [Budapest], June 4, 1988. Foreign Broadcast Information Service, *Daily Report: East Europe.* (FBIS-EEU-88-113.) June 13, 1988, 40-41.

Magyarország hadtörténete. (2 vols.) Budapest: Zrínyi Katonai, 1984.

"Military Service Reduced," MTI [Budapest], June 30, 1989. Foreign Broadcast Information Service, *Daily Report: East Europe.* (FBIS-EEU-89-125.) June 30, 1989, 33.

"Minister Horvath Interviewed on State Security," Budapest Television Service [Budapest], July 9, 1989. Foreign Broadcast Information Service, *Daily Report: East Europe.* (FBIS-EEU-89-130.) July 10, 1989, 33-34.

Mucs, Sándor, and Ernő Zágoni. *Geschichte der Ungarischen Volksarmee.* East Berlin: Militärverlag der Deutschen Democratischen Republik, 1982.

_____. *A Magyar Néphadsereg története.* (2d ed.). Budapest: Zrínyi Katonai, 1984.

"1989 Military Production to Fall 31 Percent," MTI [Budapest], January 18, 1989. Foreign Broadcast Information Service, *Daily*

Report: East Europe. (FBIS-EEU-89-012.) January 19, 1989, 37-38.

"No Joint Soviet Military Exercise in October," MTI [Budapest], August 17, 1989. Foreign Broadcast Information Service, *Daily Report: East Europe.* (FBIS-EEU-89-159.) August 18, 1989, 24.

"120 Pardoned for Roles During 1956 Events," Budapest Domestic Service [Budapest], December 30, 1988. Foreign Broadcast Information Service, *Daily Report: East Europe.* (FBIS-EEU-89-001.) January 3, 1989, 47.

"One Thousand Illegal Border-Crossing Attempts Yearly," *Nepszava* [Budapest], February 28, 1987. Joint Publications Research Service, *East Europe Report.* (JPRS-EER-87-098.) June 23, 1987, 15-17.

"Opposition Member Comments on Future Policies," *Profil* [Vienna], October 2, 1989. Foreign Broadcast Information Service, *Daily Report: East Europe.* (FBIS-EEU-89-092.) October 5, 1989, 39-40.

"Partial Withdrawal of Soviet Forces Begins," MTI [Budapest], April 25, 1989. Foreign Broadcast Information Service, *Daily Report: East Europe.* (FBIS-EEU-89-079.) April 26, 1989, 30.

Pataki, Judith. "Hungary," *Radio Free Europe Research* [Munich], July 30, 1987.

Polgár, Stephen. "Samizdat in Hungary," *Radio Free Europe Research* [Munich], May 3, 1982.

"Police Officials Discuss Country's Drug Use," *Magyar Hirlap* [Budapest], March 21, 1989. Foreign Broadcast Information Service, *Daily Report: East Europe.* (FBIS-EEU-89-061.) March 31, 1989, 37.

"Pozsgay Says 1945-62 Trials to Be Reviewed," Budapest Domestic Service [Budapest], March 22, 1989. Foreign Broadcast Information Service, *Daily Report: East Europe.* (FBIS-EEU-89-055.) March 23, 1989, 27.

"Prisoner Burns Himself to Death in Protest," AFP [Paris], July 27, 1989. Foreign Broadcast Information Service, *Daily Report: East Europe.* (FBIS-EEU-89-143.) July 27, 1989, 12-13.

Rubin, F. "The Hungarian People's Army," *Journal of the Royal United Services Institute for Defense Studies* [London], 121, September 1976, 59-66.

Sinor, Denis. *History of Hungary.* New York: Praeger, 1959.

"Spokesman on Status of Workers' Guard," Budapest Television Service [Budapest], June 15, 1989. Foreign Broadcast Information Service, *Daily Report: East Europe.* (FBIS-EEU-89-115.) June 16, 1989, 36.

"Successful Rock Composer Describes Censorship," *Magyar Ifjusag* [Budapest], March 13, 1987. Joint Publications Research Service, *East Europe Report*. (JPRS-EER-87-118.) July 30, 1987, 28-30.

"Supreme Court Rules on Punishment of Drug Related Crimes," *Magyar Hirlap* [Budapest], January 20, 1987. Joint Publications Research Service, *East Europe Report*. (JPRS-EER-87-078.) May 15, 1987, 44-46.

Treaty of Peace with Hungary. 1947.

Vali, Ferenc Albert. *Rift and Revolt in Hungary: Nationalism Versus Communism*. Cambridge: Harvard University Press, 1961.

Völgyes, Iván. "Hungary." Pages 184-224 in Daniel N. Nelson (ed.), *Soviet Allies: The Warsaw Pact and the Issue of Reliability*. Boulder, Colorado: Westview Press, 1984.

Weiss, Peter. "The Hungarian Armed Forces Today," *International Defense Review* [Geneva], August 1988, 935-38.

"Young Democrats Hold 'Sit-in' Against Police," MTI [Budapest], April 28, 1989. Foreign Broadcast Information Service, *Daily Report: East Europe*. (FBIS-EEU-89-082.) May 1, 1989, 36.

Glossary

Comecon—Council for Mutual Economic Assistance. Sometimes cited as CMEA or CEMA. Members in 1989 included Bulgaria, Cuba, Czechoslovakia, the German Democratic Republic (East Germany), Hungary, the Mongolian People's Republic (Mongolia), Poland, Romania, the Soviet Union, and Vietnam. Its purpose was to further economic cooperation among members.

corvée—Number of days each week that the serf was required to work for his lord.

entail system—Form of inheritance by which land passed to the owner's male descendents or, if he had no male heir, to the crown. Entail checked Hungary's economic development because it prevented the nobles from selling their land or using it as collateral to obtain credit.

forint—National currency of Hungary. As of July 1989, the official exchange rate was 62.28 forints to US$1.

gross domestic product (GDP)—Includes "transferred value" (cost of materials) and "newly created value" (profits and wages). "Nonproductive" activities (services) are not included in GDP; thus, it is not comparable with the Western concept of gross national product (GNP).

Hofkriegsrat—Central organ for all military matters in the Habsburg lands.

International Monetary Fund (IMF)—Established along with the World Bank (*q.v.*) in 1945, the IMF is a specialized agency affiliated with the United Nations that takes responsibility for stabilizing international exchange rates and payments. The main business of the IMF is the provision of loans to its members when they experience balance of payments difficulties. These loans often carry conditions that require substantial internal economic adjustments by the recipients.

nomenklatura—From the Latin *nomenclature*. This Russian word denotes an enumeration of important positions and the candidates who are examined, recommended, and assigned to fill them by communist party committees at various levels.

palatine—Originally created in the fifteenth century. Highest officeholder in Hungary in the eighteenth century; in theory, the commander in chief of the Hungarian armed forces.

Pannonia—Former Roman province west of the Danube in present-day Hungary and northern Yugoslavia.

Party Rules—HSWP document, which can be altered by the party
congress. The Party Rules contain sections on regulations for
admission into the HSWP, the organizational structure of the
party, the principles of democratic centralism, the role of the
Basic Organization, the tasks of the party in state and mass
organizations, and membership dues.

Petőfi Circle—A group formed in 1956 named after the nineteenth-
century poet and revolutionary Sándor Petőfi, who symbolized
Hungary's desire for freedom. Made up of liberal writers, intellectuals, and some communists, the circle generated the ideas
that led to the Revolution of 1956.

value-added tax—A tax applied to the additional value created at
a given stage of production and calculated as the difference between the product value at that stage and the cost of all materials
and services purchased as inputs.

Warsaw Pact—Political-military alliance founded in 1955 as a coun-
terweight to the North Atlantic Treaty Organization. Members in 1989 included Bulgaria, Czechoslovakia, East Germany,
Hungary, Poland, Romania, and the Soviet Union. Has served
as the Soviet Union's primary mechanism for keeping political and military control over Eastern Europe.

World Bank—Informal name used to designate a group of three
affiliated international institutions: the International Bank for
Reconstruction and Development (IBRD), the International
Development Association (IDA), and the International Finance
Corporation (IFC). The IBRD, established in 1945, has the
primary purpose of providing loans to developing countries for
productive projects. The IDA, a legally separate loan fund
administered by the staff of the IBRD, was set up in 1960 to
furnish credits to the poorest developing countries on much eas-
ier terms than those of conventional IBRD loans. The IFC,
founded in 1956, supplements the activities of the IBRD
through loans and assistance designed specifically to encourage
the growth of productive private enterprises in less-developed
countries. The president and certain senior members of the
IBRD hold the same positions in the IFC. The three institutions are owned by the governments of the countries that subscribe their capital. To participate in the World Bank group,
member states must first belong to the IMF (*q.v.*).

Index

Published Country Studies

(Area Handbook Series)

550-65	Afghanistan	550-87	Greece
550-98	Albania	550-78	Guatemala
550-44	Algeria	550-174	Guinea
550-59	Angola	550-82	Guyana and Belize
550-73	Argentina	550-151	Honduras
550-169	Australia	550-165	Hungary
550-176	Austria	550-21	India
550-175	Bangladesh	550-154	Indian Ocean
550-170	Belgium	550-39	Indonesia
550-66	Bolivia	550-68	Iran
550-20	Brazil	550-31	Iraq
550-168	Bulgaria	550-25	Israel
550-61	Burma	550-182	Italy
550-50	Cambodia	550-30	Japan
550-166	Cameroon	550-34	Jordan
550-159	Chad	550-56	Kenya
550-77	Chile	550-81	Korea, North
550-60	China	550-41	Korea, South
550-26	Colombia	550-58	Laos
550-33	Commonwealth Caribbean, Islands of the	550-24	Lebanon
550-91	Congo	550-38	Liberia
550-90	Costa Rica	550-85	Libya
550-69	Côte d'Ivoire (Ivory Coast)	550-172	Malawi
550-152	Cuba	550-45	Malaysia
550-22	Cyprus	550-161	Mauritania
550-158	Czechoslovakia	550-79	Mexico
550-36	Dominican Republic and Haiti	550-76	Mongolia
550-52	Ecuador	550-49	Morocco
550-43	Egypt	550-64	Mozambique
550-150	El Salvador	550-35	Nepal and Bhutan
550-28	Ethiopia	550-88	Nicaragua
550-167	Finland	550-157	Nigeria
550-155	Germany, East	550-94	Oceania
550-173	Germany, Fed. Rep. of	550-48	Pakistan
550-153	Ghana	550-46	Panama